PC Tuning

How To Improve Your PC's Performance—
The Smart Way!

Andreas Voss

Abacus

DATA BECKER

Contents

Contents

QuickCheck —
Get More Speed
Right Away

We wrote this first chapter so you could see what this book has to offer and then check whether and where your computer can still be brought up to speed. We're not starting right away with the most detailed hardware information. Instead, we'd like to do a quick check with you to determine where to improve your PC. Since we cannot look inside of your PC, you'll have to do it yourself. To show you what you can do, we've collected interesting tips for you in this first chapter. You can read more about each tip by following the cross-references to the appropriate chapters. We'll also talk about several interesting utilities you can use to test your PC's weaknesses. Now let's get down to business.

Solve Typical Speed Obstacles In Five Minutes

Want to bet you're not getting the most out of your system? Are you quite sure that your Windows 95 is configured for optimal performance? Are you taking advantage of every possible convenience of your PC? Are you prepared for a hard drive crash or processor failure?

You can determine whether you can improve one area of your PC or another without taking a lot of time. The following points are more fully explained later in the book so follow the cross-references to the corresponding chapters.

Checking whether Windows 95 is performing well

Have you actually asked Windows 95 how it's doing? Experienced users do that all the time—at least, every time a problem occurs. However, even beginners should know how to do this. The Control Panel will give you good information about your PC's condition. Click **Start | Settings | Control Panel...** and double-click the System icon. Then look at the information on the Performance tab. You'll find more information about system properties and related functions in the following pages.

Checking interrupts with the Device Manager

Interrupts determine when a card or port has something to say to the processor. Sometimes your computer may not have enough interrupts. You might have enough now but installing that next sound card may give you a great deal of trouble.

One thing you'll soon realize is that your PC can never have enough interrupts. Unfortunately, most users of newer PCs with Plug & Play BIOS even give away interrupts. You should make certain all is as it should be with your PC.

For example, did you know that video cards don't even need an interrupt but most PCs have one assigned anyway? So, take a look in the BIOS or in the Windows 95 Device Manager. (Check out Chapter 6 for more information.).

This version of Windows has definite problems The system properties show that some driver is creating havoc.

You should answer these questions: Are you greedy for interrupts and want to have more? Perhaps you are using SCSI? Have you enabled the two interrupts reserved for EIDE? Check the information in Chapter 6 for more options.

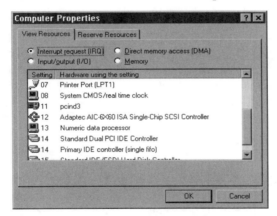

Video cards don't need an interrupt but most PCs assign one anyway. Here, IRQ 14 is needlessly used for the video card.

Calling the Device Manager and programs quickly

We could divide this tip into two: For one, you'll learn the quickest method of calling programs under Windows 95, and at the same time, you'll learn the speediest way to call the Device Manager. You've probably already been annoyed that you cannot call the Device Manager directly through a shortcut from the Desktop or a program folder.

The normal method for calling the Device Manager always goes through the dialog box properties for System, where you must then manually select the second tab for the Device Manager. The usual methods for calling this dialog box are:

◆ While holding down the a key, double-click the My Computer icon of the Desktop

◆ Right-click on the My Computer icon and select Properties in the context menu.

◆ Create a shortcut to the System icon in the Control Panel and place it in the Windows 95 Start menu (see caption from the figure below).

That brings us to the first part of the tip: Place the icons or shortcuts of your most important programs in the Start menu. To call the Start menu, use the Open command in the context (right-click) menu of the Start icon. Access to the Start menu is especially fast and convenient on Windows 95-compatible keyboards, because they have two special keys for this.

But let's get back to the Device Manager. To call the Device Manager directly from the Start menu, first create a new, empty shortcut and enter the following under Properties in the Target field.

```
C:\Windows\Control.exe Sysdm.cpl, System,1
```

This lets you call the Device Manager directly. Now all you have to do is assign an icon to the shortcut. How about the tree icon from the c:\windows\system\shell32.dll file? Now when you enable the Start menu, the shortcut appears directly over the gray dividing line after the default entry Programs. You'll find this to be much more practical.

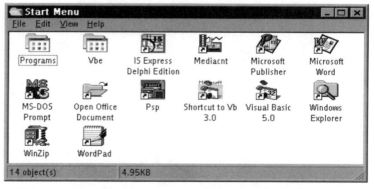

Store your most important programs as shortcuts in the Start menu;
it's the fastest, most convenient way to call them.

Hidden treasure in Windows 95 OSR2

Consider yourself fortunate if you have access to the Service Pack 2 (OSR2) from Windows 95. It includes an excellent hardware and system analysis tool that most users find superior to the Device Manager. The program is called "HwDiag" and is located in the Other\Misc\Hwtrack directory on the CD-ROM. It shows you a detailed report about the registry, gives information about allocated and free resources and all kinds of other useful information. We'll talk more about this and other analysis or benchmark programs later in this chapter.

How to get everything from the BIOS

The BIOS (Basic Input/Output System) is the first place you should check when it comes to the interrupt settings of your PC. However, you can tune up or set a lot more here than just the interrupts. We admit, at first glance everything looks pretty difficult to understand. But it's not really all that difficult, as you can discover in Chapter 6.

If you're satisfied with your boot procedure check out the different setting options in Chapter 6.

```
                              AWARD SOFTWARE, I
   Virus Warning              : Disabled    Video
   CPU Internal Cache         : Enabled     C8000
   External Cache             : Enabled     CC000
   Quick Power On Self Test   : Enabled     D0000
   HDD Sequence SCSI/IDE First: IDE         D4000
   Boot Sequence              : D,A         D8000
   Boot Up Floppy Seek        : Disabled    DC000
   Floppy Disk Access Control : R/W
   IDE HDD Block Mode Sectors : HDD MAX     Boot
   Security Option            : System      Boot
   PS/2 Mouse Function Control: Disabled    Typem
   PCI/VGA Palette Snoop      : Disabled    Typem
   OS/2 Onboard Memory > 64M  : Disabled    Typem
```

There's no need to be still booting from the C drive. You can boot from the D drive or even from SCSI, even though you have an IDE hard drive. It's no problem with this BIOS.

Modern EIDE hard drives are like nervous race horses. Everything must be perfect — especially in the BIOS. Are you using the maximum PIO mode? Do you know the correct method for registering a new drive? How do you free those darned interrupts 14 and 15 if you don't want anything to do with EIDE and prefer using SCSI? See Chapter 6 for more information.

50% more speed for $15 with a 512K L2 Cache

Depending on the type and configuration of your computer, especially regarding how much RAM you have, upgrading to 512K L2 memory cache may be a good idea. These modules cost only a few dollars. However, there are important configuration considerations. For example, pay attention if you're using more than 64 Megs of RAM because there are critical tuning traps with the L2 cache. See Chapter 4 to determine when it makes sense to upgrade, what the advantages of upgrading are and how it is connected with the amount of RAM.

High speed tuning with overclocking

All you have to do is reset a couple of jumpers on the motherboard to turn your Pentium 166 into a 200 or increase the clock speed from 200 to 225 MHz or change your PCI cards from 33 MHz. (It can be dangerous to boost clock speed but don't be so quick to ignore the possibilities. Just wait and see what all the new processors will suddenly require and what will then be possible.)

Start reading Chapter 6 to see what is really possible, how to do it and where the risks or limits are. (But first, if you buy a new motherboard, make certain it's possible to increase the system clock to at least 75 MHz—83 or 100 MHz would be better yet. Soon the old 66 MHz PCs will be forgotten. Also, anyone who has a Pentium 75, 90, 120 or 150 should think about boosting clock speed as soon as possible, because with 50 or 60 MHz, your system is hobbling along below the maximum specifications.)

FS2	FS1	FS0	BUS FREQ.
2-3	1-2	2-3	50MHz
2-3	1-2	1-2	55MHz
2-3	2-3	2-3	60MHz
2-3	2-3	1-2	66MHz
1-2	2-3	2-3	75MHz

Turbo drive already built in—this motherboard includes 75-MHz clock speed.

Is your computer running unstably since you overclocked it?

The setting of the power supply of the processor is an important minor detail that can also play a deciding role in the stability of the system. If your Pentium crashes when you boost the clock speed, check whether you wouldn't do better with the VRE power settings. See Chapter 4 to find out whether your Pentium is a VRE power type.

Maximum performance for old Pentium motherboards

Do you still have one of these second generation Pentium computers, a P75, P90 or a P100? If so, have you considered upgrading by replacing the processor? After all, now they've got these new, super fast Pentium, AMD K6 and Cyrix 6x86MX processors racing up to 233 MHz (soon even faster). In theory you could replace your old motherboard with such a processor if it weren't for one little catch. Your old motherboard, if it was built before 1996 probably supports only the multiplication factors 1.5 to 2. That would mean using a new processor up to 133 MHz and no more. It's too bad if you purchased a 166 or 200 MHz model.

It's different for Pentium 233s or K6-233s. Configured for the settings of a Pentium 100, these interpret the normal factor of 1.5 internally as 3.5 (3.5 x 66 MHz system bus = 233 MHz internal processor bus). Thus, these CPUs are the optimal upgrading tip for old Pentium motherboards. The only additional requirements are a motherboard with ZIF socket 7 (instead of 5), a stable power supply and an adapter for the dual-voltage power supply of the processors. You'll find more information in Chapter 2 and Chapter 4.

> **NOTE**
>
> **Alternatives for motherboards with maximum factor 2**
>
> If your motherboard is really only able to increase the processor clock by a factor 2, and a Pentium 133 as a maximum "normal" solution is not enough for you, then only the following models are worth your consideration. A Cyrix M1 6x86-Pr166+ works internally like a P133. However, this model uses a lot of power and gets very hot. Your motherboard should be able to manage with that.

Have better performance and fewer problems with an alternative BIOS

Are you dissatisfied with your BIOS or with the support from the manufacturer of the motherboard? Do extended booting procedures test your patience? Perhaps you have an original Intel motherboard whose BIOS prevents you from using an AMD or Cyrix processor through the CPU query. If so, it might be time to consider an independent manufacturer called MR-BIOS. This company offers alternative, motherboard-independent BIOSes that can be transferred using Flash-ROM to any supported board. For more information, see Chapter 6.

Tell Windows who's boss

Windows 95 is supposed to take care of all the work for you — few settings are necessary. However, the supposedly fantastic automatic settings for optimal usage of the hard drive are completely at the expense of performance. Plus, they also get on the nerves of many users. We're talking about the dynamic management for the swap file and the hard drive cache. Without going into detail about function or purpose, you need to remember the idea that you would prefer to switch from the automatic, dynamic settings to fixed values. These only have to be suited to the properties of your PC. See Chapter 8 to find out how to optimally adapt the dynamic management of the data cache and the Windows swap file.

Stay away from FAT32

You should keep away from FAT32 unless you have to address more than two Gigabytes on your hard drive. The new FAT32 file system, introduced by Microsoft with Windows 95b, has its tricky spots. For example, there are all kinds of problems with it and afterwards no other operating system can access the data. Furthermore, it's also considerably slower than the FAT16 (VFAT) of the old (first) Windows 95a. The main reason for this is that the administration of the many small sectors under Windows 95 reduces hard drive performance (by approximately 5%). Anyone who doesn't have to address a big hard drive in partitions over two

This small setting in the System.ini makes your hard drive cache operate optimally (for a computer with 64 Megs of RAM).

Gigabytes, for example digitial video work, should stay away from FAT32. See Chapter 8 for more information.

Windows NT 4.0 is faster than Windows 95

Contrary to popular opinion, working with the Workstation of Windows NT 4.0 (at least 32 Megs of RAM is required) is both more stable and faster than working with Windows 95. You'll notice this especially when accessing the hard drive on a SCSI system. Those who remember the reduced hard drive speed when upgrading from Windows 3.x to Windows 95 may still recall how slow Windows 95 is. Because VFAT is simply a compromise solution with much overhead, Windows NT 4.0 runs much faster, particularly with NTFS.

If your PC system is equipped with at least 64 Megs of RAM and a video card driver optimized for NT 4.0, you get 10-15% more performance than with Windows 95 running typical applications such as Microsoft Office, PageMaker or CorelDRAW (approximately 10% with a Pentium-MMX and even about 20% with 32-bit optimized processors like the Pentium Pro, Pentium II or AMD K6). That is a pretty considerable percentage that you'll definitely be able to feel. The differences, however, depend greatly on the application.

Furthermore, through genuine multitasking your system won't slow down when you're formatting a diskette in the background, burning a CD-ROM or downloading a file from the Internet. One final shortcoming of Windows NT has been solved now that an Adobe TypeManager for using Postscript screen fonts in version 4.0 for Windows NT is available.

Don't be afraid to give some thought to switching to Windows NT 4.0. We won't keep the disadvantages from you either: Games (above all, games for DOS) won't run or run unsatisfactorily, AOL with ISDN and also the MSN on-line service don't run well. However, that will soon change or there will be options for solutions.

Giving away too much RAM

You can never have enough RAM. Windows 95 really begins running properly with 64 Megs, even if Microsoft has a different opinion. Most users have only 16 or 32 Megs and most programs act as if all the RAM belonged to only them. Are you familiar with the memory hogs in your system? See Chapter 4 to find out how you can test your programs' hunger for memory.

Are you giving away more than one Meg of memory for your CD-ROM although you could be making better use of it for something else (Chapter 9)? What about your limited DOS memory? Do you have the CONFIG.SYS and AUTOEXEC.BAT files set optimally under Windows 95 (Chapter 4)?

Are you aware of what sneaks into RAM from Windows past the Autostart Group? Along with the Autostart folder, it is also possible to load files automatically through the Registry. The most important one is the subbranch Run as shown in the figure. Drivers and .DLL files are also loaded by the branch

HKEY_LOCAL_MACHINE\System\CurrentControlSet\control\InstalledFiles as well as HKEY_LOCAL_MACHINE\SOFTWARE\Microsoft\Windows\CurrentVersion\SharedDLLs. So if a program or driver seems to be hiding in your system and is called up every time you boot, take a look in these settings.

Finally, .VXD drivers located in the \windows\system\iosubsys folder are automatically loaded into memory without being called in the Registry or an .INI file. It could happen that when you uninstall a program, a .VXD file that you don't really need remains behind. Unfortunately, it's then always loaded automatically and could create problems under the certain circumstances. So, check the files in the Iosubsys folder; this could be the solution for problems with Windows 95 crashing.

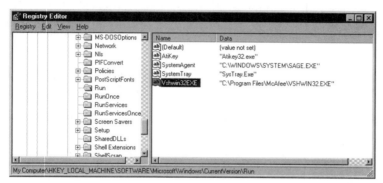

*Programs wanting to sneak into memory directly when you
start up Windows, register themselves in this Registry folder.*

Does your word processor have everything it needs?

Many programs are greedy, especially for memory. There are some programs that you should give what they need (including Microsoft Word). When we talk about memory management, cache systems, etc., we don't mean to conceal the fact from you that Word has its own cache system. Whether you are using the old 16-bit version or the new 32-bit version, Chapter 8 tells you how to set the cache correctly for bitmap and scrolling events.

The right setting for the memory cache in the Registry can speed up Word for Windows 95 and 97.

The CD-ROM slows down the hard drive with old motherboards

Something that hasn't been a topic with current motherboards can prove to be a treacherous speed obstacle with older boards: The shared connection of slow and fast devices to an EIDE port on the motherboard. The old EIDE controllers cannot work with different speeds on one port, but instead, always gear themselves to the slowest connected device. The most frequent combination could be an ATAPI CD-ROM and a hard drive, but an old hard drive could also slow down a new one.

However, many users make the mistake of assuming that this problem also exists for newer motherboards. But for the last 2-3 years, EIDE controllers have been fully capable of operating two devices that differ in speed. The only way to find out whether this is the case with your old board is to experiment. The BIOS will also give you information about this if it doesn't have the option to set PIO mode for each master and slave device at each port. See Chapter 6 and Chapter 7 for more on EIDE tuning.

The busmaster driver can help with your 16-speed CD-ROM

ATAPI CD-ROMs, the ones that are on the EIDE bus of the motherboard, really know how to hog resources. Depending on the driver, the processor load is as much as 90%. The process can really slow especially when files are copied to the hard drive. It doesn't have to be that way because your CD-ROM can communicate with the hard drive quite well without help from the processor. But you must install the appropriate driver of the motherboard manufacturer. Be sure to check this out using the information in Chapter 7.

 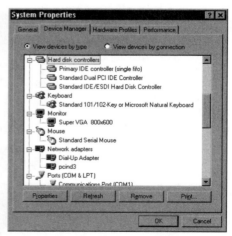

The picture on the left shows Windows 95a without a busmaster driver—not even the hard drives are detected correctly. Bus mastering is not possible. In the picture on the right, the busmaster driver has been installed. The hard drive type is detected.

Get more speed with Busmastering

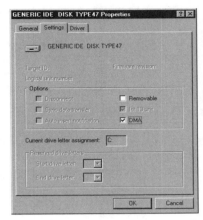

If you're a user of the Windows 95B version (also called OSR2) then you are a bit better off than the rest of the 32-bit world, at least when it comes to EIDE hard drives and CD-ROMs. By simply clicking the appropriate option in the Device Manager, you can get more speed thanks to DMA transfer. This corresponds approximately to the busmastering that can be activated through a special driver, but it works without all of that. See Chapter 7 for the details.

Thanks to the busmaster driver, Windows 95 no longer detects the CD-ROM drive

You're not alone with this problem. Windows 95 has its troubles with some Triton chipsets (to be precise, with the busmastering chips PIIX3 and PIIX4). For example, the CD-ROM disappears after the busmaster driver is activated. Solve

Enabling DMA mode for your hard drive or CD-ROM doesn't replace the busmaster driver.

this problem by patching the MSHDC.INF file. An even simpler method is to install the normal driver for the CD-ROM again. For more information on how to do that and explanations on this subject, turn to Chapter 6.

Solving speed obstacles with older SCSI hard drives

Some of the older SCSI hard drives, for example from HP or Seagate, and even some of the new ones, have the hardware write cache of the hard drive disabled. For security reasons, a write cache is always a bit of a problem. However, since even Windows 95 is using a (rather safe) software write cache, it is rather foolish and a bit overcautious not to make use of this easy, free tuning function.

How do you enable the write cache? It's no problem if you have the right program. You can get

this tool free from Seagate. In addition, Adaptec's EZ-SCSI software comes with such a function. Read Chapter 7 if you're interested.

Speed up your SCSI hard drive under DOS and Windows 3.x

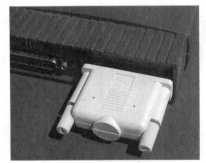

SCSI controllers with their own BIOS can address hard drives without an extra driver. The functions are built into the ROM of the card. However, you can also use the hard disk driver supplied by the manufacturer (ASPIDISK.SYS for Adaptec) as you would with controllers that don't have their own ROM. This can speed up access under DOS and Windows 3.x, since the ROM can be accessed with only eight bits, but the driver

Your ZIP drive will become more stable with such a small, active terminator.

11

can be accessed with 16-bit width. Naturally, along with the hard disk driver, the actual driver of the SCSI controller (ASPIXDOS.SYS for Adaptec) must be already loaded.

This tip won't work in Windows 95 and Windows NT 4.0. The 32-bit drivers used with these operating systems use their own routines to access the controller and the connected devices; the BIOS is only necessary for the boot procedure.

A Bomb-proof SCSI Bus

Have you ever noticed how poorly some devices are terminated on the SCSI bus? The best example of this is a ZIP drive from Iomega: when the ZIP is switched off, some computers cannot even boot. You can solve this problem by spending a few dollarsand buying an *active terminator*. Then plug it in at each end of the bus. These add-on plugs have a remarkably favorable effect on system stability. We'll also talk about a solution for the problem of not being able to actively terminate the internal part of the bus with its flat-ribbon cable. You can read more about this in Chapter 7.

How to get more data over the printer port

Iomega's ZIP drives are very popular. The ZIP drive model that uses the parallel port is especially practical because you can hook it up anywhere. Unfortunately, they're very slow (less than half the data rate of a SCSI model).

Now, while we can't perform any miracles, there are a few possibilities to increase the speed. One is to use the latest driver for the permanent linking of the device under Windows instead of the overloaded, memory-consuming Guest-Tool (see Chapter 8). Also, have you ever noticed how copy operations usually run significantly faster under DOS than under Windows 95 (Chapter 8)?

However, the parallel port itself offers the best tuning option. Switching over to the right protocol in the BIOS (Chapter 8) and an optimized setting in the Registry (Chapter 8) can make a big difference.

Hidden data garbage

You'd may be shocked if you knew how much data garbage some programs generate in the background. Word for Windows is a good example. Some files are swapped to disk several times as a temporary (TMP) file. The files are often hidden and you may not be able to find them. Unless you make the right settings, these temporary files can really impair the performance of your PC.

To solve this problem, make the appropriate settings in the AUTOEXEC.BAT. To keep the flood of temporary files from getting out of hand, tell Windows 95 delete old data garbage every time you start your computer. To do this, add the command lines shown in the figure below to your AUTOEXEC.BAT. By making a slight change (substitute *.chk and *._dd for *.tmp) you can delete all the file fragments left behind by ScanDisk or Norton Diskdoctor.

Make a backup copy of Windows on the hard drive

Here's something for all the hardware tinkerers and tuning freaks of this world who reinstall Windows 95 regularly. Create a copy of the Windows 95 directory from the installation CD-ROM on your hard drive. Although few users do this, it nevertheless has great practical advantages. You don't need to copy the entire CD-ROM, just the Win95 subdirectory, which contains all the relevant files and drivers. That works out to about 50 Megs, a small amount of disk space on today's hard drives.

These highlighted settings in DOS start files help prevent a buildup of temp files.

The advantage is obvious: whenever you need the Windows CD-ROM during an installation, you won't have to insert the CD-ROM anymore. More important yet are the advantages in case of a crash with the required reinstallation of Windows. Usually you have to link the DOS drivers for your CD-ROM and/or your SCSI controller beforehand. It's no longer a problem with a backup copy of the CD on your hard drive. You should also keep a copy of the current Windows and Programs directory somewhere on the hard drive. In case of a bigger problem, you can copy these back in Safe Mode and you'll have a completely restored system within 10 minutes. We cover the details of this operation later in Chapter 8.

TUNING OVERVIEW

Tuning is admittedly a flexible term. Computer professionals may think first about BIOS optimization and registry tinkering when it comes to tuning. However, in this book, tuning means anything that makes the PC run faster. There's no getting around upgrading with new hardware for a complete tuning job on your computer. You may ask yourself where tuning does any good or where you can do what. After all, a new, larger hard drive isn't enough to make the old one run any faster. Users with 64 Megs of RAM will rarely see any benefit in upgrading to 128 Megs.

Hardware tuning depends on the system and what it is being used for. In the following section we give you an overview of where on the system (whether hardware or software) the critical tuning options are.

Tuning table for hardware components

It's obvious that the hardware plays the most important role in the speed of a PC. However, a fast processor by itself does not make a fast machine. The greatest strength of the PC is its modular structure. It lets you replace almost every component in the computer. If you know how to make effective use of this, you can make a faster PC. The following overview gives you an idea of which PC components you can replace and which replacements are practical.

PC Component	Tuning Options	Rating
Processor	Achieve higher clock speed through a new processor or by overclocking the old processor	High, however, only if the rest of the system can keep up
Motherboard	Current Pentium boards are all equally fast, however, the new boards support new processors	Low, has more influence on system stability, unless a new processor comes with the new board.
Chipset	Replacement is only possible by replacing motherboard; overclocking with 75 or 83 MHz results in maximum performance increase	High, better results with overclocking than a faster processor!!!
L2 Cache	Increase to 512K. Exchange old motherboards with an asychronous cache for the current pipelined burst types	Medium, unless there are more than 64 Megs of RAM—then you need an appropriate Tag-RAM
RAM type (FP, EDO or SDRAM)	Exchange standard RAMs for EDO or SDRAM (only if the motherboard supports it)	Slight, Hardly any differences. SDRAMs don't result in significant advantages until system clock reaches 83 MHz
Amount of RAM	Upgrade to 32, 64 or more RAM	Very High, up to 64 Meg. After that, hardly any benefit, except for special software
Video card	Replace cards, upgrade memory	High, significant differences depend on the card. More memory only brings more color
Video add-on cards	MPEG decoder or 3-D accelerator cards	Low, Starting with the Pentium 166, MPEG cards are hardly necessary Very High, with 3-D cards!
Hard drive	Larger and/or faster type	High to very high, the hard drive is often the stumbling block with modern PCs
Bus System (EIDE or SCSI)	Change from EIDE to SCSI system, which requires replacing hard drive and CD-ROM	High, SCSI brings significant relief to the system, especially with simultaneous access to several devices
EIDE Type	Switch to higher PIO mode or Ultra DMA/33 through hard drive and/or motherboard replacement	Slight, Starting with PIO mode 3, no increase in speed, since hard drives don't even deliver the transfer rate
SCSI Type	Switch from Fast to Ultra or Ultra-Wide	Slight, unless more than one hard drive is in operation simultaneously

When hardware tuning goes wrong

Yes, there are problems and risks involved and something will frequently go wrong. The first part of Chapter 2 includes upgrading tips for older PCs. We'll list the most typical problems in upgrading (that is, replacing) PC components. There's also a separate section on overclocking (in Chapter 6) describing the most important problems and their solutions.

Configuration files

What the BIOS and the jumpers on the boards are to the hardware, the configuration files and menus are to the software, and in particular, to the operating system. Here you assign crucial settings that influence the entire performance and operation of your PC. For example, before you begin working with Windows 95 or Word 97, always check through the various Options menus (frequently the menus are also called "Extras" or "Preferences") and make all the relevant settings. However, we're not concerned so much with that here, we just want to make sure you adapt your application programs optimally to the existing hardware.

However, all the setting options aren't always so obvious to the user from the outside. Unfortunately, all too frequently the programmers have hidden the juiciest delicacies deep within the system. The most obscure veil lies over the registry file of Windows 95, which is intentionally not documented by Microsoft. Meanwhile, other sources have collected useful information. We also frequently make use of registry settings in this book.

Most experienced users probably already know where to find which system files and with which programs to edit them. If you fit in this category, you can skip this section. However, there are still many beginners who haven't had any experience with these files. This book is going to change that situation. So here's an overview of the most important files and where to find them.

Everybody needs to be familiar with these configuration files

◆ CONFIG.SYS and AUTOEXEC.BAT should be familiar to everybody. We're not going to give an extended introduction to these two files; there are other books for that purpose. But for the sake of completeness, they shouldn't be missing from our discussion. These two files can be edited with any text editor such as EDIT.COM from DOS or Notepad in Windows 95. Editing goes a bit faster with the SYSEDIT.EXE program in the Windows\System directory.

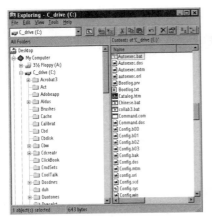 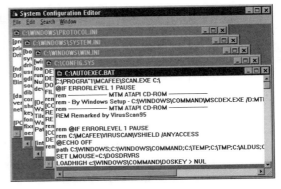

The AUTOEXEC.BAT and CONFIG.SYS files are in the root directory of the hard drive and are always good for tuning operations. The right picture shows the SYSEDIT.EXE program from the Windows\System directory, with the six most important configuration files ready to be edited.

◆ The root directory of Windows (3.x as well as 95) contains the successors to the two DOS files listed above: WIN.INI and System.ini. Here too, you see a similar division: The first file is solely responsible for software settings and the second file is, for the most part, responsible for hardware configuration. Under Windows 95 they only insure the compatibility of old programs, however, there are still some important settings that can be made here. These include the cache and the swap file. They can be edited with an text editor.

Load the SYSTEM.INI or WIN.INI file into Notepad and you're ready to edit. The individual sections are organized by subject, with headings in brackets. This is the section for 32-bit hardware drivers.

◆ The SYSTEM.DAT and USER.DAT files are the modern successors of the last two files and transfer the old legacy to the registry. This is a hierarchically structured configuration system that Windows combines from these two files or stores in them in binary format. Don't be afraid of the registry. There are almost always exact instructions for cases when you have to do something to the registry. Use the REGEDIT.EXE program in the Windows root

directory to edit the registry. Simply call the program (by typing "regedit" into the Run…
dialog box) and you're ready to go.

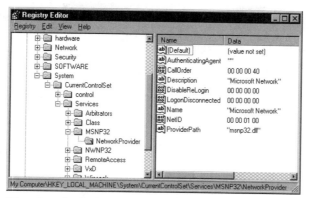

*Viewing the Windows 95 registry in the Registry Editor can at first be confusing. The settings in the
windows are hierarchically structured. You make changes only in the right window, either using the main menus
or the context menu of the right mouse button.*

NOTE

Free registry-tuning tools

The two central system files of Windows 95 are the heart of the system. Just like a
human heart, these files are also quite sensitive. It's good to have backup copies of
them. Fortunately, Windows 95 creates backups for you with each change. These backup files get
the same filenames, but with a different extension: .DA0. If your system crashes, you'll almost
always have to go to DOS to repair the damage, copying the backup copies over the main files. The
only dumb thing is that the Copy command won't work with files (original and copy) that are
protected by all kinds of file attributes. However, removing the attributes is easy: with attrib *.dat -s
-r -h you can remove the three attributes System, read-only and Hidden (s, r, h) from the three main
files. After that, you can overwrite the files. Use the same parameter with "+" instead of "-" to reset
the attributes for the files.

You can always use the old DOS commands. For example, in this case, use DOS when changing the attributes of the system files.

> **NOTE**
>
> **Windows registry tuning tools**
> You'll find other Registry tools including the ERU program (Emergency Recovery Utility) and RegClean (currently Version 4.1) on the Windows 95 CD-ROM. You can also download these programs from the Internet at the Microsoft FTP site (ftp://ftp.microsoft.com/softlib/MSLFILES/regcln41.exe).
>
> While you use ERU to back up your system files and recover them in emergencies, RegClean cleans the registry of incorrect or unnecessary entries. Deleted or changed areas are exported as .REG files and can be retrieved again if something goes wrong. Users who want comfortably to change hidden settings in the registry to coax more performance and operating convenience should use PowerToys and KernelToys from Microsoft. You can either download them from the FTP server we named earlier or from Microsoft's Internet support pages (www.microsoft.com).

System directories and seldom used configuration files

Almost everybody should be familiar with the six configuration files we've been talking about because probably no one could get by without editing these from time to time. However, there are also quite a few other configuration files that are important for tuning. You should also be familiar with the following files.

The most important system directories of Windows 95 should also be included. You can solve some of your problems with these folders, or with the files stored there. We have organized the most important items for you here:

◆ TheMSDOS.SYS file in the root directory of the boot drive. It's used for compatibility with the old DOS but it also contains interesting options for the usage of the hard drive and boot options. For more information about possible settings, please turn to Chapter 8.

◆ The \Windows\Inf directory stores the Windows .INF files. These files contain the settings and installation instructions for hardware and software. Users who want to correct defective drivers themselves will often have to manipulate the files in this directory.

◆ The \Windows\System directory is a classic. This directory contains most of the .DLL and driver files as well as a few executable programs. Windows runs programs that are located here and in the Windows directory on command, without the need for a path specification.

◆ The \Windows\System\Iosubsys directory contains the .VXD drivers (virtual 32-bit hardware drivers) that are required to operate Windows 95 compatible devices in 32-bit mode. Also, drivers are stored here in accordance with the relatively new miniport standard from Microsoft (.MPD files, *e.g.*, for ISDN and SCSI cards).

◆ In the \Windows\Sysbckup directory (hidden) Windows stores a backup copy of the most important system files (for example, COMMCTROL.DLL, WINSOCK.DLL, MPLAYER.EXE and similar ones). When a software program thinks it has to overwrite one of these files during its installation, Windows detects this the next time you start it up. Windows overwrites the file which has been illegally penetrated, using its own backup copy. What makes sense in general, can also lead to problems under the right circumstances, of course. Therefore, it is good to know where you can intervene.

Here is a listing of other important configuration files and directories. When you perform a backup of your hard drive, be sure to include these files and directories. Also, you need to become familiar with the specified filenames and their locations, because we will refer to them often in this book.

File	Location	Comment
AUTOEXEC.DOS	Root directory of the boot drive	DOS configuration file for Dual-Boot
CONFIG.DOS	Root directory of the boot drive	DOS configuration file for Dual-Boot
SYSTEM.1ST	Root directory of the boot drive	Backup copy of System.dat after first Windows installation
DRVSPACE.BIN / DBLSPACE.BIN	Root directory of the boot drive	Driver files for hard drive compression
SUHDLOG.DAT	Root directory of the boot drive	SetUpHardDiskLOG stores data from the hardware detection of Windows
DOSSTART.BAT	Root directory of Windows	A kind of Autoexec.bat for DOS mode of Windows 95
WINSTART.BAT	Root directory of Windows	Batch file for loading DOS programs or drivers before starting Windows
PROTOCOL.INI	Root directory of Windows	Parameter settings for the network
*.PWL	Root directory of Windows	Stores passwords for Windows and network logon
ShellIconCache	Root directory of Windows	Cache storage file for icon display of CD-ROM drives
ttfCache	Root directory of Windows	Cache storage file for TrueType-Fonts
ATM.INI	Root directory of Windows	Configuration file of the Adobe Type Manager
WINWORD6.INI (and similar .INI files with program names)	Root directory of Windows	Configuration file of Word 6.0 or corresponding programs

\Windows\Cookies	Storage area of cookie files from the Internet Explorer (interaction with internet pages)
\Windows\Desktop	All deletable icons or files of the desktop are copied here to appear on the desktop
\Windows\Favorites	Stores URL shortcuts (addresses of internet pages) for the Internet Explorer
\Windows\Fonts	Storage area for all system and TrueType fonts
\Windows\Sendto	These shortcuts appear in the Send to submenu of a file's context menu
\Windows\Spool(hidden format)	Temporary storage for swap files in printing and faxing operations, cause of some printing problems
\Windows\Startmenu	Contains all shortcuts of the Windows Start menu, including all subfolders in the Programs folder
\Windows\Temporary Internet Files (hidden)	Storage area for the software cache of the Internet Explorer, contains graphics, HTML files and some download files

HELP YOU SEE INTO YOUR PC

A subjective judgment such as "Well, now it's really faster" is not necessarily the best basis for successful tuning. It's better to use one of the many analysis and measuring programs which provide reliable performance data. Many of these analysis and measuring programs are shareware and available on the Internet. Also, many commercial programs, such as Norton Utilities from Symantec, are also available. We've taken a look at what is available and the following pages will introduce you to the best programs (in our opinion).

A practical look at PC measuring programs

As we said, there are all kinds of measuring and analysis programs. Each one has its weaknesses and strengths. Some are only designed for special tasks and others attempt to be the all-around solution. In searching for the right program, it helps to have an idea of the different types or to make your own categories. Then you can choose the program that is right for you.

We categorize the programs according to the following types. Some programs will belong to only one group, while others will have features from all the groups. However, the categories are useful because even the all-around programs almost always have individual modules representing each of the different types.

◆ **The "Who am I?" analysis programs**
These analysis programs display the makeup of the PC and perhaps the memory usage.

◆ **Synthetic benchmark programs**
These programs use ingenious algorithms to measure the speed of your PC or individual components. The result is a relative numerical value that is only suitable for evaluation when compared with other benchmark results.

◆ **Application benchmark programs**
These programs don't struggle with impractical algorithms, but instead use components of known applications for speed measurements. With the help of automated scripts, these application programs execute many typical actions and measure the time that elapses during these actions. Either a time value or a relative measurement is output as a result, which can be used for comparison.

Every user should have at least the first type of analysis programs to determine the state and makeup of his/her PC. The operating system already provides users with some of these programs (MSD from DOS, the Device Manager of Windows 95). However, it is also practical to have special measuring programs for special cases. For example, you may wish to determine the refresh rate or the data throughput of the serial port. We'll introduce you to some important utilities.

Chapter 1

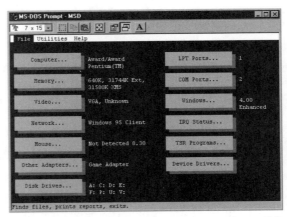

MSD included with DOS and Windows is an example of a "Who am I?" analysis program.

Opinions vary on which benchmark programs are worth recommending. Those who prefer the application benchmark programs have the advantage of very realistic testing of all the components of the PC. These programs furnish very reliable values comparing processors or devices from different manufacturers. What is more, it is extremely difficult to manipulate their results.

Unfortunately, this is not the case with the synthetic benchmark programs. We often hear video card manufacturers deceiving known benchmark programs with driver tricks. Using a manufacturer's own benchmark programs to test processor performance is also questionable. Take the results with a grain of salt (see comments further below).

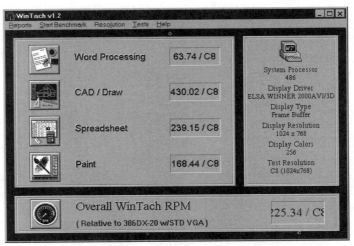

WinTach (for testing video card speed) is somewhere between a synthetic benchmark and an application benchmark program. A few built-in modules from four typical application areas are used to determine a benchmark value.

However, for fine tuning our own computers, we prefer synthetic benchmark programs. They are significantly faster and not so prone to crashes. Application benchmarks such as SysMark 32, under the right (or wrong) circumstances leave a whole battery of program actions running which can often crash the system. However, they are well suited for comparing the performance of complete PCs from different manufacturers. For example, if you wish to purchase a new PC and the dealers allow you, you can use such a program to test the actual practical aptitude of the complete machine.

However, if you then want to quickly determine the effects of BIOS adjustments, for example on hard drive performance, these programs are rather overloaded and not very useful in our opinion.

Don't believe the manufacturer's processor benchmarks

People like to show themselves in the most favorable light. This also applies to processor manufacturers. It's doubtful whether the values output by such a benchmark are actually relevant. It's not just that the high points of the processors from one's own company are highlighted but the competition always performs miserably in these tests.

Intel's iCOMP test procedure is an example. The leader of the market uses this test to try to express the performance differences between the different processor types. These are mostly based on different clock frequencies, which are by far not as noticeable in practice or in the work environment of a PC.

According to the iCOMP 2.0 procedure, a Pentium 200 is a good 40% faster than a Pentium 100. However, in reality, about 25% of the 40% improvement remains. Pretty scanty for the doubled clock frequency and much more expensive.

The MMX benchmark from Intel (IMB) is similar. The competition from AMD or Cyrix doesn't do well at all against the processor giants. However, if you take a closer look at some of the results, you'll notice that the differences are much smaller in the only relevant areas, such as image processing and video decoding. Moreover, prior tests were always performed on motherboards that had been optimized for the Intel CPUs. Once again, nothing to get excited about. The differences are actually much slighter than the manufacturer would like you to think.

The best analysis and benchmark programs

Many commercial and shareware programs are available for technical analysis and speed measurement of the PC. Since there are so many available, we'll introduce a few well-known programs. Then, we'll cover a few of the especially important programs in more detail.

The shareware programs are of course available on the Internet. Since the websites are change often and the programs are offered for downloading by several vendors, we won't be listing all the addresses. If you're interested in a program, use a search engine, such as Alta-Vista (altavista.digital.com) and enter the program name as a search item. You'll find links and other programs from the at other sites too (such as www.shareware.com and www.windows95.com). If you don't have access to the Internet, look for shareware collections such as Pegasus or shareware dealers.

Shareware programs usually have smaller tools that are used to perform quite special analyses. These include testing only memory allocation or determining the refresh rate. However, commercial programs usually offer more complete solutions. Examples here include utility collections such as Norton Utilities and others usually come supplied with a whole bundle of benchmark programs. Remember, however, that the individual components often don't do justice to sophisticated requirements.

In selecting a suitable program, don't forget that some hardware analysis tools (especially shareware programs) may run under DOS. Windows 95 makes life difficult for the programmers of such tools because direct hardware access is impossible without some trouble. For Windows users, however, such programs are often unsuitable because the allocation of resources is not displayed correctly when the drivers for say, an ISDN card are first loaded under Windows.

◆ The **Windows 95 Device Manager** of Windows 95 should be in first place because not only is it free but it also gives you truly detailed information about your system. You can get to the Device Manager using the System icon in the control panel. The Device Manager is also interesting because it displays the allocated and freed resources (IRQ, DMA, memory addresses, etc.).

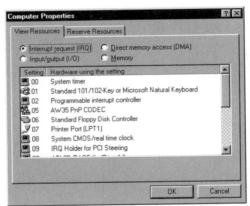

When you display the properties of the computer in the Device Manager, you can check the allocation of all four important resources in your PC and have free resources reserved in conflicts (second tab in the figure).

◆ The **HwDiag** (**Ha**rdware **Diag**nostic) program from Microsoft is available only for owners of the Windows 95b-Version (it can be found on the OSR2 CD in the Other\Misc\Hwtrack directory). A clever enhancement of the Device Manager, it creates a very extensive analysis of the system using data from the registry. Specific information (such as error messages or certain driver classes) are color coded. Be sure to take a look at this information because the program can detect logical errors in the registry, through incorrect or missing drivers. In addition, a list of all free and allocated resources is displayed at the end.

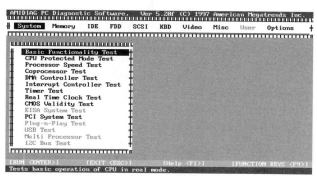

```
⊞ Hardware Diagnostic utility for Windows                          _□×
File  Edit  View  Filter  Help

   INFSection: MS_FDC_Inst
   PortDriver: HSFLOP.pdr
   Driver: C:\WINDOWS\SYSTEM\IOSUBSYS\HSFLOP.PDR
      File Size: 18999 bytes
      File Date: 8/24/1996 11:11 PM
      Manufacturer: Microsoft Corporation
      File Version: 4.00.1111
      LegalCopyright Copyright ® Microsoft Corp. 1988-1995
      FileDescription HSFLOP Virtual Device  (Version 4.0)
      Comments No Information
      SpecialBuild No Information

Class: DiskDrive
   DeviceDesc: GENERIC NEC  FLOPPY DISK
   Registry Key: HKEY_LOCAL_MACHINE\enum\FLOP\GENERIC_NEC__FLOPPY_DISK_\BIOS&*PNP0700&0B
   Current resources:
      Alloc resources:
         None
   CurrentDriveLetterAssignment: A
   Driver: DiskDrive\0002
   DriverDate:  8-24-1996
   INFPath: DISKDRV.INF
   INFSection: GenDiskInstall

Class: System
   DeviceDesc: PCI standard host CPU bridge
   Registry Key: HKEY_LOCAL_MACHINE\enum\PCI\VEN_10B9&DEV_1531\BUS_00&DEV_00&FUNC_00
   Current resources:
```

You can set the display of the Hardware Diagnostic program of Windows 95b according to various criteria or filters. In the figure, we chose display by resources. The program supplies very thorough information about the registry, linked drivers and the entire PC.

◆ **AmiDIAG** is a typical representative of the DOS analysis programs. American Megatrends (AMI) distributes AmiDIAG as shareware that can be downloaded from their website (www.megatrends.com). The program checks the individual components of the PC (ports, memory, motherboard, CPU, etc.). Along with the thorough hardware tests of the plug-in card, dealers and manufacturers will also be interested in the option for running a programmable burn-in test with the test suite, which can be supplemented with their own specialties.

```
AMIDIAG PC Diagnostic Software,   Ver 5.20f (C) 1997 American Megatrends Inc.

‖ System  Memory   IDE   FDD   SCSI   KBD   Video   Misc   User   Options

   Basic Functionality Test
   CPU Protected Mode Test
   Processor Speed Test
   Coprocessor Test
   DMA Controller Test
   Interrupt Controller Test
   Timer Test
   Real Time Clock Test
   CMOS Validity Test
   EISA System Test
   PCI System Test
   Plug-n-Play Test
   USB Test
   Multi Processor Test
   I2C Bus Test

[RUN <ENTER>]        [EXIT <ESC>]        [Help <F1>]    [FUNCTION KEYS <F9>]
Tests basic operation of CPU in real mode.
```

AmiDIAG is one of the best-known all-around DOS analysis programs to evaluate the various PC components.

◆ **Dr. Hardware** also runs under DOS, but goes one big step further than AmiDIAG. The program, currently in version 3.50, is distributed as shareware or as a CD by CDV in stores (about $15). Dr. Hardware not only gives detailed information about the entire PC, including chipsets, L2 cache, SCSI devices, etc., but it also comes with a set of benchmark programs for various components. Among the DOS programs, Dr. Hardware deserves an outstanding position. However, Windows users won't get as much benefit from it.

◆ Two additional, very similar analysis programs for DOS are **PC-Config 8.30** and **Hardware-Info 3.0**. Both of them are pretty much on every shareware CD and, like Dr. Hardware, are classics of the analysis programs. Each program has its strengths and weaknesses compared to the competition. Since these programs are shareware, you can easily pick out the right one for your needs.

◆ Along with these universal analysis and benchmark programs, under DOS there is a great multitude of small programs that specialize in evaluating individual components. These come directly from manufacturers, such as the **CPUID** program from Intel. We're only going to mention four really important and frequently cited programs here. **Landmark-Test**, which is popular in the USA, is used to compare processor speed.

Far more interesting and important are good programs for hard drives. In this category, the popular programs **CoreTest**, **HdBench** and **Threadmark** play a central role. HdBench subjects the hard drive to different performance tests and outputs a weighted mean value in Megs/sec for the crucial amount of the data transfer. This value is ideal for the actual performance of a hard drive in practice. The boundary between slow and fast hard drives is about five Megs/sec. At the dealer's, don't ask about access speed in milliseconds; instead, ask them about the mean data transfer rate of the hard drive you have selected. Threadmark is a freeware program from the well-known SCSI specialist Adaptec. In contrast to many other programs, this one measures the performance of the hard drive under practical conditions. You can download it from the Internet at the address www.adaptec.com/support/BBS_EZSCSI.html.

◆ The **Monitor Test** tool, from Nokia in Sweden, is also specialized. This is perhaps the best program for evaluating your monitor through a string of test patterns. Not only do you see all the weaknesses of your monitor, you can also optimize settings for convergence or geometry errors.

◆ There are also various programs for displaying the refresh rate under Windows. One such tool is the **Refresh** program from Hercules. The program functions with almost all cards (with S3-Chip, but not with ATI cards) and displays the active refresh rate in rough estimate or detailed analysis.

On this computer the video card was set to 100 Hz, but you could also be satisfied with 97.7

◆ The retail avenue has several representatives of the mixed analysis/benchmark program genre for Windows 95. Typical, reliable programs are **WinCheckit Pro 4.0**, from Touchstone, or Quarterdeck's **WinTest 95.**

◆ The Windows tool **Sandra** from Sisoft is especially interesting, not just because it is free of charge. The current version (97.4.1.10) is a 32-bit Win32 program (runs with the Win32 extension on Windows 3.x as well) and offers some benchmark programs along with extensive analyses. For more information go to www.city.ac.uk/~ax515/sandra.html on the Internet.

◆ Probably the best-known collection of analysis, repair and benchmark programs is **Norton Utilites** from Symantec. Norton Utilities includes several high-quality tools for Windows 95 and DOS, that every PC should have. Norton Utilities is best known for its repair and defragmenting programs, Norton Disk Doctor and Norton Speed Disk. The analysis program for DOS is called "NDIAGs," and is similar in appearance and function to the AmiDIAG program we mentioned earlier. Norton Utilities also has a thorough memory display under Windows 95.

◆ The shareware program **Meg 97 Version 3.0** from Mr. Vegas (www. mrvegas.com)is an interesting program for anyone who places value on a thorough analysis of the memory allocation of RAM and the hard drive. Registration costs only 25 dollars, and you get a software program that displays information about memory allocation under Windows 95 in clear, detailed fashion. Display occurs in tree format, and is very easy to read.

◆ **WinTune** is the benchmark program of *Windows* magazine (CMP Media) and is one of the most frequently used programs of this type. It is available as freeware from the Internet at www. winmag.com/software/wt97.htm or from one of the *Windows* magazine issues on CD-ROM. The program comes in a version 2.0 for Windows 3.x or as version WinTune 95 for Windows 95. There is also a WinTune97 version for Windows NT. Each of these versions determines the system performance through extensive tests and outputs a benchmark value for relative comparisons. The program also determines the rough system configuration and gives tips on improving performance.

◆ The **SysMark 32** test of BAPCo (a more detailed introduction follows) corresponds pretty exactly to the WinStone test and is to be viewed as the prototype of application-oriented benchmarks.

◆ Finally, we should mention the **Intel Media Bench** (**IMB**). This is a special application benchmark from Intel, which determines the MMX capabilities of a processor. The performance of the CPU is determined in four typical, MMX-relevant application areas (video, audio and image processing as well as 3-D display). However, only the areas of image processing and video decoding (especially MPEG display) are practical.

The SysMark32 test

BAPCo is an acronym for **B**usiness **A**pplications **P**erformance **Co**rporation. This is a consolidation of some important software and hardware manufacturers, with the goal of developing special application-related benchmarks that can test the performance of PC systems in a practical setting. Perhaps the most important product of BAPCo is the benchmark application SysMark32, which runs with eight well known 32-bit software programs under Windows 95 and NT 4.0 and only on x86 systems. This benchmark is the star program of its genre. The programs are:

Application	Application area	Application	Application area
Adobe PageMaker 6.0	DTP	Microsoft PowerPoint 7.0	Presentation
CorelDRAW! 6.0	Graphics	Lotus WordPro 96	Word processing
Borland Paradox 7.0	Database	Microsoft Word 7.0	Word processing
Lotus Freelance 96	Presentation	Microsoft Excel 7.0	Spreadsheet

To determine the system performance, the SysMark test copies the programs to the hard drive (the configuration of the computer including the registry is backed up beforehand) and then automatically runs all or some of the programs by script control, depending on which option you select. To rule out deviations, the runs are performed several times. If the deviations lie below 5%, the program creates a relative SysMark value, which is related to a reference system with Pentium 100. A value of 250 points means that the computer is 2.5 times as fast as the reference system. The higher the value, the faster the system.

SysMark's advantages are its practical test method and its high reproducibility. However, you pay for this with some very long processing times. On slow systems, a run can take several hours.

By the way, the SysMark 32 is ideally suited for showing speed differences between Windows 95 and Windows NT, because all of the programs run on both systems. However, users wishing to compare the different platforms of Windows NT or the supported processors (*e.g.*, Alpha processor) must resort to SysMark NT.

Shopping tips for quick buyers

Perhaps you have already used the analysis and benchmark programs we've described and discovered that your PC is way too slow. Furthermore, maybe all our tuning tips or references to all the possible hardware devices have whet your appetite for more speed and more options. Have you've already asked yourself whether you could buy something in a hurry that doesn't take that much effort and will immediately give your computer more performance and fun in your work.

Well, in principle, this is no problem. The next two chapters give you detailed advice for upgrading old PCs and buying a new one. However, we'll be happy to pick out some uncomplicated things for you in advance. We are assuming a minimum amount of $150 and a maximum of $550.

Getting the most for $150 (with the least amount of work)

Unfortunately, $150 won't buy you the world in the computer market (yet). Nevertheless, you can buy some good things.

RAM

The first and best you can do is buy more RAM. Take quick glance at the motherboard and if two slots are free head to your dealer. Buy two 16-Meg RAM modules for $150. There's no better investment for your computer.

CD-ROM drive

If your CD-ROM is running at less than 6x speed, you can get a new one with 12x or up to 20x speed.

Keyboard and mouse

This won't bring you more speed directly, but it will make you more efficient and ergonomic. We're talking about a new keyboard and mouse. The natural keyboard and the new IntelliMouse with wheels are great and together cost about $150.

Video card

2-D video cards are selling for a fantastic price right now. Buy one that has an S3-968 processor or an ET6000. They all come with four Megs of RAM. You should be able to get one for under $150. Some of the cards from the first generation of 3-D cards are also reasonably priced. However, at the most we recommend the Matrox Mystique with four Megs of RAM.

Talking about 3-D. For $150 you can get a pure 3-D accelerator card with 3-DFX Voodoo chip from Diamond or Orchid.

Removable storage devices

Get a **ZIP drive** for under $150 — especially the internal drives. That gives you a removable storage medium with 100 Megs per diskette without problems. Extremely practical, extremely reliable. If possible, get the SCSI version.

$550 worth of the best tips for quick, uncomplicated success

You can spend $550 very quickly in your favoirite computer store. Nevertheless, you can get something nice for this price and not spend the whole bundle immediately.

New motherboard with processor

Perhaps the best investment for $550—assuming you have an older computer—is a new **motherboard with processor**. For the named sum you can get a Pentium 200 MMX or AMD K6-200 with an appropriate board.

Periperhals

Buying high-quality peripheral devices is easy and rewarding. A JAZ removable drive from Iomega is tempting (see Chapter 8). How about a rewritable CD-ROM drive (see Chapter 9)?

We also recommend purchasing a really fast hard drive. You should find a 2 Gigabyte model with 7,200 rpm (rounds per minute) for under $500. The 4 Gigabyte successors are currently beyond the $550 maximum. Still, the same as with the motherboard, you should be aware that a new hard drive will bring a powerful change to your system. That's not a change that you make lightly, unless you connect the hard drive to the SCSI bus and not as a new boot drive.

Video card

Buying a new video card such as the Matrox Millenium II, will really speed up your system for low investment and risk. You'll spend about $200-300, but if you want to get rid of the entire $550, go ahead and buy the video expansion along with it.

Sound card

There is one more item that is worth its $400-500 price tag: the new sound card from Terratec, the EWS 64 (in Chapter 11). It's got everything, including digital inputs and outputs. Combined with a CD burner, you can use the sound card to make your PC into a sound studio or digital tape deck.

Chapter 2

Upgrading Tips For Older PCs

When An Old PC Deserves Another Chance

A computer you paid good money for five years ago is seemingly worth only scrap today. However, it depends on how you're using your PC. You should be honest with yourself. Do you really need the new software and hardware currently being hyped in the computer stores? If not, use your old computer with the old software. As long as you only work with documents in DOS (regardless of whether for word processing, spreadsheets or database), using even an old 286 will be acceptable. This only becomes critical when you want to work with graphics — including a graphical user interface such as Windows as well as creating and processing graphics. If you want to use graphic input devices, such as scanners, digital cameras or even video camcorders, you'll need the power of today's PCs.

When there's nothing more you can do for your old PC

A problem users have upgrading their computer systems is that old and new hardware are seldom truly compatible. This is especially true when you're trying to save money. The industry is constantly thinking up new ideas so it has new selling points. Computers that can be upgraded without problems are very profitable. In other words, dealers and manufacturers earn the most whenever we have to buy new and complete devices. In addition, continually faster innovation cycles degrade the PC you've just bought even more quickly into a useless thing.

Usually the two year rule of thumb will serve you well: A computer bought two years ago can barely be upgraded anymore. In the near future, this may even turn into a one year rule of thumb.

Here's where the problems arise, or if your computer has this equipment, then you're better off replacing than upgrading:

- ◆ Anything ticking below 100 MHz is no longer ticking properly. PCs with processors below a 486 at 100 MHz no longer perform good enough for today's software.

- ◆ Besides, everything before the 486-DX4-100 was usually a computer with a complete ISA bus or partial VL bus. That's almost the worst because there are no new plug-in cards for these bus systems.

◆ Anyone who has a BIOS without an upgrade for hard drives larger than 500 Megs is also in bad shape. There are no longer any new hard drives smaller than 1 Gigabyte for sale. While in theory, you could get the newer hard drives to run on old motherboards (see Chapter 7), this is a lot of work that usually leads to problems.

The bottom line is that if you don't have at least a 486-DX4-100 on a motherboard with a PCI bus that can use the BIOS to address today's larger hard drives, it's best to forget about upgrading the computer.

In these cases our experience has found that it is usually better to sell the old computer and use the money to buy a new one. Once it becomes a matter of upgrading the processor, motherboard and/or hard drive, replacing the computer is often the best solution.

What you can do with your old 486 ISA PC

Perhaps you have one of those time-scarred 486 SX computers and just want to breathe a bit of life into it. Well, let's have a look if this is possible. There's hardly anything new you can buy for the computer. However, newspapers usually have a section in the classifieds for used computers where you can find good deals. You could also try the weekend computer swap meets or exchanges that appear in many areas.

Your upgrading options are mainly the RAM and hard drive space. There's hardly any use in upgrading the processor or the video card.

◆ More RAM is always the first and best tuning measure. Upgrade to 32 Megs of RAM. You'll need the old 30-pin SIMMs and, unfortunately, you might have to do some hunting to find them.

◆ Look for a good (used) ISA video card. Perhaps you'll still be able to find one with the speedy S3-928 processor (for example, ELSA Winner 1000). ATI video cards are also often good choices. Be careful, however, because some old ATI ISA cards limit the maximum RAM to 12 Megs. Sometimes you can also find cards with the ET6000 chip from Tseng.

◆ Not enough space on your hard drive? If you have an IDE system, you've got a tough problem. Our recommendation is don't try to upgrade IDE. However, you can switch to SCSI. Buy an ISA-SCSI controller with BIOS support for larger hard drives (for example, the 1542 from Adaptec). Not only can you connect hard drives larger than 500 Megs, you can also add removable hard drives, such as a ZIP drive, new SCSI CD-ROMs or even a CD burner. For more on SCSI, see Chapter 7.

◆ There's not much hope for more processor speed. Read your motherboard manual to find out which processor types your board supports. The list won't be very long and you won't be able to buy them new at a store. Users who have a 486-33 should look for a 486DX2-66. This will fit into the old socket and will give you more performance immediately. Be careful because your old board probably only works with 5-volt processors. The second generation of 486DX2-66 processors often works with 3.3 volts. Things can easily go wrong, so pay close attention to the voltage type. We'll talk more about overdrive processors and other alternatives later in this chapter.

◆ Owners of VL bus computers with 486 40-MHz processors from AMD should try to get hold of an old 486 80-MHz CPU. Sometimes you can also put 486 120-MHz CPUs in these boards. Pay attention to the voltage requirements and the pinouts of the processors. Otherwise, the recommendations in this chapter apply to your situation as well.

If these tips are more of an inconvenience, why not simply buy a new PC? Plus, you don't have to throw away your old PC. It will still give you good service, for example, as a communications computer (for faxes and e-mail) or as a printer server and backup storage.

A 486-DX4 that will work

Computer models with 100, 120 or 133 MHz only had success on the market for a short time. They came on the market almost the same time as the first Pentium computers and were, for a while, a reasonably priced alternative.

The advantage over the older 486 PCs (with 33, 40, 66 and 80 MHz) was that the DX4s could be equipped with some modern PC developments, such as the PCI bus, ZIF socket type 3, PS/2-SIMM memory modules and BIOS upgrade for large hard drives. As a result, they are still quite suitable for upgrading and their performance is still acceptable. For example, Asus successfully sold the SP3 motherboard for such processors through to early 1997. It was a VIP board because it had a VL slot (VESA Local-Bus) along with the usual ISA and PCI slots.

Although slow by today's standards, there still life in them. Keep the following points in mind if you plan to upgrade one of these machines.

◆ Replacing the motherboard is hardly worth your while if your machine has PS/2 memory banks and PCI slots. Hold on to your old motherboard.

◆ You can plug a Pentium Overdrive (or compatible) into the ZIF socket. Don't spend more than $140 and your overdrive should give you decent performance increase. You can read more about this later in this chapter. Pay attention to the voltage because 3.3 volts is usually the required amount.

◆ Upgrade to 32 or even 64 Megs of RAM. This is a tremendous relief to your slow hard drive.

◆ Upgrade to SCSI. It's best to do this with a simple PCI SCSI controller (for example, the Adaptec 2940). This allows you to easily connect newer, faster hard drives and peripheral devices. Upgrading to EIDE usually brings trouble, because your old drive definitely won't get along with the new one.

◆ A new PCI video card can work wonders. Make certain to buy a fast one such as the Matrox Millenium II. The advantage is that you can continue using it in your future Pentium computer. The only reason to hold back would be if you've got your eyes on a Pentium II. In this case, AGP is the new standard (see Chapter 5 and Chapter 10 for more on video cards).

You'll find that you can work quite well with such an upgraded 486 computer. However, you might want to avoid using Windows NT or the latest 32-bit programs for Windows 95. These often call for more processor power.

We'll give you more detailed information about the individual upgrading options in the following sections.

What you can do with old P60-P100 computers

If user requirements aren't too high and a good 486 is still good enough for normal office applications, then a Pentium 60, 66, 90 or 100 will also do just fine. These models of the first and second generation of the Pentium are still very useful. Low cost upgrading options are available in many places. So if you don't have to have a power machine for 3-D animations or spreadsheets, stick with your old Pentium. Otherwise, an aging Pentium will still perform good service as a second computer on a small network.

You'll find plenty of upgrading tips for this type of computer in the next section. These can easily smooth out any bottlenecks.

INSTANT UPGRADES FOR OLD PCS

While it is true that there are fewer options for upgrading or tuning old PCs, there are a few. Granted, it usually won't boost performance as much as you would hope.

Naturally, we don't want to spend more money than we need to spend. So, we tell you mainly about measures that cost nothing or only a little bit of money or effort. In the next section we'll discuss more effective upgrading measures, which also cost more money. The following summarizes your less-expensive options:

◆ Upgrade your RAM and make sure you are using the appropriate software and an optimum system configuration.

◆ Increase the clock speed of the processor and motherboard.

◆ Be careful if you upgrade with hard drives and CD-ROM drives. There are many dangers lurking here that you can best overcome by switching to SCSI.

◆ Replace the processor with an overdrive.

◆ Replace the motherboard, perhaps at the same time switching to a newer processor.

◆ Exhaust all your opportunities for using your old hardware efficiently. For example, there are adapters that allow you to use old RAM chips with newer motherboards.

More RAM makes your old machine live again

We've said this already many times but it's very important. Increasing RAM will give your machine tremendous performance increases. However, this depends largely on the operating system or the system configuration. On modern Pentium computers the hard drive is quite clearly the speed-limiting factor. By increasing RAM, the hard drive is accessed less frequently. This will greatly speed up the entire system.

On older computers, the processor can also be a limiting factor. In this case, a RAM upgrade won't have such a strong effect. Still, upgrading RAM is always recommended — especially considering the prices to which RAM has fallen.

We recommend the following amounts of RAM:

◆ 16 Megs for working with DOS

◆ 32 Megs for Windows 3.x

◆ 64 Megs for Windows 95
Although Windows 95 will run with 16 Megs, you should upgrade to 64 Megs and then adapt your data carrier cache and swap file settings accordingly (see Chapter 8). Your PC will act as if you had bought a new one. A Pentium 166 with 64 Megs of RAM, for example, may run faster than a Pentium 200 with only 16 Megs (according to application benchmarks such as SysMark 32).

Don't use Windows 95 if your PC isn't a Pentium 90

Although virtually everyone with a PC is using Windows 95, it's possible to live without it. If you don't own at least a Pentium 90 with 32 Megs of RAM and a fast hard drive, keep using Windows 3.x. It runs significantly better and faster with old hardware than Windows 95 does.

We're familiar with only two important advantages that Windows 95 offers. They are the long filenames and the (almost) solved problem with limited system resources for Windows 3.x. Even considering software, Windows 95 hasn't brought any great advancements. Office 95, for example, differs little from Office 4.x.

Admittedly, Windows 95 operates nicer, but you could have that for Windows 3.x as well. Regardless of whether we're talking about the Taskbar, Internet Explorer or Dial-Up Networking, almost everything is also available for the old 16-bit Windows. So, be consistent. If you are going to keep your old 486 or Pentium 60, keep the old software as well.

Make certain your system is optimally configured

Pure hardware power isn't everything. You must make certain that your old PC is using optimal settings. The BIOS and the operating system play an especially important role here. At the beginning of this book you will find an overview of the most important configuration settings and tuning measures for all areas of the PC. Just because your old machine has been performing its duty for years without complaints does not mean that there is nothing more than can be optimized.

Fine tuning for your Pentium 60

Similar to tuned up 486 computers, you can still work quite well with the Pentiums of the first generation (the P60 and P66). Along with the normal upgrading options we mentioned earlier (more RAM, a good video card and SCSI connections), two additional points should be considered:

◆ These first Pentiums still work with 5 volts and produce quite a bit of heat. Also, the existing boards have very slow chipsets and won't accept any new processors, with the exception of a few special overdrives. Not a very satisfactory solution.

◆ Keep an eye on the system clock, which like the clock on current Pentium models, is limited to a maximum of 66 MHz (memory access) or 33 MHz (PCI bus). Pentium 60s and 66s differ only in the external system clock (60 MHz vs. 66 MHz). By making certain the chip has good ventilation, you can increase the system clock by switching jumpers on the board.

Overclocking the Plato board to 66 MHz

Unfortunately, increasing the system clock from 60 to 66 MHz is not documented for the most widely distributed P60 board, the Intel Plato. However, it can be done:

1. Find the appropriate jumpers on the front of the board in front of the second PS/2 slot (from the right).

2. The first post *J1H3* is connected at Position *1-2* for 50 MHz and at *2-3* for 60 MHz. To increase to 66 MHz, simply set the jumper to Position *1-2* of the second post (*J1H4*).

Why the P75 is the slowest Pentium

As an inexperienced user, you might think a higher clock speed of the processor would create a faster overall computer. However, this isn't the case. A typical example of this faulty thinking is the Pentium 75.

What can you do? Well, simply try to increase the speed of your P75 to 90 or even 100 MHz. Don't forget the ventilation. The P75, P90 and P100 CPUs come from the same production series. The Pentium 75, like the first P100 computers we were talking about, operates with a 50 MHz system and a 25 MHz PCI clock. The clock conversion from the system to the CPU clock is 1.5 (50 x 1.5 = 75). The result: In contrast to the maximum possible 66 MHz, the entire computer, including peripherals, runs very slowly. For more information about the different speeds of processors, see tabular overviews with the data of old processors and background information about setting the processor speed in Chapter 4.

Another thing that slows these systems is that Pentium-75 boards were frequently equipped with old chipsets. You rarely got modern technology with these boards. Fortunately, they haven't been used or built for normal PCs for a long time. However, notebook computers are still being sold with this Pentium. Make sure you don't buy one of these.

The speed is only Intel's recommendation for the highest possible stability. Don't panic, though, your P75 should be able to manage 90 MHz with good ventilation. Perhaps you could purchase a new cooling fan or an active cooling element and heat conducting paste. So what if the processor dies two years earlier as a result? It's already old technology—by the time it fails you'll most likely have already replaced it.

Speed tricks for P90 and P100 processors

There are still many Pentium 90 and 100 processors in circulation. Naturally, they are no longer the fastest. However, by resetting jumpers, you can squeeze the last bit of performance from these aging machines. A Pentium 90 differs from the 100 only in the clock speed set on the board. Intel produced both types in the same production line, and later tested them to determine which ones could bear the 100 MHz permanently. The processors that couldn't keep up were sold as P90s.

Users who keep an eye on good ventilation and don't care how long the processor lasts in these already aging Pentiums can play with the clock speed.

◆ Anyone who owns a P90 should check in the manual to see how it can be boosted to a P100. The old boards only know these two types. A side effect is that the system bus also increases from 60 to 66 Mhz and the clock on the PCI bus moves from 30 to 33 MHz. The Pentium 90 ordinarily works with a 1.5 clock speed of 60 MHz, while the P100 works with 1.5 speed of 66 MHz.

◆ Users who don't want to take the risk or who are having problems with the P90 at 100 MHz can try to get a genuine P100. They aren't even building these anymore so, they can be bought very cheaply as used parts for 50-110 dollars.

◆ Some old P90 processors may still have Intel's well-known Pentium bug. You may still be able to take advantage of the trade-in promise from Intel. Contact Intel for more information (www.intel.com).

You'll find more information for the proper setting of the processor speed in Chapter 4.

Caution when switching from P90 to P100

You should be very careful with older boards when you change your P90 system to the settings for a P100. The P100 is the only Intel processor designed for two clock multiplications: 1.5 and double. While the P100 on newer boards is operated externally with 66 MHz, and is significantly faster than a P90 system at 60 MHz, this was not the case with the first Pentium boards. On these, the P100 was operated externally with a 50 MHz system clock and 25 MHz PCI clock (with double clock doubling for the processor). The result was a P100 slower than a P90. So, be careful and check the documentation of your motherboard. The reverse is also appropriate: If you are running a P100 on one of those old boards, switch it to a P90 or replace the motherboard. The speed increase will be considerable.

UPGRADE COMPONENTS THAT ARE WORTH THE MONEY

The most effective—although not exactly the cheapest—way to give your computer more performance is to upgrade with new components. Who wouldn't like a new processor or a new or additional hard drive? Separating the desire and its fulfillment, however, are the expense and the uncertainty about making the right purchase. Moreover, problems lurk everywhere due to potential incompatibilities between old and new components. Often, nothing seems more difficult than properly upgrading your existing PC. The recommendations we're providing in this section will make the decisions easier for you.

A new video card works wonders

Many users underestimate the significance of two components: the hard drive and the video card. We'll go into the optimal video card in more detail in Chapter 10. Right now we'll just mention the most important things.

◆ A video card with today's accelerator cards will get your old system moving. This is an optimal tuning measure, especially for Windows. If your old computer has a PCI motherboard, then you can choose from many cards currently available. Graphic processors from S3 (type 968 or Virge), Tseng (ET6000) or Matrox (MGA) are good choices. However, these are slowly being phased out and replaced by new cards with 3-D processors (Permedia, Riva, etc.). Buy a card with no less than two Megs of RAM, and VRAM if possible. We'll tell you more about that later.

◆ Forget everything that the industry and advertisements tell you: Usable 3-D support isn't available on old PCs. The processor itself makes an important contribution in the conversion of the 3-D world. Instead, concentrate on the 2-D functions.

◆ If you only have a motherboard with an ISA or VL bus, search the classifieds or flea markets to find a high-quality accelerator card with VRAM video memory. You should have no trouble locating one, and the benefits are great.

◆ Make sure you are using the latest drivers for your video card. You should be able to find these easily from the manufacturer or the internet. Under no circumstances should you use your old 16-bit Windows 3.x driver with Windows 95. That greatly slows down the system and can make it unstable.

In Chapter 3 we introduce you to some cards worth considering.

Upgrading with new hard drives and CD-ROMs

Upgrading an old IDE computer system with new EIDE hard drives or CD-ROMs is very delicate business. You can safely assume that in the best case the new devices will be severely slowed down when operating with the old controllers and in mixed operation with the old devices. In the worst case, they won't work with each other at all. For more information, check the chapters about SCSI and EIDE (Chapter 7), hard drives (Chapter 8) and CD-ROMs (Chapter 9).

We'll give you the most important information here. If you absolutely have to have a new hard drive or a faster CD-ROM, we recommend the following:

◆ First, the most important recommendation. Switching to SCSI will open up performance reserves you might not have realized were possible for your computer. Although you can even continue using your old (E)IDE devices, we don't recommend doing so.

◆ Beware the IDEs: When you purchase new EIDE devices, it is a good idea to scrap the old ones if at all possible. At least that way you won't have any problems with incompatibilities between devices.

◆ If you have your heart set on continuing to use your old (E)IDE devices, try to connect the new ones to the first controller connection on the motherboard and the old ones to the second. These are both managed independently, so that the new devices won't be slowed down by the old ones. However, this only holds true for older motherboards. You can read more about this in Chapter 6.

In contrast to upgrading with EIDE, switching to SCSI is much easier and has a more secure future. You can continue using all the SCSI devices that you buy now on your next computer. You'll have to spend 100-175 dollars for a SCSI controller. Also the SCSI devices are somewhat more expensive than their EIDE colleagues but the SCSI products more than make up for this with a significantly greater speed potential. One aspect of this is particularly important for old, not so powerful processors. IDE devices place a great burden on the processor during their operation. CD-ROMs, for example, often burden the processor as much as 90%. SCSI devices demand much less, so that processing power is free for operating the actual software.

SCSI controllers help get your old PC back on its feet

If you decide to install SCSI devices, you'll also need to install a SCSI controller. But not all controllers are equal. You'll find more detailed information in Chapter 7. The most important question is whether you wish to install a SCSI hard drive. If so, you need a controller with a BIOS. On the other hand, if you only wish to use devices such as scanners, CD-ROMs or CD burners, a simpler controller without its own BIOS will do the trick. In this case, we recommend the Adaptec 1505 (about $50). Probably the best-known SCSI controller with its own BIOS for the ISA bus is the Adaptec 1542.

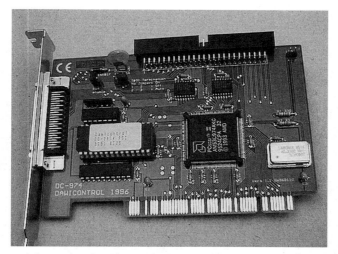

A hot price tip: The DAWI-Control DC 2974 PCI is compatible with the well-known Adaptec 2940, but costs much less.

Controllers exist for the ISA and the PCI slots, but because of PCI's popularity, you usually will only find the PCI bus models in stores. Don't bother with at the latest developments such as the Ultra or the Wide SCSI. Instead, take a normal model such as the Adaptec 2940 or the DAWI Control DC 2974 PCI from DAWICONTROL Computer Systems. Educate yourself about the configuration and connection options in Chapter 7. Your old computer will feel like its been reborn with SCSI.

A new motherboard with a normal processor is usually a better solution

It sounds so good in theory: Simply buy a new overdrive processor, remove the old processor, plug the new one into the socket, restart the machine and then enjoy the speed. Gosh, if only things were that nice and easy. Unfortunately, this is not the case—overdrive processors are only worthwhile in a few cases.

The first point is the most important: Overdrives are almost always overpriced. Sometimes they're almost as expensive as a new motherboard with a normal processor of the same value. However, this combination will give you much more performance right away, because the motherboard also makes an important contribution to speed. This is the reason that few dealers have overdrives in stock. Also, few will recommend that you purchase an overdrive.

So when does it make sense to get an overdrive and which one should you get? We'll answer the second part later. For now, overdrives are only worthy of your consideration under the following conditions:

- You have a system in which it's difficult to install a new motherboard.

- You don't trust yourself to install a new motherboard with a processor or you simply don't feel like doing it. Some dealers will do it for you for 30-50 dollars.

- For some reason you're fortunate to find an overdrive at a very reasonable price.

Getting a handle on overdrives

Overdrive processor are used to upgrade or replace old processors. They contain an internal clock increaser that converts the outer clock speed, for example, from 33 MHz with 486 processors to 83 or 133 MHz. In principle, overdrives are normal processors of the next generation, but they fit on old motherboards through integrated adapters. These adapters are necessary for the varying pin layouts and power supplies.

Currently there are three types of overdrives. You have to be really careful to make the right selection, because making the wrong selection will leave you up the proverbial creek. Here are the three overdrive types:

- For 486 processors the only really practical overdrives are the types 486-SX, 486-33, 486-40 and 486-DX2.

- For the first generation of Pentium processors, the P60 or P66 (which are also referred to simply as "Type P5"), Intel has an overdrive labeled "P5T."

- For the second generation of Pentium processors, the P75, P90 and P100 (also called "Type P54"), The proper overdrives are called "P54CT." These are available with different clock speeds. Since the beginning of 1997, there is also a model with MMX support.

The differences in overdrives lie in the type of processor socket supported, the necessary power supply (overdrives usually come with a built-in voltage converter) and the clock speed. Corresponding frequency increasers are also built into the overdrives.

The right overdrive for old 486 computers

Anyone who wishes to upgrade an old 486 has the choice between the PODP5V from Intel, which works internally with 83 MHz, and competing products from Kingston and Evergreen. The Intel PODP is based on a Pentium processor. However, it has the disadvantage of not being especially fast and only fits in certain ZIF sockets (Types 2, 3 or 6). 486 motherboards with this socket almost always have a 486 DX4 chip with 100 or 133 MHz built in. Motherboards without a ZIF socket have to go away empty handed. Compared to a 486DX4-100, the overdrive brings about a 20% speed increase. For the slight gain in performance, the price is too high at about 200 dollars.

The alternatives from Evergreen and Kingston are based on 486 processor types from AMD and are much more interesting than the PODP. The Evergreen 586 (also called the "486 Upgrade") is based on an AMD processor that works internally with 133 MHz. It costs around 160 dollars and is somewhat above a 486DX4-100 in performance. Its great advantage is that it fits on any 486 motherboard, even the ones without a ZIF socket. So, you can easily replace your old 486-33 with the Evergreen (provided the processor is not soldered to the board, which is rarely the case).

The Kingston Turbochip 133 is very similar to the Evergreen and offers about the same performance for the money. Ordinarily, you can easily use it on all old 486 motherboards. Your decision on which of the two processors you purchase should depend on availability and the current price at your dealer.

	Intel PODP	Evergreen 486 Upgrade	Kingston Turbochip 133
Processor type	Pentium	486	486
Required socket	ZIF3	486 CPU or ZIF3	486 CPU or ZIF3
Recommended for	486-33 or 486-DX2 with ZIF-2, 3, 6	All 486 types up to DX4-100	All 486 types up to DX4-100
External voltage	5 Volts	5 Volts	5 Volts
External speed	33 MHz	33 MHz	33 MHz
Internal speed	83 MHz	133 MHz	133 MHz
Clock factor	2.5x	4x	4x
Speed compared to a 486DX4-100	124 %	113 %	113 %
Internet	www.intel.com	www.evertech.co.uk	www.kingston.com
Price in dollars	220	165	165

Compare the overview of all old 486 and Pentium-compatible processors in Chapter 4.

Price tips for new 486 motherboards

Along with the overdrive processors we've been discussing, there are two other, very interesting alternatives: the old 5x86 processors from AMD (5x86-PR75) and Cyrix (5x86-PR100 and PR120). However, these alternatives require that your motherboard has a ZIF socket with at least 168 pins (Types 1, 2, 3 or 6) and that the processor is supplied with 3.3 volts from either the motherboard or an adapter, instead of the five volts typical for 486 machines.

You can still find the AMD 5x86-Pr75 for under $50. It works externally with the 33 MHz of your 486 motherboard and converts this internally through a factor 4 to 133 MHz clock speed. The performance is about the equivalent of the Evergreen or Kingston overdrive. When it comes to the price, it is the best alternative, indisputably. However, don't forget about the voltage: the processor uses 3.3 volts instead of 5. You can also achieve this with an adapter (see information box in Chapter 4). Incompatibilities hardly occur, however, the L2 cache creates problems with the AMD on some boards. These range from performance that is too low to DMA access problems with diskettes, hard drives or sound cards.

> **NOTE**
>
> **2x or 3x?—The right tuning factor for the AMD**
>
> The AMD 5x86 works internally with quadruple clock doubling. However, the factor 2 must be set on the motherboard. Most Intel boards for a 486-DX4 CPU are jumpered to the factor 3. Then the AMD will only run with 100 MHz. Make sure to switch the setting to factor 2. If your motherboard has a 40 or a 50-MHz system bus as a setting, experiment whether the processor will still run stably. This can result in a high additional performance (3 x 50 = 150 MHz or 4 x 40 = 160 MHz).

However, keep in mind that upgrading with a new CPU will only get you results if your computer has enough RAM, and above all, also has an L2 cache. Otherwise, save yourself the trouble. If you already have a DX4-100 or DX4-120, the speed gain is too slight to make the effort worth your while anyway.

Usually a 486-SX board like this one can only be upgraded with the help of a voltage adapter. A full-value 486 CPU inserted into the left coprocessor socket automatically disables the 486SX.

It's similar with the reasonably priced Cyrix models 5x86-100 and the 120. Although they're no longer being made, if you can still get a reasonably priced, used model, it's worth considering. They can be operated with 33 or 50 MHz and 40-MHz external clock (VL bus computer), they use a triple or double-speed conversion, and you get 100 or 120 MHz. The performance is just below (100 MHz) or just over (120 MHz) that of the AMD-5x86. For more information on the different 486 processor types, see Chapter 4.

NOTE

486 evolution, the trouble with voltage

Some of you may be asking yourselves, „Why can't I just replace my old 486-33 with a 486DX4?" In principle, that might work, if it weren't for the conflict with the voltage. Intel had to decrease the supply of voltage for the higher speed processors from 5 volts to 3.3 volts to keep the temperature down. Only the first generation of the 486DX2-66 still ran with 5 volts. If you can find a used model, you can replace your 486-33 with it. However, we recommend caution—there are already processors of this type in circulation that run on 3.3 volts. If your motherboard doesn't support the change, you won't be able to use the new processor. However, there is a solution: voltage adapters. For more information, see Chapter 4.

Replacing the processor

After all this discussion of the various overdrive processors and Intel alternatives (such as the 5x86 CPUs from AMD and Cyrix) you may have lost track of which type is best for which situation. The following will assist you in your decision about whether a CPU upgrade makes sense, and if so, which type of upgrade you need. Also compare the table with the relevant data about all 486 processors in Chapter 4. Of all the options, the AMD 5x86-Pr75 is the most flexible and has the best price-performance ratio.

Existing 486	Upgrade option or recommendation	Comment
SX25 or SX50 (without ZIF socket)	DX2-66, Kingston, Evergreen, AMD 5x86, Cyrix 5x86, if possible, set system clock to 33 MHz	Voltage adapter from 5 to 3.3 volts almost always necessary, coprocessor socket is useful
DX33 (without ZIF)	DX2-66, DX4-100, Kingston, Evergreen, AMD 5x86, Cyrix 5x86	Voltage adapter from 5 to 3.3 volts almost always necessary (except with DX2-66)
DX2-66 or DX2-80 (without ZIF)	DX4-100 or DX4-120, Kingston, Evergreen, AMD 5x86, Cyrix 5x86	Voltage adapter from 5 to 3.3 volts almost always necessary
DX4-75 (with ZIF)	Intel PODP, Kingston, Evergreen, AMD 5x86, Cyrix 5x86	Easy and worth your while, since a ZIF socket and 3.3 volts are present
DX4-100 or DX4-120 (with ZIF)	Intel PODP, Kingston, Evergreen, AMD 5x86, Cyrix 5x86	Hardly worth it, since there is only a minimum speed gain

Tuning up an overdrive for the P60

The P5T-overdrive from Intel, compared to the PODP, is definitely the more worthwhile purchase. However, the price, at about $250, is roughly equal to the cost of a new motherboard with a normal Pentium.

There is only one type of P5T; it's the same processor used for the P60 and the P66. The speed gain of 50-70% is attained by an internal clock doubler (i.e., 120 or 133 MHz). It has an integrated cooling fan and fits into the ZIF socket 4 of the normal P5 processor type.

You need to be careful if you upgrade a P60 with the P5T. Make certain to change the settings on the motherboard for a P66. This is the only way to squeeze the maximum performance out of it. The P5T can be operated with the maximum external clock speed without giving it a second thought (in contrast to your old P60). Some old P66 processors also wanted to have an increased voltage supply of 5.27 volts. However, you should leave these at the normal 5 volts.

Clock speed and confusion over the latest Pentium overdrives

Yesterday they were the fastest on the market, today they're already outdated: second-generation Pentiums (the P54-series, including P75, P90 and P100) are no longer very desireable. Once again, however, Intel offers an overdrive but the options are rather confusing. Users who are very careful can get an additional 50% more performance quickly. Once again you have to take a critical look at the current prices. These overdrives are usually priced above the costs of a comparable normal Pentium.

The P54CT overdrive comes in three variants for the P75, P90 and P100, differing only in the clock speed. All of the variants work with 2.5 clock doubling and increase performance by about 40%. Intel offers an overdrive special for one's old processor, perhaps leading you to think you can only use the appropriate overdrive for your old processor. This isn't the case. Your existing processor is not the deciding factor. Instead, you should know which processor type your old motherboard supports as the maximum.

If you're using a P75 on your board, Intel wants to sell you the P54CT-125 as an upgrade kit. However, if your board supports the jumper settings for a P100 (with 66-MHz system clock), you can just as easily use the P54CT-166, which is actually intended as an overdrive for the P100. You gain much more performance by doing this. The disadvantage of the two slower P54CT types (125 and 150) is that they are operated with the reduced system clock of 50 or 60 MHz. So the only reason for buying such a slow overdrive is if you are afraid to switch your motherboard to a 66 MHz system clock.

Incidentally, you have to decide exactly which type you will buy beforehand, because the overdrives themselves cannot be overclocked or rejumpered. They run internally at a fixed speed. You only have to reset the clock of the system bus, if at all possible, to 66 MHz. This is really easy to do. Check your manual, find the jumpers near the processor and reset them as documented in the manual. This will take only a few minutes.

The bottom line is to buy the P54CT-166 no matter whether it's a P75, P90 or P100. The exception here is if your motherboard doesn't let you set the system clock to 66 MHz.

By the way, compared to a genuine P166 with a new motherboard, your old board is still old with the P54CT-166. The slower asynchronous L2 cache used ordinarily on old Pentium boards acts as a powerful brake on your computer's speed. See the following section for more information.

Pentium overdrives and multimedia power

We won't saying much more to the information in the last section on the P54CT overdrive. The exception is the new ones also support MMX.

The new overdrives come in three models:

◆ With 166 and 200 MHz for a system bus clock of 66 MHz,

◆ With 200 MHz for a system bus clock of 66 MHz,

◆ A variant with 180-MHz internal and 60-MHz external system bus

Just as was the case with the P54CT, the internal clock speed is also fixed, so that overclocking is not possible. The two models with 166 and 200 MHz are meant for upgrading old P100, P133 and P166 computers. The 180 model, on the other hand, is meant for PCs with a P90, P120 and P150.

Here again, you need to set your motherboard to 66 MHz and only buy either the 166 MHz or the 200 overdrive model. The prices for these two are around 220 and 330 dollars. That means you're better off buying an AMD K6 of equal value, plus a voltage adapter (see Chapter 4).

Moreover, the BIOS of the motherboard must support the overdrive, because the overdrive registers as an overdrive, not as a normal Pentium. The 200 model only runs on a ZIF socket 7, since only this can furnish the necessary power supply of 5 Amps with 3.3 volts. The other two models will also fit in socket 5. Intel offers a tool on its internet pages (www.intel.com/overdrive/bios/download.htm) that tests the BIOS for compatibility with the overdrive. As an alternative, you can also update the BIOS (in Chapter 6).

Options for upgrading with the current processor

To be honest, we wouldn't buy an overdrive. Since we're not afraid of replacing a motherboard, we would rather advise you to replace the board and processor. Users who only wish to replace the processor don't have to buy one of the expensive overdrives from Intel.

Much more interesting and desirable is the option to insert one of these new MMX processors from Intel, AMD or Cyrix directly into your old board. It's not very difficult either. We describe the pros and cons of Pentium MMX, Pentium II, AMD's K6 and the new Cyrix 6x86MX in Chapter 4. With the individual model descriptions you will also find information about how to upgrade your old PC with one of these new CPUs. You need at least a ZIF socket 5 (socket 7 for 166 MHz and higher) and a BIOS that can be updated (most motherboards have had that kind of BIOS for years now). Make sure that the old motherboard is able to satisfy the new CPU's hunger for current and that the power supply is right. As we said, for more information, please turn to Chapter 4.

> **NOTE**
>
> **Old motherboards only go to factor 2. That means that 133 MHz is the end. Exception: CPUs for 233 MHz!**
>
> All modern processors work with internal clock speed multiplication. For this purpose, modern boards or processors have 2 contact pins (BF0 and BF1), used to set the four multipliers (see Chapter 4 for a more exact explanation). However, motherboards prior to 1996 usually don't have the BF1 pin, so only factors 1.5 and 2.0 are available. Thus, all current processors have a maximum clock speed of 133 MHz. One exception is the Pentium 233-MMX, which was intentionally set to the settings of a Pentium 100. In other words: The Pentium 233 or AMD K6-233 are the hottest upgrading tips for old P100 motherboards! For up to 133 MHz, the Cyrix M1 6x86-Pr166+ is the best alternative. Be warned, though, it uses a great deal of power, just like the AMD K6-233, and gets very hot. The motherboard has to be able to manage with a Cyrix M1.

Removing that old motherboard

Don't be afraid to replace your motherboard because it isn't difficult to do. Furthermore, it solves so many problems and is often the cheapest solution. As we've said many times, the costs of an overdrive processor are often the same as for a new motherboard with a new processor. However, motherboard replacement is only worth your while if you already have a PCI system. Only then can you continue using your old cards. What is more, with a motherboard replacement, it is easier and more convenient to replace the processor later on. Keep these points in mind:

◆ The costs for a new motherboard and processor are almost always lower than for an overdrive processor—and the performance is much better.

◆ Except for the new ATX motherboards (Chapter 3), new boards almost always fit in the old case so that's not a problem.

◆ New standard boards are equipped with a PCI bus and the memory banks for PS/2 SIMMs with a 72-pin connection. That means you will have difficulty continuing to use your old SIMMs. However, turn to Chapter 2 to find out how to do it. Watch out for the new boards with DIMM memory modules. You'll find more information about them in Chapter 4.

◆ The IDE or EIDE port may also cause problems. On your old motherboard, your old IDE drives will slow down a newly purchased EIDE drive. Only newer motherboards are able to operate EIDE devices of varying speeds at one shared connection. For more information about this and a possible solution, see Chapter 6.

A motherboard replacement is often an ideal solution and gives good results. You don't have to be the most gifted person to ever use a screwdriver to remove the old one from the case. Note or take photos of the old cable connections. Hardly anything has changed on the new boards in this respect. Also, many books are available to help you with detailed photographs and explanations.

Why a new motherboard really speeds up the old P90 or P100

Since the introduction of the 386 processors, all CPUs or motherboards work with cache chips. These place data in temporary storage for the slow RAM and allow the processor to continue working despite high clock speed. Since the 486, a first-level cache has been built into the processor with a larger **S**econd **L**evel **C**ache (SLC) on the motherboard (see Chapter 4).

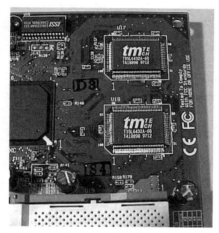

The pipelined burst cache on modern Pentium boards is usually integrated on the motherboard with two SRAM chips.

In the last few years new Pentium boards have only been using an especially quick variant of SLC, which runs in pipelined burst mode and furnishes data up to 67 Megs/second (called "pB-Cache"). Older Pentium boards with P60, P90 and P100 processors, on the other hand, usually still have an SLC, which runs under the slower asynchronous method. That just doesn't do the job. So if you bought a Pentium computer two years ago, replacing the motherboard can give you a significant speed increase, because the new pB-Cache is much faster. Unfortunately, you can only use P90 and faster processors on the new boards, not P60 processors.

Using Old SIMMs on the new motherboard

If you upgrade your old ISA computer to PCI, for example by replacing the motherboard, you probably want to continue using your old SIMM memory modules. But their 30 pins won't fit into the new 72-pin PS/2 connections. Don't worry: In this case, SIMM adapters (also called "shuttles") can help.

However, there are some things you need to consider for successful use. Only chips of the same type can be on an adapter. Also, the access speed decreases by about 5ns through the somewhat longer conducting paths, which may make it necessary to adapt the wait states in the BIOS. In other words, your computer will usually be slower than with PS/2 chips. Depending on the speed of the old memory chips (60, 70 or 80ns), you will have to buy an adapter on which the access speed of the SIMMs can be set by DIP switch. For the same reason, such constructions seldom mix with genuine PS/2 memory chips.

> **NOTE**
>
> **Make 64 out of 32—Adapters for PS/2 to DIMM chips**
> PS/2-SIMMs are actually out again, because the new 64-bit DIMM memory modules—usually as the SDRAM type—are being used more and more on the latest motherboards (see the information about memory chips in Chapter 4). But don't despair—here again, you can continue using your old chips with the help of the right adapters. Follow the compromise solution only in the configuration of the access times in the BIOS.

The increased space requirements and the weight of the finished construction can be especially critical. For example, an adapter with 4 x 4 Meg chips requires a lot of room and doesn't sit very stably in the socket. It often blocks the path for other adapters, cards or other components. If you have your heart set on installing an additional adapter (for example, for 2 x 16 Megs), you will almost always have to purchase an identical model. If you have problems finding one, try an electronics mail-order catalog.

*With four old SIMMs per adapter and two identical modules,
there's no more RAM room on this motherboard.*

Using old SIMMs as printer and fax memory

If you still have SIMM modules left over and don't think you can use them any longer, take a look inside your printer. Many manufacturers are now using sockets for standard or PS/2 SIMMs. Naturally, they don't tell customers this; instead, they try to earn lots of money through expensive and supposedly special printer memory modules. So see if your old modules will function as printer memory.

The newer models of the HP Deskjet and HP Laserjet series can be upgraded with PS/2 modules, for example, although there are a few snags to consider. You have to find out whether your printer only accepts SIMMs with parity (e.g., HP4, 4M, 4Si, Deskjet 1200) or whether it will also take SIMMs without parity (HP 4Plus, 4P, 4MV, 5P, 5MP, Deskjet 1600). Also, only SIMM modules with coding pins are accepted, which the printer users for specifying the memory capacity and access time. Many cheap SIMMs produced in Asia don't have these coding pins.

Many printers (such as the HP5 series) only accept 70ns chips and above. While 60ns chips would also run theoretically, the layout of the coding pins is different, so that the printer doesn't recognize these. All you can do is experiment.

Laser printers like the HP4 are using standard SIMMs more and more as printer memory. This is an ideal way to use your old chips. However, compatibility is not a guarantee.

THE RISKS IN UPGRADING

In theory, it could all be so easy. Buy a new hard drive or processor, install it and you're all done. Unfortunately, in this case, haste can make waste out of your computer. You see, only in the rarest of cases do the new devices run in the old environment. Traps and incompatibilities lurk everywhere. We have listed some of the important ones for you here.

The IDE risk factor

In our opinion, the worst in upgrading is the IDE or EIDE port (that is, the installation of new hard drives or CD-ROMs). In this case, what saved you money earlier now takes its revenge, because in contrast to SCSI, new and old devices only rarely run smoothly together. For more information, see the special sections on EIDE (see Chapter 6 and Chapter 7).

We'll tell you this much in advance: If possible, buy your new hard drive from the same manufacturer as the old one. Also, make certain you can return the product if necessary (get this in writing). Some new hard drives won't run with old (E)IDE hard drives. Manufacturers are constantly tinkering with the standard. For example, newer drives are operated in PIO Mode 4 or even under Ultra/DMA33. Two years ago there was no such thing.

If you run old (slow) and new (fast) devices on the same connection on the motherboard, the slower device may slow down the fast device. On the other hand, new motherboards should definitely be able to run two EIDE devices of varying speed on one connection. However, you have no guarantee that this will be true—EIDE is too prone to errors for this. So, if possible, try to run your old drive separately from the new one. Otherwise, test a mixed environment very carefully for possible influences. If nothing helps, you're better off discarding the old one or selling it.

It's very important to remember that your old motherboard often doesn't support hard drives over 500 Megs. You can read more about this in Chapter 7. Since you will have a very hard time finding a hard drive under one gigabyte any more, you won't be able to run one of these hard drives in your old computer without problems. We'll tell you more about that later.

The SCSI risk factor

As far as upgrading is concerned, SCSI is significantly easier to use. Slow and fast devices can be connected to the SCSI bus and they don't slow each other down. What is more, SCSI hasn't restricted hard drives to 500 Megs for a long, long time.

If you want to buy a brand new, fast SCSI hard drive, you may still be able to replace the controller. For Ultra and Ultra Wide SCSI (see Chapter 7), however, you will only be able to get controllers for the PCI bus.

Well, these are all marginal problems. It's much more important to know that you are running a great risk when you replace a controller, for example, if you replace an old ISA with a new PCI controller (perhaps while replacing the motherboard). If the controllers are from different manufacturers and they use different procedures for addressing the hard drives, your old data on the hard drive could be completely destroyed.

Here's an example. Earlier, you ran your hard drive on an ISA-SCSI controller from Adaptec. Now you replace the motherboard and you bought a SCSI controller from Symbios Logic. After the first connection and start of the hard drive, you can no longer access the stored data. What's even worse, the more you try to access the drive using all sorts of tricks (e.g., using some kind of tools or utilities), the more data you destroy. The problem involves the different conversion tables that manufacturers use for controlling the hard drive in the BIOS of the controller. The two best-known manufacturers, Adaptec and NCR, are unfortunately incompatible with each other. The problem occurs in both directions, that is, switching from NCR to Adaptec and vice versa.

What can you do? Stick with the same manufacturer. It is true that you could back up your data to tape and attempt to make the old drives obey the new controller by reformatting them. However, even that frequently goes wrong. Only a low-level formatting with the program built into the BIOS of the controller will help you. Save yourself the trouble and stick with the same manufacturer.

When old RAM slows your PC

Additional problems are also possible if you use your old RAM chips on a new motherboard. It's not just that the really old SIMM modules don't fit on the new PS/2 or even DIMM banks (see Chapter 4). No, the access speed and the support of the parity bits can also cause problems.

Look at the last number on the label of your memory chips. If there is a "7" or a "70" at the end, then you have 70 ns chips. In this case, your new motherboard must introduce new waitstates during memory access. There's nothing you can do about it, you have to get faster RAMs.

SIMMs with parity chips can also be critical. You can recognize these by the fact that they have 9 chips instead of 8 chips. SIMMs with a parity chip are used more and more rarely nowadays. Some boards don't really support these chips properly any more, either. Especially a mixed configuration of SIMMs with and without parity will frequently lead to a system crash. Have your dealer confirm that your new board runs with old SIMMs, and don't mix new and old chips on the same memory bank.

New processors don't get any current on old boards

It's really exciting to see what Intel and the other manufacturers are constantly coming up with for supplying power to the processor. With almost each new round of processors, the necessary voltage also changes. It even gets worse: New processors require two different power supplies. For more details, see the chapter on processors (see Chapter 4).

We'll tell you this much here: You cannot simply buy a current Pentium MMX or AMD-K6 and install it into a motherboard that is about one year old. This is true even if the motherboard supports a Pentium 166 and 200. Both the new MMX processors (see Chapter 4) and the K6 (see Chapter 5) require a second power supply for operation. And motherboard manufacturers have supported this second power supply only since the beginning of 1997. The fact that a BIOS update is also necessary for the operation of an AMD-K6 is another chapter. There is good news, though: You can circumvent the problem by using a special adapter (see Chapter 4), though the power supply components on your motherboard have to cooperate. You can read more about this in Chapter 4.

Trouble with the old CD-ROM

You've been buying several new parts for your computer, but you wanted to keep your old CD-ROM drive as a second device for playing audio CDs. Although this is a good idea, there can be some problems here too. Newer CD-ROMs and—what's even more important—the appropriate ports on the motherboard and on the sound card, only run according to the current ATAPI standard (for more information see Chapters 6, 7 or 9).

Your old CD-ROM may not work with this standard or with the ports. You could have one of those beauties from Sony or Panasonic that work according to their own, proprietary standard. Many users connected these to their sound cards. However, you can no longer do this with the new cards. If you insist on running your old CD-ROM in a new computer, you will need a compatible interface card. This should have come with your CD-ROM if you bought it separately. Otherwise, you'll have to try to get a used card.

Problems with ATX— The new motherboard won't fit in the old case

Now you say you haven't yet read the information about the new ATX form factor for motherboards (see Chapter 3). That's not so bad, unless you inadvertently purchased one of those new motherboards and didn't realize that it wouldn't even fit into your old case — even the power supply connections are incompatible. So when you buy a new motherboard, pay attention to this small, but important detail. As if that wasn't enough, a new ATX Revision 2.01 appeared in the fall of 1997. This at least put an end to the incompatibilities of some ATX cases and motherboards, regarding the design of the port cover plate.

Plug & Pray with new cards on old motherboards

New cards, for example, sound cards, only come in the Windows 95 Plug & Play standard. You can probably understand why it's called "plug and pray" instead of "plug and play" if you still have an old motherboard without Plug & Play support. In this case, you'll only have trouble with plug and play cards. On most of them, interrupt and I/O addresses can no longer be assigned without Windows 95. In this case you can only hope that the manufacturer of the card included a tool with which the installation will still function (probably under Windows 3.x). Moreover, Intel also offers an emergency solution for such cases called ICU (**I**ntel **C**onfiguration **U**tility). You can get this from your motherboard manufacturer (for example., Asus at www.asus.com/downloads/bios-dl.asp#utility) or from Intel (www.intel.com).

Never be afraid to ask your dealer anything. Always ask about compatibility when buying new peripherals if your computer is two or more years old.

Chapter 3

Recognizing Rip-offs & Buying The Best PC Possible

Some people actually buy a computer as if it were an impulse purchase. Some users found their PC in passing while shopping and simply put it into the shopping cart. That's one type of computer buyer. Others approach the matter very carefully. They search tirelessly for the latest technology, carefully weighing each dollar difference in price and comparing every bit of the specifications. However, even such careful shoppers can make bad buys. One reason is that, unfortunately, you cannot often test the equipment before buying it. Also, regardless of the reason you're buying a PC, few areas are as tough to get the right deal for your money.

In this chapter, we'll help you get your hard-earned money to the right people, for the right equipment. After reading this chapter, you should be able to clearly define the right PC for you. Also, we'll have several practical shopping recommendations that will help you find your way through this vast market.

WHERE TO BUY THE PC THAT'S BEST FOR YOU

Before selecting individual components, you have to understand two basic points. The two most important items are your purpose for using a computer and finding the right dealer (naturally, this doesn't consider price at all). The following considerations and recommendations should help you with these questions.

Think carefully about the PC you really need

In your search, keep the following in mind: The PC is a "personal" computer. That is, it can and should be "personally" matched to your needs and purposes for using it. After all, one big advantage of a PC is its extreme versatility and free configurability. For this reason, we recommend that you stay away from bundles and complete packages. These usually combine high-quality components and low-quality components and are rarely ideal for your requirements. You're better off buying in a store where they'll give you good advice and build a PC especially for you.

Closely related to this basic decision is the considering your reasons for buying a PC. Users who require the PC for graphics or video processing—perhaps even to earn money—will have quite different needs than a writer or author. Plus, gamers need to put together their "game systems" in a completely different manner from other PCs. Meanwhile, everything on the computer market has become extremely versatile. There are as many components in a PC system as there are reasons to use a PC. That means that every decision needs to be well considered.

Consider the future

Even if you know exactly for what you are going to use your PC and have already selected the right hardware and software, there's something else you need to consider. The technology continues to change quickly in the PC world. What is large and fast today maybe small and slow tomorrow.

If you buy a PC now, it is imperative that you consider the possibility that this PC may not adequate for your requirements in the future. If your system doesn't fit in with current developments, upgrading it will be extremely difficult. If possible, choose components that in your experience permit a high probability for upgrades or future compatibility. If you educate yourself about the trends and look back over the last couple of years, this is not all that difficult. In the following sections we'll give you detailed advice about which trends are important and which ones will soon land on the computer scrap heap of history. To give you an introduction, the following summarizes the most important points.

◆ Use a big tower case in ATX design.

◆ Stay away from EIDE; go for SCSI.

◆ Stay away from no name products. Brand-name manufacturers offer better driver support, repair options and compatibility.

◆ Be very careful when buying the motherboard. This part ages especially quickly, and right now there is a war going on for market shares and new standards.

◆ Consider purchasing SDRAMs (DIMM memory modules).

◆ Make future upgrades easier by not buying memory modules that are too small. Don't go near memory modules below 16 Megs.

◆ Economize everywhere except for the monitor and the video card.

Finding the right dealer/store

The last basic question is how to find the right computer dealer or store. Even if you are a champion at selecting the right components, you should place a great deal of emphasis on a reliable, accommodating dealer who gives good advice. This may cost a little extra, but you'll be paying for expertise.

If you have your heart set on buying from a big discounter, consider one of the well-known direct distributors. They frequently offer a significantly better price-performance ratio, have pretty good support, and often have high-quality goods.

Chapter 3

However, the best choice is a dealer in your area that's not too big, gives good advice, and is someone you can talk to when you have problems. The following points will help you recognize such a dealer:

◆ They carry only a selected number of products or manufacturers. These are the best products based on their experiences and are the only ones they can confidently stand behind.

◆ The equipment or manufacturers corresponds reasonably to the equipment that has been tested and approved by popular and national computer magazines.

◆ They won't talk you into buying the most expensive or newest products. Instead they'll advise you based on your needs and budget.

◆ A minimum 12-month guarantee and 24-hours on-site service and a loaner computer as part of the service for complete packages.

◆ Determine the dealer's return policy beforehand.

◆ Watch the habits of other customers. See how they are treated. Are customers buying or merely browsing? Are there any repeat customers? Is the store always empty or busy?

GENERAL TIPS FOR BUYING A PC

In this section we'll give you special tips for buying a PC. We'll also give you specific recommendations on brands and device types, each of which have been tested by the authors. We are aware that recommendations in a book will be quickly overtaken by development, however, often the easily recognizable successor models of the devices we recommend here are just as worthy of recommendation as their predecessors. You'll find additional, general information about technical details, operation and installation recommendations in the following sections for the individual device types.

Checking the number of available slots

Somehow, there's never enough room in your computer. This is especially true considering the number of plug-in cards now available — you can easily run out of slots for your new ISDN or SCSI card.

Normal boards have only three ISA slots and four PCI slots. To complicate matters, only six of these can actually be filled because at the border from ISA to PCI the slots overlap. You can either plug in only three ISA cards and three PCI cards, or four PCI cards and two ISA cards.

We're not quite certain why this problem exists. In the design of the PCI cards, the slot metal was placed right next to the alignment with ISA cards. That actually wasn't necessary. So at the contact point from ISA to PCI, two cards won't fit next to each other.

Border conflicts occur when the PCI slots and ISA meet but there's only room for one card.

ATX boards and the arrangement of components

ATX is the new form factor for motherboards. This simply refers to the different arrangement of components on the board. The main difference is the changed position of the processor. While the processor used to always be in the lower-left corner behind the cards, on ATX boards it is now in the upper-right corner under, the power supply.

ATX has four advantages: First, the ventilation and cooling throughout the computer is much better. Second, you have easier access to all the components. Third, the cable paths for hard drives and disk drives are shorter. The fourth advantage is that you can finally use long cards, which often used to be blocked by the processor's cooling fan. Sound cards or cards for receiving television on the PC are frequent examples of such long cards.

This is a classic motherboard in the BAT design.
The processor's ZIF socket is always behind the slots for add-on cards.

Chapter 3

This figure shows an ATX board. The processor no longer interferes with longer cards.

ATX also has small problems in its first version, especially when it comes to combining boards and cases. Anyone who buys a new board and a new case separately needs to pay attention to compatibility. Different models of the metal cover plates for the ports are especially annoying. Sometimes the printer port simply won't fit properly in the case. The new ATX 2.01 revision provides a remedy, under which the board manufacturers themselves are supposed to supply the right cover plates. The cases will just have uniform standard openings for the boards or ports.

NOTE

ATX doesn't just give you a higher electric bill, it can also give you a shock
In case you haven't yet noticed: If you press the off button on ATX computers, the power isn't completely shut off. Similar to a video recorder or a fax machine, the PC goes into a suspend mode. The motherboard still has a basic current. That's why, with ATX and enabled Power-Management, you can switch the computer off by shutting down through Windows 95. The disadvantage of this otherwise quite practical function is that, with about three watts of power consumption per hour, the PC increases your electric bill. Even if it is only a slight increase, this sum can add up for companies with lots of computers. The only alternative is to place an additional off switch between the network and ATX-PC. This last note applies even more than with normal PCs: when you work on the computer, for example, exchanging expansion cards, be sure to unplug the computer. Otherwise you could switch it on by touching conducting paths/wires or something similar and you could get a serious shock.

Watch out for multifunction cards and boards

More often, multifunction cards or boards are appearing on the market. "Integration" and "cost-cutting" are the catchwords. This is a nice idea in theory but in practice, however, it usually falls short. One of the most important properties of the PC, its open upgradeability or personal configurability (on the hardware level), is totally ruined by multifunction cards.

Typical examples include:

◆ By using a DSP (Digital Signal Processor), both modem and sound card functions are combined onto a single card.

◆ Sound cards with an IDE port for CD-ROMs.

◆ Video cards with add-on functions, such as an MPEG-decoder, television tuner or 3-D accessories.

◆ SCSI controllers with an integrated IDE and/or disk drive port.

◆ Motherboards with an integrated video card.

◆ Motherboards with an integrated SCSI controller.

PCs with the MediaGX processor from Cyrix are a notable example Almost everything is integrated on the board or in the processor. From sound card to video card, it's all there. You cannot upgrade anything except the memory, not even plug-in cards are possible. The video card doesn't even have its own memory, this is either inserted into the main memory using the UMA solution (see Chapter 10) or replaced by it.

The advantage of such solutions is that everybody saves money. However, this solution is programmed for disaster. It's not just that later upgrades are difficult (or impossible) and driver updates are usually harder to get. Things get especially messy when an integrated component goes haywire. Then the rest of the parts on the board also break down.

Also, integration is almost always accompanied by inferior quality and problems. Motherboards with an integrated SCSI-UW interface, for example, require a separate interrupt for each SCSI port (the 50-pin normal port and the 68-pin wide port). When using a normal UW-SCSI controller you only need one interrupt. We discourage you from purchasing such a solution. Remember its "modularity" is a big advantage for the PC.

Watch Out For Some Dealers

Unfortunately, all kinds of shady characters are rushing to the computer market. Since the profit margins in selling PCs is usually around 5-10% (sometimes even less), one can only make the big money with quantity. Especially with the large discounters, the components inside the PCs they sell can change every couple of days. Not even the salespeople see through this. Dealers sell computers according to the current price.

Some dealers usually try to save in the same areas of PC systems. If the dealer doesn't assemble your system according to your specifications, you're risking at least some inferior quality parts in the PC. If you know this, you will rarely fall for their tricks. We have listed the most important ones for you here so that you won't be the one to get taken.

Eight typical lines from questionable dealers

There's hardly an industry where customers are so dissatisfied with the manufacturers and salespeople as the computer field. It's not without good reason, either. Many dealers are only out to make quick money; by the same token, however, many customers are not prepared to pay more money for qualified advice, either. The technology continues to change so quickly that even some sales people cannot keep pace. So, instead of knowing an answer, a few salespeople use double-talk or standard explanations (and sometimes even lies) to customers. The following are some examples:

1. "Is everything I ordered in there?" you ask. "Of course it is!" the dealer winks. Don't believe this when you pick up your computer. Use diagnostic tools (see Chapter 1) to check all the components very carefully when you get home. A part may be missing or an inferior-quality replacement component has been installed. This leads directly to the next line.

2. "It's just as good..." You ordered a specific component, for example, a video card from manufacturer X but you received a different one. It may even have the same graphics processor on it. Nevertheless, the parts could differ seriously. Be very careful when components are replaced without your permission, and check the promised equivalency very carefully. Usually, the two are not equivalent.

3. "Fastest processor = fastest computer." Especially the big discounters and direct distributors almost always sell their PCs by the processor as if the processor alone were the deciding factor for the PC. Today, the peripherals are usually what determine the speed of the PC. However, these may be of inferior quality, which is how they are able to empty warehouses full of old parts. Look at all the PC's components before you buy, not just the processor.

4. "The computer has SDRAMs, it doesn't need a cache." They tried to palm off the same, completely false sentence to us earlier with EDO RAMS. Regardless of what kind of and how much RAM your PC has, it always needs an L2 cache to get maximum performance. By the way, SDRAMs will only make a PC faster with clock frequencies of 83 MHz and higher.

5. "We're out of that model, but we do have..." Too many customers are lured into the store by an especially sweet offer. Unfortunately, when you get to the store, the item is out of stock. This is the bait-and-switch technique. The dealers baits you with one item and then switches to another item. They're hoping you'll buy something else (and of course more expensive) since you're already in the store. If they're out of the advertised model, ask for a rain-check or walk out the store.

6. "We guarantee that your computer will be ready by a particular day," or "We guarantee the repair will take only three days." Make certain to get a written guarantee of the delivery date. This is especially true for service/repair work.

7. "Three-year guarantee on all of our computers" is proclaimed wholeheartedly by many price lists. The catch does not become evident until you examine the fine print: "Guarantee only applies to parts A, B, C and D." Hard drives, printers or monitors are often excluded from the extended guarantee.

    The dealer's guarantee (usually one year) is in effect for the complete PC, not that of the manufacterer (often three years). Also, when you buy single devices, the longer manufacturer's guarantee only applies if the dealer expressly transfers this over to you on his invoice. It is the dealer, and not the manufacturer, who is the binding party to the contract. Make certain you understand all guarantees and warranties before you buy the system (especially the term "limited").

8. "The OEM-version of Windows corresponds to the full version from Microsoft." This is not always the case. The OEM manufacturer has the option to buy a cheaper, trimmed-down version.

The risks of buying a complete PC

All suppliers on the market, small shops, discounters and direct distributors, offer complete PC packages. This is the easiest solution for many customers. Many people don't have the time or knowledge to select every component individually. Often several different systems—something for every price range—are available, so you take what best suits your checkbook.

While this is practical, it isn't always the best deal. We haven't yet seen a complete package that wasn't unsatisfactory in some way. Almost every manufacturer makes some compromise here. For example, a manufacturer may install the latest processor but also installs an old hard drive or a lousy video card to keep the total costs down. The worst part of such packages are almost always the input devices, i.e., the mouse and the keyboard. You may be surprised to know that the components which most directly affect the users (monitor, mouse, keyboard) are where sellers try to cut costs with inferior quality.

Have a close look at the offers in the catalogs, magazines, etc. Pay special attention to the video card, the monitor, the keyboard and the mouse. Then check the expenses with a comparable package consisting of components of your choice. This will be a bit more expensive but, surprisingly, not much more expensive.

The complete packages from the big chain stores and direct distributors are only good deals if you consider the bundled software. Admittedly, especially with the direct distributors, these are of very high quality. However, most users already have their software, and in the long run, it's best if you buy hardware and software separately. Moreover, the next version of the software may soon be available anyway.

Chapter 3

Complete PC packages are good if you can still replace individual components, such as the keyboard or the monitor (since you probably already have one). However, most dealers and suppliers will not let you do this.

Nasty motherboard traps

Manufacturers think of the most dubious savings possibilities especially when it comes to motherboards. UMA boards are one example of this (see Chapter 10), which fortunately are only seldomly distributed today. UMA boards use a part of the normal RAM for the video card integrated on the motherboard. This results in drastic performance losses to save a few dollars—pretty stupid. There's also the Cyrix MediaGX processor, with which, for example, Compaq is offering reasonably priced computers. In this case, the video card is integrated on the motherboard, and the video RAM is taken from the RAM of the computer.

Some manufacturers' economy solutions are just as great. The memory banks of their Pentium boards can be equipped individually with SIMMs. With Pentium computers, normally the PS/2 SIMMs must always be inserted in pairs, because the Pentium accesses the memory with 64-bit width but PS/2 SIMMs only have a data width of 32 bits per module.

Some manufacturers have come up with corresponding tricks to allow Pentiums to be equipped with an uneven number of modules, like 486 computers. This is only superficial because the access is converted through corresponding chips on the board. Ultimately, two accesses per module must then take place. In this way, manufacturers can save some money with these boards, but the speed plunges completely into the basement. Fortunately, there are hardly any more such boards, though you still need to be careful about the bargains offered by some discounters or what you may find on the used-computer market.

Video card frauds

Next to hard drives and especially the monitor, the video card is the favorite economy object of manufacturers or dealers. It's strange that consumers are most inclined to save money on video cards as well. Hardly anybody understands that video cards are not just important for speed, but also for the image quality, which can fluctuate greatly among the various video card types.

The manufacturers' scams to save money on video cards are almost always the same: For one, too little RAM is integrated on the card, and for another, they use a low-quality RAMDAC, the chip which controls video display. Since hardly anyone pays attention to RAMDAC, this goes practically unnoticed. We'll go into more detail about this in Chapter 10.

Here we'll just give you the bottom line: Never buy a new video card with less than two Megs of RAM. Also make certain the model you have is not trimmed down in RAMDAC. For example, Gateway used such a version of the popular Matrox Millenium in its PCs in the past. Few customers were aware that their PC featured a cheap RAMDAC, running at 175 Mhz instead of the 220-MHz RAMDAC typical for Milleniums. The result is a lower maximum refresh rate and poorer image quality. Again, see Chapter 10 for more information.

Hard drive ripoffs

The tricks involving hard drives are almost always the same ones. First, the catalogs always specify the access time as the sole criterion for the speed. But it's not at all the sole criterion, as you can read in the chapter on hard drives (see Chapter 8).

However, that's still fairly harmless. What's really rotten are the nasty scams with the size of the data cache built into the hard drive. All drives have such a cache built in, only the size is pretty variable. While beyond 256 K the amount usually doesn't have any influence on the speed of the hard drive, very small amounts (for example, 64 K instead of 128 K) have a very powerful effect. Many manufacturers are now producing series in two models. One is high quality with a large cache, one inferior quality with a very small cache. What's really nasty is the fact that the two models often differ only by a single letter or number in the drive's name. So hardly anyone will look at it unless you bring it to his attention.

The fast version with the large cache (or even an especially good, prepared copy) is now sent to the magazines or larger dealers for testing. The slow, trimmed down copies then make their way over the counters of discounters and stores that are concerned about prices. The customer purchases the latest model from Conner or Seagate in the good faith that he is getting the exact model XY1234 from the test. The customer never notices the missing letter "S" or "A" at the end of the model name.

So be very careful and check the model names exactly. Even only the slightest deviations can mean something. In particular, ask about the size of the cache and have them show you the size of the cache in the hard drive specs.

Trimmed down software

You don't really believe that someone is giving you something for nothing, do you? In particular, the big PC chain stores and direct distributors are always crowing about the software that comes with their packages. Naturally, Windows 95 always comes with it, "free." Unfortunately, the matter often has a catch-22 that these OEM versions often have a reduced range of functions. The manufacturers get the programs from, say, Microsoft at a reduced price. Both players benefit: the seller adds value to the PC and the software publisher may be able to sell you an upgrade later.

RECOMMENDATIONS FOR A DREAM PC

Now it's time for more definite buying recommendations. Now that you know and understand the information from this chapter, you're prepared to make informed decisions about what you buy. The following combinations or single components are for the most part what we ourselves use. We discourage you from buying anybody's complete package. Assemble your dream PC yourself with selected components purchased from reliable sources. This usually shouldn't pose a problem. You will see that the result is significantly better than buying from less-reliable or unknown sources. Plus your PC will be valuable for a longer time.

Chapter 3

Recommendation #1
The reasonably priced solution for the office

Most people use their PCs for typical office applications, such as spreadsheets and word processing. In addition, they may use them for a bit of database management and a graphics workshop. The performance of a modern PC is sufficient for these applications. You don't need to spend a ton of money for such a PC, in particular when it comes to processor performance. However, you won't get away without spending about $1,500 for the machine, including the monitor.

Let's get right into our first complete system, which is set up with a favorable price-performance ratio in mind.

Assemble a PC starting with the following components. Begin with an AMD K6-166 or Cyrix 6x86MX-PR166 on a normal motherboard with a THX chipset. You can also buy one of the new boards with the TX chipset, however, these are more expensive and don't deliver any better performance. On the contrary, they still have all kinds of beta bugs. The AMD and Cyrix processors are faster than the Intel CPUs at office applications, and at the same time they're less expensive. Which processor you choose depends on the current street prices. The new motherboards with a VP2 or VP3 chipset from VIA are also options for AMD and Cyrix processors. They support the CPUs better and offer more features than the Intel boards. However, we can't yet say anything about their stability and compatibility.

If financially necessary, you can use EIDE as an interface for the hard drive and CD-ROM drive—this is sufficient for limited usage. However, get a big hard drive with at least 5 Gigabytes of storage space. This creates reserve space and makes possible at least a halfway decent upgrade later. Still, even here we recommend using SCSI.

You'll have enough memory with 32-Meg standard PS/2 SIMMs (in 2 x 16 Meg modules). Use a basic model from Terratec or Creative Labs as your sound card. The sound reproduction with built-in wavetables will only benefit you if you wish to work a great deal with computer games or music programs. That hardly fits in with the purpose for using this PC.

The video card should be equipped with VRAM and without 3-D features. As an alternative, an ET6000 card with MDRAM wouldn't be a bad choice either. Spend at least $100-150 for good image quality; use at least two Megs of RAM. On the other hand, don't try to save money on the monitor, since long-term word processing can put stress on your eyes. Make sure you buy a 17-inch monitor with high line frequency, enabling a resolution of 1024 x 768 dots with 90-100 Hz refresh rate. For more information, see Chapter 10 on monitors. You can buy this type of monitor for around $700, the good ones cost about $1,000.

Have everything packed together into a tower case, if possible, with everything in ATX form factor. That creates space and always gives good ventilation. Regarding the purchase of additional peripherals such as modems, ISDN cards or extra game hardware, please refer to the appropriate sections/chapters. Another worthwhile peripheral you could buy is an Iomega ZIP drive, whose diskettes let you store about 100 Megs each. You can get the internal drives for about $100 now.

The following table shows this first office system and gives you an idea of the expenses.

Device type	Manufacturer, Name	Approximate price
Processor	AMD-K6-166 or Cyrix 6x86MX-PR166	160
Motherboard	THX board from Asus, Soyo, Gigabit or Abit; if possible, ATX-Form, or a board with a VP2 chip set e.g., from FIC	130
Memory	32-Meg PS/2-SIMMs	170
Case	Tower, if possible ATX-Form	100
Video card	Graphics processor ET6000, S3-968, S3-Virge, Riva, Permedia or similar, manufactured by ELSA, Hercules, Matrox or Diamond, minimum 2 Megs of RAM	$100-170
Monitor	17-inches monitor with minimum 82-kHz line frequency, e.g., Iiyama, Samsung, ELSA or Eizo	$700-1,000
Hard drive (EIDE)	3 to 5 gigabytes with 5400 rpm, from Seagate, Maxtor, IBM, Western Digital (WD)	$225-400
CD-ROM	6x to 12x from Toshiba, Hitachi, Plextor, Mitsumi	$50-150
Hard drive SCSI (alternative)	2 to 4 gigabytes with 5400 rpm, from IBM, Seagate or WD	$300-450
SCSI controller (alternative)	Adaptec 2940 or DAWI-Control DC 2974 PCI	$140-220
Total		$1,600-2,500

If you have any money left over for other peripherals, for example a scanner or an ISDN card, please see our recommendations in the table for the next PC.

Recommendation #2
The machine for all seasons

Since the beginnings of the PC, the golden rule has always been "The PC that will make me happy costs $5,000." It's true. Anyone who wants to have a computer at the upper end of the performance scale will have to spend this amount of money. The only question is, what should such a system look like? The answer, unfortunately, is not so easy, because it depends on how you'll be using it. Keep in mind that this recommendation is not intended for the ultimate in gaming pleasure (that's recommendation number three).

Anyone who wants computer power without limits will need a Pentium II, although this still isn't a good choice in our opinion. Also important is the application and the use of the coprocessor (floating point unit). You see, while the new processors from AMD and Cyrix are ahead of the game in normal integer performance at the same clock speed, they are significantly slower in the coprocessor performance.

So if you aren't using 3-D raytracing or time-consuming CAD applications (for which the Pentium II at 266 MHz is currently the best choice), we recommend a Pentium MMX-233. While this has a poorer price-performance ratio than the models with boosted clock speed from AMD and Cyrix, it doesn't get nearly as hot and uses much less power. Once AMD and Cyrix have a handle on the problems with clock speeds over 200 MHz, you may resort to these brands. If you really don't place any value on coprocessor performance, computer games and grand MMX performance, the top model from Cyrix's new 6x86MX is one step ahead of the competition in performance (and absolutely has the lowest price).

In choosing the motherboard, we recommend staying away from the new TX boards, because these only allow caching of up to 64 Megs of RAM, which can quickly become too little (see Chapter 4). Besides, they still have beta bugs. Soon new boards with better support for K6 and SDRAM equipment will arrive on the market. These are an interesting alternative. Above all else, however, it is important that your motherboard offers the higher clock frequencies of 75 and 83 MHz.

Bet on SCSI Ultra-Wide for the bus system. The ultra-wide costs about 10-20% more than the normal SCSI, but especially in the operation of multiple SCSI devices or hard drives, you will quickly notice the difference. Stay away from EIDE for this computer.

Based on the information mentioned earlier, it practically goes without saying that you will use an ATX motherboard with an ATX case and at least 64 Megs of RAM. You should also purchase SDRAMs, however, currently only the TVX and the TX chipsets on the Intel motherboards support this. As an alternative, you could use one of the new motherboards with the VIA chipset, VP2 or VP3 (e.g., from FIC). However, it's not yet clear just how compatible and stable these really are (see Chapter 4).

Use the finest monitor and video card. You will hardly find a better choice than the Matrox Millenium II. Only the high-quality models from ELSA, Hercules and Number Nine with 220 or 250-MHz RAMDAC offer similar performance, with sometimes better image quality. The monitor absolutely has to be 19-21 inches. The minimum is 17 inches. A line frequency (refresh rate) of about 86 kHz is very good.

After spending about $3,000 in this manner, we hope you still have enough money left over for additional peripherals. The lower section of the following table gives you some of our recommendations. You can find more information on peripherals in the following sections of the book.

Device type	Manufacturer, Name	Approximate price
Processor (fastest model)	Pentium II, Pentium-MMX, AMD-K6, Cyrix 6x86MX	$280-840
Motherboard	Boards from Asus, Soyo, Gigabit or Abit; ATX-Form, no TX chipset, 75-83-MHz system clock possible	140
Memory	64 Megs, if possible SDRAM (if the board supports it)	330
Case	Tower; ATX-Form	$100-140
Video card, 4 Megs RAM	Matrox Millenium II, Number Nine Revolution 3D, Hercules Dynamite 3D/GL, Elsa Winner Office	$250-350
Monitor	Minimum 17 inches, 19-21 inches would be better, refresh rate near 80 kHz, from Eizo, Samsung, ELSA, Iiyama or Hitachi	$900-1,700
SCSI controller	Adaptec 2940 UW	250
SCSI hard drive	4 gigabyte with 5,400-7,200 rpm, from IBM, Seagate, Quantum or WD	$450-$830
CD-ROM	12x-20x from Toshiba, Hitachi or better yet, Plextor	$110-220
Sound card with Wavetable synthesis	Terratec Maestro 32-96 or EWS-64, Sound Blaster AWE 64 Gold or Turtle Beach cards	$180-500
Subtotal		$3,000-5,350
Scanner	HP 4c	800
CD burner	Normal 2x-4x burner from Philips, Yamaha or Teac	$400-600
CD-RW burner	Rewriteable CD burner from Ricoh	550
Portable medium	Fujitsu MO (600 Meg, 3.5 inch) or Iomega Jaz drive (1 gigabyte)	$450 Media $30-100
Digital camera	From Sony, Canon, Ricoh or Olympus with at least 640 x 480 pixels	$700-1,100
ISDN card	Quicksteps from ELSA	$75-100
Modems	TQV series from ELSA or modems from US Robotics	approx. $100-200

Chapter 3

Turbo drive for Windows NT users

Windows NT users, who need unlimited computing power, may be interested in knowing that you have an additional tuning option. Windows NT supports the operation of multiple processors. For example, if you are using the right software, you can attain undreamed of speed increases with a dual processor board.

You can get good dual processor boards for two Pentiums, especially from a company named Tyan. There are also dual processor boards for the Pentium II. By the way, only the Pentium Pro is truly multiprocessor-capable. In this respect, the competition from AMD and Cyrix are at a disadvantage, because their processors can't do this.

However, the business with speed gains is a bit tricky. First of all, currently only Windows NT, OS/2 and Linux offer multiprocessor support, and secondly, it only works with special software, which is multithreading-capable. As an alternative, a second processor is useful if you perform time-consuming processing with different programs, but how often does one do that? The performance increase on the average is around 20-50%, in rare cases even a bit more. Still, for specific ranges of application this is the ideal solution.

Recommendation #3
A killer machine for game enthusiasts

Hardly any other type of program is as system hungry as the latest computer games. Nothing is fast enough, no programs need more disk space than they do. The latest technology is always in demand. Several technologies are almost only important for games, such as MMX, but especially also 3-D graphics and 3-D audio. For more details, see the following chapters of this book (see Chapters 4, 10 and 11).

Anyone who wants an optimum game PC needs a fast processor with MMX, good 3-D functions and a speedy CD-ROM. Buying a DVD might also be worth your while, since games like Wing Commander with time-consuming film sequences will, with certainty, be available on DVD. In that case, you'll also need an MPEG2 decoder card for playback of the film sequences contained on the DVD. This will cost $220-280. Normal MPEG1 cards are hardly worth your while, since MPEG1 is on its way out.

Naturally, some of the recommendations we made earlier for "normal" PCs will also apply here. However, you have to watch out with the processor. The new Intel competitors from AMD and Cyrix (the K6 or 6x86MX) are, compared to the Pentium, and especially the Pentium Pro and the Pentium II, much much worse in performance. The Pentium II leaves all the other processors in its dust with its fast L2 cache, good coprocessor and MMX performance. However, if you are using a really good 3-D accelerator card (e.g., with the Voodoo chipset), the processor clearly takes a back seat again.

Peripherals are just as important as the processor. Above all, with peripherals you need to keep an eye on optimal game compatibility with the video and sound cards. Since this topic is quite complex, we discuss it in detail in separate chapters (chapters 10 & 11). We'll tell you this much right now: Make sure you use a high quality 3-D card like the Voodoo Chip from 3DFX. Video cards, at least of the first generation with integrated 3-D functions don't get it. So stay away from Matrox Mystic, S3 Virge and whatever all the others are called. The only exceptions are models such as the Hercules Stingray 128/3D, which have a 3-D Voodoo Chip integrated on the card. We'll have to wait and see whether the first really good cards with the new 3-D processors (Riva, Permedia, etc., see Chapter 10) are worth recommending.

True 3-D is also coming into its own on sound cards. Pseudo 3-D effects, as offered by some cards (e.g., even the Sound Blaster AWE 64), on the other hand range from ridiculous to completely useless. Only newer cards with direct sound support and two speaker outputs fulfill the new requirements. Examples of this type of card are the Monster Sound from Diamond, the Maxi 64 from Guillemot and the Terratec EWS 64.

You can have better fun with games much more cheaply

A real game PC with complete equipment and the appropriate peripherals (joystick, steering wheel, etc.) will cost you between $3,300 and $5,500. For the most part, this gaming PC will still give you major headaches with new standards such as Direct X. Games for the PC are often hard to install or configure, and especially under Windows you will often have all kinds of grief with system stability. If your monitor isn't at least 17 inches, you won't have very much fun playing the games anyway.

If you actually want to use your PC only for playing games, consider purchasing a game console from Sony (Sony Playstation) or Nintendo (Nintendo 64) instead. At prices significantly lower than $300, not only do these cost a fraction of what you spend on a PC, but they will also provide you with much greater gaming pleasure. In addition, you cut costs because these consoles can be connected to any television set. It's a lot more fun playing these games on large screens.

There are hundreds of high-quality games of all kinds for the Sony Playstation. And the speed is usually much better. Nintendo's new 64-bit console incorporates a completely new high-quality 3-D graphics engine. While there aren't yet as many games available for this, that will soon change. Purchasing such consoles gives you better value for your money, especially for children. You can then spend the money you saved for buying more games.

FOLLOWING IMPORTANT TRENDS

We're going to discuss some important new developments in computers within the framework of our recommendations. We'll discuss important technical advance information and reviews, and also more general ideas and behind the scenes information about the current developments.

You've probably already been a beta tester

The pressure of competition is greater than ever before. Even large companies who once dominated their market are facing stiff competition. Only Microsoft remains a dominant single player. Perhaps, however, that too will come to an end. Every system sooner or later finds its natural enemy. The effects on the market are crucial. You need to be aware that almost all new developments—software and hardware—are put on the market while they are still in the beta (test) stage. The users are quite clearly being misused as free beta testers. You actually pay for being a beta tester by purchasing the defective goods.

The only rational conclusion from the dilemma (and that's what it really is) is to seriously consider waiting and not buying from the first generation.

No matter whether it's Office 98 or the first generation of the new motherboards with the XYZ chipset, stay away from it if you don't absolutely have to have the latest. And don't trust your most important data on the new hardware and software right away. By the way, if you have a good dealer, he or she will take care of the preselection for you. That's why you will be able to purchase the latest goods at the dealer's a couple of weeks after general availability on the market. This doesn't mean that your dealer is slow or lazy; it's a sign that you can trust your dealer.

Trends to watch

Nevertheless, right at the moment there are far reaching changes taking place in the hardware sector. Even 15 years old standards such as the connection interfaces for the mouse, keyboard and printer are being thrown out the window. In our opinion, 1997 and 1998 will see some of the farthest reaching changes in the entire history of the PC.

Naturally, this means a radical increase in the usual problems for the user—hardly have you bought your new PC before it's already completely outdated. It's not just a case of it being too slow, but new peripheral devices and plug-in cards may no longer fit into the old machine. That's pretty nasty. That's why you should educate yourself thoroughly about the most important trends discussed in this book.

Here are just a few important advance developments, which you need to pay great attention to while reading this book:

◆ Intel is currently pitting all its resources against the competition from AMD and Cyrix, which is growing stronger and stronger. In their struggle, they are employing dubious methods and innovations. Intel is attempting to divide the market into a low-priced, but relatively uninteresting SOHO area and a high-end market. Intel would like to make the Pentium market, and along with it, the Pentium-compatible competition, unappealing to the more demanding customers. This has repercussions for developments in the motherboard market and in the interfaces for plug-in cards and peripherals. The new motherboards with the TX chipset, for example, have been intentionally castrated in their maximum performance (see Chapter 4).

◆ The future for peripheral devices is quite clearly USB (Universal Serial Bus), even if the industry is still having a hard time making the adjustment. All the standards have been set for a long time, the chipsets in the second and third generations are free of defects, and many manufacturers have devices are ripe for production. USB offers many advantages. You can learn about the possibilities and the consequences starting in Chapter 5.

◆ The Firewire bus will establish itself as a second important standard for connecting high-quality peripherals and perhaps even hard drives (see Chapter 5). Sony is already selling its digital video camcorder with a Firewire interface. USB and Firewire are no competition to each other, but rather, they complement one another. Don't buy any expensive equipment, such as a video camera or a digital camera, without checking into this possibility.

◆ PS/2-SIMMs are dead; long live the SDRAM DIMMs (see Chapter 4). The new modules allow 64-bit access (and thus individually filled memory banks), and they keep up with higher system clocks without difficulties. The prices are approximately 20% higher than normal RAMs. If your motherboard allows it, get some.

◆ Which leads directly to the next important innovation: The system clock, up to now held to a maximum of 66 MHz by Intel, will soon increase to 75, 83 and then 100 MHz (see Chapter 4). Boards that don't at least support the first two frequencies will no longer be able to accept new processors within six months. Pay attention to this one, we're talking maximum speed potential!

◆ Everything is going digital, in particular photography and video processing. The prices are still much too high for the performance (except perhaps with digital video), but that will quickly change. Keep your eyes wide open.

Novelties whose time has passed

Not everything that is new is also good. And not everything that the industry thinks up meets with a pleasant reception from users. And it is the user who ultimately determines whether or not a product is successful. While it may be hard to recognize a stillborn concept at the beginning, some things can be easily seen once you look. We're at least going to take the risk. You will find detailed information in the appropriate chapters. We're just going to give really curious readers something to chew on here. So, here's our list of trends we have our doubts about.

◆ The new chipsets or motherboards from Intel for the ZIF socket 7, i.e., the Pentium class, aren't exactly a masterpiece. The intentionally integrated limitation to 64 Megs of RAM (more than 64 Megs cannot be cached, see Chapter 4) forces the system into the lower market segment on purpose. Prognosis: it's better to wait for the competition, because there will be competition.

◆ The first generation of Pentium II computers is nothing more than a Pentium Pro trimmed down for the mass market (see Chapter 4). Some of them even give worse performance at the same clock speed. Above all, the Pentium II motherboards of the first generation aren't worth very much. Once again: If you don't have to buy it, wait for something better.

◆ So far, the MMX hasn't proven itself to be a prime mover either (see Chapter 4). There are hardly any programs for it, the promised performance usually isn't delivered, and the MMX2, which we hope will be better implemented, is going to be introduced with the Pentium II successor.

◆ The DVD as a successor to the CD is another poor success. Although the technical problems have been solved for a long time, the hardware and media industries (music, film) cannot agree on standards. The first generation of the DVD player were available for only a short time before the second generation with speed doubling became available. If DVD isn't carefully driven, it will soon be a wreck on the side of the information highway.

◆ Video cards with integrated 3-D functions are supposed to be the worldbeaters. Meanwhile, almost every insider knows that it's a pure marketing gag. 3-D requires nearly unlimited power, not just from special cards, but also from the computer itself. And the supposed standards like Direct X are everything but perfect. The second generation of 3-D video cards does offer higher performance, but unperfected drivers and still-absent standards for 3-D from the software side mean there is still no smooth sailing for these cards. Take these new cards with a grain of salt (see Chapter 10).

◆ CD-ROM drives with more than 20 times the access speed, especially on the EIDE bus, should not be taken seriously (see Chapter 6). Especially due to the high processor load and the poor busmastering capability of the EIDE bus, such CD-ROMs will hardly reach the promised bandwidth in daily operation. Especially not if the data are being transferred at the same time to the hard drive. Starting at more than 12 times the speed, even a different drive procedure is to be used (CLV/CAV mixed operation, see Chapter 9), that on the inner tracks works slower than on the outer tracks. But the devices hardly deliver any advantages in practice. What is more, the mechanical requirements for the devices are increasing more and more (see Chapter 9).

Chapter
4

The Real Power In Your PC: CPUs, RAM And Chipsets

In this chapter we'll talk about your PC's processor, motherboard and RAM (main memory). These three are inextricably intertwined. In other words, it's senseless to shop for a processor without considering the other two. The constantly growing selection of processors won't make this choice easy, anyway. Increasingly, it is the other components that will improve a system's performance.

Selecting an appropriate motherboard is especially important. The chipset, those small, integrated circuits that control the interaction between the processor and the rest of the computer, is key to the system's overall performance. But users seldom consider the consequences selecting one chipset or another. A motherboard and its configuration (particularly the external clock speed) are vital to a system's performance and its stability. This chapter will help you understand the interplay between these different factors.

Finally, we'll also discuss the significance of RAM chips, explaining the traditional DRAM memory as well as SRAM for L2 caches.

The evolution of RAM technology doesn't make this any easier to understand. After all, there is EDO RAM, BEDO RAM, ECC RAM, SDRAM, RDRAM and nRAM to consider, among others. How can you know whether your system would do better with SDRAM or EDO? And what in the world are DIMMs? How large should your cache be? This chapter takes a very pragmatic look at all of these questions. And instead of excessive technical gibberish, the chapter includes a section on optimizing your memory for DOS and Windows.

BACKGROUND INFORMATION ON PROCESSORS

The background information in this section is important if you want to open the computer and install a new AMD K6 processor on your old motherboard. You'll usually have to make many settings even on a new motherboard. If this isn't done by the dealer, you'll definitely want to have this information. You'll need to know about ZIF socket types, voltage requirements, multipliers and BF pins, BIOS upgrades and more.

We've looked at catalogs, Internet pages, brochures, handbooks and tested the most important processors. Our goal was to find only the most important information for you. By reading this section, you'll be able to make thoroughly informed decisions when putting your system together. We start this section by laying out some general background information on processors and motherboards. This information will be key if you're planning on replacing your processor yourself or want to improve its performance. Another section contains hard data, comparisons, recommendations, and tips on all the current processors on the market. We've examined everything from the familiar Pentium to the racy Alpha processor. But first, let's turn to the basics that will allow you to understand what goes into tuning your system's performance.

NOTE **See Chapter 6 for more information on the BIOS configuration**
We did not want to squeeze all the information on processors, motherboards, RAM, chipsets, and motherboard and BIOS configuration into this one chapter. We've examined these issues together in a separate chapter (see Chapter 6). There you'll also find important tips on the hot topic of overclocking—increasing the clock speed of the CPU and motherboard. Don't miss it!

Closeout models and dinosaur processors

It's astonishing how long the 486 processor managed to survive in all its variations and clone-versions. However, today it is part of computing history. The few models still available are only built by clone-manufacturers; Intel no longer produces any 486 models. If you're still using a 486 or compatible processor and are considering an upgrade, definitely read the sections in Chapter 2 on upgrade options and overdrive processors.

Even the second-generation Pentium is already on its way out. The first generation of P60 and P66 (the P5) chips, as well as the second generation, the Pentium classic (the P90 through P200, or P54C chip), are slowly becoming passé. Intel will most likely leave the ZIF-7 socket arena to its competitors. Instead it will concentrate on the Pentium II and its successors, which use the new Slot One (Slot Two for the newer chips) instead of the ZIF-7 socket.

The following tables show which models are no longer players in the computer market (except perhaps in low-priced portables). You should stay away from systems with any of these processors when looking for a new computer. These tables also list processor characteristics such as clock speed and operating voltage, so you can get an idea which processor might work for upgrading your old PC. The next section includes tables showing the characteristics of current processor models. You'll also find explanations for acronyms such as ZIF and LIF.

CPU (486 models)	Socket type	CPU freq. in MHz	Bus freq. in MHz	Clock factor	CPU supply voltage	Speed relative to Pentium 100
Intel 486-SX25 (P4S)	LIF	25	25	1	5	22 %
Intel 486-DX33 (P4)	LIF or ZIF-3	33	33	1	5	29 %
Intel 486 DX-50	LIF or ZIF-3	50	50	1	5	41 %
Intel 486 DX2-50	LIF or ZIF-3	50	25	2	5	37 %
Intel 486 DX2-66 (P24)	LIF or ZIF-3	66	33	2	5 and 3.3	48 %
Intel 486 DX4-75 (P24C)	ZIF-3	75	25	3	3.3	60 %
Intel 486 DX4-100	ZIF-3	100	25 or 33	4 or 3	3.3	69 %
AMD 486-DX40	LIF or ZIF-3	40	40	1	5	34 %
AMD DX2-66	LIF or ZIF-3	66	33	2	5	48 %
AMD DX2-80	LIF or ZIF-3	80	40	2	5	56 %
AMD DX4-100	ZIF-3	100	25 or 33	4 or 3	3.3	62 %
AMD DX4-120	ZIF-3	120	40	3	3.3	73 %
AMD 5x86-Pr75	ZIF-1, 2, 3 and 6	133	33	4 (2 onboard)	3.3	77 %
Cyrix 5x86 -100 (M1sc)	ZIF-3	100	33 or 50	3 or 2	3.3	70 %
Cyrix 5x86-120	ZIF-3	120	40	3	3.3	79 %
Intel Pent. Overdrive (P24T)	ZIF-2, 3, 6	83	33	2.5	5	85 %
Evergreen 486 Uprg.	LIF and ZIF-1, 2, 3 and 6	133	33	4	5	80 %
Kingston Turbo 133	LIF and ZIF-1, 2, 3 and 6	133	33	4	5	80 %

CPU (Pentium models)	Socket type	CPU freq. in MHz	Bus freq. in MHz	Clock factor	CPU supply voltage	Speed relative to Pent. 100
AMD-K5-PR75	ZIF-5 or 7	75	50	1.5	3.52**	84 %
AMD-K5-PR90	ZIF-5 or 7	90	60	1.5	3.52	94 %
AMD-K5-PR100	ZIF-5 or 7	100	66	1.5	3.52	102 %
AMD-K5-PR120	ZIF-5 or 7	90	60	1.5	3.52	108 %
AMD-K5-PR133	ZIF-5 or 7	100	66	1.5	3.52	123 %
AMD-K5-PR166	ZIF-5 or 7	116.6	66	1.75 (2.5 onboard)	3.52	141 %
Cyrix (M1) 6x86-Pr120+	ZIF-5 or 7	100	50	2	3.3	107 %
Cyrix 6x86-Pr133+	ZIF-5 or 7	110	55	2	3.3	113 %
Cyrix 6x86-Pr150+	ZIF-5 or 7	120	60	2	3.3	116 %
Cyrix 6x86-Pr166+	ZIF-5 or 7	133	66	2	3.4- 3.6 (VRE)	120 %
Cyrix 6x86-Pr200+	ZIF-7	150	75	2	3.4- 3.6(VRE)	127 %
Cyrix 6x86L-Pr200+	ZIF-7	150	75	2	2.8 and 3.3 (Dual-Volta	127 %
Pentium 60 (P5)	ZIF-4	60	60	1	5	70 %
Pentium 66 (P5)	ZIF-4	66	66	1	5 or 5.27	76 %
Pentium 75 (P54C)	ZIF-5 or 7	50	75	1.5	3.3	75 %
Pentium 90	ZIF-5 or 7	90	60	1.5	3.3	93 %
Pentium 100	ZIF-5 or 7	100	66 or 50	1.5 or 2	3.3	100 %
Pentium 120	ZIF-5 or 7	120	60	2	3.3	106 %
Pentium 133	ZIF-5 or 7	133	66	2	3.3	112 %
Pentium 150	ZIF-5 or 7	150	60	2.5	3.3	114 %
Pentium 166	ZIF-7	166	66	2.5	3.3 or VRE	120 %
Pentium 200	ZIF-7	200	66	3	3.4- 3.6 (VRE)	126 %
Pentium Overdrive (P5T)	ZIF-4	120 or 133	60 or 66	2	5	105 or 110 %
Pentium Overdrive (P54CTB)	ZIF-5 or 7	125, 150, 160	50, 60, 66	2.5	3.3	100- 120 %

** The AMD K5 requires 3.52 volts. However, most motherboards only have a VRE setting for this use, but 3.6 volts will fry the processor.

Chapter 4

The speed or performance percentages, using the Pentium 100 as a benchmark, are only approximate and are based on the data supplied by the chip manufacturers. You'll notice that upwards of a Pentium 100, performance is raised only slightly with increased clock speeds. Thus a P200 is a mere 5% faster than a P166.

Processor sockets are a determining factor for upgrades

You may already know that ZIF is an acronym for Zero Insertion Force. This latest type of processor socket lets you remove a processor from the motherboard by simply moving a lever. The earlier LIF (Low Insertion Force) sockets, still used with earlier 486 processors, were not equipped with such a lever and required a special tool.

If your processor has such a LIF socket, it will be a bit more tricky to upgrade; however, with a bit of patience and the right tool you shouldn't have a problem.

The first ZIF sockets were introduced with the faster 486 processors (486DX4-75). The type 3 and type 4 sockets first appeared with the Pentium P5 (60 and 66 MHz). Type 5 arrived with the current Pentium chips. Then in order to accommodate the higher clock speeds of recent processors (200 MHz and up), Intel slightly changed the type 5 specifications, resulting in the type 7 socket. It is this type 7 socket over which manufacturers are currently waging a market battle.

The picture on the top shows the simple lever mechanism (closed) used with ZIF socket, and the open, unpatented design. In the picture on the bottom you can see that this design makes it very easy to upgrade to a competitor's CPU, such as the AMD K6 (here the ZIF socket lever is open).

If you're considering upgrading, pay special attention to what socket type your system uses since this will limit the processors to which you can upgrade. The current Cyrix, AMD and Intel models over 166 MHz will only work in type 7 sockets. All other Pentiums and compatibles, on the other hand, will also fit into type 5 sockets. Those who were hoping to perhaps upgrade their 486 with an AMD K5 will be sad to discover that this chip won't work in a type 3 socket, despite the chip's 486 architecture. The following table will help you determine chip-socket compatibility. For further information on a chip you should also refer to the table listing the processors' characteristics. This should give you enough information on the upgrade options for your system.

Socket type	Remarks
LIF 486	socket without lever, used on early 486 models; upgrade is more difficult, but feasible as long as the connections aren't soldered.
ZIF Type 1	486 boards, 168 or 169 contact pins (rare)
ZIF Type 2	486 board, 238 contact pins (rare)
ZIF Type 3	typical socket for 486 boards, 237 contact pins
ZIF Type 4	for the first Pentium P5 type with 60 and 66 MHz, upgradeable only with Overdrive chip
ZIF Type 5	320 pins, introduced with the P54C Pentium Classic series; found on these with up to 166-MHz clock speeds (i.e., P75-P166), on old Triton I boards for Pentiums only up to 120 MHz
ZIF Type 6	for 486 boards, 235 pins (rare)
ZIF Type 7	same as type 5 with the addition of one pin, for the Pentium Overdrive P55CT (321 pins), also supports clock speeds above 166 MHz; currently found on all Pentium boards for the AMD K6 and Cyrix 6x86MX
ZIF Type 8	processor socket for the Pentium Pro
Slot One	not actually a socket, but rather a card slot for a special Pentium II board, with a maximum clock speed of 66 MHz
Slot Two	based on Slot One, designed for the successor of the Pentium II (Deschutes), will most likely support an external clock speed of 100 MHz

If you want more technical data, check the Asus website (www.asus.com.tw/Products/TECHREF/CPU/Socket/socket.html).

Looking for counterfeit processors

It seems that more than one person has had the brilliant idea of buying slow processors and, after minor doctoring, selling them as faster chips. These crooks try to make a greater profit at our expense with manipulations such as these:

◆ Processors built for low clock speeds are relabeled as chips with higher clock speeds (for instance, Pentium 166es passing as Pentium 200es).

◆ Non-MMX Pentiums are sold as MMX Pentiums with the same or even higher clock speeds.

In these examples, the counterfeiters must remove all original markings (type identifications and the like) and apply their own. All labels and printed or engraved information are removed. Then labels are placed on the processor. The results can fool dealers and customers before the counterfeit is detected.

The easiest and best solution for this problem is to find dealers who guarantee their Pentiums as coming directly from Intel. Furthermore, you should the test the processor thoroughly. This should ideally be done before you buy it but at the very latest once you get it home. Does it seem to run reliably at the specified clock speed? Try it for a moment at the next higher clock speed. A Pentium 166, for instance, should be able to operate for a short while at 200 MHz. You'll be able to tell very quickly whether the 166 is really a 133, for example.

Can you verify the chip's supposed MMX functions by running applications that support this chip? What do system analysis programs, like Norton Utilities, tell you about the processor type? Intel has built an overclocking protection into some models of its Pentium 133 series, so that these can no longer be run as P166s or P200s.

The following tips tell how you can verify your processor model and how you might be able to detect a possible counterfeit chip.

♦ Intel applies a permanent label on the bottom of its chips. If the label on the bottom of your chip is a removable sticker, for instance, under which you find different information, you should be suspicious.

♦ Intel grinds a slight bevel into the top edges of its processors. If the casing has been ground down to remove original labeling, this bevel will appear smaller. You can check the bevel by comparing the chip to one that you know is an original processor.

The upper edge of a Pentium chip's ceramic casing is slightly beveled, so that you can tell whether a chip has been reground by comparing this bevel to that on an original processor.

If you can't quite tell whether the bevel is different, measure the chip's thickness using a pair of Verneer calipers. The housing should be exactly 2.8 mm (0.11 inches) thick. Be suspicious if it's noticeable thinner.

♦ AMD processors with a "486" label only go up to clock speeds of 120 MHz; Intel's only go to 100 MHz. If you see a chip from either of these manufacturers with a higher clock speed, you're looking at a fake. However, there is the AMD 5x86 with a clock speed of 133 MHz, which uses the 486 model ZIF-3 socket, not to be confused with actual 486 chips. Keep an eye out for suspicious offers of such processors, especially at computer swaps.

♦ Most manufacturers use some kind of coded label on the underside of the CPU. You should be able to cross-reference these codes with the technical specifications of the manufacturer (which can often be found on the Internet or in the manual). This way you can determine the model of the chip with a fair degree of certainty.

Intel's CPUID can test your processor

Unfortunately there are almost no alternatives to the above methods, which are primarily external and visual, for identifying your CPU. So far Intel has not integrated any commands into their processors that would allow you to verify their model and authenticity. There is also no software that can positively identify a processor's clock speed. Although the BIOS indicates the clock speed at boot-up, this frequency is actually determined by the motherboard settings, and not the actual system frequency.

One option that *is* available is Intel's CPUID program, which is free on the Internet. This program will determine the processor family and, for Pentiums, whether the chip contains the infamous Pentium coprocessor error. There are two CPUID versions: an earlier, multi-lingual one dating back to May 1995, and also a newer English-only version from February '96. The newer version is also able to identify Pentium Pro models. This program is not able to recognize MMX capability, however.

All you need to do is download the program, unpack it from the archive file, and run it under DOS (with no active memory managers, not even HIMEM.SYS!). With the older version you'll also need to select the language, after which the program will display a message like the one below. It's not a whole lot of information, but at least you can tell whether you've got a 486, Pentium or Pentium Pro. The program also indicates the chip's general model and its operating voltage. The program's most useful feature, however, is its ability to detect the coprocessor error.

You'll find this program on the net at http://www.intel.com/procs/support/faqs/ppfaqx2.htm. You'll also find further information on Intel processors at this address.

Correct voltage is critical for the CPU

Most computer users don't realize just how important it is that the CPU receives precisely the correct voltage. What is it that makes this voltage, the difference in electric potential across a CPU's leads, so critical? After reading this section you'll have a greater understanding of this problem, and why this is such an important detail (particularly when you're trying to tune your system).

What complicates the upgrading process is that the required voltage often changes, sometimes drastically, with nearly every new generation of processors. Even if a new processor (for instance, the Pentium MMX) happens to physically fit into an old motherboard socket, you may discover that it requires a completely different voltage than the old processor. So much for a simple upgrade.

There are two variables to consider:

1. The average and peak power requirements of the CPU (specified in watts). The amount of power required is generally greater for newer models and processors with higher clock speeds. If the CPU's power requirement is too great for the motherboard's voltage regulator, the regulator may overheat, damaging itself and the processor.

   The first generation of the Cyrix 6x86 (M1) had this problem, and soon became known as the "chip-fryer." Make sure your voltage regulator can provide the amount of power required by the CPU you want to install!

2. The CPU supply voltage (in volts). The lower the required voltage, the cooler the CPU will run. Manufacturers are therefore constantly trying to develop models with lower voltage requirements. While the very first generation of 486 and Pentium chips required 5 volts, newer processors soon ran on 3.3 and then 2.8 volts.

The voltage regulators right by the processor socket are responsible for supplying the CPU with the correct voltage. A distinction is to be made between the older, rather susceptible (these regulators run quite hot) in-line voltage regulators, and the newer **split-voltage regulators**. Most newer boards use these split-voltage regulators.

You can identify them by their distinctive coils, found directly behind the ZIF socket (as in the picture below). They run cooler, and are therefore better-suited for supplying power-hungry CPUs like the Cyrix or AMD chips. If at all possible, you should get this type of board for these types of processors.

The picture on the left shows an in-line voltage regulator. It produces a lot of heat and needs cooling fans. It may not be able to handle more power-hungry chips like Cyrix or AMD processors. The picture on the right shows a split-voltage regulator. It's found on newer motherboards and can supply the greater amounts of current required by power-hungry chips.

Given a good cooling system, the wattage requirement is generally not a limiting factor (with the exceptions of certain processors such as the first Cyrix 6x86 M1 models, or the AMD K6-233 with its maximum power usage of 28 watts and 10 amperes). The processor supply voltage, on the other hand, is always extremely critical. The greatest problem with increasing processor clock speeds

87

is that the chip runs hotter. To lower the operating temperature, the chip needs to run at the lowest possible voltage. At the same time, at higher voltages the processor is less susceptible to interference, and will be more stable.

The following is an example. To transmit data, any given pin connector of the chip will either contain a high or low voltage signal (the difference in electric potential across the connector). The smaller the difference between these high and low voltages, the greater the likelihood that some type of interference will cause the signal to be misread. Chip manufacturers therefore strive to build CPUs that will remain stable at the lowest possible voltage. This leaves some headroom to possibly raise the voltage in order to achieve greater clock speeds, without causing the chip to overheat.

Processors have for some time now run on no more than 3.3 volts; the 5-volt days of the first 486 and Pentium chips are already long gone. A Pentium 66 running at 5 volts would get hot enough that you could actually burn your fingers on it. To make the higher clock speeds of the Pentium 166 and 200 possible, Intel introduced its VRE models, which utilize 3.4 to 3.6 volts, rather than the standard 3.13 to 3.46V. These chips thus require a small increase in voltage to maintain stable operation at these higher clock-speeds. The following section explains how to determine the supply voltage required for your processor.

VID2	VID1	VID0	CPU VOLTAGE	CPU TYPE
1-2	1-2	1-2	2.5V	AMD3
1-2	1-2	1-2	2.7V	AMD1
2-3	2-3	2-3	2.8V	P55C
2-3	2-3	1-2	2.9V	K6-200
1-2	2-3	2-3	3.2V	K6-233
2-3	X	2-3	3.4V	STD
2-3	X	1-2	3.5V	VRE

The CPU voltage supply settings are usually controlled by jumpers on the motherboard. Good motherboards will have labels for the different voltage positions printed right on the board (like this Asus TX97).

The AMD K6 is a good example of the effect that the processor's operating voltage has on its maximum cock speed. While 166 and 200-MHz models will run on 2.9V, AMD recommends a core-voltage of 3.2V for its K6-233 chip. As you'll learn in our chapter on increasing processor clock-speeds (see Chapter 6), it can be prudent and even necessary to slightly raise the CPU voltage (for instance, to the VRE standard) when trying to increase the clock speed. This will often prevent stability problems, and a voltage increase to the right of the decimal point is usually not a problem.

Running a processor at too low a voltage will not damage the hardware in any way, but it can make your system unstable. Increased voltages, on the other hand, will raise the processor's temperature, which can be countered with a good CPU cooling fan. If you're going to raise the processor's clock speed, it is best to have a standard-type CPU, so that you still have the option of increasing the supply voltage to the VRE standard.

The latest development for core-voltages is the dual-voltage processor, of which the Pentium MMX (P55C) was the first. Since it is not yet feasible to run the entire processor with a lower voltage of 2.8 to 2.9V, the critical in- and output (I/O) sections of these chips are run at the usual 3.3V.

The actual processor core, which accounts for about 90% of the processor's power demand, runs at a lower voltage. The advantage of this compromise is clear: these types of chips can be run at higher clock speeds without significantly increasing their operating temperature. The disadvantage is that old motherboards with their simple voltage regulators will only be able to accommodate these chips with special adapters.

At this time, all the new CPUs for the ZIF-7 socket are dual-voltage types (Pentium MMX, AMD K6 and Cyrix 6x86MX, also called "multimedia processors"). If you're interested in the more detailed numbers on the required processor voltages for the individual models—say you're building your own system or want to upgrade an old one—then please refer to the appropriate tables below. We've listed the same data for older processors earlier in this chapter.

Now what do you do if you want to install a new AMD K6 or a Pentium MMX 233 in your old motherboard with no dual-voltage support? Either you spend a lot of money on a new motherboard (you may have better luck selling your old processor together with the motherboard), or you spend a lot less on an adapter, which can be had for about 65 dollars.

You should be able to get adapters for the ZIF 5 and ZIF 7 sockets from sources on the Internet. This adapter will provide 2.5, 2.8, 2.9 and 3.2 volts for dual-voltage CPUs. If your system has a VRM socket for the voltage regulator, there's an even easier solution. All you need is a new VR module (available from Madex for about $10), which controls the processor's core voltage. You can find further information about these various adapters on the Internet by searching for "Voltage Regulators."

> **NOTE**
>
> **From 5 volts to 3.3—Adapters for 486s**
> There were already plenty of voltage problems when upgrading to the 486. The switch from 5V to 3.3V was just as significant as the current change from single-voltage CPUs to dual-voltage chips. If you want to use new 3.3V processors on your old 486 or Pentium 60/66 motherboard with a 5 volt supply, you'll have to use an adapter. In addition to Ironwood Electronics, you can also check with Aries Electronics, both on the 'net.

Finding the correct voltage

While the new MMX processors are grouped rather clearly and consistently into specific voltage types, things are quite a bit more complex with the Pentium Classic. The small (but nonetheless significant) difference between the lower standard voltage and the higher VRE voltage is anything but obvious. However, as with its 486 chips, Intel (and most competitors) prints codes on the underside of its CPUs that contain several pieces of information. This label not only specifies the correct processor voltage, with Pentiums it also indicates whether the chip possesses multi-processor capability, since not all of them do.

Take a look at the underside of your Pentium and look for a label such as SY016/VSS (as in the picture below). The three-letter combination to the right of the slash indicates the processor type, verified by Intel after its manufacture through a series of tests. Intel produces almost all Pentiums in the same series, and then tests to learn at which clock speed the processors are still stable and reliable and whether it performs satisfactorily in a dual-processor configuration. The code to the left of the slash indicates the production series. For more detailed information on this label and your Pentium chip, see Intel's Pentium reference table on the Internet (www.intel. com/procs/support/faqs/ppfaqx2.htm).

The code on the CPU's underside specifies the processor type. The three letters to the right of the slash are of special interest. By the way, "iPP" simply means that your chip is a Pentium P54C.

In any event, the significance of the three letter code is as follows:

- ◆ The first letter indicates the voltage class: "S" for standard or "V" for VRE.

- ◆ The second letter indicates the timing-specification: "S" for standard or "M" for "minimum valid MD timing."

- ◆ The third letter indicates whether the processor is dual-processor-capable: "S" for standard and "U" means that the chip was not tested for dual-processor capability.

So what's the bottom line? Basically any letter to the right of the slash that's not an "S" is a bad sign. The best processor type is a SSS, the worst is the VMU type. An SSS will be the best candidate for overclocking, since it has the greatest tolerance for increased voltages and clock speeds, although dual-processor capability won't really be an issue.

If you're buying a Pentium Classic rated at 166 or 200 MHz, make sure you get a chip with the "double-S." However, most 166s and 200s are VRE chips, so your chances won't be good.

Processors are slaves to the clock

The frequency generator governs the speed of the processor and the other motherboard components. Within one clock cycle, the processor can execute one command. With a faster clock cycle (i.e., more commands per second), the computer will be able to perform any given task more quickly. Therefore clock speed and the related elements should be prime considerations when tuning your system. By skillfully tweaking the motherboard and processor frequency, you can obtain the greatest performance increase—for free. However, it's extremely important to know the limitations of the system if you don't want to barbecue your computer.

From this little quartz circuit, oscillating at a mere 14.31818 MHz,
the different motherboard frequencies are produced
through an array of mathematical somersaults.

On today's motherboards, the frequencies for almost all of the system's components are generally produced (or rather converted) by a single IC called the *PLL frequency generator*. (PLL is an acronym for Phase Locked Loop). A small quartz crystal produces a rock-steady base frequency of about 14.31 MHz, which is then converted to the various required frequencies through a series of feedback-loops, phase-shifts, divisions, and other tricks. Usually this one chip provides the clock frequency for not only the processor (i.e., the system bus), but also for the PCI bus, the I/O chips (which are the system's connection to the outside world), and in the future also the USB bus.

*This little PLL chip, right by the ZIF socket, converts the base frequency
of the quartz crystal to the various frequencies for the motherboard.
The old type of chip shown here (with the ICS label) does not support a 75 or 83-MHz system frequency.*

The **system bus** is the most important of these frequencies. It is the processor's external frequency, which is also used for communication between the L2 cache and main memory. The system bus frequency is extremely important, in certain respects more important than that of the processor! The PCI bus is usually linked with the system bus at a factor of ½. Since its specifications max out at 33 MHz, the system bus may run at no more than 66 MHz, according to Intel.

Nevertheless, 75 or 83 MHz and even more are perfectly feasible today, and these frequencies are slowly being implemented. We'll talk more about this in Chapter 6. Some newer boards have found a clever way around this limitation by linking the PCI bus (like the ISA bus, with its 8.3 MHz) to the system bus *asynchronously*, which allows the PCI bus to run at a constant 33 MHz.

What's particularly significant and also quite interesting is how the processor gets its own clock frequency. We'll discuss this in greater detail after we cover the basics. The 486DX2-66 was the first CPU to use an increased internal frequency (2 x 33-MHz external frequency = 66-MHz internal frequency). This little trick is commonplace for all modern Pentiums and compatibles.

These CPUs are equipped with their own PLL circuits to obtain the desired internal clock speed. Through a set of special pins (the BF pins), the processor senses the system bus frequency, and then sets its own internal frequency accordingly. This is necessary because generally processors with different operating frequencies are manufactured in a single production run.

Otherwise it wouldn't be possible to run essentially identical models at 133, 166 and 200 MHz. There has to be some way of basically telling the processor what CPU type you want it to be. It is this system that lays the groundwork for *overclocking* (see Chapter 6).

Clock calculations

The method through which processors actually get their internal clock frequency is simple, but also quite clever. As mentioned above, modern CPUs have built-in PLL circuits that make it possible to create the desired frequencies from the base quartz frequency. Two variables need to be taken into consideration when determining the internal CPU frequency:

1. The system bus frequency, external to the processor.

2. The multiplier with which the processor is to replicate the system bus frequency internally.

If the system is using an external 50 MHz, for instance, and the multiplier is 2, then the desired processor speed is 100 MHz. A 66-MHz bus with a multiplier of 1.5 would also result in a 100-MHz CPU frequency. However, these two systems would perform quite differently, the 66-MHz PC having the distinct advantage. These combinations are an open invitation to system tuning. And as mentioned, the system bus speed can be even more important than the processor speed.

The correct multiplier can be determined by the user, using the BF pin settings. This is how the processor knows whether it's supposed to use a factor of 2 or 2.5, for instance. Current Pentium models for the ZIF-7 socket are therefore equipped with two special pins, BF0 and BF1, each of which can contain either a low- or high-voltage signal. This means there are four possible multipliers (2 x 2 = 4; it really is only a *little* multiplication).

NOTE

Caution with old boards—they often have no BF1 pin!
Motherboards manufactured before 1996, for the first generation of Pentiums, were often only equipped with the BF0 pin, so that the maximum multiplier would be 1.5 or 2. Current processors, therefore, won't be able to exceed 133 MHz! The one exception is the Pentium 233 MMX, which converts the BF setting for the P100 (1.5) to 233 MHz.

On most boards, the BF pin settings are made using jumpers or DIP switches near the ZIF socket. Usually the necessary information is printed right by the jumpers or pins, indicating the correct setting for each multiplier. This information should also be available in the literature that came with your hardware. Some new boards, such as the ones by Abit, allow these settings to be made through the system's BIOS—hence *jumperless motherboards*.

This picture shows the BF pin layout. The setting is made using
jumpers next to the ZIF socket—it determines the CPU multiplier.
You may have to refer to the motherboard literature for the correct settings.

It gets a little trickier, however. With two BF pins you can select between no more than four multipliers. The second generation of Pentiums (the P54C, or Pentium Classic) interprets the same settings as 1.5, 2, 2.5, and 3. Using a 66-MHz bus (by far the most desirable), this results in processor frequencies appropriate for a P100, P133, P166 and a P200. The "in between" Pentiums, such as the P120 and P150, result from a bus frequency of 60 or 50 MHz. The new Pentium MMX (P55C), on the other hand, interprets the same BF pin settings as multipliers from 2 to 3.5. That gets us processor speeds from 133 to 233 MHz. In other words, there can be no MMX chips below a P133. The new multiplier settings were not simply shifted over from the old. Rather, the setting that was previously used for the P100 (multiplier of 1.5) is now used for the P233 (multiplier of 3.5). In other words, a Pentium 233 MMX or an AMD K6-233 on any older or even most new motherboards will have to be configured like a Pentium 100.

> **NOTE**
>
> **They took away the Pentium 133's BF1 pin**
>
> Many users who bought a Pentium 133 and then wanted to overclock it to 166 MHz discovered that this is no longer possible (at least with the newer models). The reason: to protect itself against counterfeiters, Intel cut the P133's BF1 pin out of the circuit, eliminating the 2.5 and 3 multipliers. Consequently, the P133 can only be configured with a multiplier of 1.5 or 2 (resulting in a P100 or P133). The only possible tuning option remaining for such a chip is to increase the system clock speed to 75 or 83 MHz, which will give you the equivalent of a P150 or P166.

Finally, the question remains: How will it be possible in the future to select clock frequencies of 266 MHz and faster? One possibility is to use a new interpretation of the BF pin settings, the way the MMX chip does. Even simpler would be the introduction of a third BF pin (as is already the case with the Pentium II). By just adding one more pin (BF2), we could choose from eight multipliers ($2^3 = 8$). This type of processor could be operated at one of many different clock frequencies. Today some manufacturers, such as GigaByte (GA 586-ATX), are making boards for normal Pentiums that have a BF2 pin, and thus support multipliers of up to 5.5. However, that doesn't mean that you can overclock a normal Pentium by a factor of 5.5, since the chip wouldn't even be able to read this setting. Instead, the extra pin is intended for future processors, such as the AMD K6-266.

NOTE

Three BF pins, but there are nine multipliers, rather than eight—how so?
The very newest Pentium boards support three BF pins, for processors such as the new AMD K6-266. However, there are actually nine possible multipliers (1.5, 2, 2.5, 3, 3.5, 4, 4.5, 5 and 5.5). How is this possible, when there are eight possible values (23 = 8)? The trick is this: 233-MHz processors actually interpret the 1.5 setting as a multiplier of 3.5. The BF setting for these values is the same, the CPUs just interpret the setting differently.

Here follow several examples for possible clock speed combinations. They're intended to demonstrate that any given processor can be run in different ways, and that the default configuration of some CPUs results in unacceptably slow system- and PCI-bus frequencies.

CPU-speed in MHz	External speed in MHz	Multiplier	BF-Pins in use	PCI-Bus speed in MHz	Remarks
75	50	1.5	1	25	Pentium 75 (too slow due to the 50-MHz system bus)
90	60	1.5	1	30	Pentium 90
100	50	2	1	25	Pentium 100
100	66	1.5	1	33	Pentium 100 (alternative config.)
120	60	2	1	30	Pentium 120
150	60	1.5	2	30	Pentium 150
150	75	2	2	37.5	Pentium 133 overclocked
166	66	2.5	2	33	Pentium 166 standard
187.5	75	2.5	2	37.5	Pentium 166 overclocked
207	83	2.5	2	41.5	Pentium 166 overclocked
233	66	3.5 (i.e. 1.5)	2 (like P100)	33	Pentium 233 standard, config. like P100
266	66	4	3	33	AMD K6
300	66	4.5	3	33	Pentium II, K6?
333	66	5	3	33	Pentium II?, K6?
366	66	5.5	3	33	Pentium II?, K6?

Chapter 4

NOTE

System slackers—stay away from the Pentium 75, 120 and 150!
As explained farther below, with processors over 100 MHz, the system and PCI bus clock speeds are much more important than just the processor frequency. Conversely, this also means that you should by all means avoid all models and configurations that use a 60, or even worse, 50-MHz system speed (i.e., a 30 or 25-MHz PCI frequency). Such systems are, in a sense, slowed down artificially. You should only get a P120 or P150 if you're planning on overclocking it to a P133 or P166, which these CPUs should easily take.

MMX technology and Intel

In early 1997 Intel announced its next milestone in processor development called MMX technology. MMX integrates a new set of 57 on-chip commands, the kind which would be used by multimedia applications (graphics, audio, video and 3-D imaging). According to Intel, this set of new commands increase peak performance up to 400% and result in an average increase of easily 50-100%.

After taking a quick look at the technology, you'll see why MMX works. Processing pictures and sounds (pictures also make up videos) usually requires the processing of 8-bit data (or multiples of such), which are generally generated by digitizing analog signals. You're probably familiar with color scans, most of which are digitized with a color-depth of 8 bits, in the three RGB colors. Another example is audio files that have been digitized with 8, 12, or often 16 bits (CD-quality). When processing such files, the same commands typically have to be applied over and over to 8-bit segments of data, for instance, in sharpening a graphics image or digitally reducing the volume of a wave file.

MMX was introduced to process these repetitive operations more quickly. Special 64-bit registers (little caches in the CPU that help it process data) are used to store 8 x 8-bit data segments, all of which are then processed by the same command in one fell swoop. In other words, one command is applied to several data segments (in the past, each data segment had to be commanded individually). It's easy to see that this method, also known as SIMD (Single Instruction Multiple Data), saves quite a bit of time. A few other tricks are used to further increase performance. These Intel processors also have two MMX pipelines, which means that they can process two MMX commands simultaneously (i.e., 16 x 8-bit data segments). The new chips by AMD (the K6) and Cyrix (6x86MX) each have only one MMX pipeline.

Intel Corporation's MMX logo

Now for the catch: to prevent MMX from throwing a wrench into the works of existing operating systems and applications, it was necessary to integrate the MMX technology into the existing processor structure, so that its commands would be readily accessible. Instead of using its own physical registers, MMX uses those of the co-processor (FPU). This, in and of itself, is neat, except that it now is no longer possible for MMX and FPU commands to be executed concurrently. What's even worse is that an Intel processor takes a whopping 53 clock cycles to switch from MMX to FPU operation. The Cyrix MX and AMD's K6, on the other hand, can do this in just one cycle, since they have a dedicated MMX unit, allowing the switch to take place much more quickly. This helps make up for the otherwise somewhat inferior performance of these chips in terms of their FPU or MMX operation.

So what are the practical ramifications of this switching? According to Intel they're minimal, since FPU commands and MMX data are only seldom processed at the same time. But let's look at the example of a 3-D application: first the FPU has to calculate the spatial coordinates for a given object; only once this calculation is finished does the MMX render a surface onto the object, and of course this now happens *much* faster.

Unfortunately this little hangup affects the MMX's performance more often than Intel would care to admit. That MMX technology doesn't do much for 3-D computer games (in which the above scenario happens all the time) is no longer a secret.

To clarify once again: MMX does not affect the performance of the operating system. The OS doesn't use the type of data in which MMX specializes. Even the applications that can take advantage of MMX processing have to be programmed especially for MMX-support in order to reap its benefits. Although there are several such applications (such as Photoshop 4 and Corel 7), they only make use of MMX's advantages with a few filters and other special functions that really won't get used a whole lot.

Applications don't even have to have direct MMX capability. A program can simply utilize a driver for a 3-D accelerator card, for example, that supports MMX. Under Windows 95 this could happen through the Direct 3D interface, for instance (see Chapter 10 for information on 3-D graphics and cards).

So what's the last word on MMX? MMX is most appropriate for the low-cost multimedia PC market. MMX's additional performance is intended to replace the more costly expansion hardware (such as 3-D accelerator cards) used by the pros. Unfortunately MMX's advantages are minimal particularly in the arena of computer games. The general lack of software support for the new technology is another good reason not to spend money on it. Currently there are very few games with MMX support, and those that have it use it only for limited parts of the program (as in the game POD).

If you're trying to decide between a Pentium Pro and the new Pentium II because you're hooked on computer games, you're better off with the Pentium Pro. The Pentium II has a very slight performance advantage over a "normal" Pentium MMX anyway—another reason not to spend the extra money.

Chapter 4

> **A note on MMX motherboards**
> **NOTE** Contrary to rumors, Intel's new TX chipset has no special MMX support. In other words: a MMX CPU won't run faster on one of these new motherboards compared to an old 430HX board. MMX technology is an application software issue and not hardware or chipsets.

The next generation of processors called the MMX2 is scheduled to debut in mid-1998. These processors are to resolve the drawbacks of MMX1.

FACTS, DATA AND TUNING TIPS FOR TODAY'S PROCESSORS

Everyone wants the fastest, most sophisticated, and of course the most expensive system. In past years the measurement was always quite simple: Intel always had the best processors and the clock frequency was the single most important factor. Today, users are looking for non-Intel processors. New manufacturers are now competing successfully with Intel.

What's the benefit of all this to the user? Most noticeable, this competition is driving prices down considerably. In particular, Intel had to introduce its Pentium II at a low base-cost. Other Pentium models have become much more affordable. The competition, of course, must keep pace, and strives to keep its prices at least 20% below those from Intel. Let's hope the trend continues.

One disadvantage for the prospective buyer is that it's getting more difficult to choose from the huge selection of processors. Not only will there soon be four to five Intel competitors, but Intel itself keeps producing different variations on its models. Furthermore, Intel is currently marketing three models (Pentium, Pentium Pro and Pentium II). The competition adds to this barrage with its P-rating, which is supposed to indicate a processor's performance relative to that of an Intel CPU. It's easy for consumers to feel increasingly overwhelmed and confused.

If you're looking for a new PC or want to upgrade your old system and you're interested in the most for your money, you must become familiar with many technical details and differences between the available processors. Otherwise, you could easily be stuck with a system that's already outdated in just a few months (not one to two years, the way it used to be).

Most users aren't interested in technical details of the inner workings of a processor. However, it's getting more important to understand the significant differences between CPUs and which chips are suited for what type of applications. Therefore, we've included information on the strengths and weaknesses of the most current processor models in this chapter. Don't worry, we won't barrage you with a great deal of technical details except for what is essential information that will allow you to upgrade your system intelligently. You'll come away with a clear picture of what type of system will be right you.

Intel's counterattack is the Pentium MMX

We intend, however, to look specifically at the new MMX model compared to the competing chips by AMD and Cyrix and Intel's earlier chips. After all, we still need to consider the processor that could currently be called Intel's base model, the P55C.

The P55C's continued success rests entirely on the Socket 7 system. This chip, just like the ones by AMD and Cyrix, is bound to this socket, and precisely that is Intel's dilemma. In order to keep the competition at bay, Intel must abandon the ZIF Socket 7 and move on to new technology (see our section on Intel's strategy below). Therefore, it's unlikely that Intel will develop another Pentium MMX after the recently announced top-of-the-line model, the Pentium 266.

Intel now makes many of the new P55C models in plastic casings instead of the typical ceramic ones (like the shown one here).

Perhaps we should take another quick look at the P55C's capabilities. The Pentium, a 32-bit processor with a 64-bit memory bus, is now four years old. Intel won't introduce a true 64-bit processor until the end of the millennium—a project that's code named Merced. In any event, now that the old Pentium Classic (P54C) has been updated and overhauled, the new Pentium, with its larger L1 cache and large number of other performance-enhancing features, compares pretty favorably with the competition. It fares particularly well with respect to its MMX and coprocessor (FPU) performance, and beats the competition at equal clock speeds.

Under Windows 95 the new Pentium delivers about 10-15% more speed compared to the old model. That means a P166 MMX is about as fast as a Pentium 200 Classic. However, that's only the case under Windows 95; under NT and DOS (e.g., for computer games) the difference is quite minimal. Nevertheless, today there is very little reason to buy a P200 Classic, unless you get an exceptionally good deal on it.

The question for you is quite simple: why and when should you purchase a Pentium MMX? The answer is: only if you're mostly using programs other than typical office applications, and only after the price relative to that of competing CPUs has finally dropped.

> **NOTE**
>
> **Determing the best CPU to overclock**
>
> Intel's chips do have clear advantages over its competitors': their high quality and their low power consumption. An Intel Pentium will run considerably cooler and use less juice than an AMD K6 with the same clock speed. While the competition tries to squeeze as much from its chips as it can, Intel processors always have a good safety margin. This also leaves more headroom for tuning measures. A Pentium 166, for example, can be overclocked to a higher speed than a comparable AMD or Cyrix, and it will be more stable. However, we strongly recommend that you do not overclock your PC's CPU.

Chapter 4

Compared to the competing chips by AMD and Cyrix, the Pentium maintains its advantage only with DOS games, MMX and FPU applications. In all other areas the competition wins, and at better prices! As soon as the competition has CPUs at 266 MHz (or faster) for the ZIF Socket 7, as well as optimized chipsets, the Pentium's days will indeed be numbered.

There is one arena in which the Pentium's chances are still quite good: portable computers. The new Pentium MMX released in late 1997 is being manufactured with 0.25 μ technology and runs with a core voltage of only 2.5 volts. For notebook users, the chip's low heat production and low use of electricity make this Intel Pentium a good choice.

The following table lists the most important technical data for the Pentium MMX. All models are dual-voltage chips and therefore require separate supply voltages for the processor core and its I/O sections. As a comparison, we've also listed the same data for the AMD K6 and Cyrix 6x86MX.

CPU model (P55C)	Pentium 166 MMX	Pentium 200 MMX	Pentium 233 MMX	AMD K6	Cyrix 6x86MX
Comparison with Pentium MMX, same clock speed, integer performance	n/a	n/a	n/a	about 10% faster than Pentium	about 10-15% faster than Pentium
Comparison with Pentium MMX, same clock speed, coproc. performance	n/a	n/a	n/a	about 20% slower	about 15-40% slower
Internal clock speed in MHz	166	200	233	166-233	150-187.
External clock speed (system bus) in MHZ	66	66	66	66	66 or 75
Multiplier	2.5	3	3.5*	3.5	2 or 2.5
Core voltage	2.8	2.8	2.8	3.2	2.8
I/O voltage	3.3	3.3	3.3	3.3	3.3
L1 cache in Kilobytes	2x16	2x16	2x16	2x32	64
Data and code cache separate	yes	yes	yes	yes	no
average power consumption in watts	6	7	8	10 - 17	12
Peak power consumption in watts	13	16	18	17 - 28	ca. 21
Manufacturing process in μ	0.28	0.28	0.28	0.35	0.35
Transistors per CPU in millions	4.5	4.5	4.5	8.8	6.8

* Since older as well as most new boards only use multipliers from 1.5 to 3, these motherboards must be set to a multiplier of 1.5 (setting for P100) when used with a P233 processor. This CPU is programmed for a multiplier of 3.5 with this BF pin setting, and will thus operate at 233 MHz.

Upgrade options, overdrive processor and MMX for everyone

As mentioned in Chapter 2, Intel offers Overdrive processors as an upgrade option. These are expensive but simple upgrading solutions. Simply insert it into your ZIF socket (which must be at least a System 5) and you're set.

Intel also has matching MMX Overdrive models besides its old Pentium upgrades (the P54 series, i.e., P75, P90 and P100). Their prices are noticeably higher than those of the normal processors. Chapter 2 rates these upgrades and what you should consider if you're thinking of getting one. Here is just a quick summary: if you are thinking of this type of upgrade, be sure to get the largest model with 200 MHz internally (i.e., the model for the P100, P133 or P166). Chances are that you can configure your motherboard for a P100 (with a 66-MHz system bus frequency), so that your system and PCI bus will be operating at their full potential.

You can probably get a normal Pentium MMX with the newest motherboard for about the same amount of money. Or you could opt for an AMD K6 or a Cyrix 6x86MX. Below, in the sections on the respective processors, you'll find the necessary information for upgrading old motherboards with these CPUs.

If you're set on keeping your old motherboard, we recommend you get a Pentium MMX 166, 200 or 233, or as an alternative a Cyrix 6x86-PR200 (though the K6's power consumption may be too great for your old board). Since your old motherboard is probably not equipped with a dual-voltage regulator, you'll need to use an adapter of the type described earlier.

By the way, not only P75, P90 and P100s can be upgraded with an Overdrive or a new CPU, but also P120, P130s or whatever. If you're not sure about how the selected clock frequencies or multipliers are converted, you'll want to refer to our section on processor clock frequency above.

It's crucial to remember that old motherboards can only use the multipliers 1.5 and 2, since they only utilize the BF0 pin. In other words, 133 MHz is as fast as they'll allow the processor to go. The exceptions to this rule are the Pentium 233 MMX and the AMD K6-233. Let's look at an example: you upgrade an old P100 system with the P233 MMX, using one of the adapters we mentioned. With the same settings as for the P100 chip (with a multiplier of 1.5), the P233 will run at 233 MHz under the optimum configuration. It may seem odd, but the only other thing you may need to do is change a few settings for your old memory chips in your BIOS. This operation is described in Chapter 6.

The Pentium II isn't the brightest star in the processor sky

The Pentium II uses the processor core of the Pentium Pro and the MMX capabilities of the new Pentium. What's new is that the L2 cache, which was integrated in the Pentium Pro and thus also ran at the processor's clock speed, has now been segregated. The cache now runs side by side with the processor on a small card, and at only half of the processor's clock speed. The advantage of this arrangement is that it lowers Intel's production costs. The disadvantage is that, as a result, the processor is slower than a Pentium Pro with the same clock frequency! Even MMX can't help that. You'll find more information on this topic in our section on L2 caches in this chapter.

The new Pentium II (left) plugs into Slot 1 architecture (right), rather than the familiar ZIF socket.

The only advantage that the Pentium II offers over the other models is that it is available in clock frequencies of 233, 266 and even 300 MHz. And with Intel's switch to 0.25 μ manufacturing technology, we may see clock speeds of 400-500 MHz in 1998! We'll see if the competition can keep up. AMD and Cyrix are currently struggling to produce enough chips above the 200-MHz level.

> **NOTE**
>
> **A note on the Pentium II's cache**
> Pentium II supports 512 Megs of RAM. To be more specific, the L2 cache tops out at this memory limit. While it may seem incredible, some servers are already equipped with 640 Megs or more! The performance of such systems will suffer radically because the cache can no longer service the system's memory properly. Although this should not be an issue for most users, it may be for power users, who perhaps operate large company servers.

When compared with the Pentium 233 MMX, Pentium Pro 200 and the AMD K6-233, the Pentium 233 MMX comes in about 10% slower than the rest, which all perform similarly. The Pentium II is perhaps about 5% faster than the K6-233—on a good day. Only at 266 MHz does the PII start to clearly pull away from the competition. Since the processor core of the Pentium Pro was overhauled for the Pentium II, Intel was able to remedy the old 16-bit weakness with Windows 95. Under Windows NT the Pentium II gains a little more of an advantage, beating the normal Pentium by about 20%. However, even here the PII 233 is still equivalent to a Pentium Pro 200. In other words, considering it's lower clock frequency, the old Pentium Pro is actually faster than the new Pentium II. Aside from MMX (which the old Pentium also offers) and the new motherboard design (which was primarily aimed at the competition), the PII has nothing new that benefits the user.

Intel has extensive information available on its processors available www.intel.com/pressroom/archive/releases.

So Intel's competitors, AMD and Cyrix, just about keep pace with the Pentium II—the differences in the integer performance are barely noticeable. However, the Pentium II fares better under DOS (with games), as well as with applications that utilize the coprocessor (FPU). These allow the new Intel chip to shine. Currently there simply isn't anything better for game addicts, thanks to the chip's good FPU and MMX technology, although the second pick would still be the Pentium Pro.

Since the PII still has to contend with a 66-MHZ system bus, the advantages of the chip's high clock speeds (even 300 MHz) are minimal, except with highly processor-intensive operations. The PII 300 is only marginally faster than the PII 266, but it costs well over $600. The slight increase in performance does not justify the considerably higher price.

What else is interesting about the PII? Its MMX performance corresponds pretty closely to that of the normal Pentium—the same 57 commands, 2 pipelines and FPU-dependent operation . The chip's MMX performance, like that of its FPU, beats that of the AMD and Cyrix competitors by a good 25%. But then, who really needs MMX?

For professionals, the PII's advantages come to bear in other areas. For one, the chip is dual-processor capable (though not for multi-processing, like the Pentium Pro). For another, the new 440LX-chipset motherboards are equipped with the new AGP bus for video cards—see Chapter 5 for information on the AGP bus. This development promises a large performance gain for 3-D applications.

NOTE

The best chipset for the PII

The first motherboards for the PII use the old 440FX chipset from the Pentium Pro (sometimes called "Natoma"). This chipset is neither the fastest, nor does it have SDRAM, Ultra-DMA or AGP support. Since the fall of 1997, PII 440LX motherboards (440BX for servers) have been equipped with all of these wonderful features. So if you're in the market for a PII and motherboard, be sure to get one of these new boards. Also, the success of AMD and its K6 has forced Intel to lower its prices considerably.

With the PII it's particularly important to use the right motherboard. Like the Pentium Pro, the PII is able to load new micro-code through its BIOS to correct minor errors. Intel has patented its new Slot One board design, which replaces the ZIF socket, so the competition won't be able to immediately produce clones. Although it uses a lot of power (up to 40 watts for the 300-MHz version), you can install up to a PII 266 on an ATX board without additional, active cooling (though it's certainly better to use it). However, the rather clunky case and large heat-sink occupy a lot of room on the board.

NOTE

Software tuning for the Pentium II

Sometimes programmers come up with very resourceful ideas. A case in point is the little software proram for the Pentium Pro and PII called "FastVid," which increases the data-transfer rate between the processor and the PCI bus from 8 to 90 Meg/sec! However, it only runs under DOS, with the DOS4GW memory manager in the same directory. It speeds up the display of graphics for comuter games very noticably, allowing animation to be much more fluid. You can find a lot of information on FastVid, as well as the program itself, on the internet at http://web.inter.nl.net/hcc/FastVid.

The PII's successor, with a clock speed of over 400 MHz and a 100-MHz system bus, has the potential to deliver the long-hoped for breakthrough in performance. This chip may hit the market in mid-1998. Until then Intel will most likely do its best to increase the PII's clock speed and to lower its power consumption. Also, it plans to introduce a special version of the PII for portables, since the current model is too large for this application. Perhaps the next generation will draw on the virtues of the Pentium Pro and again get an integrated L2 cache running at the full processor speed. Only then would we be able to truly recommend purchasing the PII.

CPU model	Pentium II 233 MHz	Pentium II 266 MHz	Pentium II 300 MHz
Internal speed in MHz	233	266	300
External speed (system-bus) in MHz	66	66	66
Multiplier	3.5	4	4.5
Voltage	2.8	2.8	2.8
L1 cache in kilobytes	2 x 16	2 x 16	2 x 16
L2 cache (on the expansion card) in kilobytes	512 (soon also 256)	512 (soon also 256)	512 (soon also 256)
Data and code cache separate	yes	yes	yes
Power consumption in watts	35	38	40
Manufacturing process in μ	0.35	0.35	0.35
Transistors per CPU in millions	7.5	7.5	7.5

In July 1987 Intel introduced a special version of the PII that was intended for servers. This model can also apply ECC error correction to the L2 cache. This increases overall system stability, which is particularly important for servers. This is a unique feature; other processors currently have ECC error correction only for main memory.

The Pentium Pro is in many cases still the chip of choice

All the talk about the Pentium MMX and Pentium II has overshadowed the Pentium Pro. The integrated L2 cache, running at the full processor frequency, provides the necessary performance. For servers, Intel recommends using the PPro in multi-processor configuration.

The Pentium Pro may remain the processor of choice, especially if you're running applications under Windows NT that don't use MMX or wouldn't be much faster with MMX. You don't need MMX except for image processing (and few programs currently support MMX fully). Although the chip's clock speeds are lower than those of the Pentium II, you can make up for this a bit by overclocking it to 233 MHz (with a good cooling system). And the 16-bit shortcoming really isn't an issue with this type of processor: Windows NT really is the operating system of choice anyway.

Thanks to its integrated L2 cache, the Pentium Pro is the fastest processor at its respective clock speeds.

Chapter 4

If you're a power-hungry user, you may want to consider running the Pentium Pro under Windows NT with four CPUs. The Pentium II can be configured as a dual-processor. Another argument for absolute power users is that while the Pentium II maxes out at 512 Megs of main memory, the Pentium Pro handles up to 768.

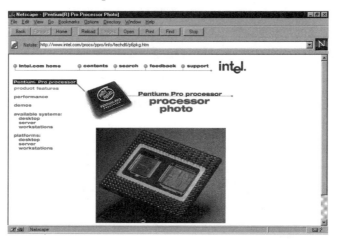

You'll find detailed information on the Pentium Pro at Intel's Web site: http://www.intel.com/procs/ppro/info/index.htm. Also, in this picture note the L2 cache, integrated in the housing (to the left).

Rumors indicate Intel is planning to further develop the Pentium Pro. Intel may be planning to release a model with MMX support. Recently, it also introduced a version with a 1-Meg L2 cache. As always, it's important to carefully weigh Intel's products against competing hardware.

> **NOTE**
>
> **Using the Pentium Pro with the new Pentium II motherboard**
>
> New motherboard and memory developments don't apply to the Ppro's Socket 8 system. AGP video cards and SDRAM chips would be particularly desirable. You can forget Ultra-DMA for IDE hard-drives, on the other hand; after all, who wouldn't use SCSI instead? Don't worry, though, there's a way to extend the life of your PPro. Adapter cards allow the Socket 8 chip to be plugged into the the PII's Slot 1, which lets you use your Pentium Pro on a new PII motheboard. You just have to be sure to avoid compatibility problems with the re-loadable BIOS microcode. It's best if you can test the board's compatibility with your chip before making the purchase, or to make sure you have the option of returning the chip. These adapter cards are available from Tekram. You can find information on these at the company's Web site: http://www.tekram.com/MAINBOARDS/P2/P6F40K-A5.html.

By the way, Intel seems interested in doing the opposite as well: allowing Pentium Pro users switch to a Pentium II, using an Overdrive chip. However, this chip will only provide better performance if it's running at least 300 MHz and you truly are utilizing MMX to its potential. Also, the motherboard must support multiplier settings of 4 or 4.5 to utilize the higher processor speeds.

A close look at the K6 from AMD

AMD really *has* outdone itself with the K6 and the chip is currently Intel's number one enemy. The K6, the product of a collaboration with the Texan chip-maker NexGen, has the stuff to really put Intel under pressure.

The new K6 is pin-compatible with the Pentium, since it was developed for Socket 7, which is exactly where AMD is waging its battle against the market leader. We described Intel's reaction to this offensive in the previous section. What's interesting is that AMD has licensed the MMX technology from Intel and built it into its K6. For most observers this seems like an odd arrangement.

The K6, as a Socket 7-compatible CPU, will run on most motherboards (and also on some Socket 5 boards). All that's needed is the appropriate BIOS version and the proper processor supply voltage (see info box).

There's little question that AMD has done *all* its homework with the K6. At equal clock frequencies, it is 10% faster than a Pentium MMX, and is almost as fast as the Pentium II (about 3% difference). The new Cyrix is even a tad faster, and that with a lower clock speed. When it comes to the coprocessor (FPU), however, the K6 has to yield to the might of Intel. Here the Pentium II is still number one (20% faster, on average). More or less the same holds true under DOS (games) and with MMX applications. In these areas the K6 clearly takes the back seat. Its slow FPU and single MMX pipeline (Intel has two) drag the chip's performance down in these areas (by about 25%). Even the fact that the K6 can switch much more quickly between MMX and FPU commands can't make up for these handicaps. However, MMX performance highly depends on the application that's running, and in the important arena of image processing the K6 almost keeps up with the Pentium MMX. In other words, the chip's MMX handicap is relatively insignificant in practice. And for computer games you'll want a good video card, anyway, so these apparent shortcomings really don't affect the chip in any significant way.

The K6, like the Pentium II, is able to make the most of the 32-bit environment under Windows NT, pulling even farther ahead of the regular Pentium (by up to 20%). Again, that goes for the integer performance, which is what counts for "normal" programs such as business applications. Under Windows NT the K6-233 is pretty much on par with the Pentium Pro 200 and the Pentium II 233, so it really is a hot processor.

NOTE

When is the K6 the right choice for you?

The decision whether to go with the K6 depends on for what you'll be using it. For normal business applications (integer performance) the K6 is the better and cheaper(!) choice. However, the same can be said for the Cyrix 6x86MX. What gives the AMD chip the edge is that it's encountered less trouble than Cyrix's. It's also already available with a 233-MHz clock speed, and its FPU performs better than the Cyrix coprocessor. The Pentium MMX should only come into question if you'll be utilizing the FPU and/or MMX heavily. Furthermore, the Pentium II is the right choice only if you've got a deep pocket and a need for performance delivered by high clock frequencies. The final argument for the Intel chips is their support for multi-processor operation. The K6 is a single-processor chip. For normal users the K6 is currently the best choice, particularly if you'll be using it on a motherboard with improved AMD support.

From a technical viewpoint, the K6 owes its performance to a number of factors. The L1 cache, for instance, was increased to 64 K (Intel only uses 32 K). For the faster processing of x86 code, the K6 utilizes a RISC core, while the Pentium still processes the commands natively. The K6 uses two decoder units to translate the x86 commands into RISC commands, which are then parallel processed (six at a time) at a high speed. This may be the reason that the K6 often does so well in pure, synthetic benchmark tests (such as the Norton SI). The RISC processing of x86 commands offers all sorts of tuning possibilities for new software, which might be written in such a way as to make the translation of x86 commands into RISC instructions more rapid. The motherboard chipsets that are currently still optimized for Intel processors can also be modified to enhance performance with the K6. Given such improvements, AMD should be able to make things even hotter for Intel.

There are a few downsides. The AMD chip's biggest problem is still its high power consumption—almost 30 watts for the 233 model (see our table). Next to the Pentium II, it's currently the most power-hungry processor, more than even the Cyrix, whose predecessor gained the title of "chip fryer." However, with its move to 0.25 µ manufacturing technology last year, AMD should be able to solve this problem. This will also enable the chip to run at significantly higher clock speeds. Furthermore, the new AGP graphics bus, as well as probably higher system bus frequencies, will be introduced together with the new chipsets (such as the AMD640AGP), developed by AMD and other manufacturers. These developments should allow AMD to truly come into its own, from which all of us can benefit.

> **Toss that old Pentium, gimme an AMD K6!**
>
> **NOTE** Many users would probably like to trade their old Pentiums for a speedy K6. And yes, it's possible, even with many older motherboards! Unlike the Cyrix 6x86MX, the K6 is a bit more accomodating, since it's driven with the ususal 66-MHz system frequency throughout. What's more challenging is the chip's power consumption - it's as hungry as the old Cyrix M1 CPUs. Therefore, if your motherboard supports a 6x86 M1, the voltage regulator will do fine with the K6. It's best if your board has a split-voltage regulator. You don't necessarily need a BIOS update (the K6 will run on old boards), but without it you won't be able to utilize certain performance-enhancing features, such as write-allocation. The K6 supports Asus starting with the BIOS version 0202. If your original Intel motherboard refuses to work with the new chip, simply use MR BIOS (see Chapter 6). What's more important is the correct processor supply voltage (dual-voltage). The K6 233 is particularly unusual in this respect, since it requires the unusual core-voltage of 3.2 V (which only newer boards supply), even though it will generally also run at 2.9 - 3.1 volts. Don't despair if your motheboard isn't equipped with a dual-voltage regulator; all you need is an adapter. With older motherboards you'll also need to check the maximum possible multiplier setting, since such boards often only support factors of 1.5 or 2. Other than that, nothing should stand in the way of your upgrade to a K6.

Chapter 4

The following table lists the most important data for the currently available K6 models relative to the Pentium and the new Cyrix (the latter are only average values). Be sure to note the high power consumption and unusual voltage requirements of the K6 233. Like the new Pentiums, the new AMD CPUs are dual-voltage processors, and require different voltages for the processor's core and its I/O section. Please refer to the info box for more information and for upgrade options with existing motherboards.

CPU model	AMD K6-166	AMD K6-200	AMD K6-233	Pentium MMX	Cyrix 6x86MX
Comparison with Pentium MMX at the same clock speed—integer performance	about 10% faster than P166-MMX	about 10% faster than P200-MMX	about 10% faster than P233-MMX	n/a	about 10-15% faster than comparable Pentium
Comparison with Pentium MMX at the same clock speed—coprocessor performance	about 20% slower	about 20% slower	about 20% slower	n/a	about 15-40% slower
Internal clock speed in MHz	166	200	233	166-233	150-187.5
External clock speed (system bus) in MHz	66	66	66	66	66 or 75
Multiplier	2.5	3	3.5	2.5-3.5	2 or 2.5
Core voltage	2.9	2.9	3.2	2.8	2.8
I/O voltage	3.3	3.3	3.3	3.3	3.3
L1 cache in kilobytes	2x32	2x32	2x32	2x16	64
Data and code cache separate	yes	yes	yes	yes	yes
Average power consumtion in watts	10	12	17	6-8	12
Peak power consumption in watts	17	20	28	13-18	21
Manufacturing process in μ	0.35	0.35	0.35	0.28	0.35
Transistors per CPU in millions	8.8	8.8	8.8	4.5	6.8

NOTE

Getting full performance with the right motherboard

As mentioned, the K6 doesn't quite live up to its full potential on motherboards with Intel chipsets. Given the right conditions, with a faster system bus speed, SDRAM and Ultra-DMA support, it could do much better. This requires new chipsets, and you won't be getting those from Intel. However, AMD and other manufacturers, such as VIA, have already done their own thing, and developed special chipsets. Starting last fall, new versions even support AGP.

Learning lessons from the old Cyrix 6x86 (also called MI)

Cyrix's first real Pentium clone, the 6x86 M1, was actually just starting to gain market acceptance. The company's experiences with the first models had been rather unsettling, and Cyrix had just released its new "L" version (low voltage) of the M1 when the new 6x86 MX (or M2) was introduced. The old 6x86 consequently faded into history. However, we want to take a quick look at it for this discussion of current CPUs. After all, this chip was the impetus for several beneficial developments:

◆ The development of better voltage regulators that could easily handle processors with higher power consumptions.

◆ The P-rating, the performance evaluation relative to Intel's processors, as determined by standardized benchmark programs. A 6x86 PR200+ is at least as fast as an Intel Pentium 200, even though the clock frequencies are different.

◆ The introduction of the 75-MHz system bus frequency.

The first versions of the M1 suffered extreme heat buildup and various stability problems. The chip's power consumption was too great for many motherboards, and some of the old in-line voltage regulators simply burned out. Thus the processor's nickname, "chip fryer." However, Cyrix was able to reduce the processor's power consumption with each revision, and was able to completely resolve the problem with revision 2.7. The 6x86L was the first dual-voltage version of the M1, running on the usual 2.8 and 3.3 volts. At the same time, many motherboard manufacturers began switching to the new, more powerful split-voltage regulators. The new 6x86MX is also a dual-voltage chip, and it uses significantly less power than its predecessor (as well as the AMD K6). You'll find further technical data on the 6x86 in the tables in this chapter.

For buyers on a budget, the 6x86L is probably the best processor for business applications, offering the highest performance/price ratio (among the non-MMX processors). Its FPU performance, on the other hand, leaves a lot to be desired, lagging considerably behind Intel's.

The 6x86 also experienced early problems with various operating systems and applications, which you ought to consider before making your purchase. Microsoft Windows NT 4.0, for example, will turn off the L1 cache's write-back mode of the 6x86, since the chip is very sensitive to reflections on the motherboard. This leads to a severe drop in performance. As a solution, Cyrix will exchange the old processors, and it has also made a patch for NT available (DirectNt—see our info box). However, this patch can also lead to instability. Starting with revision 2.7, or the new 6x86L model, Cyrix has solved this problem as well.

NOTE

Tuning pitfall—6x86 PR166+ chips configured as Pentium 166s will crawl along at 66 MHz

The Cyrix 6x86 Pr166+ must be configured on the motherboard with a multiplier of 2, like a Pentium 133. The chip can only read multpliers of 2 and 3, so if it's configured like a P166, with a multiplier of 2.5, the CPU will run at 1:1 with the external clock speed of 66 MHz. Since most BIOS versions don't even recognize clock speeds of 66 MHz, the lowest registered clock speed will be assigned, usually 75 or 80 MHz.

Chapter 4

What's particularly important about the M1 is that it was the first chip to introduce a higher system bus frequency. The 6x86 PR200+, which, like all 6x86 chips, only recognizes multipliers of 2 and 3, was the first processor to run at an external clock speed of 75 MHz. Vobis has this model in its lineup, and even offers special motherboards for the chip, which link it asynchronously to the PCI bus. This allows the PCI bus frequency, which is usually set at 37.5 MHz, to be held to the permitted maximum of 75 MHz.

Since then, several other manufacturers have started to offer motherboards with 75 and 83-MHz support—after all, the future belongs to systems with faster system clock speeds. This is also an important potential tuning opportunity with regard to overclocking of Chapter 6 for more information on this topic).

NOTE

Tuning tips for the M1—special programs light a fire under the old Cyrix 6x86
The M1 has several special functions that are intended to be activated by an appropriate BIOS. When this is not the case, or for those who want to be doubly sure, IBM and other manufacturers offer little software tools that can increase performance. However, the effect isn't very pronounced. This seclection of programs includes DirectNt, which re-activates the L1 cache under NT 4. There are also various tools for configuring the M1. You can find more information on these tools as well as links to related sites at http://web.inter.nl.net/hcc/FastVid. You'll have to select the subdirectory for Cyrix processors, since this is a Web site with frames (see screenshot).

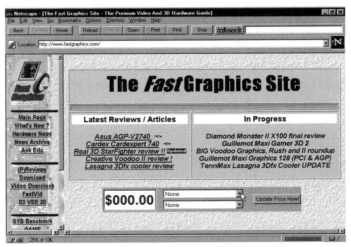

You'll find information and download links for optimizing the old Cyrix 6x86 processor at www.fastgraphics.com.

Despite great performance, the Cyrix 6x86MX struggles

The Cyrix 6x86MX, first called M2, is a collaboration between Cyrix and IBM. It was originally meant as a Pentium-clone for the ZIF Socket 7 and is aimed primarily at Intel's Pentium MMX top models and the AMD K6. However, after National Semiconductors bought Cyrix in July 1997, the future of the 6x86MX is unclear.

The performance of the 6x86MX, particularly in the integer range (operations that don't include the coprocessor) and under Windows 95, is impressive. The "MX" in its designation indicates that the processor also supports MMX commands. It currently has the highest performance/cost ratio of all Socket 7 processors for normal business applications, where the coprocessor is not used. It's faster than the AMD and the Pentium, and the PR233 approaches the performance of the Pentium II 233, which has a higher clock frequency. In other words, at equal clock speeds, the 6x86MX is faster than all other x86 processors.

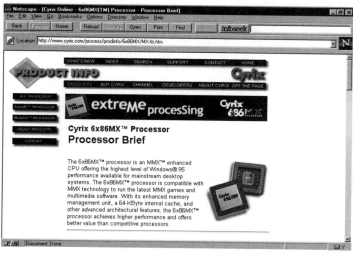

The Cyrix 6x86MX is headed toward an uncertain future

However, the 6x86MX continues to fight an uphill battle. The serious problems faced with the first Cyrix models on many motherboards scared away many dealers and customers. Unfortunately the new version still has an important disadvantage: the chip's coprocessor (FPU) is considerably slower than those from the competition (including the K6).

Cyrix and IBM have done their homework with the new processor. The L1 cache in particular, which was increased from 16K (in the M1) to 64K is a main reason for the chip's increased performance. According to Cyrix, a 6x86MX-PR200 is about as fast as a Pentium MMX 200.

The Cyrix can, on average, boast a good 10-15% more performance than its Intel counterpart. It's even slightly higher than the AMD K6. When you consider that the clock speed is lower than that of the benchmark processor, it's clear the Cyrix indeed performs well. However, when the coprocessor (FPU) is used, the Cyrix loses its advantage. It's up to 50% slower in its coprocessor operation than the Intel chips and 20-30% slower than an AMD K6. The Cyrix is therefore not the chip of choice for CAD applications, 3-D animation and computer games that use FPU functions frequently. It does slightly better in its MMX performance.

Although the Cyrix only has one instruction pipeline (Intel has two), it can switch much more quickly between FPU and MMX operation, just like the AMD K6. Still, as with the K6, the Cyrix's poor FPU performance keeps its MMX performance below the level of the Pentium's. Depending on the application, the Cyrix may keep pace with the K6, but usually falls a little behind.

The following table shows important Cyrix 6x86 data. The table shows the PR166 can be run at 2 x 75 as well as 2.5 x 66 MHz. The best setting is determined by the user and the motherboard (see our comments below the table). If operation remains stable, the 75-MHz setting is better.

CPU model	6x86MX PR 166	6x86MX PR 200	6x86MX PR 233	Pentium MMX	AMD K6
Comparison with Pentium MMX at the same clock speed—integer performance	about 10 - 15% faster than P166-MMX	about 10 - 15% faster than P200-MMX	about 10 - 15% than P233-MMX	n/a	about 10% faster
Comparison with Pentium MMX at the same clock speed—coprocessor performance	about 15-40% slower	about 15-40% slower	about 15-40% slower	n/a	about 20% slower
Internal clock speed in MHz	150	166	187.5	166-233	166-233
External clock speed (system bus) in MHz	75x2 or 60x2.5	66	75	66	66
Multiplier	2 or 2.5	2.5	2.5	2.5 to 3.5	3.5
Core voltage	2.9	2.9	2.9	2.8	3.2
I/O voltage	3.3	3.3	3.3	3.3	3.3
L1 cache in kilobytes	64	64	64	2x16	2x32
Data and code cache separate	no	no	no	no	no
Average power consumption in watts	10	11	12	6-8	10-17
Peak power consumption in watts	19	20	21	13-18	17-28
Manufacturing process in μ	0.35	0.35	0.35	0.28	0.35
Transistors per CPU in millions	6.8	6.8	6.8	4.5	8.8

Depending on the motherboard and expansion cards you're using, it could be critical to run at least the PR233 with a 75-MHz system frequency (in the table you can see that the PR166 can also be configured this way). If the motherboard doesn't include an asynchronous link to the PCI bus, you may have problems with some cards or memory chips (see the overclocking information in Chapter 6). However, this is unlikely. The processor is rated for 75 MHz and the entire system will run noticeably faster this way. The best solution is to select one of the new motherboards with a chipset optimized specifically for the Cyrix.

Using SDRAM will give you even greater performance and stability benefits with computers operating at a 75-MHz system bus clock speed. The PR233, in particular, achieves some of its performance from the higher system frequency. But even at equal clock speeds, it clearly beats the Intel and AMD chips in integer operations.

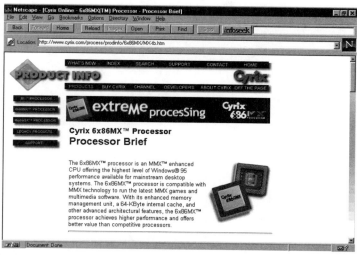

You'll find technical information and benchmark test results on the Cyrix website.

If you're looking for an affordable PC to use with the usual range of business applications, and you're not planning on running applications that rely heavily on the coprocessor, you can save a lot of money using the Cyrix. In this case, it's actually the best choice in terms of its performance/price ratio. Furthermore, the 6x86MX will become even more appealing as Cyrix releases true 200 or 225-MHz chips. Remember, to truly appreciate this chip's performance you have to compare it to competing processors with the same clock frequency, and when you do that, it even beats the Pentium II!

However, we have the same reservation about the Cyrix as the AMD K6: if you're a power user and are running a wide variety of software, particularly applications that rely on the FPU, you should stay away from this processor. Also, if you're interested in running Windows NT on a multi-processor system, the Cyrix will be a dead-end. Like the K6, it is designed only for single-processor operation. In such instances the Pentium II is the better choice. Game addicts will also want to steer clear of the Cyrix, since its DOS performance can't touch that of the Pentium II, even the K6 is better.

NOTE **Improving your system with an upgrade—switching to the 6x86MX**

Like the K6, the new Cyrix chip raises the question of compatibility with old motherboards. As with the K6, chances are very good that the upgrade would work. The first considerations ought to be the chip's supply power, the correct system frequency (75 MHz), and possibly a BIOS update. However, a new BIOS is only necessary if you want to squeeze as much performance as possible out of the processor. If you're using an original Intel motherboard, you'll want to switch to MR BIOS (see Chapter 6). If your motherboard doesn't support a 75-MHz system speed (asynchronously, if possible), you won't gain much by using the PR233 model and should opt for a different one. With regard to the chip's supply power, you should note that the new Cyrix requires dual-voltage (2.9 and 3.3V). If your old motherboard doesn't have such a regulator, you can simply use an adapter. However, it's important that the board's voltage regulators are stable enough to supply the power-hungry chip without any problem. The new Cyrix does use less power than its predecessor, and even uses 30-40% less than the AMD K6, so the old Cyrix problems have finally been banished. The only other potential obstacle is the limited availability of multipliers (1.5 or 2) on old motherboards.

The 21164PC processor from DEC for Windows NT 5

You're probably already familiar with DEC by using its Alta-Vista search engine on the Internet. DEC, also called Digital, has developed the Alpha processor, an extremely powerful CPU that shames competing models from Intel, AMD and Cyrix. One big reason for the chip's prowess is that it's already available in versions at over 500 MHz. The Alpha failed to gain broad market acceptance until recently because it lacked a supporting operating system. (It only ran with a special version of Windows NT.)

DEC may change all that with the release of its slightly modified Alpha called the 21164PC. The 21164 has a slightly larger L1 cache than the large Alpha and a segregated L2 cache. While this lowers production costs, it only lowers performance by about 10%. The DEC chip also has a form of multimedia extension called "MVI." Unlike MMX, DEC limited its multimedia functions to video acceleration and audio coding. MVI is much more effective than its Intel counterpart. You can play MPEG2 movies with AC3 digital audio from DVD video using a 21164 without any additional hardware. Also, DEC's MVI runs parallel to the coprocessor unlike Intel's MMX.

If Microsoft does support the 21164 with Windows NT 5.0 as announced, the chip will acquire a huge selection of software immediately and an extremely critical operating system. Windows NT 4.0 is already available in a version specifically for the Alpha processor and in early August 1997 Microsoft introduced special versions of Excel and Word 97 for the chip. Also, DEC has announced plans for a software-emulator for Pentiums called FX32!. It's rumored to be quite good and runs extremely fast on the 21164. This means almost any x86 program (DOS and Windows) will be able to run on the DEC processor.

Comparing the performance of a 21164PC with an internal clock speed of 433 MHz to a 233-MHz Pentium II or Pentium MMX makes the Intel chips look extremely slow. The DEC chip can boast up to four times the performance of the Intel processors in coprocessor operations.

CPU model	DEC 21164PC
Compared to Pentium MMX at the same clock speed—integer performance	about 100% (533-MHz version vs. Pentium 233 MMX)
Compared to Pentium MMX at the same clock speed—coprocessor operation	about 400% (533-MHz version vs. Pentium 233 MMX)
Internal clock speeds	400, 466, 533 and soon 600 MHz
External clock speeds (system bus)	26 to 133 MHz (128-bit bandwidth)
Core voltage	2.5V
I/O voltage	3.3V
L1 cache	16K (code) and 8K (data)
Data and code caches separate	yes
Power consumption	28 - 37 W

It's clear that the 21165PC offers a compelling alternative for power users. It may be perfect for 3-D rendering, complex CAD operations or processing long video sequences. The one disadvantage is that the DEC processor needs its own motherboard. However, with an L2 cache of up to 4 Megs and SDRAM support, DEC has definitely done its homework. All other components can be selected just like with a normal PC, for instance an Adaptec 2940UW-SCSI controller, or a Matrox Millennium graphics accelerator.

The very best thing about the DEC chip, however, is that its price should become competitive with those of the lower Pentium II models.

Chapter 4

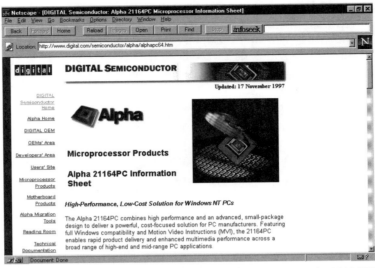

You'll find well-organized and highly detailed information on the 21164PC on the Internet at http://www.digital. com/semiconductor/alphapc64.htm.

Centaur's Pentium clone for portables

Intel seems to be lagging about one or two years behind its PC processor development when it comes to chips designed for notebooks. Portables with fast Intel processors are exceedingly expensive, so this is an area in which it can be particularly beneficial to take a look at the competition. Centaur (a subsidiary of the memory-chip manufacturer IDT) developed a Pentium clone for notebooks in a remarkably short period of time. Of course this chip, known as the IDT-C6, can also be used in affordable normal PCs.

The C6 is a Socket 7 chip, just like the competing processors from AMD and Cyrix. Its main distinguishing features are its small size, low price and low power consumption. It also supports an MMX-compatible instruction set. Thanks to a large L1 cache, a 200-MHz C6 can keep pace with a Pentium of the same clock speed—and that in spite of the chip's simple design. The new Pentium 200 MMX notebook processor, dubbed "Tillamook," will most likely be much more expensive than the Centaur version (you'll find information on the Pentium MMX later in this chapter).

So if you're looking for a new, affordable notebook, keep an eye out for the Centaur chip. It's clear that Intel can no longer rest on its laurels in this market niche, either.

Inside Info And Tuning Tricks For Chipsets, The L2 Cache And More

Everyone seems to consider only the processor and RAM as the important elements of a PC. However, the right motherboard and its configuration are also important. However, they receive less attention because they can't be sold as easily on over-simplified hype (200 MHz is faster than 166 MHz, 48 Megs of memory are more than 32 Megs). When considering the motherboard, we're concerned about things entirely different. These aren't as simple and obvious as the processor clock speed, for instance.

Don't panic because there's only a few things you need to understand. For example, how does the chipset affect the motherboard's performance; or the L2 cache, which resides on the board except in Pentium Pro and Pentium II systems? Are you aware of the catch with Tag-RAM? We'll learn that the size of this component on your motherboard has an important affect on your system's performance when you're using large amounts of RAM. This section deals with these, as well as the motherboard and its most important components. However, we won't cover the configuration of the BIOS and jumpers (and overclocking) until Chapter 6. Here we're mainly concerned with making the correct motherboard choice and the possible hardware additions, for instance, L2 cache memory or Tag-RAM.

The motherboard determines the system's stability and speed

It's hard to believe how many ads you see from computer stores and mail-order outfits that boast: Pentium XYZ with huge amounts of RAM, large hard drive, giant monitor and other goodies for a price of "next-to-nothing." You rarely hear one word about the motherboard. However, after reading this section, you'll realize that there's more to consider when considering a new system.

The motherboard is the basis for communication between all of the PC's components. It converts and distributes the electrical power, provides connection points and drives the processor with the correct clock frequency. Also, don't forget the BIOS, which controls all of the PC's basic functions. It's all too clear that any shortcomings in this part of the system will affect the performance of the system as a whole.

Like software applications, motherboards have version or revision numbers. This number is usually printed right onto the board, though it can sometimes be hard to find. A 1.0 version (such as this new Asus TX97E) is usually a source of trouble.

When buying a motherboard, it is absolutely crucial to inquire about the board's chipset and revision. The chipset is the group of microprocessors on the motherboard that is responsible for the coordination between the processor, memory and the peripherals (such as the expansion cards). You'll see that all of the currently available chipsets have their strengths and weaknesses.

If you bought a Pentium II system early in 1997, for instance, you may have an ancient chipset (the 440FX) that offers neither satisfactory performance nor enough expansion options. Too bad if they didn't warn you about that first, because new boards became available later.

Now, how do you pick the right motherboard? The first rule is to stick with name-brand boards. When manufacturers use the same chipset, the performance differences will only be marginal. Stability, quality and BIOS support are more important. Motherboard manufacturers to consider include Asus, Abit, Soyo, Gigabyte and Tyan. Asus in particular has managed to virtually establish itself as the standard. The familiar P55T2P4 board might not be the very fastest or have the latest goodies, but it'll run a long time without any problems.

Choosing the perfect motherboard

Choosing the right motherboard can be tricky. The sheer number of manufacturers is confusing without listening to their techno-babble. We currently recommend a board from either Asus or Abit. Both build stable boards with tight quality control. The pros consider boards from Asus as the standard. However, the new boards with the 430TX chipset are being received with some suspicion—the first problems have already surfaced. However, before we get to the new models, let's discuss the basics that make a good board.

Be sure to buy from a well-known manufacturer with good support. Unfortunately, today support means primarily the Internet. Other support services are becoming less common. So check out the manufacturer's homepage before you make your final selection. See if their support for EIDE drivers and, most importantly, BIOS updates is what you need.

◆ Is the board also available with ATX form-factor? ATX has important advantages for handling and cooling the PC. Unfortunately not all boards are available in this format.

◆ The BIOS type that the board uses is less important. The performance remains about the same whether Phoenix, AMI, Award or even MR BIOS is used. However, Award is more frequently used, particularly on high-quality boards and by well-known manufacturers. Phoenix is uncommon, while MR BIOS is more of a solution for pros, which can also be used for upgrades (see Chapter 6).

◆ Does the BIOS support the new ACPI power-management function of the PC97 Microsoft standard? This function offers software-based control of the system's power-management and boot functions. Not only does it enable the PC to be shut down by the software and make bootup faster, it even allows a network administrator to manage and re-boot another PC over the network.

◆ What's the configuration method for the motherboard? Through good old-fashioned jumpers or completely through the BIOS?

◆ It's very important to look closely at the different possible configurations in the board's Plug-n-Play and PCI BIOS (see Chapter 6). Can you assign the interrupt for each PCI slot manually, not just automatically? Many boards don't allow this, which can lead to serious problems in configuring the PC.

◆ What chipset is being used (THX, TVX, TX or maybe one of the new non-Intel versions)? How will this affect the board's characteristics?

◆ Does the motherboard support all the current processors? This requires not only the right BIOS but also the right, stable supply-voltage. Be sure to refer to the information earlier on standard and VRE voltage settings as well as dual-voltage support for the newer processors.

◆ What type of voltage regulator does the board use? Are they the old, in-line regulators or the new, significantly better split-voltage types?

◆ Does the motherboard support the up-and-coming system clock speeds of 75 and 83 MHz? It should, at the very least, support 75 MHz. Does it perhaps have a turbo-setting with 68 MHz, similar to the boards by Abit?

◆ Does the board have four or even eight/nine multiplier settings (two or three BF pins)? You get nine multipliers instead of eight with the BF2 pin because 233-MHz CPUs re-interpret the setting 1.5 as 3.5.

◆ How much and what kind of RAM does the board support? Can the BIOS be configured for access times lower than 60ns when using SDRAM?

◆ How large is the L2 cache and can it be enlarged. Most importantly, how much RAM can it cache? The latter is such an important consideration that we'll specifically cover it in a separate section later.

◆ USB and infrared ports should be easily upgradeable—at least through a plug-in module— so that you'll still be able to use them next year with new peripherals.

◆ For you pros: will you want to run a multi-processor system? This narrows the choice of motherboards significantly. Tyan, for example, is a well-known manufacturer of high-quality multi-processor boards.

These are the most critical points on the way to buying a new motherboard. We'll discuss how to correctly configure your motherboard with jumpers and/or the BIOS in Chapter 6.

Our choices for standard PCs

At this point we only recommend motherboards for ZIF Socket 7 (Pentium and compatibles) systems or perhaps also Socket 8 (Pentium Pro) systems. The Pentium II has been on the market for a short time and we're still waiting for the new boards that will be optimized for these chips. Furthermore, Socket 7 is likely to remain the standard for most PCs for some time to come, thanks to AMD and Cyrix (see the previous section).

Chapter 4

We have three specific recommendations: the Asus P55T2P4, the Soyo 5BT5 and the Abit IT5H. All these boards range between $100-$140. The Asus maintains the dominant market position. Many pros wouldn't consider buying any other board. Soyo also produces very sophisticated and highly compatible boards. Some of its older boards from Abit were plagued with compatibility problems. However, Abit seems to have solved these problems and is trying to compensate by producing high-quality boards with a number of new, innovative features. The new boards by FIX, with the new VP2 chipset, are also very interesting, although it's still too early to say much about their compatibility and long-term stability.

> **NOTE**
>
> **Tuning tip for AMD K6 and Cyrix 6x86MX owners—the new motherboard by FIC with the VP2 chipset**
>
> Most AMD K6 and Cyrix 6x86MX owners are really driving their Porsches in second gear—without the right motherboard, you just can't run at full speed. However, VIA now has the first optimized chipset, the VP3, and FIC has developed a motherboard to match: the BAT model PA 2007 and the ATX model PA 2011.

As we mentioned, the P55T2P4 is a classic, with stable performance and flawless construction. Asus's Internet support (www.asus.com) is also very good. The board is now in its 3.x revision and shows the company's long-term commitment to the series. This motherboard is available in several versions. The standard BAT version is the most interesting since it supports the new system bus frequencies of 75 and 85 MHz. The otherwise identical ATX version does not yet support these. There is also a version with an integrated Adaptec 2940UW SCSI controller, which we do not recommend (more on this topic in our SCSI chapter in Chapter 7).

Compared to the Asus boards, the Abit IT5H seems exotic. It's most prominent feature is that most of the settings are made using a special BIOS program. One exception is the size configuration for the L2 cache is still set using jumper as on the Asus boards. What's more appealing about the IT5H is that it offers a turbo mode of 68 MHz, in addition to the new bus speeds of 75 and 83 MHz. Systems are guaranteed to remain perfectly stable in this mode. Plus they'll run just a bit faster. There is currently no ATX version of the IT5H. If you opt for an IT5H, make sure you *don't* get a version lower than revision 1.5, since there were problems with these earlier boards. Also, version 1.5 still used an old in-line voltage regulator, so you may be risking a meltdown if you run an AMD K6 233 on one of these boards. Abit will shortly release version 2.0, which will be equipped with a split-voltage regulator and will also support ECC RAM, so it would definitely be worth waiting for one of these new boards.

Otherwise, all boards use the proven, non-limiting 430HX chipset and support all of the new Socket 7 processors by Intel, AMD and Cyrix up to 233 MHz. Flash-BIOS upgradability, stable voltage regulators (unfortunately still in-line regulators with Abit) and cacheable memory up to 512 Megs are all givens.

Why it's important to understand chipsets

We believe the chipsets are second in importance only to the CPU. They coordinate all the interaction between the processor and the rest of the world. Chipsets are not necessarily the same. There are important differences that not only affect the system's performance, but can also limit a PC (for instance, by restricting its upgrade options).

Chipsets generally consists of two such processors on the motherboard, which can easily be identified by their labels.

In the past a few chipset manufacturers battled in the market. However, Intel has managed to dominant this market since the introduction of its Triton chipset. Two Triton II versions called 430HX and 430VX (THX and TVX) in particular were found on virtually every motherboard. The market has changed recently with manufacturers such as Sis or VIA offering alternatives to Triton. Let's first look at the Intel chipsets—the THX, TVX and the new TX (430TX).

The difference between THX and TVX is small, but significant. You should understand this difference so no one can sell you a TVX board without your knowledge. This chipset has two additional functions that, in practice, are fairly useless. It supports multi-processor operation and also the newer, faster SDRAM. However, it is also considerably slower in its RAM access than the THX. Since SDRAM has no added benefit at the usual system frequency of 66 MHz, and very few users run multi-processor systems, 90% of all motherboards have THX chipsets, which is exactly what you should buy. Unless you have a specific need for one, don't let anybody sell you a TVX board.

NOTE

The best chipset for the Pentium Pro and Pentium II
The right chipset also makes a big difference with the Pentium Pro and especially the Pentium II. As we mentioned, you should stay away from the current Natoma chipset—get one of the newer boards released in the fall of '97 (or more recently) instead.

Intel's new TX chipset for the Pentium has a built-in performance trap

The problem with the 430TX is that it intentionally limits the maximum amount of RAM that can be cached to only 64 Megs. In other words, if you install more than 64 Megs of RAM in your system, its performance will take a noticeable drop. This is truly a joke considering today's low RAM prices and memory-hungry 32-bit applications.

The few advantages that the TX chipset—and the boards that use it—include SDRAM support and the new Ultra-DMA/33 EIDE port. However, as we said, you don't need either of these.

Windows 95 encounters problems with the TX chipset recognizing ATAPI CD-ROMs on the second EIDE bus when a Busmaster driver is used (see Chapter 6). In the meantime new drivers have become available that fix this problem. You should be able to download them from the Web site of your motherboard manufacturer (www.asus.com, for instance).

Another problem with the TX chipset is that it runs at 3.3 volts instead of the normal 5 volts. This has caused serious problems with some ISA cards and hard drives. Before buying such a board make certain it will work with your other components. Otherwise, you may be in for an unpleasant surprise. You probably won't need to worry about this problem with newer systems since the manufacturer already knew of the problem and likely has fixed it by now. But be careful with older systems.

The TX chipset offers a few trick features, but for speed it's no better than its predecessor, the THX.

> **For notebook users: USB only with the TX chipset**
>
> **NOTE** USB is the the hottest recent development in the peripherals realm (see Chapter 5). It's particularly interesting to notebook users, since it allows many devices to be attached externally (such as CD-ROM drives or digital cameras). However, be aware that USB is currently only available for new notebooks with the TX chipset; so check before you buy, or you may be kicking yourself two years down the road.

Some manufacturers, such as Asus, add some features to their TX97 models. These features include CPU temperature sensors or voltage monitoring functions for different system components. However, these features are probably more useful for a network administrator in a large company than an individual user. Most of us will want to go with the proven THX boards (see our recommendation above).

Finally, the TX chipset has nothing to do with MMX or its enhancement. The motherboard actually cannot affect this function. MMX is intended solely to be used by software to process certain types of data more quickly.

The new TX97 boards by Asus have a temperature sensor built into the ZIF socket that sits under the CPU and registers its temperature. Although this usually is entirely unnecessary, it can come in handy when overclocking.

New chipsets from VIA, AMD, Sis and others

This tip is especially important if you have (or want to get) an AMD K6 or Cyrix 6x86MX. For the first time in a long while you can again get great motherboards with powerful chipsets that are *not* from Intel. The move is led by Sis and VIA, who are working closely with AMD and Cyrix to develop better support for their processors.

The first of these products is the Apollo VP2 chipset by VIA, which was released in the summer of 1997. AMD is offering its own version called the AMD640. FIC has also started delivering the first boards with the VP2 chipset, the PA-2007 (BAT version) and the PA-2011 (ATX). The special thing about these is that the BAT version is already available with a 1MB L2 cache, and the corresponding ATX version should become available in the fall.

The VP2 chipset has several special features to make it different from Intel chipsets:

◆ An L2 cache of up to 1 MB. This results in better performance than with Intel TX boards, especially under Windows NT.

◆ Special support of AMD K6 and Cyrix 6x86MX processors, in particular through a special L2 cache access method called "linear burst." This improves performance up to 5% over Intel boards.

◆ SDRAM and Ultra DMA support—the same two features that distinguish the TX chipset.

◆ ECC memory support.

◆ Unlike Intel's TX chipset, the L2 cache can service up to 512 Megs of RAM. No 64 Megs limit here.

◆ Enhanced power-management features following Microsoft's PC97 standard (ACPI, or Advanced Configuration and Power Interface).

Chapter 4

The really hot development hit the market in the fall of 1997. This was the VIA VP3 and the AMD640AGP. It features an increased system bus speed of 100 MHz as well as the new AGP graphics bus.

To prevent the higher system bus frequencies of 75 MHz and faster from destabilizing the PCI bus, the latter is run asynchronously. This means it's not linked to the system bus directly at a 50% frequency ratio, which should prevent any trouble with some PCI cards.

Similar chipsets are expected from other manufacturers, such as Opti, Ali, SiS or ITE. It promises to be a hot year.

Turbocharger and the right L2 cache

The Level 2 cache was introduced with the first 386 system over 33 MHz, some years ago now. The reason is that the processor runs much faster than the relatively slow RAM chips that make up the system's main memory. There have been many attempts to deal with this problem; many of them are less than satisfactory, such as a processor wait-state, utilizing CPU timeout-loops. However, the best and most widely accepted solution has been the use of a small, extremely fast buffer between the CPU and RAM.

The L2 cache is integrated directly into the motherboard (except on Pentium Pro and Pentium II systems). These little static-RAM (SRAM) chips do not require unending refresh cycles to retain their data, unlike conventional RAM. Instead, a constant closed circuit current is used. Therefore, these chips allow access times of just under 10ns. Unfortunately their production costs are much higher and they require more power, so they are not suitable for main memory.

Most motherboards now include 512 K of integrated, onboard SRAM memory for their L2 caches.

The three types of L2 caches are possible but only one is used for today's motherboards:

◆ asynchronous (as-L2 cache)

◆ synchronous (s-L2 cache)

◆ pipelined burst (pB-L2 cache)

These three types differ slightly in the SRAM chips they use. A more important difference is in the way they operate or are organized. The slowest and also least expensive type is the asynchronous, which, not surprisingly, cannot keep up synchronously with the processor's clock frequency. The synchronous type can, however. Until two to three years ago, it was used on most motherboards, before being replaced by the pB-L2 type. Although this type of SRAM is no faster than the synchronous type at system frequencies up to 66 MHz, it is less expensive to produce. As its name indicates, the CPU accesses the data in this type of L2 cache in bursts. With each burst, data is read in contiguous packets, or successive steps. Only the first access step is a little slower than with the synchronous type, each successive access then generally occurs at the processor clock speed—in the BIOS configuration this is described, for example, with numeric combinations like "3-1-1-1." The configuration of the cache's burst access is an important system-tuning consideration (see Chapter 6).

NOTE **Tuning your system with the right type of L2 cache**
Up to a 66-MHz system clock speed, a synchronous cache is the best choice for maximum speed. However, these types of motherboards aren't readily available. Although, pipelined-burst caches are almost as fast, and with future system frequencies of 75, 83 or even 100 MHz, they're the better choice—synchronous caches can't keep up at these speeds. If your old Pentium motherboard is still equipped with the Triton 1 chipset (Neptune), for example, you're probably working with a lame asynchronous L2 cache. In that case you can boost your system's performance noticably even by just switching to a new motherboard. Conversely, if you're considering plugging a new processor into your old motherboard, you should keep in mind that the lame L2 cache is going to put the brakes on your new CPU. As to the ideal size for your L2 cache, please read our section below.

An interesting approach was taken with the L2 cache for the Pentium Pro and Pentium II. Integrating the L2 cache directly into the processor case is the optimum solution for achieving the highest possible speed, since the cache can run at the full processor frequency. After all, otherwise it's only running at the system bus's usual 66 MHz.

However, Intel discovered that the L2 cache could only be produced at a reasonable cost for up to 150-MHz clock speeds. The internal L2 caches in 200-MHz PPro chips literally comes at a high price. What's more, the PPro can only be tested after the processor core and the L2 are assembled. If even one of the two components is defective, the whole thing has to be tossed, and this results in a relatively high attrition rate. This is why the Pentium II has the L2 cache mounted on a card next to the processor, running at half of the CPU's clock frequency. This way even a 300-MHz Pentium II can make do with the less expensive 150-MHz L2 memory. Consequently, the Pentium II is about 25% cheaper to produce than the Pentium Pro.

Determining how much cache is necessary

Many PC users are wondering how much cache is necessary. It's important to remember that the cache's size actually matters less than its access technique and access time. Adding more memory to the cache will only improve your PC's performance if it *is* the bottleneck in your system, and this only happens when large amounts of RAM are used.

Chapter 4

One rule for the proper cache size is quite simple. It's proportional to the size of the system's main memory. If you have lots of RAM, you'll need a larger cache. You won't need more than a 256-K L2 cache with up to 64 Megs of RAM. In this case, upgrading to 512K will only increase your PC's performance less than three per cent. In other words, you aren't likely to notice a difference in normal use. However, if you have more than 64 Megs of RAM, 256K won't be enough to cache all of main memory, resulting in a marked decrease in performance. In this case, it's definitely time to upgrade. However, there are many nasty pitfalls to avoid, as you'll learn below.

> **NOTE**
>
> **Darned cheapskates—PCs without L2 caches!**
>
> It's hard to believe, but it happens again and again: some manufacturers come up with lame excuses not to include L2 caches at all. This happened first with the introduction of EDO RAM, which is supposedly so fast that the L2 cache becomes unnecessary. The same thing will probably happen when SDRAM starts to be used more widely. This cost-cutting method is also frequently used on notebook systems; lower-priced Pentium 120 models in particular are often still sold without L2 caches. Don't believe anything to the contrary; regardless of what kind of system you have or what kind of RAM you're using, your PC will run much too slowly without an L2 cache. Manufacturers probably save around $30 by leaving out the cache, which is much too small a sum to justify torturing users with such inadequate systems. If you've got one of these, all you can do is hope that it's upgradeable.

A few final thoughts on cache-size and upgrade options. Since early in 1997 almost all up-to-date boards have been shipped with 512 K of L2 cache; until then 256 K was standard. Most older models allow for upgrades. These upgrades are usually done using a COAST module but can also be done through small, bi-directional memory chips. COAST modules, resembling PS/2 SIMMs, are plugged into a separate socket near the ZIF socket. Both of these solutions are very inexpensive ($20 for 256K). This is really cheap enough so that you should definitely upgrade if you think that your system would benefit. As mentioned above, if you have less than 64 Megs of RAM you really won't notice a benefit. Be sure to get the right type of COAST module if you opt for this type of upgrade—the following tip will explain.

You can upgrade your motherboard's L2 cache from 256 to 512K using this kind of coast-module.

> **NOTE**
>
> **Is it worth it?—new motherboards with 1-Meg L2 caches**
>
> In July of '97 the first motherboards with the new VP2 chip by VIA appeared. One of their special features is that they support 1 Meg of L2 memory. The company FIC is already selling the first such board (the PA-2007). It offers a performance increase of about 5% vs. a board with a 512-K L2 cache, though this depends on the application and operating system. This motherboard, or rather the VP2 chipset, also offers other advantages—see our section on chipsets and motherboards, see the information this chapter—and it's a worthwhile alternative to Intel chipsets.

Tag-RAM costs manufacturers money and users headaches

The function of Tag-RAM is closely related to that of the L2 cache. This little SRAM chip coordinates the exchange of data between the cache and main memory. If there is too little Tag-RAM, the L2 cache will only be able to service a limited amount of RAM. Unfortunately, most manufacturers (knowingly) provide an insufficient amount of Tag-RAM (the 8K8 type) on their motherboards, so that no more than 64 Megs of RAM can be cached. This is not to be confused with the 512 K required for the L2 cache when the system is using more than 64 Megs of RAM (see previous section). Although these two work together, they're separate chips.

You can upgrade your Tag-RAM using this upgrade socket near the coast-module and the ZIF socket.

Larger Tag-RAM chips (16K8 or 32K8) only cost around five dollars, so it's truly a mystery why manufacturers try again and again to cut their costs on such items, at the computer user's expense. But then, a dollar saved is a dollar earned.

In any event, if you want to upgrade your system's memory to more than 64 Megs, it's crucial you make sure that the Tag-RAM on your motherboard is sufficient. Otherwise upgrading your L2 cache to 512 K won't do a thing. Fortunately, some manufacturers have provided a small upgrade socket for an additional Tag-RAM chip, allowing you to simply add another (16K8 or 32K8). As an alternative, you can upgrade your Tag-RAM using a special coast-module (revision 3.0), which contains an additional Tag-RAM chip along with the L2 cache upgrade. However, it's important to know that you can only use one of these two upgrade options—either the upgrade socket *or* the coast-module with the Tag-RAM. In practice, the coast-module option is generally the more affordable one. Be sure to verify that the coast-module you're considering includes a Tag-RAM upgrade.

Chipsets can limit the size of your RAM

It seems that many manufacturers don't trust users with more than 64 Megs of RAM—why else would they build so many hurdles and traps above this level? Indeed, insufficient L2 cache and Tag-RAM aren't the only factors that can limit the use of more RAM: there are all sorts of chipsets that just won't play along.

With the first Triton I chipset, three or four years ago, it was perhaps still forgivable that only 64 Megs of RAM could be cached. However, the fact that Intel has reverted to this practice with its new 430HX (Triton III) is truly incomprehensible. After all, the two current (Triton II) chipsets, the THX and TVX, allow 512 Megs of RAM. Perhaps to no one's surprise, there is a motive behind this self-imposed speed limit, as discussed earlier.

The moral of the story is to keep your fingers off old motherboards with Triton I chipsets and, of course, the new TX boards. It's better to stick with the proven and still more or less up-to-date THX models.

The Pentium II's L2 cache stops at 512 Megs

Speaking of RAM limits thanks to limited L2 cache support: the Pentium II has a similar pitfall. In this case it's neither Tag-RAM nor the motherboard chipset that's to blame. Instead it's the processor, or rather its integrated L2 cache. The Pentium II by design isn't at all fond of RAM above 512 Megs. It's not just that RAM above this level isn't cached; even the memory below this limit will no longer be cached, bringing the whole system to its knees with a 50% drop in performance.

All right, you're thinking, "Yeah, who's ever going to use that much RAM anyway?" Admittedly, it'd be a bit much for a home-system, but intensively-used servers, for instance for large networks or Internet servers, can easily require 640 Megs of RAM. For such systems the Pentium Pro is the only choice, which supports RAM up to 768 Megs.

WHAT YOU NEED TO KNOW ABOUT MEMORY

RAM is the elixir of life for any PC, and with every new piece of software, it becomes more precious. Fortunately, after years of artificially high prices, RAM prices have finally fallen to reasonable, and hopefully stable, prices.

However, this is no reason to run out and buy as many of the familiar PS/2 SIMMs as you can afford. Just as with all other hardware items, developments are happening in the RAM world, and they've never been as far-reaching and rapid as right now. While this is good news on one hand, it is also rather frustrating, since last year's hardware is already outdated. This is doubly annoying with still rather pricey RAM chips. You probably recall the switch from standard to PS/2 SIMMS just five years ago, that came with the introduction of the Pentium. A similar thing is happening right now with SDRAM.

In this section we're going to first cover the different RAM types currently in use, just enough so that you understand their advantages and disadvantages. We'll talk about configuring your RAM using the BIOS farther below, in the Chapter 6 on BIOS and motherboard tuning. The chapter on optimizing your RAM for the software you're using may be of the most interest to you however. It contains all of the important tips for getting the most out of RAM with DOS, Windows, and a number of software applications. Remember that a poorly configured Windows system with 64 Megs of RAM will run no better than an ideally optimized 32 Meg system, so stay tuned.

The 64-bit straightjacket

Few things are as aggravating as no longer being able to use the RAM chips that you bought at a premium on your new motherboard. This happened to many users about four years ago, with the introduction of PS/2 SIMMs. The cause for this change was the Pentium with its 64-bit wide memory bus (even though the Pentium is still a 32-bit processor). The standard 30-pin SIMMs, with their 8-bit transfer-width, that had been used until then were not suited to the Pentium—their use was limited to 486 systems with 32-bit memory buses. Therefore the switch was made to PS/2 SIMMs, with 72 pins and a data-width of 32 bits. PS/2 SIMMs thus have to be used in pairs to make 64-bit access possible with Pentium systems.

The old 30-pin 8-bit SIMMs (below) had to make way for the new 32-bit PS/2 SIMMs (above), because the Pentium uses 64-bit memory access.

The current introduction of DIMM memory is also related to the optimization of memory bus access. This new memory type permits 64-bit access to a single module, as explained below.

By the way, if you still have old SIMM chips and really want to use them, refer to the tips in Chapter 2.

NOTE

Is the 128-bit memory bus on its way, or what's next?

Memory access just can't happen fast enough. There are two ways of making it as fast as possible: a higher clock speed and/or wider data transfer. Current technology permits 64-bit transfer, which is what the Pentium and all other current processors use. However, the next processor generation will not include a 128-bit bus—if anything, the development is in the other direction. The reason is that a 128-bit bus would be extremely complex and also less reliable, especially at higher clock speeds.

As explained below, RDRAM—which is particularly fast—makes do with a mere 8-bit bus. However, this bus permits clock frequencies of 600 MHz and more, which more than compensates for the smaller bus width. Development will most likely continue in this direction.

Differences between DIMMs and SIMMs

Probably very few PC users ever wondered about the term SIMM until suddenly these new DIMM chips appeared on the market. Unfortunately DIMMs are often equated with SDRAM, but they're not the same thing. Although SDRAM is currently being built in DIMM form, so is EDO RAM, setting the stage for potential fraud: It's possible that unscrupulous dealers will sell EDO DIMMs disguised as more expensive SDRAM. This is something you'll want to watch for very closely.

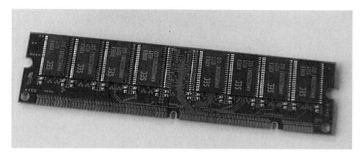

*This is an example of a DIMM bar. This 64-bit IC's 178-pin contact
strip with its two gaps make it somewhat larger than the older PS/2 SIMMs.*

So what's under the hood of one of these DIMMs (**D**ual **I**nline **M**emory **M**odule)? Quite simply, in contrast to SIMMs (Single Inline Memory Module), they have a contact strip with two sections. In other words, the 178 pins of the new 5.2-inch module are split between two successive contact strips. Otherwise the new modules look like the old, they're simply a bit bigger. The slots (memory banks) have been modified a bit for the new chips, and they're easier to open and close than the old ones. The real purpose behind the new format is that the modules can operate individually under 64-bit access. This allows you to also use an odd numbered combination of modules on a Pentium motherboard, also making it easier to combine modules of different sizes.

The handy clips on the sides of these DIMM memory banks make it much easier to install your modules.

Chapter 4

NOTE

The 5-volt trap—the correct voltage for your DIMMs

As if the confusion between SIMMs and DIMMs wasn't enough, there are even different types of DIMMs, such as buffered and unbuffered modules (though only the latter are commonly used). Furthermore, older DIMMs require a supply voltage of 5V and newer ones run on 3.3V. To make things worse, depending on your motherboard, only one or the other type will be supported. You should stay away from the 5V type, because it's on its way out. Therefore, when shopping for a motherboard, make sure it supports 3.3V memory modules, and don't let a dealer sell you 5V DIMMs. The latter have only one remaining advantage: there are special boards which allow you to use both SIMMs and DIMMs together, but only the 5V kind. However, 5V SIMMs are basically no longer available, and 5V DIMMs are disappearing as well. Luckily the different DIMM types have different contact-strip spacings, so they're easy to tell apart. But that doesn't make it impossible to buy the wrong type.

By the way, the first boards with DIMM memory banks had barely hit the market when special adapters appeared that make it possible to use the old PS/2 modules. If you opt for this solution, make sure that your BIOS isn't configured for the faster SDRAM access.

When to use FP RAM, EDO RAM or SDRAM

Those shopping for a new system today have three different types of RAM to choose from: FP RAM, EDO RAM and the new SDRAM. However, the latter two are only supported by newer motherboards with TX chipsets or older motherboards with TVX chipsets. All the other chipsets that are coming out, such as for the AMD K6 or the Pentium II, will also support SDRAM.

To answer the question of appropriate RAM type or to make a recommendation, we'll have to discuss the characteristics of these three types. However, we can say right off the bat that, with the current standard system frequency of 66 MHz, there is virtually no difference between these three types. Therefore, if you're planning on keeping your system in its stock configuration for some time, you may just want to buy the least expensive type of memory—surprisingly the cheapest often seems to be EDO RAM, otherwise it's FP RAM.

> **NOTE**
>
> **One left, two down—RAM modules are structured like tables, making certain access tricks possible**
>
> Memory is structured like large spreadsheet tables: lots of rows and columns that are grouped into pages. Each resulting cell in this table receives one bit of information. To access specific data, the memory controller must know the page, row and column address and specify it to the DRAM ("Get me the info from cell E26 on page 15"). Since sequential data is often stored in neighboring areas, access can be speeded up by specifying the addressing information (page or row) only once—then the data from that page or row, for instance, can be transferred in one batch.

Here are short, not-overly-technical descriptions of the three types of RAM:

1   DRAM stands for Dynamic RAM and refers to all types of normal PC main memory modules in use today. Unlike SRAM, used for the L2 cache, the cheaper DRAM loses its information very quickly if its cells aren't continually refreshed with cyclical refresh-pulses. These superimposed refresh-cycles slow down the access to the memory and cost processor time. On the other hand, DRAM is less expensive to manufacture and it produces less heat during operation.

2   FP DRAM stands for Fast Page mode DRAM. This is the type of standard RAM most commonly used today; its access time is slightly lower than that of the previously used DRAM. The trick used with FP RAM is that the memory modules are able to remember the currently active memory page (see sidebar above). So when data within the current page needs to be accessed, only the row and column addresses have to be specified. Older BIOSes will have to be specifically configured for the use of FP RAM, while this is the default setting with newer ones (see Chapter 6). FP DRAM is commonly available in 60 and 70-ns access times.

> **NOTE**
>
> **Caution!—70-ns chips are too slow for modern PCs**
>
> FP DRAM in particular can be found in 60 and 70-ns versions these days. It's crucial that you only use 60-ns memory chips in your modern Pentium system—they are essential for the performance of PCs with 66-MHz system buses. 70-ns memory is barely adequate for 60-MHz system buses (P120 or P150 systems). Good dealers will have a testing device that can verify memory chip access times. The indicated values are somewhat approximate—it's possible that a 60-ns chip will give a reading of 65ns, but that ought to be the maximum. The access time is also indicated by the last number printed on the chip. You'll see something like "xx-60" or "xx-6." Buy 50-ns EDO RAM if you can find it at a good price. This type of RAM will keep up with your system even if you overclock your system bus to 83 MHz.

3. EDO RAM stands for Enhanced Data Output RAM (sometimes also called "Hyper Page Mode"). With this variant, as the name indicates, data can be read more quickly from the memory. EDO RAM is a version of FP RAM, in which output data for the processor is kept ready longer, so that new data can be written even as the current data is being read. This was made possible through a small change to the column address signal (CAS). EDO RAM is usually available with 50 and 60-ns access times. There is also a new version of EDO RAM, called BEDO RAM. The "B" stands for Burst, and this type of RAM really does speed up access. However, BEDO has no chance of gaining a market foothold, because Intel does not support the format and because the market has apparently already opted for SDRAM.

NOTE

EDO RAM only works on certain systems!
If you're thinking of using EDO RAM, you should know that your motherboard and BIOS need to support these. This is only the case with newer Pentium boards—486 motherboards with EDO support really don't exist. While it's possible to use EDO RAM with such boards, you will not be able to benefit from their greater performance.

4 SDRAM stands for Synchronous DRAM. This type runs synchronous to the external processor frequency, without wait-cycles. However, it can only do this up to 100 MHz. Its 10-ns access time is significantly below that of the other types of DRAM. Furthermore, almost all modules include 2 K of cache-RAM, which speeds up access even more. SDRAM is currently being produced primarily by Samsung, and as one would expect, they're more expensive than other types of DRAM. Unfortunately, SDRAMs use more power and consequently run hotter. All SDRAM modules are produced in DIMM format and thus support 64-bit operation. Therefore they also don't necessarily need to be used in pairs.

Now to the practical facts. SDRAM is clearly the format of the future, since it won't be long before even Intel will break its strict 66-MHz system bus frequency limit and raise it to 75, 83 and then 100 MHz. FP and EDO RAM just can't keep up at these speeds, requiring lots of wait-states, for which even a fast L2 cache can't compensate.

NOTE

Mixing your EDOs and FPs—it's possible, but...
On most boards it's possible to mix EDO and FP RAM, though never on the same bank. In other words, you could use two EDOs on bank 0 and two FPs on bank 1. Depending on your BIOS version, the EDO modules will then simply be addressed like FPs. Newer versions of BIOSes can address these types individually and correctly for each memory bank.

However, you probably knew that a big BUT was on its way: for the still standard 66-MHz systems, the greater cost of SDRAM is not justifiable. Just like EDO RAM, it fails to bring a noticeable improvement in performance. You may remember the big discussion about EDO RAM, when it first came out two years ago. At the time, some PCs were even sold without L2 caches, because EDO was supposedly fast enough on its own. Nonsense—you're left with a meager 2% increase in performance. There are two reasons the advantages of SDRAM are still negligible. For one, an L2 cache is perfectly capable of keeping the processor running at capacity at system clock speeds of up to 75 MHz. In this case the slower RAM modules really don't slow the processor down. Secondly, and more importantly, no BIOSes are currently available that can actually use the low access times made possible by SDRAM. The best any BIOS can provide is support for 50-ns access times (such as MR BIOS, see Chapter 6). We're still a ways off from the possible, and eventually necessary, 10-ns access time.

> **NOTE**
>
> **Where and when SDRAM will truly shine**
>
> SDRAM really starts to make sense with the introduction of the AGP bus for new graphic cards. These cards have to access main memory at high speeds for the necessary 3-D calculations. At that point normal DRAM will simply be too slow. Speaking of video cards: SDRAM is replacing DRAM and VRAM even on conventional video cards, to no one's surprise.

Again, remember that the type of RAM used for normal PCs is not all that important. SDRAM is only worth the extra money if you're planning on using the chips in a future system or if you're going to fully utilize upcoming technologies such as AGP (see sidebar). If, however, you want to keep the PC in its current configuration or perhaps sell it at some point, you're better off not spending the extra money for the SDRAM.

You'll find more information on SDRAM and RAM in general at the Web sites of different chip manufacturers, like IBM (www.chips.ibm.com/products/memory), Siemens (www.siemens.de/semiconductor/memory/index.htm) or Micron (www.micron.com).

Problems in using SDRAM

It seems that SDRAM technology is still experiencing some growing pains—there have already been reports of the first problems with the new memory modules. Apparently the production tolerances or specifications of different manufacturers haven't been perfectly coordinated yet, and some users have encountered incompatibility problems in using different SDRAM chips on the same board. It makes sense, then, that most SDRAM today is still sold directly on new motherboards. Motherboard manufacturers generally bundle their boards with a 32-Meg module, whose compatibility with the board is assured. If you, the user, then want to upgrade to

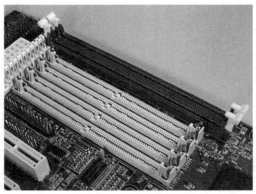

On this type of board you can use either DIMMs or SIMMs, but not both!

64 Megs and get an SDRAM DIMM from another source, you may be in for a nasty surprise.

Even if a board has both SIMM and DIMM sockets (such as the Asus TX97-E), **do not** try to use both types of memory modules at the same time! This is only possible with 5-volt modules, which are extremely hard to come by. If you try it anyway, you'll ruin the chips. Even if you do manage to get at some 5V modules, if you're using different types of RAM, your motherboard will treat all of the modules just like the slowest one in the chain. Therefore there won't be any advantage in using those SDRAM chips.

Parity bits and ECC make your system more stable

Until two to three years ago, all memory modules had a parity bit. This was easy to see, since the modules always contained an odd number of chips—usually nine instead of eight. The last, odd-numbered bit is used as a check-bit to catch errors, through check-sum analysis. When parity modules are used with the Pentium's 64-bit memory bus, there is an 8-bit checksum word for each 64-bit data word.

Since the parity bit had only been used for the memory test at bootup, and the quality of today's RAM chips is high enough to virtually rule out hardware defects, parity-bit chips have more or less fallen out of use. With these kind of modules you'll need to make sure that the bootup memory test is disabled, otherwise your system will lock up. It's important to emphasize that the parity bit only offers a means for error *detection*, not error correction. Thus an error message at bootup simply means "This memory chip is dead."

> **NOTE**
>
> **RAM with or without parity?—it's a matter of chipsets**
>
> Your chipset determines which type of RAM you'll need. The old Saturn chipset for 486 boards, for instance, requires parity chips. The old Neptune and the more current TVX chipset for the Pentium do not support parity checking. Only the THX and Natoma chipsets for the Pentium Pro/II can use either, and to some extent even ECC. if you're going to use chips both with and without parity on the same board, you'll generally need to disable parity or ECC support in your BIOS. It's also possible to use parity chips on boards that don't support parity checking at all. However, to take advantage of the ECC function, you'll need DRAM with true parity bits, not the kind of DRAM that permits parity checks through an integrated logic circuit.

Most current motherboards or chipsets can use error correction code (ECC) to correct memory errors during operation—for instance under Windows—through the use of the parity bit. These boards include, for example, the Natoma and THX chipsets for the Pentium II and the regular Pentium. Make certain that you get real parity modules when buying memory for such systems to ensure that your ECC will function properly (see sidebar above). Unfortunately, it's a given that this type of memory is more expensive than modules without parity.

> **Ideal for servers—Pentium II with L2 cache ECC**
>
> **NOTE** Intel now offers a special version of the Pentium II, which is able to use ECC on the L2 cache. Together with the ECC used in the Natoma chipset, this ensures a very high level of operating stability. Intel, of course, sees this as a good reason to charge quite a bit more money. Nevertheless, such a Pentium II is just the right thing for a hefty network server. You'll find more information on the Pentium II on earlier in this book.

ECC is not just an error detection method. It also corrects errors that are detected, which is a large step forward. However, only 1-bit errors can be corrected; 2-bit errors are simply reported to the operating system by the BIOS through an NMI signal. However, (currently) all operating systems—from Windows 95 to NT and OS/2—react to such a signal by locking up. The settings that determine how the PC will react in case of an error are made in the BIOS (see Chapter 6). If possible, you should select the configuration that automatically corrects 1-bit errors, without displaying a message. 2-bit errors should be handled without any notification, so that the operating system does not crash. If your motherboard can't be configured this way, then you won't be able to use ECC.

By the way, using ECC takes a little bit of processing power; you can expect a performance drop of about 2-5%. However, the increased system stability is well worth this low price.

Memory tuning with Interleave

You may remember the interleave method from the old 386SX-NEAT systems. This method is also used with many new DRAM video cards (see Chapter 10). It improves memory access by alternately addressing paired memory banks. This way the DRAM refresh cycle occurs between accesses, thereby saving time. This way the relative access time is lowered by about 10ns. However, the prerequisite is that the processor can access memory banks that are paired. On the motherboard this means, for example, that banks 0 and 1—each with two sockets—must be completely populated.

> **The interleaving advantage—only possible with the right chipset and**
>
> **NOTE** **memory type**
>
> Interleaving was particularly popular on 486 motherboards with the Saturn chipset, for example. Intel's current Pentium chipsets don't use this technique anymore, although there are some competing products that do, for instance one by SiS. Most likely the new Pentium chipsets developed by Intel's competitors will use every trick in the book to boost performance, and interleaving will surely be one of them. Unfortunately interleaving is not possible with EDO RAM, because of its slightly different operation.

If you plan on using interleaving, you'll need to be careful which RAM modules you use on your motherboard: you might get 32 Meg using 2 x 16 Meg or 4 x 8 Meg modules. However, only the latter combination will populate both memory banks, which is necessary for interleaving to work. This means your PC will actually run a little faster with the 4 x 8 Meg modules than the 2 x 16 Meg ones. However, the disadvantage is that you won't be able to upgrade the PC to 64 Megs without scrapping the old modules. Since the advantages of interleaving are lessened through the use of fast L2 caches, it's generally better to leave your upgrade options as open as possible. Best, of course, would be to fill both memory banks by using 4 x 16 Meg modules, giving you 64 Megs and the ability to interleave.

If you're using an AMI chipset BIOS, you can activate interleaving using the *Interleaved Memory* command. Award and Phoenix don't have this command—they sense when the memory banks are fully paired and enable interleaving automatically (see Chapter 6).

Fast futures—RDRAM and more

For the next couple of years SDRAM will most likely be the top-notch RAM type for fast PC systems. However, its fate is already sealed, and its time on the market will be limited, because it's simply too slow for the next generation of high-speed processors, with fancy codenames like Deschutes and Merced.

The new type of RAM for the turn of the millennium will almost certainly be RDRAM, or at least be based on the technology developed by the California company Rambus. RDRAM is currently being used by Silicon Graphics for high-end workstations, as well as some console game systems like the Nintendo 64. What's likely to ensure the success of this new technology is that Intel and Rambus have formed a strategic alliance to develop a memory type for the new Intel processors based on RDRAM.

Whether this new RDRAM-type memory is going to be called "Direct-RDRAM" or "nDRAM" is pure speculation. What's more important are the current and future performance figures:

RDRAM is already about ten times faster than normal DRAM, which is based on entirely different technology. To accommodate a much higher clock rate—currently already up to 600MHz—the memory bus was narrowed to 8 bits. This decrease in complexity has two advantages: lower RAM and motherboard production costs and increased bus operating stability (see the information regarding different bus widths). Of course new motherboards and memory controllers will have to be developed—currently the data rate for RDRAM is already at 600MB/sec, which is supposed to be raised to 1.6GB/sec for the new Intel processors. However, to achieve such rates the data bus will probably have to be widened from 8 to 16 bits. On the Rambus home page, at www.rambus.com, you'll find more information about this technology

The development of RDRAM is not good news for the other manufacturers, because the Intel-Rambus tag-team may very well develop a memory-chip monopoly. European and Asian chip manufacturers aren't about to take this lying down, and have already formed a kind of counter-consortium, comprised of companies like NEC, Siemens and Mitsubishi. Their goal is to develop an open alternative memory standard. This new chip-type is called SLDRAM, and its performance should be comparable to the Intel/Rambus product (high clock speed, narrow bus, etc.). The advantage of this open standard would be that any manufacturer could produce this type of RAM without paying licensing fees. However, the U.S.-based Intel/Rambus force is farther along with its product development, and Intel will be sure not to support SLDRAM with its processors. The cards thus seem to be stacked against the new open memory standard. You can find more information on SLDRAM at the www.sldram.com and www.scizzl.com Web sites.

Battling RAM Shortage

In this section you'll find a selection of the best memory-optimization tips for DOS and Windows. We had a tough time deciding which chapter should discuss the software cache settings (Smartdrive, or rather VCache32) and the Windows swap-file. Both are closely connected with memory and hard drive operation and therefore need to be discussed in that context. We finally opted to include this material in the hard drive chapter, starting in Chapter 8. After all, in today's systems, the hard drive is even more critical than RAM, with a greater effect on performance. Lower RAM prices and new, less complicated software have eliminated many of the RAM hurdles.

Therefore this chapter will deal with only with the basic settings for the system's main memory under DOS and Windows. The hardware-related configuration for RAM timing is covered in Chapter 6. It simply would have been too confusing to cover all aspects of RAM use and configuration in this section.

Since the introduction of Windows 95, most people have been able to stop worrying about memory optimization. Remember the days of DOS, when you struggled to squeeze every single kilobyte from your lower DOS memory? There were all sorts of tools like Quarterdeck's QEMM and Microsoft's Memmaker that you could use in your quest for more available memory. Luckily this is no longer an issue—under Windows 95 there no longer is a memory limit or resource problems, like there still were under Windows 3.x. And DOS is now only used for computer games, and even there memory use is rarely an issue. The fact that DOS is only used to run games, and the help of special memory managers like **DOS4GW.EXE** that can use the once so hard-to-get-at memory above 1 Meg, make things quite simple today. No one needs to fumble with cryptic configurations of EMM386.EXE anymore, and thankfully there really isn't much that still needs to be taken into consideration. The few remaining points are discussed below.

Please remember that the settings covered in the hard drive chapter (Chapter 8) and the BIOS chapter (Chapter 6) also affect your system's memory. You'll need to take all of these considerations into account if you're going to get the most out of your PC.

Determining how much RAM Windows requires

Yes, the question is getting old, and everyone has a different answer, and Microsoft's is usually lower than most. Of course you want to spend as little money on more memory as necessary, but maybe, if you just knew for sure, maybe 32 Megs of RAM would finally do it, or perhaps 64 Megs?

First, consider ignoring Microsoft's recommendations. Sure, Windows somehow does manage to run on 8 Megs of RAM. However, it operates much better with at least 32 Megs of RAM. Plus if you're working with two or three applications at the same time and don't want to have to keep waiting for the hard drive, you'll find that even 64 Megs are sometimes barely enough. We were skeptical until we used the tool described earlier to discover just how memory-hungry 32-bit applications really are.

Since then we've upgraded all our systems to 64 Megs of RAM. Even our small Pentium 133 network PC became a little sprinter. Considering the very low price of RAM prices today, there's no reason not to upgrade to 64 Megs. If you then also optimize your cache and swap-file settings, as described in Chapter 8, you won't recognize your own PC. Don't even consider running Windows 95 with less than 32 Megs, that is, unless you have a lot of time and patience.

RAM and resource doublers

You may remember that SoftRAM released the first RAM doubler for Windows 3.x and Windows 95 about two years ago. It promised to double the amount of available physical memory through software-based RAM data compression. This sounded good enough to many people and the software sold quite well, for a while. However, several test results soon confirmed that the program had no effect.

What's strange is that several such programs are still available. Quarterdeck, a well-established company, is still selling its own RAM doubler (MagnaRAM), claiming it significantly improves performance.

What these programs essentially do is compress the data in the Windows swap file. There's nothing wrong with that, but aside from decreasing the size of the swap file, there is really no positive effect. MagnaRAM is no exception. You're much better off spending the money on real RAM.

There is another class of RAM doublers that, under Windows 3.x, can have a much more significant effect by increasing the system resources. DoubleRAM is one such program. As described below, Windows 3.x has a problem managing limited memory areas, which get too small awfully quickly when multiple applications are in use. This type of resource doubler allows the system to run more smoothly and more stably. However, switching to Windows 95 solves these problems completely.

Determining if HIMEM, EMM386 or QEMM are still necessary

The days of memory managers are virtually over. Since almost all of today's games run under Windows (some in DOS mode), those good old memory managers no longer need to be used. It's a good thing, too, because those entirely cryptic commands and the management of that critical range of memory between 640 K and 1.024 Megs—the adapter segment or UMB—were anything but easy.

The only thing that's still needed, is the DOS, or rather Windows driver HIMEM.SYS, which Windows 95 loads automatically at startup (even without it being included in the CONFIG.SYS file). This driver configures the memory above 1 Meg as extended memory and allows Windows, as well as any compatible DOS games, to run in protected mode. All 32-bit programs, like Windows 95, as well as almost all computer games use protected mode. There is also a 64 K memory segment directly below the first 1024 K, the HMA, that HIMEM.SYS makes available to DOS.

NOTE

Qemm 386, still the best? Who still needs the one-time super-memory-tool?

Quarterdeck's Qemm was once the state-of-the-art memory optimizer. It combined the functions of Himem.sys and Emm386.exe into a driver named Qemm386.exe. In addition to the many slick functions that squeezed every possible kilobyte of memory from the UMB, Qemm 386 provided an excellent analysis program (Manifest). However, because of Windows 95, Qemm is no longer important to most PC users. Only those who are still running old DOS applications under Windows 95 will be able to use the current version of Qemm (version 8) to get the most out of their PC, but for that, it is still the best thing you can get.

The only reason to include the line DEVICE=PATH\HIMEM.SYS in your CONFIG.SYS is if you want to boot your system in DOS mode for playing computer games. The "path" is the directory in which the driver is found—usually C:Windows. It's fine, however, if you load the driver like this every time you start your system, because Windows 95 does so anyway at bootup.

The IFSHLP.SYS driver belongs to HIMEM.SYS; it is also loaded by Windows 95. It was first introduced with Windows for Workgroups and is a protected mode driver for the entire file system. It allows Windows 95 to use 32-bit hard disk access and file-caching. You can load this driver just like HIMEM.SYS using the device command in your CONFIG.SYS.

You'll only need the EMM386.EXE DOS driver if you're using old DOS programs that cannot use protected mode and for which there isn't enough DOS memory. This driver does two things. First, it allows the memory in the adapter segment (the UMBs, between 640 and 1,024 K) for drivers—this is known as loading drivers high. This frees up more of the lower DOS memory (up to 640 K). Second, EMM386 can configure the memory above 1 Meg according to the old LIM/EMS standard, also known as expanded memory. Until about 1993 this was a common method for making more memory available to DOS applications like MS-Word. EMS is an alternative to XMS, the memory management method used in protected mode with the HIMEM.SYS driver.

You'll also run into the terms EMS and XMS, or expanded and extended memory, under Windows 95. Remember that, first of all, EMS is only used by a few old DOS applications, and that any memory segment can be used either through EMS or XMS, but usually not both. In other words, any memory that has been reserved for EMS use will not be available to Windows.

If you don't have such old DOS programs requiring EMS, use the NOEMS switch with the EMM386 device driver call to deactivate this function. This will also gain you another 64 K in the

Chapter 4

UMB to load other drivers and memory-related DOS programs high. Otherwise this 64 K segment would be reserved for the management of EMS memory in the UMB.

CONFIG.SYS command lines and optimizing memory

Below you'll find two sample CONFIG.SYS files. One is for new Windows 95 or new DOS games that support protected mode. The second is for pure DOS programs that need a maximum amount of memory within the first 1,024 K of RAM (and of course all sorts of DOS hardware drivers, for instance for the CD-ROM).

By removing the NOEMS switch in the EMM386.EXE line and replacing it with Ram, you can activate EMS. However, in that case you should also specify the amount of memory after the Ram parameter—usually 4 Megs will be enough. Since today EMS memory is used very seldom, and probably only on old systems that were optimized a long time ago, we won't delve any farther into this topic—and to be honest, most of us got tired of this DOS memory mess a long time ago. Several books address this in detail, if you are really interested.

One more thing about the information below. You may notice that we've removed the lines with which Windows 95 normally activates the codepage function. It's also entirely antiquated and only eats memory unnecessarily. The lines in the first table are the few things that you might, at the most, want to add to your Windows 95. Everything else should go (except perhaps special drivers). If you're working exclusively under Windows, you could actually do entirely without a CONFIG.SYS and AUTOEXEC.BAT.

Config.sys for Windows 95***	Remarks
device=himem.sys /testmem:off	DOS memory manager
device=ifshlp.sys	Protected mode driver, file system
dos=high,umb	Loads DOS into high memory
installhigh=keyb.com gr,,keyboard.sys	DOS keyboard driver (German)
fileshigh=20	DOS file-access parameter
buffershigh=20,0	DOS file-access parameter
set path=a:\;c:\windows;c:\command.com	Directories for important files
shell=a:\command.com a:\ /e:512 /p	Directory containing Command.com
***You'll need to complete the path information for your drivers, consisting of the folder or directory names in which the drivers are located (for intance, device=c:\windows\himem.sys).	

Config.sys for DOS-Programs***	Remarks
device=himem.sys /testmem:off	DOS memory manager
device=emm386 noems	DOS memory manager
dos=high,umb	Loads DOS into high memory
device=aspix**.dos.sys /d	Driver for SCSI controller**
device=cddrive.sys* /d:cdlw0	Driver for CD-ROM*
install=mscdex.exe /d:cdlw0 /l:e /m:16	DOS CD-ROM software driver
installhigh=keyb.com gr,,keyboard.sys	DOS keyboard driver (German)
install=smartdrv.exe 2048 2048	DOS software cache program
fileshigh=50	DOS file-access parameter
buffershigh=20,0	DOS file-access parameter
set path=a:\;c:\windows;c:\command.com	Directory containing Command.com
shell=a:\command.com a:\ /e:512 /p	

** x for 2, 4, 6, 7, or 8—the names of the SCSI controller used in your system, for instance from Adaptec. You can find more information on page <!5!> of Chapter 7.

* The name of the DOS CD-ROM driver will vary depending on the manufacturer and whether you're using a SCSI or ATAPI.

***You'll need to complete the path information for your drivers, consisting of the folder or directory names in which the drivers are located (for intance, device=c:\windows\himem.sys).

Chapter 4

NOTE

Drivespace—the additional hard drive capacity may reduce the amount of RAM for DOS and Windows

If you're running Windows with a hard drive that has been compressed using Drivespace or Doublespace, the Drvspace.bin driver is also loaded under DOS, so that you'll still be able to access the compressed drive(s). (The names of these drivers are different for licensing reasons, but the programs are actually identical.) However, depending on the driver or version used, up to 110 K of conventional DOS memory will be used by the driver. The way around this problem is to use the line Devicehigh= Dblspace.sys /Move in your Config.sys to load the driver high. However, you won't be able to do this without Emm386.exe: the 110 K will fit into the adapter segment, but not the HMA. Without Emm386.exe and Drvspace.sys we only had 478 K of available DOS memory; with both of these drivers installed this number jumped to 619.

It's also a good idea to use a simple command in your AUTOEXEC.BAT to delete all unnecessary .TMP files on your hard drive with each bootup. You'll find more information on this procedure in Chapter 1.

DOS memory tricks

Here are a few tips if you still want to optimize your CONFIG.SYS and AUTOEXEC.BAT and squeeze out that last kilobyte.

◆ Whenever possible, use DEVICEHIGH= to load all drivers and programs into high memory. Some will fit into the 64 K HMA that HIMEM.SYS makes available. However, if there are several such programs, you'll need to use EMM386.EXE to activate the UMB.

◆ If you're using EMM386.EXE to activate the UMB, you may encounter memory conflicts with cards that use the UMB to store their ROM data. Most SCSI cards do this, for instance. In this case you'll need to use the parameter Emmexclude=xxxx-yyyy to exclude the memory range from use by programs.

◆ SCSI drivers can also be loaded into high memory, contrary to what most manuals will tell you. Adaptec, for instance, claims that its Aspdi driver (usually) cannot be loaded high. This isn't necessarily true. You can use DEVICEHIGH to load all SCSI drivers high after the HIMEM.SYS and EMM386.EXE calls. This goes for the controller driver (Aspixsys.dos) as well as the scanner or CD-ROM driver (SJIIX.SYS or ASPICD.SYS).

◆ Using INSTALL= in your CONFIG.SYS, you can launch memory-resident programs, like keyboard drivers, that are usually loaded from the AUTOEXEC.BAT. When such programs are started from AUTOEXEC.BAT, the memory defined for each program's environmental variables is reserved. Usually this is 512 to 2,048 bytes, so with several programs it really starts to add up. That's why install is a better alternative.

◆ DOS will load as many of its components into the HMA (high memory area) and the UMB as possible with DOS=HIGH,UMB. This is enough reason that your CONFIG.SYS should always include this line.

◆ Use FILES= to specify the maximum number of files that can be open at the same time. The default value is 20; the only time you'll need more (under DOS) is when you're running a database. Each higher value uses another 64 bytes of memory. Make use of high memory with FILESHIGH.

◆ BUFFERS=X,Y is used to define a kind of antiquated software cache. The first number defines the file buffer, the second value the secondary buffer. This function has become redundant through the use of true caches such as Smartdrive. You'll want to reduce the parameters to 10,0. Use 20,8 under DOS and without Smartdrive. You can also use BUFFERSHIGH to use high memory for this function.

◆ DOS reserves 96 bytes of memory for each drive letter assignment. With LASTDRIVE you can determine the number of drive letters. By default, five drive letters (through E) are reserved. Use LASTDRIVE=X to specify the last drive in your system ("x" is the drive letter, without the colon).

◆ Stacks are reserved memory segments in which data is stored during an interrupt. This information is then used to restore the settings after the interrupt has been processed. If the system runs out of stack memory, it crashes. To prevent such crashes, reserve additional memory, almost 2 K worth. However, all new and most older PCs don't need this extra memory. You can verify whether yours does by using STACKS=0.0 to set the value to zero. If you don't get any kind of message about a stack overflow, you can keep using this setting.

◆ Although this function isn't directly memory-related, it's good to cover it here. It's a good idea to define your path in your CONFIG.SYS rather than your AUTOEXEC.BAT. In the latter file, the path definition is limited to 137 characters—this limitation doesn't apply to set PATH= in CONFIG.SYS.

◆ Use the DOS command MEM /C/P to view the amount of used and available lower and upper DOS memory. With these two parameters the function also displays the programs currently resident in memory page by page, instead of all scrolling past at once. If the listing is too long to view at once, simply press (Enter) to view the next page. Unfortunately, this doesn't make it possible to view all of the information at once. You can get a kind of hardcopy using mem /c >filename.txt, which will save the text in a file with the specified name. You can then use a text editor or word processor to view the information, like this:

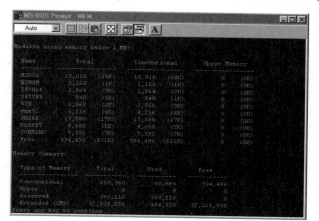

Using MEM /C>FILENAME.TXT (where filename can be any desired DOS name) displays
the name of memory-resident programs and drivers under DOS.
Thanks to HIMEM.SYS and EMM386.EXE,
several programs could be loaded into high memory.

> **NOTE**
>
> **Better than the original—saving memory with alternative programs**
> Another, often overlooked way to save memory is using alternative programs and drivers that are available as shareware. The best-known is probably 4DOS, a replacement for Command.com, the DOS command interpreter. However, there are also many alternative keyboard drivers. Not only do these programs use less memory, they often also perform better. Just take a look at a shareware CD-ROM or at the www.shareware.com or www.windows95.com Web sites.

DOS memory tricks under Windows 95

All the above optimization tricks also essentially apply for the DOS 7 or 7.1 version used by Windows 95. However, there are a few special considerations that won't be of interest to non-Windows 95 users:

◆ As described in Chapter 8, MSDOS.SYS is normally used to load a number of drivers. These should be disabled if you're not using them.

◆ Windows 95b (also known as OSR2) uses a faulty HIMEM.SYS. Instead of using the normal 1 K of conventional memory under DOS, the faulty driver gobbles up 44 K. Microsoft has acknowledged the bug and the most simple solution to the problem is a patch file (Iosysupd.exe or D33818.exe) which you can download from http://www.microsoft.com/germany/support/archiv.htm or http://www.vobis.de/bbs/support/brett19/ on the World Wide Web. This patch file will fix the faulty driver. You may have heard that it's possible to use DEBUG.EXE to fix the file but we don't recommend this method. Microsoft's fix is much easier and safer.

◆ There is only one DOS driver that's really still useful under Windows 95 and that is the keyboard driver. You usually won't need either a mouse driver or a CD-ROM driver. However, for the few times that you do need them, you'll want to include them in your Start files. Simply use REM to deactivate the driver calls (for instance, REM DEVICEHIGH=C:\DRIVERS\MOUSE.SYS) until you need them. Better yet, use DOSSTART.BAT to activate these types of programs.

◆ Under Windows 95 you don't need codepages (DIDSPLAY.SYSand MODE) or the country code driver (COUNTRY.SYS). You're better off removing these drivers and saving that much more memory.

◆ Losing DOS memory by using DRIVESPACE: as mentioned above using Drivespace under Windows also causes the corresponding driver to be loaded under DOS. If you don't optimize your memory, this can easily reduce the available DOS memory to 450 K, so you may again want to refer to the info box above.

◆ DOS drivers that you'll only need for specific DOS applications and that can be launched in a Windows 95 DOS session don't have to be loaded from your CONFIG.SYS. Windows can define specific CONFIG.SYS and AUTOEXEC.BAT files for a DOS application through its Properties settings (right-click the icon of the EXE file and select Properties). The mouse driver is one such example. Remember that Windows 95 makes most functions—the mouse, CD-ROM, network—available to the DOS window without requiring any additional DOS drivers, which also saves memory.

◆ Have you ever used DOSSTAR.BAT or WINSTART.BAT? These two batch files in the Windows directory are used to start memory-resident programs after shutting down or before starting Windows. We can't think of a good use for WINSTART.BAT. You'd use it to load DOS TSR (Terminate and Stay Ready) programs that are supposed to remain active for the Windows session. However, you can use DOSSTAR.BAT to launch drivers for your mouse, keyboard or sound card. Many manufacturers, such as Microsoft with its Intellimouse, use this method to automatically load drivers. This way these drivers don't have to be loaded into memory when Windows 95 boots, but they'll be activated whenever you access DOS. Perhaps, this isn't such a bad solution.

A question of resources under Windows

There are three good reasons to switch from Windows 3.x to Windows 95:

◆ Long file names

◆ Nicer environment

◆ Better resource management

It wasn't unusual under Windows 3.x to get that annoying "Insufficient memory" message despite the 32 Megs of RAM in your system. It still happens under Windows 95, but much less frequently. The key to this are resources: finite memory ranges that Windows uses to manage the graphic display of windows or the execution of command calls. Consider these as lists in which commands and objects are processed. If the list fills up, it's curtains. For instance, if too many windows are open, the resource memory for the GDI (Graphic Device Interface) may run out, even though other memory is still available—Windows will grace you with an error message and may even crash.

The most critical and limited resources under Windows 3.x were, for instance, the user and GDI resources, responsible for the display of windows and for command calls. For these, Windows 3.x used four 16-bit memory areas, with 64 K each. That's not very much, as you may suspect.

The amount of resources still available is specified as a percentage. It'd be more accurate if separate percentages were given for both the user and the GDI resources, but since the lower value is generally the critical one, that's the one that is displayed. The operation of Windows becomes compromised when the available resources fall below 30-40%. Under 30% things get critical, and usually the system crashes.

Chapter 4

Windows 95 uses several tricks to control these resource problems. These tricks are quite effective, especially when you're running 32-bit applications. For one, these applications can benefit fully from the new 32-bit user resources, which max out at a generous two gigabytes—that's vastly more than was available under Windows 3.x. For compatibility reasons Win95 still uses 16-bit GDI resources, but many things that previously used GDI resources are now managed by the nearly unlimited user resources. Therefore, the resource issue is much less of a problem under Windows 95.

However, if you're using large amounts of resource-gobbling 16-bit applications, it's possible to create that "artificial memory shortage" even under Windows 95. There are many shareware tools that you can use to monitor your system's resources. Also, Windows 95 includes a tool called "System Resource Meter" that you can minimize in the System Tray of your Taskbar. You can also display the available resources by right-clicking My Computer and selecting **Properties**. If you're often receive the "Insufficient Memory" message, use these tools to check your system's resources.

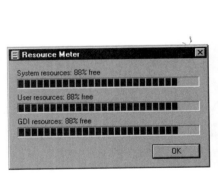
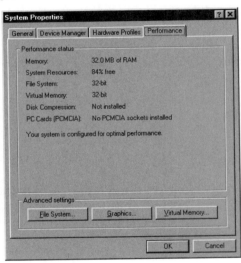

In the left picture the system resources are being monitored, an important capability even under Windows 95. This is very easy when using the System Resource Meter (this utility has to be installed extra). The right picture shows the Performance tab under System Resources. This resource information only reflects the lowest of all current values.

Memory optimization for Windows 3.x users

Finally, we'll also list the best memory settings for Windows 3.x. The following settings almost all apply to the [386enh] section of the SYSYTEM.INI file. You'll find following the individual descriptions a listing of the settings the way they should be entered under [386enh].

◆ **Freeing the monochrome memory segment**. One of those unfortunate DOS-inheritances is that two areas between 640 K and 1 Meg are reserved for video cards: one for color cards and the other for monochrome cards. If you're using a color VGA card, you should make the monochrome memory area available for Windows: enter VGAMonoText=Off in the [386enh] section of your SYSYTEM.INI file. You'll also have to add Device=monoumb.386 to activate the Monoumb.386 driver in your Windows\System directory.

◆ **Disabling EMS**. Even under Windows 3.x there were virtually no applications that used EMS (Expanded memory). If you're not using any of these programs, you can disable the memory that Windows usually reserves for EMS, and make it available to other applications. The entry ReservePageFrame=False corresponds to the NOEMS parameter used with Emm386.exe and supplements it under Windows. NoEmmDriver=On can be used as an alternative, but it's best to simply use both, just to make sure.

◆ **Optimizing the DMA buffer size** won't get you more memory, but it'll help make better use of the memory that is available. All devices that use DMAs (older CD-ROM controllers and current sound cards) are normally assigned only a 32-K data buffer. Often this is not enough, and with large amounts of data the devices will report an error. If you encounter this problem, use DMABufferSize=64 to double the buffer size.

◆ **Optimizing the breakpoints**. Windows uses breakpoints to securely process multiple actions and programs. It reserves a multiple of 4 K of memory for these breakpoints. The standard setting is 358 breakpoints, but with the use of several demanding applications this can be too little. Even though it will use a little more memory, you should increase this value to 768. Even higher values are possible, but they always have to be multiples of 4. The corresponding entry is in your SYSYTEM.INI.

Here's the optimized [386enh] section of the SYSTEM.INI with all of the settings we've discussed. We haven't included other values, such as the ones entered by Windows.

```
[386enh]
VGAMonoText=Off
Device=monoumb.386
ReservePageFrame=False
NoEmmDriver=On
DMABufferSize=64
MaxPBs=768
```

Please note also that the settings for the cache and the swap-file, both of which are closely related to memory-optimization, are discussed in our hard drive chapter, starting in Chapter 8

Norton Utilities and finding memory-thieves in your applications

You'd be surprised if you knew just how much memory some applications use. Sometimes you can't help but wonder what those programmers did to create such memory-hogs. While the 16-bit version of Word for Windows 6.0 used a mere 1.7 Megs of memory, the almost identical 32-bit version, Word 95, eats up a whole 8 Megs! Excel 95 gobbles even more: 9.5 Megs. How can you tell, you ask? A marvelous application displays all of this information: The System Information program (SysInfo.exe) in Norton Utilities 2.0 for Windows 95.

As the picture below shows, this application neatly displays all of the programs and drivers that are currently in memory. It not only displays the amount of main memory used, but also differentiates between 16 and 32-bit applications. This can be very useful information, since the 16-bit applications can be quite a bit more troublesome than their more stable 32-bit colleagues.

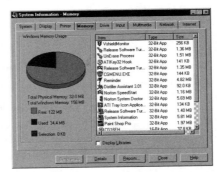

The Norton Utilities System Information indicates exactly how
much memory a given application is using.
Some of these figures may make you nervous.

Unfortunately this utility can only show the memory used by any given file, such as an EXE or DLL file. Since Word for Windows really consists of not only WINWORD.EXE, but a number of DLL files as well, the amount of memory used by the application as a whole is really higher than indicated above. It'd be great if Norton made its next version able to display the total amount of memory used by an application—perhaps using a before-and-after comparison when the application is launched. However, if you want to, you can actually do this with the current version of System Information, since it lists the complete memory allocation in detail. In any event, the utility is highly recommended. We've used this program to identify several memory-hogs, that we then removed from our system. It's great for testing shareware programs—you'll find that even some tiny little applications, which perhaps do nothing more than display the time of day, can consume inordinately large amounts of memory.

By the way, as discussed in the our first chapter, Windows 95 automatically loads any driver that's found in \WINDOWS\SYSTEM\IOSIBSYS, even if it's not in the registry or an INI file. You can use your System Information to check which VXD files are contained in this directory, and whether some of these are perhaps not needed. Things get tricky, of course, when old hardware components or applications have not been uninstalled in their entirety.

Chapter 5

Increasing Performance With A Better Data Bus

If you've read the book straight from the first page to this point, you've probably noticed that we've been trying to shift your focus on the most important tuning consideration from the processor to the PC's other components. The often-overlooked bus systems—the data thoroughfares connecting the PC's different components—are a prime example. There are many data buses in a PC so we'll talk only about those that directly connect the processor and motherboard to the peripherals. The newest developments in this field, such as USB, AGP and Firewire, are currently very hot topics.

We won't be mentioning SCSI or EIDE much in this chapter because these are primarily high-capacity data-storage buses. These types of buses really need to meet a different set of requirements so we've covered them in a separate chapter (Chapter 7). Another data bus that warrants discussion is the 64-bit connection between the processor and main memory: the system bus. However, characteristics of and tuning measures for the system bus have been discussed in an earlier chapter (see Chapter 4), so we won't repeat that information here.

This chapter will provide you with essential information and tuning options for the PCI, USB, AGP and Firewire buses. Don't underestimate the significant effect these components have on a PC's performance. An optimized data bus between the processor and the expansion cards—especially the video card—can truly work wonders for your system's overall performance.

EXPANSION CARDS AND OPTIMIZING THE DATA BUS

The data bus between the processor (or motherboard) and the expansion cards has a critical effect on the overall performance of a PC. You may remember the drastic improvement that the switch from ISA to PCI brought. Optimizing the expansion card data bus will particularly benefit hard drive controllers (SCSI or EIDE) and, most of all, video cards.

PCI is slowly reaching its limits—at least it's easy to get that impression since the otherwise highly proven system is already being replaced by the AGP (Advanced Graphics Port) for video cards. This is not to say that PCI is at its end; today's systems generally don't come close to using its full potential. You can significantly increase your PC's performance by optimizing your expansion card bus. We'll explain how to do this and discuss what AGP has to offer.

The limitations and future of the PCI bus

PCI has been used for several years and it's clear that no other system or data bus has proven its effectiveness as thoroughly. It's also likely that PCI will still be with us for some time to come. It's only for video cards, whose performance has become more critical to the system as a whole, that a new standard, the AGP, is being added. We'll talk about the AGP in more detail later.

PCI is a 32-bit data bus for all types of expansion cards. It's advantages over the ancient ISA bus have been the topic of much discussion and are well-known. Here we've assembled the most important information, plus some interesting facts of which you may not have been aware. This information lets you, perhaps for the first time, correctly configure your BIOS and use special cards, like TV or video cards.

- ◆ The PCI's increased speed over the ISA bus is made possible by three items: 32-bit (instead of 16-bit) data transfer, 33-MHz (instead of 8.3-MHz) clock rate and several technical refinements, such as a more direct connection to the system bus and a burst mode for memory access. In theory, this makes it possible to achieve data transfer rates of up to 132 Megs/sec, but in practice this only reaches around 40 Megs/sec, because any given card can't hog the entire bandwidth for itself. Posting is another refinement that's particularly important for the improved performance. Posting is a type of cache memory in which the processor can temporarily store data, even if the PCI card can't process it at that moment. When it's ready, the card can retrieve the data from the posting independently, while the processor goes about its business. You can control this posting function to some degree through your system's BIOS (see Chapter 6).

- ◆ The clock speed of the PCI bus is usually linked to that of the system bus with a factor of 0.5. Newer motherboards that support independent, asynchronous PCI bus clock speeds are becoming more and more important. The PCI specification maxes out at a clock speed of 33 MHz. This also means that the system speed can't exceed 66 MHz. Higher system bus clock rates, like 75 or 83 MHz, would violate the PCI standard, because with a factor of 0.5 they would result in a PCI bus speed of 37.5 or 41.5 MHz. This will cause significant problems with many PCI cards (see Chapter 6). However, higher PCI bus clock speeds will most likely be introduced in the near future.

- ◆ The PCI bus is (supposedly) fully Plug and Play compatible. Although this is generally the case, it doesn't always work flawlessly. Still, the PCI's Plug and Play capability is significantly better than those of the ISA bus. Most system BIOSes allow you to configure the Plug and Play characteristics (see Chapter 6).

- ◆ With its new hardware specifications (PC97 and PC98), Microsoft is planning a step-by-step replacement of the ISA bus in favor of the PCI bus. The PC98 specification supports only PCI and possibly AGP. Most ISA hardware, such as sound and ISDN cards, is being switched to PCI. The bottom line is that ISA will soon be gone. If you're going to buy any expansion cards, such as an audio card, get PCI versions if at all possible.

◆ Currently up to five PCI slots are possible on one motherboard, four of which can be run in Bus Master operation. The first motherboards equipped with PCI buses often only supported one or two Bus Master slots. If you have one of these boards, check which ones are the Bus Master slots, and use these for your SCSI controller or video card. Using a Bus Master-capable card in a non-Bus Master slot will cause a drastic drop in performance.

◆ This is one of the most important performance factors of the PCI bus. Bus Master is the DMA-like capability to exchange data directly with main memory and, very importantly, with other PCI cards *without* help from the processor. These functions must be supported by the operating system. Under Windows 3.x they were called DCI; under Win95 they're known as DirectDraw. They make it possible, for instance, for PCI television or video cards to directly insert their images into the RAM of a video card, without any kind of connection cable (see Chapter 10).

DMA channels and interrupts are also handled differently under PCI than ISA. The DMA channels are actually no longer needed, because of PCI's Bus Master support. This allows you to use all of the DMA channels for the few remaining ISA components (such as sound cards and the printer port). PCI also uses its own interrupts, INT A through INT D. These are converted into normal IRQs—such as INT A into IRQ 10—for the other system components. This conversion is handled entirely by the BIOS, so interrupts cannot be configured on the PCI card. It's important to know that PCI cards cannot use the lower 8-bit IRQs (0-7); only the upper ones are available (8-15). This means that EIDE systems may run out of upper IRQs—yet another reason to use SCSI instead (this saves one upper interrupt).

◆ PCI components can be connected to the bus through expansion slots or through direct connections on the motherboard. One typical example of such a connection is the two EIDE controllers that are connected to the PCI bus on most normal motherboards. There are also boards where an onboard SCSI or even UW-SCSI controller is connected directly to the PCI bus. Thanks to the shorter connection paths, these yield even higher performance than when expansion cards are used. The possibility of utilizing PCI Bus Master here is a significant tuning opportunity, especially with EIDE controllers. The well-known Bus Master driver uses precisely this opportunity (see Chapter 7).

It's clear that the PCI bus has much more to offer than its innocuous cards and slots would lead you to believe. The configuration of its Plug and Play and Bus Master functions offer you plentiful tuning opportunities. The BIOS configuration for PCI is covered in the BIOS chapter (Chapter 6).

The most common PCI bus mistakes and speed-bumps

The broad capabilities of the PCI bus coupled with most users' lack of knowledge can often result in problems or unnecessarily decreased performance. Most such errors occur time and time again. We've collected the ones that are the most important to avoid:

◆ **Stay away from PCI-VL combination boards**: Many such VIP (VL-ISA-PCI) boards are still in use, such as the SP3 by Asus. They were quite popular for 486 systems for some time, although VIP Pentium boards were produced as well. It's important to note that as soon as you use a VL card on this board, you're making the entire PCI bus slow down to VL bus speed. Good boards only slow down when the VL bus is really being used, but on many boards the PCI bus runs at the slower speed whenever a VL card is present. If you're using this type of system, toss your old VL video card and replace it with a real PCI card. Currently you should be able to get a decent price selling your VL video card, since they're in relatively high demand for older PCs.

◆ Try to **set the PCI bus to the highest possible clock speed**. The maximum PCI clock rate is 33 MHz, corresponding to a system bus rate of 66 MHz. However, the P75, P90, P120 and P150 can only work with a PCI bus speed of 30 or even 25 MHz. If you're using one of these chips, try to increase the external clock speed (see the section on overclocking in Chapter 6).

◆ Use **Bus Mastering**, especially between PCI cards. Are you considering buying a MPEG, TV or video card? If so, only settle for one that can use Bus Mastering to communicate directly with the video card—using DCI under Windows 3.x or DirectDraw under Windows 95. This maximizes performance, and you won't need a troublesome cable connection between the two cards. Stay away from ISA to PCI combinations. You'll also find more information in the chapters on the individual card types.

◆ Have your **BIOS settings** for the PCI bus been optimized? Did you know that there are over half a dozen PCI bus BIOS settings that you need to check for optimum configuration? You'll find more information on this topic in the BIOS chapter in Chapter 6. Please also be aware that not every PCI card needs its own interrupt, although this is the way the BIOS is usually configured. The video card is a typical example.

Good reasons not to buy some ISA cards

We've mentioned that the days of ISA are over. Microsoft's new PC97 and PC98 specifications have clearly put the pressure on the ISA bus in favor of PCI. This raises the question: should you still buy any ISA cards, and if so, which? Also, are some cards only available in ISA format?

Until recently many types of cards, such as ISDN or sound cards, were only available as ISA cards. However, much of that has changed. These two card types in particular already have PCI versions on the market. Although they won't increase performance, these new expansion cards are easier to configure, and the consistent use of the PCI bus results in a PC that is more stable overall. One interesting PCI sound card is the Monster Sound by Diamond (see Chapter 11).

PCI versions of active ISDN cards are currently becoming available; passive PCI ISDN cards should be available by the time you read this. But you may want to hold off on these initially. Further PCI candidates include low-cost SCSI controllers—PCI versions are currently available in the $50 to $100 range, such as the Adaptec 2910.

Chapter 5

Why AGP is the new data bus for fast 3-D graphics

Sure, the whole world is normally three-dimensional so it's no wonder that computer audio and graphics would try to be as real as possible. Unfortunately, 3-D graphics computing is a very demanding operation that pushes all modern PC systems to their limits. This is true for the PCI bus as well, which is too slow for high-resolution 3-D graphics with its maximum throughput of 66 Megs/sec (in practice it's closer to 20 Megs/sec).

In response to this problem, Intel collaborated with the leading manufacturers of video cards and defined a new bus standard: AGP, the Accelerated Graphics Port. The AGP bus isn't a replacement for the PCI bus, but rather an additional video card slot to be used in parallel with the PCI bus. Initially the new bus will run at the usual 66-MHz system clock speed and will be linked to the PCI bus. The improvement is that AGP has four times the bandwidth of PCI (about 266 Megs/sec) and can even double this throughput in 2x mode. This should provide ample reserves for the 3-D applications of the future.

AGP also uses many other tricks to make this high throughput usable. The most important of these is akin to PCI's Bus Master, the ability to directly exchange data between the card and main memory without involving the CPU.

Another great benefit of AGP is that future 3-D video cards will be less expensive than those now available. This is because these cards won't need the usual additional memory for 3-D data. On previous PCI 3-D cards, on-card memory was required to store spatial-coordinate data (Frame and Z-buffer) and surface-texture data, because it would have been too slow to use the PC's main memory for this data. However, AGP's throughput to main memory is so high that this is no longer a problem, that is, with the right DRAM modules. AGP cards can therefore do without the additional 3-D memory. As a matter of fact, it is now possible to store greater numbers of and more highly detailed surface textures than with the usual 2 to 4 Megs of 3-D memory.

The close integration of AGP and PCI also makes for a high degree of downward-compatibility. This is particularly important for Bus Master transfers between PCI cards and an AGP video card. After all, if you've paid all that money for a fancy new video card, it should be able to use DirectDraw to exchange data directly with the video components.

NOTE

The hardware race—Intel is also building its own AGP card

Intel won't be shortchanged, and is using its AGP knowledge to develop a card for its new standard. Given the company's business acumen, it's no surprise they've picked a good partner in Real3D, which has been building flight simulators for the military. Chances are good that the new card will be a hot product.

After all this theory you're probably wondering about the practical advantages of AGP, as well as software/hardware support. Most companies have already developed video cards with AGP connections, and initially they should cost about $50 more than their non-AGP counterparts.

Thanks to its compact construction, the AGP slot is actually a bit smaller than a PCI slot, so the additional slot and card don't take up much extra room on the motherboard.

In practice, the actual performance boost depends heavily on the motherboard (memory type, system bus speed; see sidebar), as well as the application being used, in particular with 3-D functions. With normal 2-D applications, AGP cards are only about 10-15% faster than a PCI equivalent. With a board using a 66-MHz system bus, it's hard to increase performance any further. Therefore, if you're just using 2-D applications, such a motherboard and new AGP card may not be worth your money. However, as soon as 3-D graphics are involved, AGP more than pays for itself, although its performance potential will only be used fully with upcoming boards, memory modules and the right applications.

NOTE **Full AGP support only with extra-fast DRAM**
As mentioned above, AGP utilizes the PC's main memory for its 3-D calculations. This requires the fastest possible DRAM for maximum performance, especially since the CPU and the PCI bus also access RAM directly. The prescription therefore reads: SDRAM and a high system clock rate. However, even SDRAM with a maximum clock speed of 100 MHz won't be able to use AGP to its limit—RDRAM, on the other hand, may make this possible (see Chapter 4). As long as the system clock speed crawls along at 66 MHz, AGP will just be running at idle. This means that the first AGP cards may need to have some on-card memory after all, if they're going to achieve significantly higher performance.

Chapter 5

The other thing that's essential is AGP support by the operating system and, most importantly, the motherboard manufacturers. Intel is trying to enhance its Pentium II chip (only starting with the new 440LX chipset) with AGP, thereby leaving the Socket 7 systems and—so hopes Intel—AMD and other Intel competitors in the dust (see Chapter 4).

However, Intel's competitors already unveiled their own AGP-capable chipsets and motherboards in late 1997 (see Chapter 4), which should drive prices down and make AGP more accessible in general. Therefore switching to the new system, or waiting for a short while first, is a good idea, especially because the extra money you spend will then be saved on the traditional 3-D accelerator cards you won't need to buy. Finally, there's the question of operating system support. Not to worry, with its next version of Direct X, or DirectDraw 5, Microsoft Windows 95 (98) will also support AGP. Windows NT support for AGP should be close behind. If we've managed to really whet your appetite for AGP, you can find more information at these websites: http://www.agpforum.org and http://www.intel.com/pc-supp/platform/agfxport.

NOTE **The bottom line—who really needs AGP and why?**
The information presented above makes it clear that AGP is only worth the extra money if you use extensive 3-D applications. The performance of the PCI bus with a PCI 3-D card is fine for simple 3-D applications such as games or normal 3-D rendering software. AGP will only make a significant difference if you're doing complex 3-D animation. However, the first-generation boards won't be able to truly utilize AGP's potential—things should get much more interesting around the middle or end of 1998.

THE USB DATA BUS WILL PERFECT YOUR PC

The current developments in the hardware market are frightening and fascinating at the same time. Everything is changing and the peripherals in particular. For the first time in many years, the old connection systems were replaced with at least two new standards: USB (Universal Serial Bus) and Firewire. This means that if, in one or two years, USB is established as the new standard for virtually all peripherals with a low transfer rate, it'll be impossible to plug a current printer, keyboard or even mouse into your computer—the connectors won't fit. Anything you buy now that doesn't comply with USB will very soon be outdated. More than ever, having the right information can save you a lot of money down the road.

What USB is to "normal" peripherals like keyboards, mice, printers and perhaps scanners (those with relatively low resolutions), Firewire is to devices with particularly high data transfer rates. This affects first of all video processing equipment, although hard drives and other high-capacity storage devices can also be connected by Firewire. USB and Firewire are, without a doubt, the duo of the future.

USB (Universal Serial Bus) and its advantages

USB (the Universal Serial Bus) will soon change the PC as we know it—already it is being advertised as the *must have* feature for new systems. USB is essentially a new, general standard for connecting peripheral devices with a maximum data throughput of 1.5 Megs/sec. These peripherals include the mouse, keyboard, printer, monitor, speakers, scanner, joystick, modem, telephone and data storage devices with relatively low transfer rates (such as 8x CD-ROM players). All the typical devices with different specialized connectors that you've been plugging into your PC will now be connected with the same USB connector. What's more, you'll be able to connect them to each other. Here are the most important features and advantages of this new system:

◆ USB is an open, industry standard defined in the fall of 1995 by seven companies (Compaq, DEC, IBM, Intel, Microsoft, NEC and Northern Telecom). Since then 250 companies have aggreed to the standard. All the preparations and technical developments for the introduction of USB have been completed—all we're waiting for now is the release of the first products.

◆ USB will completely change the way peripherals of all types are connected to the PC. Old standards like the serial and parallel ports are gone. Up to 127 USB devices can be connected through this bus system using a small, four-pin connector. They can also be connected to each other. The keyboard and monitor in particular will act as hubs for the connection of other devices—so no more crawling around under the desk, trying to plug in your joystick or modem.

◆ Thanks to USB, many devices will no longer need special connection cards—no more SCSI cards and no more speakers or joysticks plugged into audio cards. What's best is the new Hot Plug and Play feature: you can plug in any device while the system is running, and the operating system will automatically detect its presence.

◆ Devices that run on a low voltage won't need power cords, since the USB cable is equipped with a 5-volt power connection. This is enough to run speakers and digital cameras, for examples.

◆ USB cables and connectors are simple and they're inexpensive to produce. The connectors have four data pins and two supply-voltage pins, and they're asymmetrical so they can't be plugged in the wrong way.

◆ USB supports a high-bandwidth transfer mode (12 MBit/sec) and a low-bandwidth transfer mode (1.5 MBit/sec). This makes it possible to connect both slow and fast devices—even ones that use different bandwidths within one of these transfer modes, such as a mouse and keyboard. This feature in particular lends USB its quality of (near) universality.

◆ PC-related telecommunications will also benefit from the new standard: USB provides interfaces for most common telephone standards, such as ISDN. This will makes it easier to connect and operate telephones, modems and other communication devices to your PC.

A close look at this list of features makes it clear why USB really is the definitive standard of the future. So if you're shopping for a new PC, by all means make sure that it supports USB or, at the very least, that you'll be able to add it later. If you're curious about USB, visit www.intel.com/design/usb and www.intel.com/design/usb/tour/overview.htm on the Internet.

USB is nearly here

It's true that the switch to USB is taking longer than initially was expected. However, that's not very surprising considering the broad impact of this change. What's more, users will only really benefit from USB once the entire PC and all the peripherals support it. Nevertheless, the changeover to the USB bus will most likely get underway no later than the end of 1998.

Some manufacturers are already selling complete PCs with full USB support, such as IBM, Compaq, Toshiba, Siemens, Sony and Dell. Other heavyweights, like Gateway and Vobis, are close behind. Peripheral manufacturers also already have USB mice, keyboards, modems and monitors ready to ship.

Altec Lansing has also released the first USB bus loudspeakers. While these USB peripherals initially will cost about 5-20% more than the conventional equipment they are replacing, prices should soon be comparable. After all, the new equipment is actually easier to manufacture.

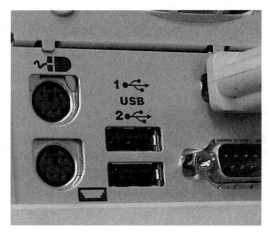

DELL's current models already include two USB sockets on the back of the PC case.
The conventional connectors are also still there and will be with new PCs in the near future.

If you're in the market for a monitor, you'll probably want to get one that already has a USB connector—remember that the monitor, along with the keyboard, will act as a USB-connector hub for other peripherals. It would be too bad if you'd have to get yet another monitor only because the one you've just bought wasn't equipped with USB.

Knowledge and equipment you'll need for USB

Unfortunately you can't just run out, buy a USB mouse, and hook it up to your old PC. Even if you have a new system that has a USB, you still need an operating system that supports the new bus; all system components have to be coordinated with one another. So what do you need and what will make USB work?

First, USB must be supported by the motherboard. Intel's current chipsets (430HX, 430VX for the Pentium, and 440FX for the Pentium Pro/II) all have USB support. Its new chipsets (430TX and 440Lx), as well as the competition's (VIA and SiS), support USB entirely. While the first version of Intel's chipsets encountered some USB support problems, their new products are trouble-free. In other words, you should be able to use USB with any new motherboard.

NOTE

Optimal combination with pitfalls—USB for notebooks

USB should be of special interest to notebook users, where it may prove even more useful than with PCs. After all, notebooks have to use more external devices than desktops. Unfortunately, USB notebook support only starts with Intel's new 430TX chipset for Pentiums. This should be an important consideration if you're shopping for a new portable.

Microsoft has already integrated USB with its Service Pack 2.1 (OSR 2.1) for Windows 95b. Unfortunately, there's currently no driver that gives old versions of Windows 95 USB support, and since OSR 2.1 isn't available for individual sale, we'll have to wait for the release of Windows 98 for USB support (more on this just below).

You can check whether your Windows 95b version is OSR 2.0 or OSR 2.1 by looking at the list of devices in your Control Panel's Add New Hardware wizard. If you see "USB-Support" in this list, you have the right version. You can also check the version number of NTKERN.VXD in Windows\System\Vmm32. This file should have a version number of 4.03.1212 or higher.

USB support for Windows NT is a little more tricky. It's unlikely that a USB driver will become available for Version 4.0, although NT 5.0 should have integrated support. However, Microsoft still has some work to do because Plug and Play is a central part of USB and Windows NT still doesn't even support PnP.

By the way, if you want to buy or upgrade a PC with a USB keyboard, you need to make sure that the BIOS supports this keyboard. Otherwise, you'll only be able to use a conventional keyboard to make BIOS settings, and that's not exactly the idea.

Upgrading—equipping older or current systems with USB

Don't worry, you don't have to toss your old PC just because it doesn't have USB sockets soldered to the motherboard. Most boards have had USB support since mid-1996 but some manufacturers have simply omitted the connectors to save money. Using a little module that plugs into a socket on the motherboard (see illustration) you can make these connections quite easily.

Chapter 5

USB adapter sockets on an older motherboard with an Intel HX chipset (left) and a newer board with a TX chipset (right). You can get the USB adapters from your motherboard manufacturer.

You can add USB support even if your old chipset doesn't support it directly. Soon you'll be able to get PCI expansion cards that'll add USB to your system.

Two great advantages of USB

It's true that it doesn't seems like a big difference whether you connect your keyboard and mouse to a USB rather than a PS/2 socket. However, the advantages of USB have less to do with comfort or ease of use and more with the following:

◆ **Saving resources**: similar to the SCSI bus, the USB controller is the only item that needs to use resources from the motherboard (such as an IRQ)—none of the devices hooked up to the USB require any further resources. You may know from experience how often you're limited in the number of devices you can connect by the available system resources. USB will put an end to that. You can connect up to 127 devices to a USB! And they'll only use one IRQ!

◆ **Great advantages for scanners, digital cameras and video-conferencing**: USB is going to be particularly advantageous for imaging devices. Up to now, this type of data frequently had to be transmitted through the parallel port, which is really too narrow and inflexible. SCSI is also not flexible enough, since it doesn't support Hot Plug and Play, and it's also too expensive. USB will change all of this.

Simple video-conferencing cameras, for instance, won't need framegrabber cards anymore and won't have to be connected to the parallel port. This will lower costs for the user. USB will also lower the costs for scanners, while offering performance comparable to SCSI. USB is going to be especially useful with digital cameras. In the future you'll be able to upload the pictures directly through a USB cable connected to your keyboard or by plugging the photo memory cards into a slot on your keyboard.

◆ **Faster Internet access thanks to USB cable modems.** Cable modems, which send and receive data over coaxial television cable, are just making their advent. This technique not only dramatically increases the available bandwidth, but also helps take some of the load off the telephone network. Most upcoming cable modems will likely be equipped with USB connectors.

Firewire is the bus for huge amounts of data

USB and Firewire (also known as 1394) are the two data buses of the future. While USB is for devices that transmit lower amounts of data, Firewire is the system for high-end devices like digital video recorders, TV set-top boxes, hard drives and high-performance networks. The two buses are similar in many ways, for instance in the shape of their connectors, but Firewire is technically much more advanced and powerful. Without going into the technical differences, we'll mentionFirewire's most important characteristics. If you're shopping for a new entertainment PC that complies with Microsoft's PC97 specifications, you're bound to encounter Firewire. Also, if you've ever used a Sony digital camera, you've already used Firewire. These cameras are the first equipment to use the new high-end data bus.

A closer look at the Firewire scenery

Firewire is a serial bus system based on the 1986 initiative number 1394 from the IEEE (the international committee that's responsible for computer standards). Apple Computer was a major force in the development of the new standard; the company had been searching for an affordable replacement for the SCSI. Apple and SGS Thomson own essentially all of the patents of the 1394 specification, finalized in the fall of 1995. The name Firewire is Apple's trademark for the 1394 bus but the two companies have licensed the specification so that other manufacturers have been able to develop 1394 products as well.

So, what does Firewire do for the average user and what is it intended for? Well, Firewire is foremost the perfect solution for connecting any and all types of video devices to each other and/ or to a PC. Unlike USB, Firewire devices can also exchange data without the presence of a computer; for instance, a digital camcorder will be able to send its images to a stationary digital video recorder. the following summarizesthe most important features of Firewire:

◆ Like USB, Firewire uses simple, inexpensive cables and connectors. The data connection consists of two independently shielded two-pole conductors (four altogether), with a two-conductor supply line carrying 8-40 volts at up to 1.5 amperes. This allows smaller devices to be operated without separate power cords.

Chapter 5

The picture on the left shows a Firewire connector. The picture on the right shows a firewire socket

◆ The 1394 specification defines three different signal rates that can be transmitted simultaneously over the same line: 100, 200 and 400 MBit/sec. This is up to 30-times the rate permitted by the USB. However, at this point, only devices with up to 100 and 200 MBit transfer rates have been built. Digital video recorders are currently just using the 100 MBit rate. However, that's still 12.5 MBit/sec more than a normal SCSI controller could manage.

◆ Unlike USB, Firewire devices can also exchange data without being connected to a PC. It's even possible to build complex networks of interconnected devices or groups of devices.

◆ The first PCI expansion cards are already available for Firewire, such as the 1394 to PCI AHA 8940 adapter, from Adaptec. However, at the current time it's only being sold to OEM clients for professional video-processing systems, not to end-users.

◆ You can connect up to 63 devices to such a Firewire-PC adapter, each with a cable length of up to 4.5 meters (14.5 feet).

◆ Like USB, Firewire supports the connection and disconnection of devices during operation; in other words, it also supports Hot Plug and Play.

◆ Microsoft supports Firewire with its PC97 and PC98 specifications, as well as with drivers for its new versions of Windows 98 and Windows NT 5.0. Windows 95 and Windows NT 4.0 drivers are also available for devices currently in use, such as video-processing hardware. The PC97 and PC98 specifications require at least one Firewire connector for the new "entertainment" PCs, which gives you an idea of how ubiquitous this new bus will soon become.

These facts still don't tell the whole story, although it's easy to see that Firewire is a hot new development. At this time, there's nothing else like it. However, most important for the normal, pragmatically oriented user is how Firewire really performs, and what benefits it has for them right now.

First use for firewire is digital video

Firewire is no longer the future-babble of select techno-heads. Sony digital video recorders were the first devices with 1394 connectors and have been available since late 1995. In the spring of 1997 Panasonic also released its DV camcorder, the NV-DE3. The digital output of these devices complies with the Firewire standard. The only thing they don't have is the supply voltage connection, so the connectors and cables consist only of the four data-conductors.

Digital output on the back of a Sony DV camcorder

The first PC expansion cards with Firewire connectors are also already available. With these you can transfer digital data from these video recorders to your PC. These expansion cards are currently available from Sony, Fast, Miro and Adaptec. The Firewire connection can also be used to transfer the video data, with no drop in quality, to the stationary Sony DV recorder.

Using the different 1394 expansion cards, it's possible to transfer individual images or whole video sequences directly from the camcorder to your PC's hard drive. This data then still has to be decoded before it can be edited, because the DV format does not support direct processing.

The transfer of digital video data requires a high-performance bus like Firewire, since the usual data throughput of 3.5 MByte/sec for peripheral connections is tough to exceed without serious complications. Firewire is the perfect solution for this problem, offering a high degree of flexibility at a relatively low cost.

It's impressive to see just how fast and easily a Sony Firewire capture board can write individual images from a running video tape to a hard drive. At the same time, the recorder can be fully controlled by the PC using the LANC interface.

If you're in the market for a digital camcorder, you should under no circumstance consider one without Firewire (like the one by JVC).

Firewire and the future

Although the use of Firewire is currently limited to transfering DV data, it should broaden significantly this year. Soon all entertainment PCs will be equipped with a 1394 connection, in accordance with Microsoft's specifications. You can expect the following Firewire devices to become available in the near future, all of which should offer near top-notch performance:

◆ High-quality color printers for photo and video images

◆ Hard drives and external removable data storage media

◆ PC to PC networking cards

◆ Music synthesizers for MIDI and Digital Audio

◆ Set-top boxes for televisions, especially for digital TV

◆ DVD players

◆ High-quality satellite decoders

◆ High-quality digital video conferencing systems.

Firewire will, for the first time, allow TV, video and the computer to truly merge into one system. It will also make affordable solutions for powerful hard drives and local networks possible, as well as the distribution and processing of video data. The computers and entertainment systems of the future will be dependent on Firewire. If you're at all interested in this area, you should insist that any equipment you buy in the future support this standard.

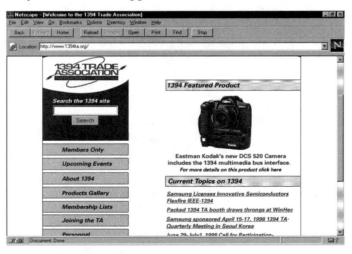

You can also find more than enough information on Firewire on the Internet. The Web sites with the best information are http://www.adaptec.com/serialio, http://www.1394ta.org and http://www.computervice.com/DV-L/Firewire.html.

BIOS & Motherboard Tuning—From Correct Configuration To Overclocking

We could call the BIOS the subconscious of the PC because it breathes the necessary life into your PC when you turn it on. BIOS, of course, doesn't stand for "life" but means **B**asic **I**nput / **O**utput System.

BIOS is so important because it's responsible for the booting process of the PC and for configuring the basic PC hardware. By "basic hardware," we mean the motherboard with its components and the processor. Only the variable peripherals (plug-in cards, modems, mouse, etc.) are later configured with their own drivers or BIOSes.

Configuring the BIOS is critical to the stability and performance of a PC. Both aspects must be considered because they frequently oppose one another. Today's optimal BIOS configuration isn't as critical as it was a few years ago. Manufacturers then rarely delivered reasonably preconfigured motherboards. But today, Auto-Detect, Auto-Config and Plug & Play are the modern buzzwords which show that the BIOS saves the user a lot of work.

However, most manufacturers play it safe during preconfiguration and reduce performance in favor of system stability. Anyone who really knows their way around and likes to experiment can increase speed and get more options from their PC. These optimization and configuration settings are what we'll talk about in the first part of this chapter. Such intrusions into the BIOS preconfiguration are particularly important when you use atypical hardware, for example, a new Pentium-compatible CPU from AMD and Cyrix or unusual plug-in cards such as television cards. These frequently do not work properly with the standard settings.

The software configuration of the BIOS is closely connected to the hardware configuration of the motherboard. This covers all the settings concerning clocking and the supply voltage of the CPU and the system bus. The buzzword "overclocking" is currently heard everywhere because only recently a few motherboards make it possible to drive the PC beyond the preset specifications. This clearly brings more performance, but also many problems. The latter can often be brought under control by skillfully configuring the BIOS and motherboard. The last section of this chapter will show you exactly how you can overclock your PC and what can be the advantages, but also the risks, of so doing.

PRACTICAL TIPS ON SELECTING AND OPTIMIZING THE BIOS

Before talking about manipulating the BIOS and motherboard, we'll give some basic information on the BIOS. You can skip this section if you're familiar with the types of BIOSes, how they work and what to look for when buying a BIOS (or motherboard).

Flash ROM, EEPROM and CMOS

BIOS is software which must be enabled immediately when turning on the computer to perform a basic configuration and control the boot process. Because storage media such as diskettes are unusable for this purpose, the BIOS software is stored in a small ROM (**R**ead **O**nly **M**emory) chip and permanently integrated on the motherboard.

So the ROM component can be modified with the BIOS software, EPROM or (more recently) EEPROM components are used. EPROMs (**E**rasable **P**rogrammable **ROM**) can be written only with special equipment called EPROM burners. However, EEPROM chips (**E**lectrically **E**rasable **P**rogrammable **ROM**) can also be programmed by supplying an increased voltage (usual 12 V) to the computer. EPROMs have also recently been called "Flash ROMs."

An EPROM doesn't look much different from other computer chips.

You can update the BIOS (as may be necessary when changing a processor) only if the BIOS on your PC contains a Flash-ROM component. Flash-ROMs are common on current motherboards. However, make certain when buying a new motherboard that it has this very important feature. You'll find more practical information on the topic of BIOS updates in the following section.

> **NOTE**
>
> **Get a replacement BIOS for making changes**
> Anyone who wants to experiment with the BIOS, perhaps even to test an entirely different one, such as the MR BIOS, should if possible have a second BIOS chip available for testing. For this, take the current chip to an electronics store and buy an identical, empty EEPROM. Your PC dealer or the electronics dealer can load your present BIOS into this component for you in a corresponding device. You can then change the chips on the motherboard as you desire. Should you ruin a component, you will still have a replacement.

Close by the EEPROM-BIOS component (to the lower right with the AWARD label) you'll usually find a jumper (upper center), with which the flash component can be switched into write mode.

The BIOS not only contains data and commands that are permanently programmed but it must also be sent special information by the user. This includes information such as the time or the properties of the hard drive. All these user-definable settings must be stored on the motherboard and adjusted with the permanent data of the BIOS. The special RAM component used to store this data is called the CMOS (**C**omplementary **M**etal **O**xide **S**emiconductor). Because the CMOS requires a constant supply of current, a small battery is included on the motherboard. This battery was formerly housed with the clock chip in a separate, small housing (usually with the label DALLAS).

> **NOTE**
>
> **Knowing the CMOS-BIOS—Backing up and deleting at will**
> The data in the CMOS can be manipulated via the BIOS control settings, and also backed up completely via a special program, in case of accidents. How you delete the CMOS settings all at once, and why that can be necessary, you will learn in the following sections

BIOS manufacturers

The BIOS market consists of three main companies: Award, AMI (American Megatrends) and Phoenix. The motherboard manufacturers purchase the components of the BIOS software from one of these three and then modify it to their specific boards. The company from which the BIOS originates is usually not important to the user. Because the three differ only slightly, you won't need to worry about it when buying your board (unless you use some special hardware). We will discuss what you need to look for soon.

BIOS-Manufacturers	Internet address
AMI (American Megatrends)	www.megatrends.com
Award	www.award.com
Phoenix	www.ptltd.com/home.ht

The decision for or against a BIOS manufacturer is, of course, already made for you by the manufacturer of the motherboard. The only way to choose a particular BIOS producer is to buy the motherboard that uses that BIOS. Award recently has assumed a dominant role in the realm of high-performance boards. But in terms of performance it doesn't differ from the competition. AMI BIOSes are merely somewhat easier to work with, particularly when you have the WIN BIOS version of AMI , which can be configured with the mouse and known window controls. Award BIOSes, on the other hand, can only be manipulated from the keyboard, but are generally better documented. (We'll talk about an independent producer called MR BIOS next.)

NOTE

The "S"uper Pentium?—A gimmick with the Award BIOS

The Award BIOS has a small peculiarity: It displays not only a Pentium when booting, but a "Pentium-S." "S" stands for the SL-processor series, which has expanded power-management capabilities. This feature was introduced a few years ago by Intel in the 486-CPU, but has meanwhile found general use in all processors. Don't worry then, if your BIOS does not indicate the presence of the SL capabilities, they are there nevertheless.

An alternative, independent BIOS is MR BIOS

You do have an alternative but keep in mind that you may have compatibility problems with the motherboard. The one alternative independent BIOS you currently have is called MR BIOS. It has certain advantages and expanded options compared to Phoenix, AMI and Award. You can get more information on MR BIOS — including how to select the correct version for your motherboard — by visiting the MR BIOS website (http://www.mrbios.com). MR BIOS is available as shareware from the Unicore website on the Internet (www.unicore.com).

Chapter 6

Visit the MR BIOS website (http://www.mrbios.com) for more information on this alternative BIOS.

MR BIOS runs on all the important boards that are now available and is programmed into the Flash-ROM of the BIOS with the tools supplied. This will overwrite the old BIOS so make certain to back up the original BIOS first. You may want to consider buying a second EEPROM for these experiments.

MR BIOS not only offers more setting options but also increases system performance and clearly speeds up the booting process. MR BIOS can, however, be important to survival if you want to use a non-Intel CPU on an original Intel motherboard (for example, an AMD K6). When the Intel BIOS reads the CPU-ID, it may refuse to boot if no original Intel processor is present. This problem is solved by using MR BIOS.

MR BIOS is available as shareware from the Unicore website on the Internet (www.unicore.com).

Jumperless motherboards

Until recently, the central settings of the motherboard were always made using jumper bridges. However, more jumperless motherboards have appeared recently. Most settings on these boards are made from the BIOS alone. Only the size of the L2 cache is still usually set using jumpers. A pioneer of this new technology is Abit. Its current motherboard, IT5H, is recommended for this among other reasons (see Chapter 4).

Jumperless motherboards can make it easier for anyone wanting to experiment because it is no longer necessary to unscrew the computer case and change jumpers. You'll need to consider whether such a feature is important. Meanwhile, more companies are entering the jumperless market.

The Cyrix 6x86MX and AMD K6 need special support

Although you can depend on all BIOS versions supporting an Intel processor, the CPUs from AMD and Cyrix may require special BIOS versions and chipsets. If you have or buy such a processor, carefully consider the corresponding BIOS support (see Chapter 4).

Fortunately, most motherboard producers offer special BIOS versions for the AMD and Cyrix processors when necessary. For example, you'll need to use BIOS Version 202 for the Asus board P55T2P4. Your dealer can then update them using Flash-ROM.

Chapter 6

BIOS with built-in SCSI support for SymbiosLogic

Anyone who flirts with SCSI but is intimidated buy the higher cost compared to EIDE should know that a few motherboard or BIOS producers (for example, Asus with Award) offer built-in SCSI BIOS support. It's therefore possible to use inexpensive SCSI controllers from Symbios Logic (formerly NCR) that use the Sym810 SCSI chip. Because this controller no longer needs its own ROM-BIOS (such as, for example, the controllers from Adaptec), they are clearly cheaper than the competition.

Keep in mind these are otherwise full-featured Fast-SCSI controllers for the PCI bus. Compatibility and performance are not necessarily inferior to the expensive controllers found in standard operating systems. Naturally, the drivers are perhaps not so finely tuned and you may not all the performance offered by the expensive branded models. Nevertheless, they cost less than half as much. See Chapter 7 for more information on SCSI.

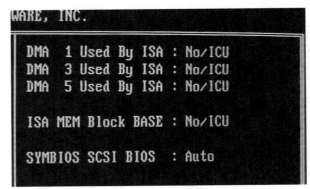

On many motherboards (here T2P4 from Asus) you can enable the support for Symbios Logic SCSI controllers in the "PNP and PCI Setup." Anyone using an Adaptec controller or EIDE can disable the function. Auto does this automatically.

A basic course on BIOS manipulations

Now we're getting into the most important basic BIOS tunings. First, however, there are a few things you need to look for before continuing. On the next few pages we'll summarize the most important functions if you're a beginner. We'll also talk about adjusting the BIOS, backing up your CMOS RAM data and correcting any errors you may make.

Determining whether speed or stability is more important

When tuning the BIOS you often will need to choose between top speed or stability. Many settings can increase performance but often at the cost of the system's reliability. A typical example concerns the timing values for the main memory. The correct setting can push your RAM modules to their performance limits, which will increase both the system's speed and failure rate. The EIDE or PCI functions offer similar questions. It's also a critical issue with overclocking.

No one can tell you whether speed or stability is more important. It greatly depends on your situation. For example, configure entirely for system stability if your PC is used mostly for business. In this case, a computer crash and data loss are the last thing you need. On the other hand, a crash is more of an inconvenience than a disaster if you use your PC mostly for entertainment. In this case, what matters most is that the hardware is not damaged.

A basic rule to follow in BIOS tuning

There are many settings in the BIOS and changing just one can make a big difference. If you change several parameters at the same time, you easily forget what was changed and may not be able to find the cause of problems. Therefore it's better to proceed one step at a time. Make one change and then test your PC's performance. If the test was satisfactory then continue with the next change.

It is also a good idea to take notes. You may also be able to print the current screen (depending on the BIOS and your printer) by pressing the (Print Screen) key. Unfortunately, this won't always work with some laser and ink-jet printers.

```
                    ROM PCI/ISA BIOS (PI55T2P4)
                        BIOS FEATURES SETUP
                        AWARD SOFTWARE, INC.
 Virus Warning             : Disabled ° Video  BIOS Shadow  : Enabled
 CPU Internal Cache        : Enabled  ° C8000-CBFFF Shadow  : Disabled
 External Cache            : Enabled  ° CC000-CFFFF Shadow  : Disabled
 Quick Power On Self Test  : Enabled  ° D0000-D3FFF Shadow  : Disabled
 Boot Sequence             : C,A      ° D4000-D7FFF Shadow  : Disabled
 Swap Floppy Drive         : Disabled ° D8000-DBFFF Shadow  : Disabled
 Boot Up Floppy Seek       : Disabled ° DC000-DFFFF Shadow  : Disabled
 Floppy Disk Access Control : R/W     °
 Boot Up NumLock Status    : On       °
 Boot Up System Speed      : High     °
 IDE HDD Block Mode        : Enabled  °
 Typematic Rate Setting    : Enabled  °
 Typematic Rate (Chars/Sec) : 30      °
 Typematic Delay (Msec)    : 250      °
 Security Option           : System
 PCI/VGA Palette Snoop     : Disabled ° ESC : Quit         : Select Item
 OS/2 Onboard Memory > 64M : Disabled ° F1  : Help    PU/PD/+/- : Modify
                                      ° F5  : Old Values  (Shift)F2 : Color
                                      ° F6  : Load BIOS  Defaults
                                      ° F7  : Load Setup Defaults
```

A printout of the Award BIOS from an HP Laserjet. The incorrect frame functions result from the improperly applied character set; the important information is not affected by this.

Standard and unconventional solutions for getting into the BIOS

To access the BIOS on most simply press the (Del) key during booting when you see the message "Hit Del to enter Setup" on the screen. Some manufacturers attempt to block the user from gaining access to the BIOS. The table following below lists alternative key combinations to enter the BIOS on these PCs.

BIOS	AMI	Award	Phoenix
Standard key combination	Del	Del	Del
Alternative combination (for old motherboards)	F1	Ctrl Alt Esc / Ctrl Alt	Ctrl Alt Esc / Ctrl Alt

You might want to also try the following keys. These keys have to be pressed simultaneously during a brief period of the booting process.

Ctrl + Enter
Alt + F1
Alt + Ctrl + Insert

Alt + Enter,
Alt + Ctrl + F1
F10 (for example, in the case of Compaq),

The BIOS version on some basic PCs may let you do little more than set the date. In these cases, a special diskette is included that has a form of a BIOS program with which you can set further parameters from DOS. An example of this would be the IRQ reservation of the various plug-in slots (the PnP and PCI-BIOS).

If you fail to get in using either the Del key or the key combinations in the table, the only alternative left is to remove the keyboard plug. Then the next time you boot up, your PC may show an error message and requires you to press a key to enter the BIOS. Simply plug the keyboard back in and try again to enter the BIOS.

Restarting the computer using the Ctrl key

Your PC should not be damaged when you change the parameters in the BIOS Setup. In the worst case, your PC may not start because the control of a system component cannot synchronize with the other components. The computer then is locked up and the screen remains dark.

When this happens, you may be able to reset the BIOS to its default values by holding down the Insert key and turning on the computer. This ensures that the board is returned to the basic configuration it received at the factory. However, this also will delete your custom settings.

Your work will be more difficult if this method won't work or if the BIOS is protected by a password. In this case, you must delete the CMOS RAM by disconnecting it or shorting the battery.

Back up the CMOS configuration data of your BIOS

You can use various programs to back up the data of the CMOS RAM (the user-specific settings, not the BIOS). Then, in case of troubles, you can use the backup to restore the original settings. You should always back up data before beginning any tuning experiments and after completing the configuration.

The best known program for backing up the BIOS is probably the Rescue tool of the Norton Utilities from Symantec. Use it to back up all important settings of DOS, Windows 95 and the CMOS data. In case of a serious problem you can write back the data from the backup diskette using your Windows 95 emergency startup diskette.

Another program for backing up CMOS data is AMI Setup (although it can be used only for the AMI BIOS).

Beeps and identifying errors

You've certainly heard the beeps emitted by the BIOS during booting when an incorrect configuration or a problem is detected. An incorrect configuration can also be the faulty connection of important components such as the keyboard.

Although most beep tones are simply alarm signals, others refer to specific errors depending on the length and sequence of the beeps. The manual for you motherboard should list the beep codes. The following tables list the most important signals for BIOSes that use such error codes.

AMI BIOS error codes			
Tone	Error present	Tone	Error present
1 short	Refresh error in the RAM	9 short	BIOS checksum error (BIOS possibly defective)
2 short	Parity error in the RAM	10 short	Write/read access error, CMOS RAM
3 short	Error in the first 64 K of memory	11 short	L2 cache error
4 short	Defect in the timer component	1 short, 3 long	DOS and Extended Memory test error
5 short	Processor addressing error	1 long 2 short	No video card found
6 short	Process error in protected-mode test (gate A20 or keyboard-controller failure)	1 long 3 short	No monitor found
7 short	Processor error	1 long, 8 short	Graphics memory addressing error
8 short	Graphics memory addressing error		

Chapter 6

Award BIOS error codes			
Tone	Error present	Tone	Error present
1 short	Everything o.k.	1 long, 2 short	Viceo card addressing error
2 short	Slight error which is usually indicated by a message on the screen. Can continue the boot process with [F1] or (according to the motherboard) enter the BIOS	1 long, 3 short	Keyboard controller addressing error

Phoenix-BIOS Plus and Version 1.x error codes (Dashes indicate pauses)			
Tone	Error present	Tone	Error present
1-1-3	CMOS error	3-4-1	Video card addressing error
1-1-4	BIOS checksum error	3-4-2	Screen-retrace test error (screen control)
1-2-1	Timer error	4-2-1	Timer error
1-2-2	DMA-controller initialization problems	4-2-2	Shutdown/restart test
1-2-3	Read or write error in DMA-page register	4-2-3	Protected Mode test error(Gate A20)
1-3-1	RAM-refresh error	4-2-4	Protected Mode test error (false interrupt)
1-3-3 or 1-3-4 or 1-4-1	Error in first 64 K of RAM	4-3-1	Error in memory above the first 64 K
1-4-2	Parity error in first 64 K of RAM	4-3-2	Timer error
3-1-1 or 3-1-2	DMA-controller error	4-3-4	Real-time clock error
3-1-3 or 3-1-4	Interrupt-controller error	4-4-1	Serial interface test error
3-2-4	Keyboard controller error	4-4-2	Parallel interface test error
3-3-4	Video card addressing error	4-4-3	Coprocessor test error

Error codes of the Phoenix BIOS 4.0 (Dashes indicate pauses)			
Tone	Error present	Tone	Error present
1-2-2-3	BIOS checksum error	1-3-1-1	RAM-refresh error
1-2-3-1	Timer error	1-3-3-1	General RAM error
1-2-3-3	DMA-cntroller error	1-4-2-1	CMOS error

What to do when you get a BIOS error message

The first thing to do when you get a BIOS error message is to relax. Some PCs will run despite the error(s). If not, you probably will only need to change individual components. The first rescue or analytical steps in the case of error messages should be as follows:

◆ **RAM and L2 cache error**: Press down firmly on the memory chips or pull them out and reinstall them. If that doesn't help, change them individually to find the defective chip.

◆ **Processor error**: Remove the CPU from the socket and check the contacts. Then put it back. If the error message still appears, change the CPU as a test.

◆ **BIOS and CMOS errors**: Press the BIOS chip down firmly and attempt a restart. If this works, reload the default BIOS settings using the Load BIOS Defaults command and reenter all settings. It might be a good idea to carry out a BIOS update using the Flash-ROM (see below). For CMOS errors, check all plug-in cards and connections, because improperly installed devices contradict BIOS settings and cause the messages. If nothing helps, try to get a new BIOS chip from the manufacturer.

Using special tools to change secret settings

The manufacturers—for understandable reasons—don't want users to set or even have access to everything in the PC BIOS. Many parameters, for example, the configuration of the L2 cache or the timing settings for the main memory, are not accessible on most modern boards. But that doesn't mean that possibilities are not available—there are merely no menu commands.

Special programs are available to access additional and hidden settings. The most popular may be AMI Setup. It's a shareware program available on the Internet (www.sysopt.com/bios.html). It offers access to hidden functions and also the convenient setting of all standard functions using DOS.

You'll find the shareware tool AMI Setup useful for conveniently changing nearly all motherboard settings if you're using AMI BIOS.

The Award BIOS equivalent is called TweakBIOS and it's also available as shareware from the Internet (www.miro.pair.com/tweakbios/index.html). This program lets you change the Chipset Feature BIOS settings on motherboards with THX, TVX, TX and FX chip sets from Intel (all currently available Pentium, Pentium Pro and Pentium II boards). It can check the timing values for memory access to main memory and the L2 cache very nicely and can make any changes needed. The program even displays the different settings for FP and EDO RAM.

TweakBIOS lets you change the Chipset Feature settings in the Award BIOS
(in particular the RAM timing data and second-level cache).

BIOS updates through Flash-ROM

As mentioned, motherboards now include Flash-ROM, which allows users to easily update a BIOS. It's good that only few users use it because a BIOS update only makes sense when there are problems and always involves the risk of damaging the motherboard. Keep the following in mind:

◆ Only update a BIOS when problems are present that the manufacturer says can be solved by an update or if a new processor (for example, AMD K6, Cyrix 6x86MX) needs special functions to run.

◆ Always get the BIOS update from the producer of the motherboard and not from that of the BIOS. The motherboard manufacturer always uses special versions specially adapted to his board. The BIOS producer may not have that same version.

◆ The best source of BIOS updates is the Internet.

◆ It is absolutely necessary that you use **only** exactly the BIOS version released for your motherboard. Don't use the BIOS for a similar board (for example, Asus P55T2P4 and XP55T2P4) unless the manufacturer expressly states that the version for both boards is identical.

◆ The BIOS version number appears briefly in the upper left during booting. The number to the lower left during booting indicates only the type of motherboard.

```
 Award Modular BIOS v4.51PG, An Energy Star Ally
 Copyright (C) 1984-95, Award Software, Inc.

#401A0-0105

PENTIUM-S CPU at 166MHz
Memory Test : 65536K OK
```

```
Press DEL to enter SETUP
06/10/96-82430HX-PI55T2P4C-00
```

The picture on the left shows the number that is displayed during booting. It corresponds to the version number (in the case of the Award BIOS — here 0105). The number appearing at the lower left-hand edge of the screen, on the other hand, only designates the motherboard model (picture on the right).

◆ You'll need a special program for the update. It's probably a diskette labeled as the flash diskette. Always make a backup copy of the old BIOS before making the flash update.

The procedure of the flash update is rather simple and identical for most motherboards. It's based on the application of an elevated burning voltage. The Flash-ROM chip can be written with data only at this higher voltage. For resetting to the write mode, you'll find a jumper on most motherboards near the BIOS chip (this is the JP18 for Asus motherboards). It must be reset from disabled to enabled. Many boards also come without jumpers, the burning voltage being enabled by the update program. After a successful update, make certain to put the jumper back in the old position for the normal operating voltage.

After you have enabled the write-mode jumper, you still must call the flash-writer program (called PFLASH.EXE for Asus). The PC must be in Real Mode for this purpose so make certain to disable all memory managers (HIMEM.SYS and EMM386.EXE). The best procedure for this is to boot from a diskette on which you have only the flash program and the BIOS update files from the manufacturer. (In other words, make certain the diskette doesn't include CONFIG.SYS and AUTOEXEC.BAT.) The program surfaces of the flash writer are all kept rather simply in text mode. Normally you have only two or three functions: back up old BIOS into a file, write new BIOS from an update file and, possibly, a further function which is not needed (for the initial writing of the boot block in the BIOS).

NOTE

BIOS update for tech-freaks—DMI-configuration utilities

Many producers equip their motherboards or your BIOS with another configuration option, the DMI (Desktop Management Interface). A DMI utility which comes with it, MIFD (Management Information Format Database), makes it possible to swap data with a 4 K memory area in the BIOS Flash-ROM. The BIOS stores information on the CPU, clock frequencies and memory chips, for example, in this database. These can be read with the DMI program. The purpose of the program, however, is to enter information such as series numbers or owner and manufacturer data into the MIFD, which could be of interest for companies for security reasons. The DMI has little to offer the average user, however.

It's absolutely necessary that you first back up the old BIOS. Then select Update from the menu. The program will ask for the path and the file name of the BIOS file and will then begin the burning operation. If problems arise, <u>do not</u> shut down or reset the computer for any reason. If you do, you may not be able to boot it and will no longer be able to update. Try to repeat the process and, if that doesn't help, reinstall the BIOS. The report of CMOS-checksum errors when you first boot up after that is normal because you'll have to enter all configuration data anew after the update.

Everything is good if you can access the BIOS and can enter settings there. Once in the BIOS, first use the Load Setup Defaults command to enable the default settings. But if everything seems to go wrong nevertheless, as a last resort, turn to your dealer or directly to the manufacturer for a new BIOS chip. You may be in luck if your motherboard has a recovery function. When this is enabled (usually by setting a jumper), the motherboard will attempt to read a BIOS file from the diskette into the damaged Flash-ROM. However, it remains to be seen whether this works. Only a few motherboards have such a function and you'll need a new chip for those that don't.

Company	Internet address	Company	Internet address
Soyo	http://www.soyo.com	Asus	http://www.asus.com
Tyan	http://www.tyan.com	Abit	http://203.73.138.1/html/emain.htm
Gigabyte	http://www.giga-byte.com	Elitegroup	http://www.ecs.com.tw
		Siemens Nixdorf	http://www.sni.de/public/pc/service/softw_de.htm

MAKING LIFE EASIER—SETTINGS FOR SAFETY AND CONFIGURATION

The first part of this section summarizes the settings that are not so important for performance. These settings are concerned with security (password, virus-protection, etc.) and miscellaneous basic configurations.

We'll start with an overview of a typical BIOS main menu and we'll use the Award BIOS. It has become the standard BIOS for all the high-quality motherboards. The settings, subdivisions and designations for AMI and Phoenix BIOSes are very similar so you should also be able to find your way through these by following our information.

An overview of the BIOS

When you reach the BIOS using the keys or functions described in the table on 178, you'll see the main menu. Then you can access each of the main functions by using the arrow keys.

The following picture shows the most important main functions or menus. The ones you'll use most often are the submenus BIOS Features Setup, Chipset Features Setup and PNP And PCI Setup (below, for the sake of simplicity, written standard or lowercase).

Press the (Pg Up) or (Pg Dn) keys or the arrow keys to move between the different options Press (Esc) to leave each menu and, eventually, the BIOS. You'll be prompted whether to save any changes. Press (Y) to save or (N) to exit without saving.

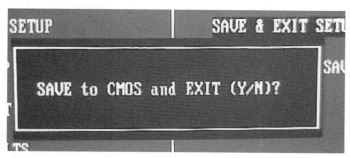

Select the individual submenus with the arrow keys from the main menu of the Award BIOS. The settings of the second, third and fifth menus are very important.

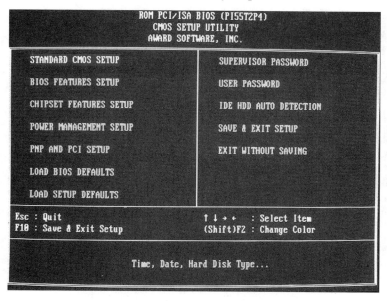

All the submenus in the main menu of the AMI BIOS are listed one beneath the other. Otherwise the organization and designations are pretty much like those of the Award BIOS.

```
          Standard CMOS Setup
          Advanced CMOS Setup
         Advanced Chipset Setup
         Power Management Setup
        PCI / Plug and Play Setup
            Peripheral Setup
         Auto-Detect Hard Disks
           Change User Password
        Change Supervisor Password
  Auto Configuration with Optimal Settings
  Auto Configuration with Fail Safe Settings
          Save Settings and Exit
           Exit Without Saving
```

AMI's Advanced CMOS Setup corresponds to Award' BIOS Features Setup. The Advanced Chipset Setup corresponds to the Chipset Features Setup of the Award BIOS.

The built-in Virus Warning will protect the boot sector of your hard drive

If you switch the Virus Warning in the BIOS Features Setup to Enabled, the BIOS will monitor the boot sector of the hard drive. This is easily done by the BIOS because the boot sector is always the logically first sector of a partition. If a program tries to write to the boot sector, a warning will appear on the screen and the user must confirm the access. Rarely is there a need to rewrite the boot sector (the exceptions being the installation of a new operating system and some anti-virus software). Therefore make certain this option is set to Enabled.

This provides protection against the boot-sector viruses which, as the name suggests, infect the boot sector of disks. Keep in mind, however, this won't provide protection against all viruses — only against boot-sector viruses. A specific anti-virus program (for example, McAfee Anti-Virus, Dr. Solomon's Antivirus Kit, etc.) provide more comprehensive protection against other viruses.

```
  Virus Warning              : Disabled
  CPU Internal Cache         : Enabled
  External Cache             : Enabled
  Quick Power On Self Test   : Enabled
  Boot Sequence              : A,C
```

The Virus Warning is set by default to Disabled. Set it to Enabled, and you have a defense against write accesses to the boot sector of the hard drive.

> **NOTE**
>
> **Virus warnings and operating system setup**
>
> Each time you install a new operating system, it will access the boot sector to store its files there. To prevent problems with the virus-warning function, merely switch it off during the OS setup.

BIOS password offers some protection for your PC

The BIOS usually offers two password functions. The first is USER PASSWORD. It's a query during boot-up against unauthorized use of the computer. The second is SUPERVISOR PASSWORD and it provides protection against unwanted manipulation of the BIOS itself. You'll find both functions in the main menu of the BIOS. You can optionally enter one or both passwords. Also, the two passwords don't have to be the same. In computers with only one password function, the supervisor password is usually used.

The user password is used to prevent other people from accessing your computer. The query appears before the operating system boots so it also guards against curious individuals who think they can work around the password protection on a hard drive by booting from a diskette. Without setting a supervisor password, the road into the BIOS is wide open and anyone can make changes there. Only the user password can be changed without knowing the old one.

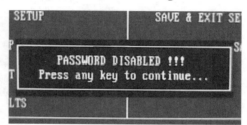

The left picture shows the password settings in the main menu of the BIOS. The right picture shows the old password can be disabled by pressing a key such as [Spacebar].

What to do when you forgot your BIOS password

Quite frankly, one of the dumbest things to do when working on your PC is to forget the BIOS password. Although you'll no longer be able to boot for PC if you forget the user password, it's still possible to get around this problem or delete the password. However, this also proves that BIOS protection by password is a superficial security measure. Real security can be achieved only by combining various methods and perhaps encrypting your data carriers. These are your options for password rescue:

1   If you have an AMI BIOS, you can read the password with the aid of AMI Setup. Unfortunately, that won't be much help if you need the user password (for booting). This tip thus only makes sense for a forgotten supervisor password.

2   Many motherboards with the Award BIOS will accept the following general passwords: LKWPETER, AWARD?SW, 589589, aLLy and SWITCHES?SW.

3   Otherwise, the last resort is to delete your personal data from the CMOS chip by removing the motherboard battery. Removing the battery is quite simple on the newer motherboards. It's done either through a jumper or DIP switch on the motherboard (see your manual) or by removing the battery for a short time (30 minutes at the most is usually long enough).

However, be very careful when removing the batter. The spring that keeps the battery in the holder breaks easily when bent upward. The correct procedure is to push out the battery in a forward direction by holding down the surrounding plastic ring (see the following picture).

Carefully remove the battery in a forward direction (careful, the spring breaks easily)
or reset the jumper beside it according to the manual to delete the password information.

If your motherboard has a jumper available for deleting the CMOS RAM, this will always work in the same way. Open the jumper (probably near the battery) and turn on the PC briefly and then turn it off again. Return the jumper to its original position and then reboot. Unfortunately, this will not only delete the password but all the settings (for the hard drive, for example). These settings will have to be reentered.

You may have to take a different approach with old boards. The battery often cannot be removed. If this describes your board, contact your local computer technician or dealer for assistance.

Do not forget the password if the battery is built into the DALLAS chip with the system clock. Otherwise, the battery cannot be removed and if no delete jumper is present, you can toss the board.

BIOS write protection for diskettes

Use the BIOS to prevent all write accesses to your floppy drive using the Floppy Disk Access Control command. This will change diskettes to a read only status. You'll find this in the Award BIOS's BIOS Features menu (or under System Security in the AMI BIOS). This function makes sense for two reasons. First, to protect important diskettes (boot diskettes, for example) from viruses on the hard drive. Second, you can make it impossible for others to transfer your data to another diskette.

To enable the write protection, you have to change the basic setting R/W (Read/Write) to Read Only. In the Chipset Features Setup you also have the option of disabling the drive completely, so that will also be unable to load any software. You'll find more information on that in a later section.

```
Boot Up Floppy Seek       : Disabled
Floppy Disk Access Control : R/W
Boot Up NumLock Status    : On
```

The Floppy Disk Access Control option lets both reading and writing access to the floppy drive.

Keyboard optimization for nimble fingers

You can set the reaction time of the keyboard in the BIOS. The default values are suitable for everyday use or average typists. However, experienced typists should enter different values. First, change the Typematic Rate Settings to Enabled so you can change the Typematic Rate and Typematic Delay settings.

The Typematic Rate setting is the critical value because it determines how many entries per second you can make. The setting of 6 is probably low for experienced typists and makes the keyboard too awkward. Increase it to the maximum value

```
Typematic Rate Setting      : Enabled
Typematic Rate (Chars/Sec) : 30
Typematic Delay (Msec)      : 250
```

of 30. The Typematic Delay setting determines the delay time in milliseconds between two keyboard entries. Use the lowest setting of 250 msec there.

When Protected Mode makes sense

This information is more important for older computers but can also be used for newer PCs (if it's still available). This option affects the BIOS-controlled switching of the processor from Real Mode (DOS operation) into the Protect Mode (Windows operation) using the A20 signal. In early computers (286es) this was accomplished by the (slow) keyboard controller. Only later was a special, rapid data line introduced with the A20 gate, over which the chip set can switch the processor into the Protected Mode without using the keyboard controller. The Protected Mode is of course important only for Windows, because, by using it, main memory beyond one Meg can be addressed. The switch-over is not important for DOS programs that work exclusively in the first 1024K.

If an option such as Fast Gate A20 or something similar is available in your BIOS, make certain to set to Enabled. Then the transition occurs through this rapid port instead of the slow keyboard controller.

BIOS OPTIMIZATION FOR STARTING THE PC

Another task for the BIOS is coordinating the boot process. The boot data for this purpose are stored in a special location called the boot block. It usually doesn't need to be updated during a normal BIOS update.

Meanwhile, PCs today have several boot options. You can still choose between diskette and hard drive as the initial boot medium. But now you also can give SCSI hard drives precedence over EIDE. On some boards you can even determine the EIDE partition from which you boot. Beyond this really simple selection of the boot drive, other settings determine the booting speed. The disablement of the superfluous function tests which run when you switch on the computer (memory, diskettes, etc.) can clearly retard the starting operation. The most important settings relative to booting are summarized below.

Speeding up the boot process

The booting process of an average PC lasts too long (SCSI computers are even worse). However, there are a few settings in the BIOS that we can use to speed up the starting process. One example is the hardware function tests. Most of the relevant settings are found in the BIOS Features Setup menu.

◆ The Boot Up System Speed setting influences the clock `Boot Up System Speed    : High` frequency of the computer. This was introduced in 486 computers for reasons of compatibility, for example, with old games. When the PC was intentionally slowed the system clock was reduced from 33 to 8 MHz because otherwise some games would no longer run. This setting obviously has no affect in most Pentium PCs. But if the setting is available on your PC, make sure it is set to High and not to Low.

◆ Quick Power On Self Test is found in nearly all BIOS `Quick Power On Self Test  : Enabled` versions. It controls the memory test which occurs when you turn on the PC. In the On or Enabled setting, the memory is tested only once. On the other hard, repeated testing is carried out when Off or Disabled is set. If you test your memory thoroughly after you buy it and then have no problems, keep the value set to Enabled.

◆ Memory tests on old motherboards: The settings Above 1MByte Memory Test, Memory Parity Check Error and Memory Test Tick Sound have a function similar to the Quick Power On Self Test entry on most of the current Pentium boards. However, these are found almost exclusively on old 486 boards. Set all these parameters to Disabled to speed up the booting operation.

> **NOTE**
> **Hardware versus software solutions during the memory test**
> Assuming you did not buy your RAMs at a Hong Kong flea market, you can expect problem free operation. RAMs are rarely defective nowadays and likewise do not fail during operation. Continual memory tests are superfluous. Besides, the Himem.sys memory manager of Windows 95 checks the RAM again during start-up, and that is more relevant to practice than the BIOS. To avoid this test, you have to call Himem.sys with the "/testmem: off" switch.

Get rid of those annoying floppy drive default settings

Depending on the BIOS, you'll find three or four settings for the floppy drive that influence booting. Because the floppy drive is seldom used, you can optimize these settings to speed up the booting process.

◆ **Disable the floppy as the boot drive**: You can determine the primary boot drive with the Boot Up Sequence setting. If you retain the standard setting A,C", the computer will always attempt to boot from any diskette present in the floppy drive. If it isn't a boot diskette, an error message will appear and you'll be asked to remove it. Instead, select the C,A (or a similar combination) setting and you'll boot from a diskette only if the hard drive fails. If at some time you want to start from a diskette, simply change the boot sequence again in the BIOS first.

Chapter 6

◆ **Removing the initialization of the floppy drive motor:** The Boot Up Floppy Seek option lets you specify whether the BIOS will look for a floppy drive when it boots and initialize it by resetting the drive heads. This is hard on the drive heads. Setting this option to Disabled will not impair the use of the drive (see the following illustration).

```
HDD Sequence SCSI/IDE First: IDE        D4000
Boot Sequence              : D,A        D8000
Boot Up Floppy Seek        : Disabled   DC000
Floppy Disk Access Control : R/W
```

◆ **Switch the drive letters:** The assignment of the drive letters is important only for old PCs which have a 5.25 drive and a 3.5 drive. In this case you have the ability to switch the letters A: and B: between 3.5 and 5.25 drives. You do this by enabling the Swap Floppy Drive function in BIOS Features Setup (see the following illustration).

```
Swap Floppy Drive          : Disabled
```

Use this feature in BIOS Features Setup to switch the drive letters of the floppy drives. The setting is obviously not important for PCs with only one floppy drive.

◆ **Further control over the floppy drive:** While the above option is only a software trick with the drive letters, the Chipset Features Setup menu offers more extensive control over the floppy drives. Using the options shown in the chart, you can completely shut off the floppy controller on the board or switch the standard assignment of the drive letters. This sometimes isn't a bad idea for security reasons. See the following illustration:

```
Onboard FDC Controller     : Enabled
Onboard FDC Swap A & B     : No Swap
```

Booting options from CD-ROM and SCSI

Current boards, for example, those with the TX chipset, offer extensive options for selecting a boot drive. You can not only choose between the floppy drive and all EIDE hard drives (and partitions), but even boot from an ATAPI CD-ROM. You must first have a CD-ROM with booting capability (to create such a CD-ROM, see the corresponding tip in Chapter 9).

```
SCSI ID:LUN NUMBER #:# 0:0 - IBM      DORS-32160
SCSI ID:LUN NUMBER #:# 1:0 - IBM      DORS-32160
SCSI ID:LUN NUMBER #:# 2:0 - PIONEER CD-ROM
SCSI ID:LUN NUMBER #:# 3:0 - PLEXTOR CD-ROM

A BOOTABLE CD-ROM IS DETECTED IN YOUR CD-ROM DRIVE...

The boot sections on your bootable CD-ROM are:
  0. DEFAULT ENTRY
SCSI ID:LUN NUMBER #:# 5:0 - IOMEGA  ZIP 100
```

Only special CD-ROMs, such as those of Windows NT 4.0, are recognized as bootable CD-ROMs, if the BIOS settings in the boot sequence were changed to CD-ROM.

Furthermore, it is now possible with these boards to define attached SCSI hard drives as the boot drive. Previously EIDE was always ahead of SCSI. You'll find all the needed settings in BIOS Feature Setup and, as mentioned, unfortunately only on current motherboards. Ask your dealer or supplier whether a BIOS update can provide your old board with these functions. These are very practical functions.

```
HDD Sequence SCSI/IDE First: SCSI
Boot Sequence              : A,C
```

On the new motherboards you can finally specify that EIDE drives no longer be placed ahead of SCSI drives in the boot sequence.

Hard drives almost never need a boot delay

In the case of old hard drives, the PC could boot more quickly than the hard drive is able to start up and react to queries from the BIOS. Therefore, BIOSes have entries like Delay for HDD or Hard Disk Pre-Delay. These can be used to purposely delay the booting operation for a few seconds to give the hard drive a chance to start.

But let us make it quite clear: The hard drives of the last three or four years have no need to diddle around like that, but come immediately up to speed. So, switch such settings to Off. Set a delay to On only if you have problems.

Some BIOSes have a corresponding setting option for SCSI hard drives. The options have names like Delay for SCSI Devices. Here, too: Disable with Off unless problems turn up.

No More Trouble With EIDE—All The Important Hard Drive And CD-ROM Settings

The most important devices configured using the BIOS are probably (E)IDE hard drives and ATAPI CD-ROMs (see also Chapter 7 and Chapter 9). The BIOS contains many settings for these devices — ranging from initial installation to fine tuning.

You'll find additional information on the topics EIDE and Power Management or Resource Saving further below in this chapter.

Leave the HDD utilities in the BIOS alone

Hard drive utilities are usually found in the main menu of old BIOS versions but seldom in current BIOSes. These are little programs for testing and formatting IDE hard drives. The critical thing about these utilities is that they perform low-level formatting and are intended only for old MFM,

Chapter 6

ESDI and RLL drives. Low-level formatting is always done by the manufacturer and should not need to be done again. You're risking damaging the hard drive when working with these utilities. This is especially true for an EIDE drive. Therefore, our advice is to not use them. Use only the High Level Format of the operating system to format a hard drive. Don't confuse these HDD utilities with the IDE HDD Auto Detection we'll talk about in a later section.

Registering EIDE hard drives in the BIOS

The days when correctly registering an EIDE hard drive in the BIOS was a difficult task are fortunately now past. Nearly everything is now automatic thanks to the Auto-Detection function. The first motherboards with this feature had a simple recognition function that showed only the hard drive data. Motherboards now use proper autoconfiguration. In other words, they enter the data determined automatically in CMOS RAM. Follow these steps to register your hard drive in the BIOS.

1. Install the hard drive(s) and correctly set it to Master or Slave (more on that in Chapter 7). Also write down the data for security or control of your hard drive from the enclosed documentation. The data on cylinders, heads, sectors and the size resulting from these values are important. The data for precompensation (Precomp) and Landing Zone (Landz) are not needed because they are entered automatically by the BIOS.

2. Turn on the computer and enter the BIOS. Then select the IDE HDD Auto Detection option from the menu. The BIOS will immediately and automatically determine the type of hard drive(s) that is connected. Problems will arise only if you want to run old and new hard drives with different PIO-Modes in mixed operation. If the Auto Detection function can't handle it, you'll have to enter the values manually (see below).

Registering an (E)IDE hard drive is done in the main menu under IDE HDD Auto Detection.

3. If the functions are detected, the possible operating values (LBA, LARGE, NORMAL) are displayed in a list. See the next sidebar for an explanation of the operating modes. In 99% of all cases, select LBA and confirm the choice.

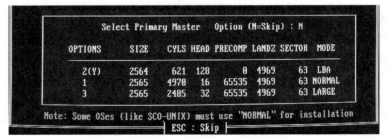

Newer BIOSes detect the data for a hard drive automatically and suggest the correct operating mode (here it's option 2 with LBA). The PIO mode is not entered here but later in the Chipset Features menu.

> **NOTE**
>
> **The agony of choice—The correct (E)IDE mode**
>
> The agony of choosing one of the various hard drive modes for (E)IDE drives first arrived with hard drives larger than 504 Megs and the EIDE specifications. More information on this can be found in Chapter 7. Very old MFM or ESDI hard drives are registed manually in the standard BIOS without reference to an EIDE mode (see figure below). But EIDE hard drives over 504 MB can't address a BIOS directly (Standard Mode); a special Translation Mode is necessary for such drives: Large = Extended CHS; LBA = Logical Block Addressing. LBA is the newer and more widely compatible method, which should be used whenever possible. LARGE should only be used if the hard drive was previously run on a different computer and the stored data must not be lost.

4. The hard drive data are automatically recorded into the standard settings of the BIOS by the Auto Dectect Utility. When you leave the BIOS, you only have to remember to save the changes.

5. You'll find a few more EIDE settings in the BIOS that can tune the drive's performance. However, adjust these only after saving the first registration and restarting the computer. These other options are explained in the following sections.

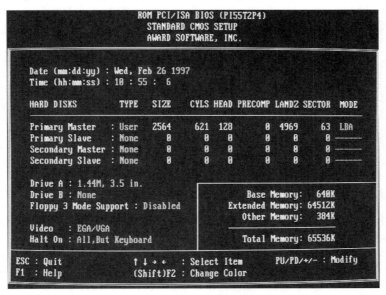

The hard drive values are now permanently entered in the standard BIOS. The hard drive data can also be entered manually in this menu, though this is normally no longer necessary.

6. Once all the BIOS settings have been entered, the hard drive must still be partitioned and formatted by the operating system. Remember, DOS and Windows 95 can only address

Chapter 6

partitions with a maximum size of two gigabytes with VFAT. Only FAT32 and NTFS are capable of more. You'll find further information on this in Chapter 8.

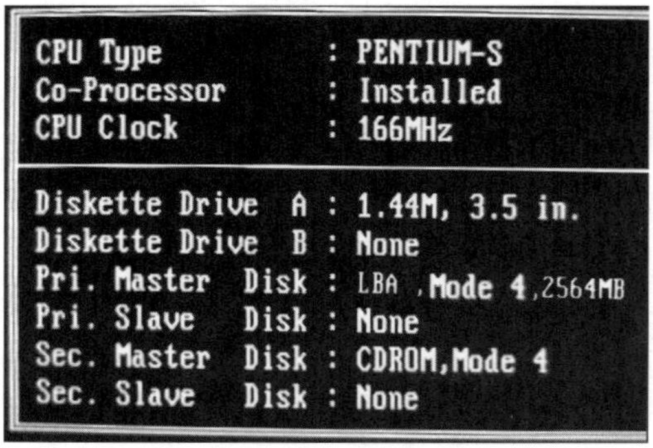

```
CPU Type           : PENTIUM-S
Co-Processor       : Installed
CPU Clock          : 166MHz

Diskette Drive  A  : 1.44M, 3.5 in.
Diskette Drive  B  : None
Pri. Master  Disk  : LBA ,Mode 4 ,2564MB
Pri. Slave   Disk  : None
Sec. Master  Disk  : CDROM,Mode 4
Sec. Slave   Disk  : None
```

All registered hard drives are displayed during booting (shown here as Master and Slave).

Registering your CD-ROM in the BIOS

◆ Installing an ATAPI CD-ROM (EIDE mode) is normally quite simple regarding the BIOS. In most cases you do not have to report the CD-ROM to the BIOS separately. Some newer ATAPI CD-ROMs support PIO modes 3 or 4, which means that it can be driven on the same EIDE port with a hard drive. However, you should avoid this whenever possible and attach the CD-ROM to the secondary port.

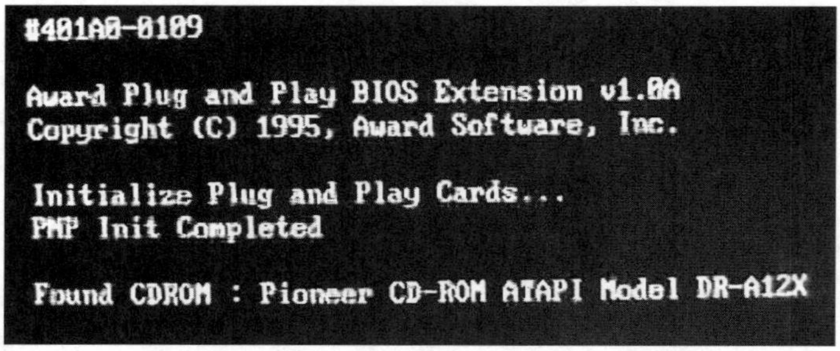

```
#401A0-0109

Award Plug and Play BIOS Extension v1.0A
Copyright (C) 1995, Award Software, Inc.

Initialize Plug and Play Cards...
PNP Init Completed

Found CDROM : Pioneer CD-ROM ATAPI Model DR-A12X
```

The new Atapi CD-ROM is normally recognized and enabled automatically by the BIOS using Plug & Play.

◆ Install the CD-ROM and hope that your BIOS will recognize the unit during boot-up and deliver its full functionality to the secondary port (for example, the 32-bit mode). That's all that is usually necessary. You may still have to work with the PIO mode in the BIOS (see the next three tips on hard drive and EIDE tuning). A message should appear the first time you boot on the screen telling you the device was properly recognized and initialized. You still need to install the driver in the operating system before you're done. Chapter 9 has more information on configuring the CD-ROMs under DOS and Windows.

```
CPU Type          : PENTIUM-S
Co-Processor      : Installed
CPU Clock         : 166MHz

Diskette Drive A  : 1.44M, 3.5 in.
Diskette Drive B  : None
Pri. Master Disk  : LBA ,Mode 4, 2564MB
Pri. Slave  Disk  : LBA ,Mode 4, 2564MB
Sec. Master Disk  : None
Sec. Slave  Disk  : None
```

If the CD-ROM supports a PIO mode, that will also be shown in the boot menu.

NOTE

Slow-down danger—Problems with high-speed CD-ROMs

BIOS settings can have a significant influence upon the speed of new high-speed CD-ROMs (for example, 24x). The data throughput of such CD-ROMs can exceed 3,000 Kbytes/sec, which is already too much for the lowest PIO mode. This becomes critical if an ATAPI CD-ROM is the only EIDE equipment in a system (for example, if you otherwise use SCSI hard drives). Depending upon the CD-ROM type or driver used, many BIOSes will fail to enable the rapid 32-bit mode needed for the hard drive (see next section). The result is an obvious slow down in the CD-ROM's output. You can get around this problem only if you either use all SCSI drives or run an EIDE hard drive with the CD-ROM, for the BIOS will then enable the 32-bit mode. You will (hopefully) see that SCSI is essentially free of such problems.

Chapter 6

Fine tuning your hard drive with more BIOS options

After you have installed the hard drive in the BIOS and entered the correct data, check these additional EIDE settings that fine tune the operation of the unit. Most of these options will be found in the BIOS Features Setup. Also most are relevant only for DOS and Windows 3.x because Windows 95 and NT take care of hard-drive functions with special 32-bit drivers instead of through BIOS functions.

◆ **More rapid data transfer thanks to Block Mode**: Depending upon the type, EIDE hard dives can transfer several 523-byte sectors at a time (according to type: 2, 4, 8, 16 or 32 sectors). This significantly increases access to DOS and Windows 3.x. It also at the same time relieves the processor of its workload, which needs to transfer less address data. The settings are irrelevant under Windows 95 and NT because they use their own driver functions. The names of the settings are IDE HDD Block Mode (Award), Multi Sector Transfer or Multiple Sector Settings (Phoenix or AMI). They should be set to Enabled or HDD, respectively. However, often you'll also have to enter the maximum block number of which the hard drive is capable to enable them. HDD Max or Enabled or Auto read this value from the hard drive. If this option is not in your BIOS, look for it in your hard drive manual or find the correct value by experimenting (values that are too high lead to obvious problems during operation).

NOTE

Problems with block mode

Enabling the EIDE-block mode also has disadvantages because the PCI bus is blocked during operation of the hard drive. Running critical applications in the background (for example, data transfer or burning CDs) can lead to crashes. For modems, a modern, buffered interface should be present for compensation (16550A or compatible). If the dreaded buffer overruns occur during CD-burning or data transfer, disabling the block mode is recommended.

| IDE HDD Block Mode Sectors : HDD MAX | Boot |

Use HDD MAX to enable the maximum block by block transfer of sectors that your hard drive can handle.

◆ Enabling the 32-bit transfer-mode can still be set in old BIOS versions. This is a standard mode on newer boards and is active providing a hard drive is connected. Many BIOS versions do not enable it if only an ATAPI CD-ROM is connected to the EIDE port. The result is that fast 24x CD-ROMs cannot reach full speed in the 16-bit mode. The only remedy is to enable the function in the CD-ROM driver (not all brands have it) or connecting an additional EIDE hard drive.

In any case, this mode was not the standard for older motherboards and hard drives so it may be enabled or disabled. In this operating mode, data are transferred between controller and EIDE hard drive with a full 32 bits. Both devices must have a compatible set of commands. Enabling the setting in the BIOS avoids having to use special software (under DOS and Windows 3.x), that the drive or even the CD-ROM use in the 32-bit mode. Such drivers used to be supplied by the producers of the first EIDE controllers.

If the IDE 32-Bit Transfer Mode option (or similarly named option) is still available, set Enabled. Because problems can then occur in operation (for example, with Windows 3.x), you need to keep an eye on the function and possibly disable it.

Get more speed and resources from the correct EIDE mode

In Chipset Features Setup you'll find all the settings which control the operating mode of both EIDE ports on the motherboard. There you can set the PIO and/or Ultra-DMA mode (only on newer motherboards), and even turn off one or both EIDE ports. This is particularly important for SCSI users who can free up two IRQs for other devices by disabling the unneeded EIDE ports.

◆ Using the command Onboard PCI IDE Enable you can specify whether both (Both), one (Primary or Secondary) or neither (Disabled) of the two EIDE ports on the motherboard is available for hardware. SCSI users should switch to Disabled, to free up IRQs 14 and 15. Anyone running EIDE drives on only the first port should disable the second port using Primary to gain IRQ 15. Also frequently encountered are SCSI computers using only the second port for a ATAPI CD-ROM. In this case the setting Secondary is correct, thus releasing IRQ 14.

198

◆ Only on the most recent mother boards (with 430TX, 440LX, VP2 and similar new chip sets) is it possible to use IDE Ultra DMA Mode to enable the new operating mode of special EIDE-Ultra/DMA hard drives. The Auto option is usually available, which enables the motherboard to recognize and correctly set the operating mode automatically.

◆ It's also possible to set the various PIO modes (0, 1, 2, 3 and 4) of EIDE hard drives for each individual port and to specify each master and slave device. Use the IDE0 (or 1) Master (or Slave) PIO/DMA Mode options for this (see chart). In the Auto setting, the BIOS attempts to determine the PIO mode automatically. However, that doesn't work very often. Furthermore, it definitely slows down the booting process. It's better to set all values manually.

Be aware in this case there is no clear gain in speed beyond PIO Mode 3. On the contrary, PIO Mode 4 is even more susceptible to disturbances. If you have problems or operate old and new devices together on a single port, it may be a good idea to try a lower setting. It is true that two fast EIDE devices cannot be driven on a single port on old motherboards. However, recent models have been able to run master and slave devices with different settings.

```
Onboard PCI IDE Enable      : Both
IDE Ultra DMA Mode          : Auto
IDE0 Master PIO/DMA Mode    : Auto
IDE0 Slave  PIO/DMA Mode    : Auto
IDE1 Master PIO/DMA Mode    : Auto
IDE1 Slave  PIO/DMA Mode    : Auto
```

The settings for the various operating modes of EIDE hard drives are usually found in the lower right of the Chipset Features Setup *menu. The default* Auto *setting is very convenient (if it works), but is not always the best approach.*

Tuning tips for configuring EIDE devices and connections

The EIDE settings in the BIOS permit several configuration options and some can be considered tuning tips.

◆ If you run only devices configured as Masters (on one or both ports) in the BIOS, but the mode of all EIDE devices on both (Master and Slave) is set to Auto, the result will be a slowdown during booting. The reason is that the motherboard will wait for all connected Master and Slave devices to report back. Because the latter is not present, time is needed before the motherboard finally realizes there's nothing there. You can prevent that by setting the value for each concerned port to the lowest mode (0). But that won't work for any Slave devices present. Use the Disabled option if it's offered by your BIOS. Manually selecting the PIO mode for the devices present instead of the Auto setting can lead to a booting speedup.

◆ If you are running two EIDE hard drives, but no CD-ROM, you must decide whether to run them in a Master-Slave combination on the first port or as a Master-Master combination using both ports. We recommend the first approach. The second approach produces no speed advantage and you'll also be using a second precious interrupt. Furthermore, the processor burden will increase with simultaneous use of the two drives because the CPU is now continuously working with two IRQ requests and coordinating two ports.

◆ Windows 95 often fails to detect an ATAPI CD-ROM on the secondary port. However, if this also happens without installing the EIDE Busmaster driver from the manufacturer (see next tip), configure the CD-ROM as a Slave device. You may be surprised that this generally works better than when it is set correctly as a master or single. Another problem with ATAPI CD-ROMs and the 32-bit mode of the BIOS was mentioned earlier.

◆ Problems can occur recognizing a CD-ROM under Windows 95 after installing the EIDE bus master driver. Windows has a bug in the .INF file for the EIDE port (MSHDC.INF) and so the chip controlling this function (PIIX3 or PIIX4 = PCI ISA IDE Xcelerator) of the Triton-II or Triton-III chip set (430HX/VX or 430TX) is often not correctly recognized.

As a result, many BIOSes disable the apparently unneeded secondary port during the next bootup. Then the CD-ROM is no longer available for Windows 95 nor can it be installed. Intel has a patch available for (MSHDC.INF) (but only for Intel boards) at its website. New busmaster drivers to solve this problem should be available by the time you're reading this book. These will be available from Intel (http://developer.intel.com/design/pcisets/busmastr/index.htm) or from your motherboard producer or their website. A further but not so satisfactory solution: In the Registry, you can exchange the busmaster driver (ideatapi.mpd) for the original driver (esdi_506.pdr), but for the secondary port only. Simply look for the first driver name and replace, in the branch, the suboption labeled Secondary. See also Chapter 7.

TWEAKING RAM, ROM AND THE L2 CACHE THROUGH THE BIOS

Correctly choosing the RAM settings and the PCI bus are two of the most important aspects of the BIOS. But here, too, today's motherboards have made your work easier: RAM chips have auto-configuration settings. All you need to know is the access speed of the DRAMs to configure these settings.

Besides the timing settings of the DRAMs and L2 cache, we'll also include all the settings concerning RAM in this section.

The shadow RAM still provides benefits under DOS

Enabling the shadow RAM function(s) in the BIOS used to be one of our favorite tuning tricks. However, these settings are now irrelevant in Windows 3.x and Windows 95. For both the functions of the computer's own BIOS (System BIOS) and the BIOS for the video card (Video BIOS) are addressed using their own drivers under both operating systems. The slow BIOS functions are no longer used.

However, shadow RAM still makes sense under DOS (and thus for boot-up and computer games without their own drivers). Many functions under DOS, (for example, the graphics display) are developed using the BIOS. Any direct access to the ROM BIOS will occur with a slow data width of only 8 bits. The shadow RAM function simply copies the data of the System-ROMs and/or Video-ROMs to the same address and, in a manner of speaking, doubles the available RAM of the normal main memory. The entire copying action occurs in the adapter segment between the first 640 and 1,024 K of RAM.

The shadowing of the System-ROM is enabled by default on most of today's motherboards. A menu command for this is rarely found today. Otherwise, it is called System ROM Shadow, System BIOS Shadow or System Shadow. The shadowing of the video card BIOS can be enabled using Video ROM Shadow, Video BIOS Shadow, Video ROM BIOS Shadow, Video Shadow or the like. All these options are found in BIOS Features Setup.

```
Video   ROM BIOS   Shadow   : Enabled
C8000  -  CBFFF   Shadow   : Disabled
CC000  -  CFFFF   Shadow   : Disabled
D0000  -  D3FFF   Shadow   : Disabled
D4000  -  D7FFF   Shadow   : Disabled
D8000  -  DBFFF   Shadow   : Disabled
DC000  -  DFFFF   Shadow   : Disabled
```

*Video ROM BIOS Shadowing leads to an accelerated graphics
display only under DOS. However, enabling the function is worth it for that alone.*

Besides the System-ROMs and Video-ROMs, the ROMs for other plug-in cards (for example, SCSI controllers or network cards) can also be selectively enabled. But for this you must know in which memory segment the address of the ROM lies. BIOSes enable the shadowing of three, six or ten address blocks. However, we strongly advise against enabling this function. First, most functions of the cards are always enabled by usually using special drivers (for which reason you should always use them if possible). Another reason is that problems arise frequently after the shadowing of plug-in cards.

Enable the cache function for the graphics BIOS

Many motherboards today have another option for accelerating the graphics display under DOS besides to the shadow RAM function. Use the Video BIOS Cacheable menu option to enable a caching of the Video ROMs. Enable this function using Enabled.

```
Video BIOS Cacheable        : Enabled
```

The menu selection for enabling the cache function of the video BIOS is found under Chipset Feature BIOS.

Unwanted memory restrictions

Most BIOSes contain one or two settings that, for reasons of compatibility, can be used to control memory size.

This concerns the function Memory Hole at 15M - 16M or Memory Hole at (Award) or ISA LFB Size (AMI) in the Chipset Features BIOS. The Phoenix BIOS, on the other hand, ignores this. This option can be used to disable the installed memory beyond a certain amount. This really weird-sounding function makes sense only if you want to use one of those very rare and old ISA cards which require their own address range above a certain amount of memory.

Naturally, this is a reasonable solution only in extreme cases (if you absolutely have to use such a card). Therefore, you should definitely set the function to Disabled.

Set the OS/2 Onboard Memory > 64M option to Enabled only if you want to run the operating system OS/2 Warp with more than 64 Megs of RAM. Otherwise, OS/2 cannot address memory beyond this limit. In all other cases, set the function to Disabled.

Standard settings for DRAM

The following options listed aren't so important today's boards because they're enabled either by default or automatically. Nevertheless, they're quite important for understanding later tuning tips . If you have an old board, you may find an useful tip.

Finally, if you have not yet read Chapter 4, some of these terms and concepts may be new. Chapter 4 talks about the basics on memory chips not explained here. So, refer to Chapter 4 if you don't understand something.

◆ Special support for Fast Page DRAMs no longer needs to be set in current BIOSes. Because FP-DRAMs have been standard for the past three or four years (see Chapter 4), the support is enabled by default on all motherboards. Found only on old boards are corresponding options like DRAM Page Mode or Fast Page Mode DRAM (AMI) or Fast DRAM (Award), which should likewise be set to Enabled (assuming of course that you use FP-DRAMs and not normal DRAMs on such an older computer). If you have PS/2 RAMs, you can proceed with confidence.

◆ **Using interleaving**: As we mentioned in Chapter 4, you can speed up memory access by enabling the interleave technique. The prerequisite for this is a symmetrical population of the memory banks (see Chapter 4 for an explanation). Whereas the Award and Phoenix BIOSes recognize such a constellation of the memory population automatically and enable the interleave factor without any action on the part of the user, this must be done manually in the AMI BIOS. The corresponding entry (designations are somewhat variable, but always something like Enable Interleave Function or Interleaved Memory) will be found in the Advanced Chipset Setup main menu.

◆ Also relevant only for old boards is enabling the Hidden Refresh. All DRAM require a continual refresh current pulse so you won't lose your data. This was done previously by the DRAM controller on the motherboard, which added to the workload on the processor. This was eliminated later by memory chips with their own refresh logic. They took care of the refreshing operation. On older boards, enabling this function must occur first on the memory chips. The result is a definite gain in speed. More recent BIOSes have this function enabled by default. The corresponding function is called Hidden Refresh (AMI) or DRAM Hidden Refresh or Decoupled Refresh (Award) and should be set to Enabled.

More speed by optimizing DRAM access

The timing settings of the main memory (DRAM) is an important and complicated options in the BIOS. You'll see that with a few changes in the manufacturer's default settings it is possible to get a good 5% more performance out of most PCs. That is about as much as you'll get by expanding the L2 cache from 256 to 512 K.

Chapter 6

```
                    ROM PCI/ISA BIOS (PI55T2P4)
                       CHIPSET FEATURES SETUP
                        AWARD SOFTWARE, INC.

  Auto Configuration      : 60ns DRAM    Onboard FDC Controller   : Enabled
  DRAM Read Burst Timing   : x222         Onboard FDC Swap A & B   : No Swap
  DRAM Write Burst Timing  : x333         Onboard Serial Port 1    : COM1,3F8H
  RAS to CAS Delay         : 3T           Onboard Serial Port 2    : COM2,2F8H
  DRAM R/W Leadoff Timing  : 6T/5T        Onboard Parallel Port    : 3BCH/IRQ7
  DRAM Turbo Read Leadoff  : Disabled     Parallel Port Mode       : Normal
  DRAM Speculative Leadoff : Enabled      ECP DMA Select           : Disabled
  Turn-Around Insertion    : Disabled     UART2 Use Infrared       : Disabled
  Turbo Read Pipelining    : Disabled
  Peer Concurrency         : Enabled      Onboard PCI IDE Enable   : Primary
  PCI Streaming            : Enabled      IDE 0 Master Mode        : Auto
  Passive Release          : Enabled      IDE 0 Slave  Mode        : Auto
  Chipset Global Features  : Enabled      IDE 1 Master Mode        : Auto
  16-bit I/O Recovery Time : 1 BUSCLK     IDE 1 Slave  Mode        : Auto
  8-bit I/O Recovery Time  : 1 BUSCLK
  Video BIOS Cacheable     : Enabled      ESC : Quit     ↑↓→← : Select Item
  Memory Hole At 15M-16M   : Disabled     F1  : Help     PU/PD/+/- : Modify
  DRAM are 64 (Not 72) bits wide          F5  : Old Values (Shift)F2 : Color
  Memory parity SERR# (NMI): Disabled     F6  : Load BIOS  Defaults
                                          F7  : Load Setup Defaults
```

Nearly all the settings concerned with the main memory's timing values are found in Chipset Features Setup.

The basis for all the settings described below are two technical peculiarities of the memory chips: First, they're constructed in rows and columns that are combined to form pages. Addressing memory therefore requires transmitting page, row and column addresses. These can be optimized through several tricks (for example, burst accesses). Second are the necessary refresh cycles which each DRAM must implement and which slow down actual access. The setting options summarized below always either use tricks during local access or optimize the refresh behavior of the DRAMs. A further tuning factor is, of course, the L2 cache and its cooperation with RAM. We have summarized those settings relevant to the L2 cache at the end in another section.

Finally, most time-relevant settings in the BIOS are shown in the time unit processor cycle (for example, 5T or 5CCLK for clock). Rarely will you find concrete data, such as milliseconds or nanoseconds.

◆ **Auto-configuration**: With the first option in the Chipset Features Setup, Auto Configuration, you can set all essential timing values of the motherboard DRAM. You need only select the access speed (usually only 60ns or 70ns or rarely 50ns). You can change the following options individually only in the Disabled settings. Most boards are conservatively set for 70ns chips. Because this is no longer current, definitely check the settings on your board and correspondingly enter the following settings.

◆ **Refresh setting**: Many motherboards define the DRAM refresh values as the time interval needed for repeated accesses to memory regions of the same type. An example is two sequential row (RAS is an acronym for **R**ow **A**ddress **S**trobe) or column accesses (CAS is an acronym for **C**olumn **A**ddress **S**trobe). The entries will are then called DRAM RAS or CAS

Precharge Time or something similar. The time interval between a line and a column access is used as a measure against other motherboards. (DRAM RAS to CAS Delay; frequently also split into two options as Fast RAS to CAS Delay and RAS to CAS Precharge/Refresh Time). However, it doesn't really matter which of these your motherboard uses. What is important is that these time intervals be low and be indicated in processor cycles (3T, 4T, etc.). The time interval between these accesses is called the Precharge Time. It directly determines the intervening refresh time, for which there is yet another entry in some BIOSes, such as Refresh RAS Assertion. Here, too, set the values low.

```
DRAM CAS Precharge Time : 1 CCLK
```

The refresh cycles on the older 486 motherboards were often set by the CAS accesses. The proper settings depend greatly upon the type of DRAMs (access time, structure), but nearly always lie between 1-4 cycles. Pure CAS access can usually be set to 1-2 cycles, the RAS access to 2-3 cycles. The direct refresh assertion (Refresh RAS Assertion) should be established at 3-4 cycles. The lower values are usually valid for EDO RAMs with 60 ns. FP DRAMs with 70ns, on the other hand, use the higher ones. The best approach is to start from the default values and to try reducing them one at a time by one unit. Raise it again if problems appear.

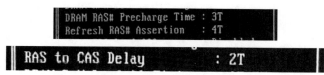

```
DRAM RAS# Precharge Time : 3T
Refresh RAS# Assertion   : 4T

RAS to CAS Delay         : 2T
```

Usually the RAS access on the time interval between RAS and CAS access is used as the measure for the refresh setting on recent motherboards. There is frequently also a separate entry for the definition of the refresh time: Refresh RAS Assertion. The values indicated above are recommendations for 60-ns EDO RAMs.

Setting the waitstates: As described in the following Note box, PCs with fast processors must insert wait cycles for memory access. Concrete settings for waitstates are found mostly only on old 486 and Pentium computers. In these cases, the settings usually have names similar to Read WS Options or DRAM Write WS Options and can be set between 0 and 4 waitstates. For 60ns chips, 3 wait states are usually correct but 4 works well for 70ns chips.

On new PCs, however, the wait states are set automatically using the DRAM speed of the BIOS. The options are called DRAM Speed or DRAM Read/Write Waitstates. Either the settings Slow, Normal and Fast or concrete access times (50, 60, 70, 80ns) are available. Either keep the waitstates low or select the fastest memory type. If your PC crashes, try raising the setting again.

NOTE

Waitstates and what's behind them

Depending on the clock frequency of the processor or system bus, normal DRAMs may not be able to respond to each memory access by the processor. For that reason it's necessary to introduce waitstates for the processor to slow the PC. The motherboard tries to keep waitstates small or eliminates them. Important factors for this are the access speed of the DRAMs (for example, 70ns are adequate for a system-clock frequency of 60 MHz) and the type of the L2 cache. In 486es and the first Pentiums with L2 caches and memory-access methods that were not yet so optimized, the waitstates had to be set in the BIOS. Pentium PCs with a 66-Mhz system bus, 60ns DRAMs and pipelined-burst L2 cache rarely need waitstates. Iff they do, they're set automatically using the DRAM access settings.

◆ **Optimization by burst access**: The correct settings for burst access offer a second tuning possibility with the refresh settings. These two settings mutually determine one another. If the access rates are already set very high, that should not be exaggerated for the burst. The settings for the leadoff and other accesses are in most BIOSes distributed over several options. if possible, set the lowest values offered. You can always raise them again in case of problems. The table on page 207 lists the most important designations and values for you. Corresponding figures will be found above or right below the table. The indicated values are only recommendations so they may not operate depending on the type of memory and motherboard you have. Don't be afraid to experiment here to find what works.

NOTE

First find, then nail down the burst access

The CPU or the L2 cache can access memory (DRAM and cache-SRAMs)more rapidly through burst access. Connected data are thereby divided up into packets loaded into a hopper to accelerate transfer. An analogy is picking apples. The harvest is faster when the trees are in rows and you pick with a basket. You look first for the correct row of trees and fill the basket in a single trip down that row. Only then do you get another basket and begin again. The CPU or the L2 cache does something like that with the main memory. You stuff four accesses into a single packet of the type "xyyy." "X" is the leadoff access and lasts the longest (for example, five cycles), because the complete memory address must be transferred (that corresponds to looking for the row of trees in the example). For the next three accesses (yyy) only the column addresses are still used, permitting these three data bits to be transferred in two cycles each. The resulting access is indicated as 5-2-2-2. The values for the leadoff (x) and the remaining accesses (yyy) are usually entered separatedly in the BIOS and differ in each case according to the memory type (FP, EDO or S DRAM), access speed and chipset. The Intel 430FX (Natoma) for the Pentium Pro/II, for example, works with a leadoff of seven (instead of five as in the case of the Pentium 430HX).

The recommended BIOS settings in the table below are valid for 60ns chips. The default settings from the manufacturer, intended for reliability, are selected more conservatively. For 70ns chips you'll usually have to increase the values by one cycle. EDO RAMs, in comparison with FP DRAMs, respectively tolerate one cycle less during all read accesses. Only very few BIOSes provide separate settings for the two types of memory. Only if you use a special tool, like TweakBIOS, will the settings for FP and EDO DRAMs be displayed separately (see information in this chapter). If you enlarge your memory (for example, to 128 Megs), you may have to reduce the burst timing, because the additional management overhead for the large amount of memory reduces access.

Designation	Remark	Setting
DRAM Read Burst Timing	Burst Read access, relatively dependent upon memory type. 70-ns chips also need x333 for EDO	x222 (EDO RAM) x333 (FP DRAM)
DRAM Write Burst Timing	Burst Write access; relatively independent of DRAM-type, can be one cycle faster than Read access	x222 (Standard is x333)
DRAM R/W Leadoff Timing (also individually)	Setting for initial access (x). The Read(R) is less dependent upon the DRAM type than the Write (W) access	R=6, W=5 (R=5 for EDO) (R=7, W=8 is default value)
DRAM Turbo Read Leadoff	Accelerates the Leadoff Timing in a manner similar to Speculative Leadoff (next entry), because under certain conditions it is not forced to transmit the complete access data. Operates only rarely and is often mutually exclusive with the following option	Disabled (enable as a test at a system-clock frequency of 60 or 50 MHz)
DRAM Speculative Leadoff	Enables a Leadoff access even when the complete address data were not transmitted. This option and Turbo Read Leadoff (last option) are mutually exclusive on fast systems	Enabled (Default is Enabled)
Turbo Read Pipelining	Similar to the last two options; gives motherboard chipset renewed access to the processor if the first data was not yet transferred completely	Enabled (Default is Disabled)
Fast EDO Path select or Fast EDO Leadoff	Only in some BIOSes and EDO RAMs, speeds up multiple Leadoff accesses; Mutual influence with regard to Read Burst Timing settings	Enabled (Disabled if Read-Burst accesses too slow)

Chapter 6

```
Auto Configuration      : 60ns DRAM
DRAM Read Burst Timing   : x222
DRAM Write Burst Timing  : x333
RAS to CAS Delay         : 3T
DRAM R/W Leadoff Timing  : 6T/5T
DRAM Turbo Read Leadoff  : Disabled
DRAM Speculative Leadoff : Enabled
Turn-Around Insertion    : Disabled
Turbo Read Pipelining    : Disabled
```

This picture presents the default settings of an Award BIOS (in this case, an Asus T2P4 motherboard) for 60-ns DRAMs, which are not the speed optimum.

```
Auto Configuration      : 60ns DRAM
DRAM Read Burst Timing   : x222
DRAM Write Burst Timing  : x333
RAS to CAS Delay         : 3T
DRAM R/W Leadoff Timing  : 6T/5T
DRAM Turbo Read Leadoff  : Disabled
DRAM Speculative Leadoff : Enabled
Turn-Around Insertion    : Disabled
Turbo Read Pipelining    : Disabled
```

This picture shows the improved timing values (three values were changed). They run nearly all 60-ns DRAMs (FP and EDO) in a stable manner and about 5% faster.

Finally, there are also error-correction settings in the Chipset Features BIOS for a few BIOSes with **ECC-capable chipsets** These boards automatically recognize whether RAMs with Parity (72-bit width) or without parity (64 bits) are inserted. It's only possible if true 72-bit RAMs are used employ the ECC-error correction of 1-bit errors in the BIOS by enabling the Memory parity SERR# (NMI) option.

```
DRAM are 64 (Not 72) bits wide
Memory parity SERR# (NMI): Disabled
```

If 64-bit DRAMs are used without parity, as in this case, the BIOS will recognize this automatically and switch the ECC-error correction to Disabled.

A few SDRAMs settings are frequently not optimized

SDRAM settings in the BIOS are found on only the few boards that are able to provide true support to the new memory chips (see Chapter 4). However, no manufacturer has yet been able to make full use of the possibilities of SDRAMs. While access speeds up to 10 ns can be addressed, they cannot thus far be exploited on any motherboard known to us. The best settings are still 50 ns and are limited to a few extra options for the definition of the refresh times.

The SDRAM settings on most motherboards therefore depend on the auto-configuration settings of the DRAM-access speeds. If you're eager for a tuning experiment, disable the auto-configuration and change the settings of the few SDRAM options manually to the lowest possible values.

As a rule, the refresh times, as in the case of normal DRAMs (see above), are given in processor cycle using the RAS- and/or CAS-accesses (SDRAM RAS# Timing or SDRAM CAS# Latency).

Using the auto-configuration defaults with the lowest access time (usually 60 or 50 ns) as a point of departure, attempt to reduce these values. The SDRAM Speculative Leadoff function speeds up the first part of the burst access for normal DRAMs, so if possible, set it to Enabled.

Turbo loader for the memory—setting and optimizing the LI and L2 caches in the BIOS

We already discussed the function and design of the L2 cache in Chapter 4. In this section we'll deal with the actual configuration of the cache chips that, even on modern motherboards, are not nearly as versatile as RAM. One or two settings for the L1 cache are occasionally integrated into the processor. However, these are restricted to enabling or disabling the cache and selecting the operating mode.

```
Auto Configuration        : 60ns DRAM
DRAM Read Burst Timing     : x222
DRAM Write Burst Timing    : x222
DRAM R/W Leadoff Timing    : 10T/6T
DRAM RAS# Precharge Time   : 3T
Refresh RAS# Assertion     : 4T
Fast EDO Lead Off          : Disabled
Speculative Leadoff        : Enabled
SDRAM RAS# Timing          : 3T/5T/8T
SDRAM CAS# Latency         : 3T
SDRAM Speculative Read     : Disabled
```

The automatic defaults for SDRAMs (in the case of an Asus TX97 motherboard) do not get the maximum from the fast SDRAM chips; these should be changed.

The most important settings in the BIOS for the two caches are explained below. Most current BIOSes allow their enabling or disabling in the BIOS Features Setup. This makes sense only if an old but still used DOS game simply refuses to run at the high speed of a Pentium.

◆ You can affect the on or off setting of the L1 or L2 cache using the CPU Internal Cache or External Cache options in BIOS Features Setup. Set both options to Enabled.

◆ The working mode of the cache on some 486 motherboards can be set either to the slow Write Through Mode or the fast Write Back Mode. In the more modern Write Back Mode, write accesses to the CPU are buffered in a working memory of the L1/2 cache by first gathering together the address data and then transmitting it asynchronously (independently of the CPU) to the main memory. In the obsolete Write Through Mode, write commands are sent to the memory unbuffered and separately, which doesn't make proper use of the principle of a cache and is clearly slower.

In any case, only the last of the 486 series (for example, the Enhanced AMD 486-120WB) as well as all Pentiums are in a position to use the cache in this mode. If a corresponding option is available in your BIOS for one or both caches, attempt to set them both to Write Back (WB). If only one can run in this mode, let it be the larger L2 cache.

You should be aware that the 486 processors absolutely require a motherboard or BIOS that permits enabling of the Write Back Mode, because the operation of the PC is otherwise very unstable. In the case of current Pentium motherboards, the function is enabled by default.

```
CPU Internal Cache    : Auto
External Cache        : Write Back
```

Both caches should be active if possible on 486 boards and running in the Write-Back Mode.

◆ A few motherboards have settings for the amount of memory which can be cached. In some AMI BIOSes, there may be an Above 16 MByte Cacheable entry. If you have 16 or fewer Megs of RAM, set this option to Disabled and the PC will then run a bit faster. Cache is used better for small amounts of memory using this function. You must switch the settings to Enabled when you have more memory. Otherwise, your PC will run very, very slow.

◆ Modern L2 caches likewise work in Burst mode, which can rarely be configured in the BIOS. A few special tools such as AmiSetup and TweakBIOS let you change the default BIOS values. If a setting of the burst access values in the BIOS is possible, the command will usually be called Pipeline Cache Timing or similar name. In that case, you can choose from several options such as Fast, Faster or Fastest.

Set the fastest timing possible, which is in part possible only for small caches. Anyone going from 256 to 512 K must often reduce the values. The burst-accesses of modern L2 pipelined-burst caches occur in two groups of four of the type xyyy / zyyy, which should amount to 3-1-1-1 / 1-1-1-1 for 256 K and 3-1-1-1 / 2-1-1-1 for 512 K. The asynchronous L2 caches of old 486 and Pentium boards operate, on the other hand, only with a slow access of the type x-3-3-3.

◆ The option CPU Fast String (or Fast String Move) is also found in the BIOS of some Pentium Pro or Pentium II systems. This enables the String Move command mode of the L1 caches in the processor, which leads to increased performance. Therefore, always set this option to Enabled.

THE OPTIMAL BIOS SETTINGS FOR ISA AND PCI BUSES

The BIOS contains many settings for the ISA bus and the PCI bus. However, very little speed advantage can be gained from tuning these settings. The manufacturer usually always used the best settings as the default configuration. It's very important to understand the options and the mechanisms associated with them in case of problems with the PC or unusual hardware configurations. For example, many MPEG cards use bus mastering to send data to the video card over the PCI bus will not work until some PCI settings in the BIOS have been changed.

The settings described below are grouped by topic and found for the most part in the Chipset Features BIOS (Award) or Advanced Chipset Setup (AMI). As in the earlier sections, the wording can differ depending on the motherboard. Also, certain settings are not even present in some configurations.

Rarely used settings for the ISA bus

Settings for ISA cards or the ISA bus are almost gone from current mother boards. Not only has the ISA bus become much less important, it's also relatively uncomplicated and needs little configuration. One item still relevant is the use of resources (IRQ, DMA, etc.) by ISA cards. It's set in the Plug & Play BIOS and we'll talk about it more later.

The ISA bus is rather unassuming. If the corresponding settings are still available in your BIOS (usually in Chipset Features Setup), they mostly concern the coupling to the system clock. Remember that the ISA bus should be clocked at the most with only 8.3 MHz. One function was already discussed in the section on memory settings (see the information in this chapter): it is possible to block 16 Megs of the main memory for a few particularly stubborn ISA cards. But now a brief description of two frequently occurring options:

◆ The clocking of the ISA bus can still be set (usually) only on old 486 boards, where the subdivision ratio relative to the external system clock (in the case of 486es, 33, 40 or 50 MHz) must be entered. For the usual 33 MHz, this is one fourth the external processor clock. The option is usually called ISA Bus Clock; as a setting, you have to select the fraction of the external processor clock (PCLK). A bit of testing is required.

```
ISA Bus Clock         : 1/4 PCLK
CPU Internal Cache    : Auto
```

In the case of the 33 MHz external processor clock, the clock rate of the ISA bus should be set to ¼ (8.25 MHz). A setting of $^1/_3$ (11 MHz) lies outside the specification. It would have a speed-up effect on the PC as a whole only by using an ISA video card.

◆ It's possible in many BIOSes to define a wait cycle for ISA cards. However, this is necessary only with very old cards or those of very poor quality that are unable to deliver your data as quickly as it can be processed by the fast CPU. This can result in system crashes or lockups. Defining an extended recovery time for data I/O (I/O = Input/Output) gives the card more time to get ready for the next transmission. The names of the settings options are 16-Bit I/O Recovery Time and 8-Bit I/O Recovery Time for 16-bit or 8-bit ISA cards and are found in Chipset Features Setup. The times are entered in system cycles and must of course be longer for 8-bit cards than for 16-bit cards. It may be possible to achieve improved performance here using reduced values (except for sound cards).

```
16-bit I/O Recory Time    : 5 BUSCLK
8-bit I/O Recory Time     : 8 BUSCLK
```

The default settings for the recovery time of ISA cards on older motherboards specify five cycles for 16-bit and eight for 8-bit cards.

◆ A few ISA cards require memory addresses in the adapter segment (between 640 and 1024 K) because they must, for example, use it to address their own ROM-BIOS on the card. But because the regions of the adapter segment are also used for shadowing or as DOS expansion memory, problems arise frequently with such cards. For this purpose, you can have a memory block reserved from all other functions in the Plug & Play BIOS by defining a starting address and a block size (up to a maximum of 64 K). The command for this is ISA MEM Block BASE.

```
DMA  1 Used By ISA : Yes
DMA  3 Used By ISA : Yes
DMA  5 Used By ISA : Yes

ISA MEM Block BASE : No/ICU
```

If you enable it, the option ISA Mem Block Size will be displayed just below it. Use ISA MEM Block BASE to select the starting address of the adapter segment (for example, D800). Then determine the size of the memory block using ISA Mem Block Size. A large memory block will border upon the maximum upper starting address.

Reserving a memory block in the adapter segment for ISA cards usually remains turned off. You'll find further settings which control the interaction of the ISA and PCI bus immediately below in the section on the configuration of the PCI bus in the BIOS.

Setting the timing of the VESA Local Bus in the BIOS

Since we are busy with the settings for outmoded bus systems, we should also mention the VL bus. If you still have such a computer, set the timing of the VL bus in the BIOS as a function of the internal processor frequency. Use the Local Bus Timing option for this, which you nearly always set to ¼ the processor frequency. You can experiment with higher rates, but these usually lead to problems.

BIOS settings for busmastering, burst access and more

Today's PCs have several settings for the PCI bus. This bus also has many functions (see Chapter 5) that let you optimize and configure it precisely. Most settings for this area are found in Chipset Feature Setup. An exception is the Plug & Play configuration, which is in its own section.

First, let's consider the configuration of the PCI functions. Most of the settings described below should already have been set correctly in the BIOS by the manufacturer. However, check them anyway — optimizing the PCI bus is one of the most important PC tuning factors. When you use exotic hardware cards, such as video capture card or MPEG cards, you'll often need a fairly extensive knowledge of the BIOS settings. That should, however, no longer be a problem if you have read the background on the PCI bus in Chapter 5 and the following recommendations. The first two setting options are still concerned with the interaction of the PCI bus with the ISA bus. Next we'll talk about those options specific to the PCI bus.

◆ Defining the latency time of the PCI bus occurs in the Plug & Play menu of the BIOS. Use the PCI Latency Timer entry to establish (in clock cycles of the PCI bus) how long a PCI card may tie up the bus before releasing it for data transmission by another card or the ISA bus. If a small latency time is selected, the PCI card must release the bus to others more quickly. This can be important with time-critical processes on the ISA bus (for example, with audio or network cards). If you use a PCI card requiring a high bandwidth with the fewest possible interruptions (for example, a video capture card), the value may need to be increased. The default value in the Award BIOS is 32 and is somewhat higher in other BIOSes. The bandwidth extends from 0-255 but settings of 30-40 are optimal for most PCs and BIOS versions. In case there are problems with certain cards or time-critical processes (hard drive recording, video capture, etc.), experiment with these settings.

◆ Another entry which regulates the interaction of PCI and ISA cards is PCI/VGA Palette Snoop in BIOS Features Setup. In the Enabled setting, it allows an ISA card to synchronize its color palette with a PCI video card. This is necessary, for example, in the case of ISA-MPEG or VGA-TV converters. Otherwise, strong color

```
PNP OS Installed    : Yes
Slot 1 (RIGHT) IRQ : NA
Slot 2 IRQ          : NA
Slot 3 IRQ          : 11
Slot 4 (LEFT) IRQ  : NA
PCI Latency Timer  :  32 PCI Clock
```

The latency-time settings of the PCI bus are not in Chipset Features Setup but are found in the Plug & Play menu.

errors result on the monitor or viewer, or the ISA card may not work. In all other cases, if you have no ISA cards which exchange data directly with the PCI video card, we recommend setting the entry to Disabled because it will act as a brake on performance.

```
PCI/VGA Palette Snoop    : Disabled  Typem
```

This function, necessary only for ISA cards that exchange data with PCI video cards, should normally be disabled.

◆ Like the CPU and the L2 cache, PCI cards can also access memory through burst mode or be addressed from the CPU. On many mother boards, burst mode for the PCI bus is enabled by default and is no longer found in the BIOS on new Pentium boards. If present, the entry names are usually PCI Burst Mode (AMI-BIOS) or CPU to PCI Burst (Award). Switch these to Enabled. Only the very first PCI cards (for example, video cards with the S3-928 chip) sometimes have problems with that.

```
CPU to PCI Burst Write  : Enabled
PCI Burst to Main Memory: Enabled
```

Not only can the CPU address the PCI bus in burst mode, but the PCI bus can also address the memory. The option of enabling or disabling both settings is still found only on older motherboards.

◆ Less frequently encountered is an option like Max. Burstable Range. The value entered there determines the size of the data blocks which are transferred to the PCI bus in burst mode. The setting in this case is 0.5 KBytes and should normally not be changed. Larger values no longer lead to higher performance for the most part, but only to data losses on many PCI cards.

◆ The busmaster controller of the PCI bus allows PCI cards to carry out many actions automatically without processor support. It's possible using the Peer Concurrency function to access not only the busmaster controller but the processor can also simultaneously access the PCI card. That is very important for the exchange of data with graphics and video cards and should be set to Enabled. Only old PCI cards have any problem with that, which you'll quickly notice.

Chapter 6

◆ A comparable function which enables a rapid transfer of data by the block to the PCI bus is PCI Streaming. Also switch this to Enabled.

◆ What busmastering is for the PCI bus, DMA operation is for the ISA bus. To prevent an ISA card from being able to block the simultaneous operation of the PCI bus through DMA mode, switch the Passive Release function to Enabled. This function can lead to crashes on the PCI bus if the ISA card using DMA (sound cards, some SCSI controllers) transfers too much data.

◆ Using the Chipset Global Features function, PCI bus mastering is simultaneously applied to all PCI slots, which allows maximum speed but at the same time also assumes maximum compatibility among the PCI cards used. This point is critical when using an MPEG card and video capture card if they use bus mastering to write data into the graphics memory. If you do have problems with such cards, then switch the function to Disabled. This somewhat increases the CPU loading during operation, but leads to a stable PC.

```
Peer Concurrency        : Enabled
PCI Streaming           : Enabled
Passive Release         : Enabled
Chipset Global Features : Enabled
```

These four most important settings for the PCI bus should (in the case of a typical Award BIOS (Asus T2P4-motherboard)) be set to Enabled.

◆ Only Phoenix and Award BIOSes exploit the capability of the PCI bus to receive data transferred from the processor using a buffer. So in these cases, the CPU will not have to wait for the PCI bus in order to execute a transfer; it can deposit data in a temporary buffer (postings), from which the PCI controller can fetch it independently. That unburdens the CPU. The function is enabled using the options CPU/PCI Memory Write or CPU to PCI Write Buffer. This option is the default on many motherboards and is therefore no longer found in the BIOS.

◆ The setting CPU/PCI Write Delay is still found only in the Award BIOS. There the wait cycles (in processor cycles), which the processor must insert before it can again transfer data to the PCI bus, are defined. It should be set to the lowest possible value.

◆ Only rarely, in the case of a few Award BIOSes, is it still possible to set the PCI-clock frequency relative to the system bus. This is normally permanently coupled to the system bus with a factor of 0.5. The entry is called PCI Clock Frequency (or the like) and is useful particularly for overclocking the system bus (see the information in this chapter), to hold the clock frequency of the PCI bus to the recommended 33 MHz.

TIPS AND OPTIONS FOR INTERFACES AND PERIPHERALS

We cannot forget that interfaces on the motherboard still have an important role to play. We cannot ignore the BIOS here either because and it has several interesting options that can give your PC that extra bit of performance.

The following tips concern all settings for floppy drives, printer ports or serial interfaces. You won't get greater speed from these tweaks, but you can solve many IRQ problems by cleverly manipulating the resource assignments.

Turbo tape and gaining 15% more speed

If you run a QIC80 or Travan Streamer drive on the controller of the floppy drive, you can gain 10-15% during data transfer by changing BIOS settings for the floppy controller. The trick is simple: Change the diskette capacity in the Standard CMOS Setup from 1.44 to 2.88 Megs. It does have one disadvantage however. You'll need to change the default in all programs for formatting from 2.88 to 1.44 Megs, whenever you work with normal diskettes.

```
Drive A : 1.44M, 3.5 in.
Drive B : None
Floppy 3 Mode Support : Disabled          Base Memory:    640K
                                          Extended Memory: 64512K
                                          Other Memory:    384K
Video   : EGA/VGA
Halt On : All,But Keyboard                Total Memory: 65536K
```

If you run a floppy streamer, set the default under Drive A in the Standard CMOS Setup from 1.44 Megs to 2.88 Megs. Data transfer will then take place more quickly.

Save on resources, solve problems—Advantages from interface configuration

Many users pay little attention to the fact that you can configure the interfaces (the serial ports, printer port, mouse port, infrared connection) in the BIOS. It is normally correct, of course, that these be left in the default setting, but here are examples of solving problems by making changes:

◆ If possible, use the PS/2-mouse connector available on most of today's motherboards. The mouse run more quietly and you'll open a serial interface for other devices. For many BIOSes, you must still explicitly release IRQ12 for the mouse port. The command is called PS/2 mouse function control or something similar. Most current motherboards support such use automatically.

Chapter 6

> **NOTE**
>
> **The mouse business—When the PS/2 connector is absent**
>
> Most motherboards provide complete support for a PS/2 mouse, even if there is no plug present. But it is possible to install one; located right beside the keyboard connector is usually a four- to six-pin plug bar, on which a PS/2 adapter can be installed for $5 - $75. Ask your dealer.

◆ Change the assignment of the serial interfaces (COM1 to COM2). Frequently the COM1 interface is equipped with a nine pin connector; the COM2 port with a 25-pin connector. Depending upon what device you want to connect to the available cable, it can be helpful to change the two interface designations for the operating system. For that you need only switch the default values for the two interfaces in the BIOS.

```
Onboard Serial Port 1    : 3F8H/IRQ4
Onboard Serial Port 2    : 2F8H/IRQ3
Onboard Parallel Port    : 3BCH/IRQ7
```

The assignment of the COM1 and COM2 designations in the operating system can be interchanged quite easily in the BIOS using these settings.

◆ The interrupts are already very scarce especially on EIDE computers. However, if you need to install another plug-in card but don't have a free IRQ, consider whether one of the two serial interfaces can be disabled. Remember, you can disable any port in the BIOS. The only requirement is that the new plug-in card can be configured to IRQ3 or 4.

◆ Of course, a normal motherboard (LPT1 and LPT2) do not two parallel interfaces. However, a second printer port can be installed for a few dollars using a small plug-in card. Manuals are rarely included with these inexpensive cards and often the configuration is difficult. Because the cards are usually configured as LPT1, simply set the original printer port to LPT2. To do this you must change the resource assignment for the command Onboard Parallel Port Mode from 378H/IRQ7 or 3BCH/IRQ7 (default settings) to 278H/IRQ5.

Most recent motherboards have infrared support built-in but it's seldom used. Also, few boards have integrated the necessary connectors or transmitters. Nevertheless, the IrDa-port (Infrared port) for many PCs is enabled in the at the factory. That leads to two unpleasant problems: First, it occupies the COM2 interface (which no longer functions for modems, etc.). Second, the IrDa-mode also reserves one of the DMA channels. Therefore, set the UART2 Use Infrared option in the BIOS to Disabled. The setting should be Enabled only if you want to exchange data with a printer or notebook using infrared and have a transmitter for your motherboard.

UART2 Use Infrared   : Disabled

Normally the infrared support in the Chipset Features BIOS should be disabled, as it is here.

Turbo drive for the printer port

The parallel interface can be used for more than just printing. The parallel transfer of data using the printer connection give acceptable performance for network connections and connecting data storage media (ZIP drives, for example) or scanners.

However, the LPT mode normally used for the parallel interface is no longer adequate for all these new applications. Nevertheless, it does allow a transfer of data at a maximum rate of 300 K/sec with a data width of eight bits. The transfer is already bi-directional in the LPT mode. Many users misunderstand this.

It's possible on all motherboards to reset the working mode for the parallel interface from the conventional LPT mode to the EPP or ECP standard. That occurs in the Award BIOS, for example, in Chipset Features Setup. EPP and ECP were defined at the beginning of the 1990s by several manufacturers including Intel, Zenith, Hewlett Packard and Microsoft. Not only was the data-transfer rate increased to 0.5 - 2 Megs/sec, several devices (up to 128 in the case of ECP) could also now be controlled individually. That made it possible, for example, to put together a small network.

ECP is an expansion of EPP and uses an additional FIFO-buffer control similar to that used for the serial interface. Whereas EPP was developed only for non-printer terminal equipment, ECP also supports corresponding printers. But to be able to make use or EPP or ECP, however, the terminal equipment must also support the protocol. That is a crucial point that is often overlooked.

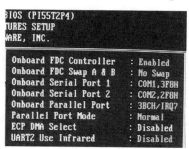

BIOS (PI55T2P4)	
TURES SETUP	
WARE, INC.	
Onboard FDC Controller	: Enabled
Onboard FDC Swap A & B	: No Swap
Onboard Serial Port 1	: COM1,3F8H
Onboard Serial Port 2	: COM2,2F8H
Onboard Parallel Port	: 3BCH/IRQ7
Parallel Port Mode	: Normal
ECP DMA Select	: Disabled
UART2 Use Infrared	: Disabled

Normally, you need to set the parallel-port mode to Normal, because EPP or ECP is supported by only a few devices, but occupies an additional DMA channel.

It's acceptable for most current printers to leave the parallel port mode set to the standard LPT-port mode. Bi-directional communication with the printer is also possible in that case. Only if you connect devices such as a ZIP drive, streamer or scanner is it worthwhile to change the setting to EPP or, best of all, directly to ECP. In any case, that should be mentioned in the owner's manual accompanying the device.

There is, however, one catch. The computer in EPP/ECP mode will need a free interrupt and possibly also a DMA channel to operate. In fact, nearly all boards already reserve an interrupt for the standard mode (the default is IRQ 7), even though that is usually not even necessary for printing. A DMA channel, on the other hand, is not needed for the LPT mode. Reserving a DMA channel for EPP/ECP mode is usually no big deal, because pretty much only ISA cards still use one.

```
Onboard FDC Controller    : Enabled
Onboard FDC Swap A & B    : No Swap
Onboard Serial Port 1     : 3F8H/IRQ4
Onboard Serial Port 2     : 2F8H/IRQ3
Onboard Parallel Port     : 3BCH/IRQ7
Parallel Port Mode        : ECP+EPP
ECP DMA Select            : 3
UART2 Use Infrared        : Disabled
```

To squeeze the maximum performance from the printer port, change the entry under Parallel Port Mode from Normal (LPT Mode) to ECP+EPP. At the same time, a DMA channel (usually 3) must be entered under ECP DMA Select.

Windows 95 will also have to load a different driver when the setting is changed to EPP+ECP, otherwise this will not work. Thanks to Plug & Play, the driver change normally occurs automatically. The next time the computer boots, Windows will recognize the protocol change and correspondingly install the driver. Exactly the reverse will take place if you want to change back again the old LPT mode.

BIOS and USB support

Finally, we need to mention there are very few USB settings in the BIOS. Aside from enabling USB and maybe also a setting allowing the use of a USB keyboard, there are no further settings in the corresponding BIOSes. So, if you use USB or a USB keyboard, set the value to Enabled.

```
USB Function          Disabled
USB KeyBoard Support  Enabled
```

Only very few motherboards already possess complete USB support which, above and beyond these settings, must still be enabled in the BIOS.

Very important is the USB keyboard support seen in the picture. Many BIOSes support USB but do not provide full support to a USB keyboard with the same functions as a regular keyboard. The result is that when your computer locksup and you must get into the BIOS, it's only possible with a conventional keyboard which you must then connect to the computer. This is at best an inconvenience so you should be aware of this important detail.

THE GREEN SOUL OF THE PC—BIOS POWER MANAGEMENT UNDER THE MAGNIFYING GLASS

By using the Power Management Setup menu you can improve the power consumption of your PC.

The power-management functions of desktop PCs critically examined

Today's motherboards have a main menu in the BIOS that can be used to enable the various power-saving functions. However, the settings are not changed until power management is enabled in the operating system. So it's pointless to enter values in the BIOS if you have not also enabled the corresponding driver under DOS or Windows. For example, the POWER.EXE driver must be incorporated as a DEVICE command in the CONFIG.SYS under DOS and Windows 3.x. Power management in Windows 95 is enabled using the Power control panel.

If you work all day with your PC, we advise against enabling this function. Depending on the motherboard and the programs running, that Windows 95 becomes relatively unstable with power management. With Windows NT 4, an enabled power management even leads to massive problems, because it doesn't support a corresponding BIOS function.

The following commands have the following meanings (see figure further below):

♦ Using the command Power Management, you can essentially enable the power-saving mode for the first time. Choose between Disable, Min Saving, Max Saving and User Define. The last three settings enable the power-saving mode, in which case, for the first two options, default values for the remaining commands have already been entered in Power Management Setup. The setting Min Saving or User Define seems to make the most sense, because the longest reaction times can be enabled. When all is said and done, a desktop PC should not continually power down after not being used for a few minutes. Max Saving may make sense only when the PC is seldom used.

♦ Using the Video Off Option, you can select the steps to cover when a connected monitor is put to sleep. We generally advise against this function. If your monitor doesn't have its own power-saving mode, it also doesn't use the BIOS functions too much. But if it has a green function, select this instead. Only, for example, if you work under DOS and are therefore unable to activate the monitor's own mode due to lack of a driver, does it make sense to tun off Always On and switch on Susp, Stby → Off. In that case, the monitor will be powered down in the three usual steps (Suspend, Standby, Totally off).

♦ Under the Video Off Option, if one of the settings for enabling the monitor power-saving mode was selected, you must also specify the method by which that is to take place under Video Off Method. The available options are V/H SYNC + Blank, DMPS and Blank Only. The first option disables the vertical and horizontal line signals and switches the screen to black. This also activates the same actions in monitors with their own power-management system. DMPS is a setting only for modern video cards and monitors which support the

Display Power-Management Signaling Standard. In this case, the BIOS uses the DPMS-capable video card to put the monitor to sleep. With Blank Only, the screen is switched to black, but the line signal is not disabled. This setting is for old monitors without their own sleep mode and, like a normal screen saver, merely prevents the image from being burned into the tube. It doesn't save on power.

◆ Use the Suspend Switch command to enable the use of a power-saving switch on the motherboard. If you apply a switch to the corresponding contact on the motherboard, you can switch the computer into sleep mode at the press of a button, which we personally consider to be the best of all the possibilities for making intelligent use of power management. If your case doesn't have such a switch, you have two alternatives. First, you can misuse the turbo switch present on many housings and connect it to the suspend plug, or you can buy an additional switch in an electronics store and lead this to the outside through a small hole. The second alternative is a software solution, not directly comparable but with the same effect—enable the Standby command in the Windows 95 Start menu, as described later.

◆ Use Doze Speed (div by) and Stby Speed (div by) to determine what timing factor of the computer operation is reduced in the Doze Mode (the first powering down step of the motherboard) and Standby Operation (the second step of powering down). If the values 8 and 32 are selected, as in the example, the system frequency will be reduced by a factor of eight in the first enablement stage (Doze Mode), thus to 25 MHz in the case of a Pentium 200. In the Standby mode and then also in the Suspend mode, the frequency is reduced by a factor of 32 (to 6.25 MHz for a Pentium 200). This sufficiently reduces the power consumption of the processor without shutting it down completely.

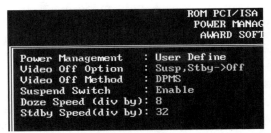

These settings in the Power Management Setup should provide a good starting point for most desktop PCs. For current monitors and video cards, the Video-Off Method can also be set to DPMS, but V/H SYCNC + Blank leads to the same result. With the setting Video Off Option Always On, the Video-Off method will have no effect.

◆ Use the lower settings in the ** PM Timers ** area to define the timing behavior of Power Management: at which times the usual three stages (Doze, Standby and Suspend) will be enabled. Using HDD Power Down, you can set the time (unfortunately, usually only from one to 15 minutes) after which EIDE hard drives are powered down. These values are much too low in our opinion, because a shutdown of the hard drives after a maximum of only 15 minutes is much too soon. We advise against enabling this option. Besides, SCSI hard drives are not affected by this. For Doze, Standby and Suspend Mode, you define the time (in values from one minute up to four hours) after which the first, second and third stage of the power-saving mode is enabled. These are freely selectable only if you selected User Define as the value under Power Management (above). Normally you should select really high values here (for example, one hour).

NOTE

And so it goes—Power-saving mode for SCSI hard drives

SCSI hard drives cannot be switched to the sleep mode from the computer BIOS, but they can be put to sleep. You simply need a special program, like that from Adaptec in the familiar EZ-SCSI program pack supplied with your SCSI controllers.

◆ The connections by which the computer is powered up from the Suspend Mode are defined using the options in the ** PM Events ** area. The four most important (COM1, COM2, Real-Time Clock, PS/2-Mouse Port) interrupts that are usually used are listed in the lower left . However, in the area to the upper right you can check the enablement function for each individual interrupt from 3-15. Normally, enabling the serial interfaces or of the mouse port is enough; the keyboard operates at IRQ1, of course. Defining an additional IRQ on the right side makes sense, for example, with the use of a fax or ISDN card, if the computer is employed as a communications server.

```
                    ROM PCI/ISA BIOS (PI55T2P4)
                      POWER MANAGEMENT SETUP
                       AWARD SOFTWARE, INC.

  Power Management    : Min Saving    IRQ3  (COM 2)      : Disable
  Video Off Option    : Always On     IRQ4  (COM 1)      : Enable
  Video Off Method    : V/H SYNC+Blank IRQ5 (LPT 2)      : Enable
  Suspend Switch      : Enable        IRQ6  (Floppy Disk): Enable
  Doze Speed (div by) : 8             IRQ7  (LPT 1)      : Enable
  Stdby Speed(div by) : 32            IRQ8  (RTC Alarm)  : Disable
                                      IRQ9  (IRQ2 Redir) : Enable
         ** PM Timers **              IRQ10 (Reserved)   : Enable
  HDD Power Down      : Disable       IRQ11 (Reserved)   : Enable
  Doze Mode           : 1 Hour        IRQ12 (PS/2 Mouse) : Enable
  Standby Mode        : 1 Hour        IRQ13 (Coprocessor): Enable
  Suspend Mode        : 1 Hour        IRQ14 (Hard Disk)  : Enable
                                      IRQ15 (Reserved)   : Enable
         ** PM Events **
  IRQ3  (Wake-Up)     : Disable
  IRQ4  (Wake-Up)     : Enable        ESC : Quit        ↑↓→← : Select Item
  IRQ8  (Wake-Up)     : Disable       F1  : Help        PU/PD/+/- : Modify
  IRQ12 (Wake-Up)     : Enable        F5  : Old Values  (Shift)F2 : Color
                                      F6  : Load BIOS  Defaults
                                      F7  : Load Setup Defaults
```

You use the settings in the ** PM Events ** area to set the interrupts (and thus the devices attached to them) which, when active, will cause the computer to exit the power-saving mode and resume normal operation.

```
              ROM PCI/ISA BIOS (PVI-4SP3)
                POWER MANAGEMENT SETUP
                 AWARD SOFTWARE, INC.

Power Management   : User Define    IRQ3  (COM2)       : Enabled
Video Off Option   : Susp,Stby->Off IRQ4  (COM1)       : Enabled
Video Off Method   : DPMS           IRQ5  (LPT2)       : Enabled
Suspend Switch     : Enable         IRQ6  (Floppy Disk): Enabled
Doze Speed (div by): 8              IRQ7  (LPT1)       : Enabled
Stdby Speed(div by): 32             IRQ8  (RTC Alarm)  : Disabled
                                    IRQ9  (IRQ2 Redir) : Enabled
    ** PM Timers **                 IRQ10 (Reserved)   : Enabled
HDD Off After      : 10 Min         IRQ11 (Reserved)   : Enabled
Doze Mode          : 20 Sec         IRQ12 (PS/2 Mouse) : Enabled
Standby Mode       : 10 Min         IRQ13 (Coprozessor): Enabled
Suspend Mode       : 10 Min         IRQ14 (Hard Disk)  : Enabled
                                    IRQ15 (Reserved)   : Enabled
    ** PM Events **
PCI Master Activity: Enable
COM Ports Activity : Enable        ESC : Quit         ↑↓←→ : Select Item
LPT Ports Activity : Enable        F1  : Help         PU/PD/+/- : Modify
HDD Ports Activity : Enable        F5  : Old Values   (Shift)F2 : Color
DMA Ports Activity : Enable        F6  : Load BIOS Defaults
VGA Activity       : Disabled      F7  : Load Setup Defaults
```

On older computers, in this case a 486 motherboard, more general designations are used for the predefined group to the lower left, instead of IRQ numbers. That was so a beginner could easily determine to which interrupt the LPT or COM port was connected.

A Power-saving annoyance with Windows 95

If you're interested in saving power, experiment with the power-management settings in the Windows 95 control panel. All too frequently, the compatibility mode for APM 1.0 standard (**A**dvanced **P**ower **M**anagement) in the Advanced Settings is not enabled, even though that is nearly always the correct setting. Moreover, the Disable Automatic Charge-Status Query checkbox on a PC should be enabled, because it is not necessary in this case to check a battery continually for its charge, as in the case of a notebook.

Select the Power Control Panel, allow Windows to control power management and click [Advanced], to enable these settings.

You can also have the Standby Mode command displayed in the Start menu. To do that, select the Advanced tab, as shown in the figure, and enable the Display Standby-Mode in the Start menu checkbox. This command replaces the Suspend switch on the housing and is a very practical means of putting your PC on standby.

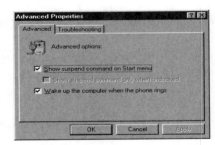

This is how to enable the option. The command Standby Mode will then be displayed in the Start menu.

This picture shows how the new command can be used to put the PC to sleep with a mouse click.

The power-management functions of new boards and operating systems

The current power management systems do leave something to be desired. Intel and Microsoft seem to be aware of this. Microsoft has for that reason defined a PC97 specification (there's already an upgrade: PC98) which provides, among other things, expanded power-management functions. The new power-saving standard is called ACPI (**A**dvanced **C**onfiguration and **P**ower **I**nterface) and contains more flexible and extensive power-saving functions for the PC. This must, of course, be supported by the operating system, which will first take place with Windows 98.

As is so frequently the case, hardware development is again ahead of the software department. The first motherboards with ACPI support are already available. These are boards with the new Intel Pentium chipset 430TX (for example, the Asus TX97). But VIA also already supports ACPI with its VP2 chipset. Of course, there is still little to be gained with these functions, but that will quickly change as soon as Windows 98 comes out. One of the best improvements associated with that will be OnNow, which means that in the future the PC will be ready for operation in a few seconds right after being turned on, without booting. In other words, just as though it had been in the power-saving mode.

PLUG & PLAY BIOS—AWAY WITH WASTED IRQS AND RESOURCE CONFLICTS

All PC users should be familiar with the Plug & Play BIOS (PNP and PCI Setup). Assigning the interrupts for the individual plug-in cards of the ISA and PCI buses are set here. Since this is perhaps the most frequent source of resource conflicts, configuring these settings correctly is very important.

Not only can you avoid or solve resource conflicts here, but you may be able to free wasted resources for other equipment. Unfortunately, most BIOSes simply throw away interrupts in the base settings with which they are delivered. We'll talk about this in more detail soon. First, let's turn to the general commands in PNP and PCI Setup.

Away with auto-functions—You'll be better off entering the interrupt settings for the PCI bus yourself

One of the great advantages of the PCI bus is its Plug & Play capability (often abbreviated to PnP). However, you may still experience problems relying on PnP. The function is good for starting the first functions and driver calls when installing a card, for example, but then we recommend checking it carefully after that.

Because PnP is helpful only if a compatible operating system is installed (currently only Windows 95), it's nice that the function can now be disabled on a few motherboards.

Chapter 6

> **NOTE**
>
> **What's an INTA?—The somewhat different interrupts of PCI**
>
> The good old resources, like DMA channels and interrupts, are now history for the PCI bus and are relevant only for the ISA bus. DMA channels were actually replaced by bus mastering. And the PCI bus uses its own procedure for interrupts. There are four interrupt signals available for each slot, called the INT A-D# or INT 1-4#. But because most cards and operating systems work through the conventional IRQ system, the interrupt signals can be mapped to IRQs. This makes scarcely any difference to the user, except that he will be confronted with the INTx# concepts during the configuration of many cards and/or BIOSes. Most BIOSes likewise continue to display interrupts instead of INT# assignments during PCI-PnP configuration, just as Windows 95 will have nothing to do with INT# in the Device Manager. For the most part, all PCI slots are configured to use a common INT number (for example, INTA#), so that all cards (when necessary) must be set as a group to this INT number. But in the BIOS, a conventional IRQ for each slot will still be assigned for compatibility reasons. It makes little difference to the user, so long as everything operates well.

The basis of PnP is the PnP and PCI Setup menu in the BIOS. This is where the permanent assignment of interrupts to the individual slots of the PCI bus can be established before installing the card. Furthermore, certain interrupts can be reserved for the ISA bus to avoid conflicts with ISA cards. The same is true for the DMA channels, which are relevant only for the ISA bus. The BIOS ignores other resources, such as memory addresses. Even if the operating system finds no multiple assignments, a resource conflict is still easily possible despite PnP-BIOS. Unfortunately, that happens frequently.

```
                 ROM PCI/ISA BIOS (PI55T2P4)
                      PNP AND PCI SETUP
                    AWARD SOFTWARE, INC.

Slot 1 (RIGHT) IRQ : NA        DMA  1 Used By ISA : Yes
Slot 2 IRQ         : NA        DMA  3 Used By ISA : Yes
Slot 3 IRQ         : 10        DMA  5 Used By ISA : Yes
Slot 4 (LEFT) IRQ  : NA
PCI Latency Timer  :  32 PCI Clock   ISA MEM Block BASE : No/ICU

                               MCR SCSI BIOS       : Disabled

IRQ  3 Used By ISA : No/ICU
IRQ  4 Used By ISA : No/ICU
IRQ  5 Used By ISA : Yes
IRQ  7 Used By ISA : Yes
IRQ  9 Used By ISA : Yes
IRQ 10 Used By ISA : Yes
IRQ 11 Used By ISA : Yes
IRQ 12 Used By ISA : No/ICU
IRQ 14 Used By ISA : No/ICU    ESC : Quit        ↑↓→← : Select Item
IRQ 15 Used By ISA : Yes       F1  : Help        PU/PD/+/- : Modify
                               F5  : Old Values  (Shift)F2 : Color
                               F6  : Load BIOS Defaults
                               F7  : Load Setup Defaults
```

The interrupt and DMA channels for the ISA and PCI bus are defined in PnP and the PCI-Setup BIOS. Reserving resources for the ISA bus is valid only for old ISA cards without Plug & Play capability.

Let's return to the settings in the PnP and PCI Setup menu.

◆ If a PnP-capable operating system (currently only Windows 95) is not used, it makes little sense to enable the PnP function in the BIOS. Therefore, recent motherboards let you switch off the PNP operating system support. The command PNP OS Installed (in the upper-left corner of the PnP and PCI Setup) should only be set to Yes when Windows 95 (or a successor) is being used. The No setting, on the other hand, is better for Windows NT or Windows 3.x.

◆ The very important assignment of interrupts or INT numbers (see the above information box) occurs with the entries Slot 1 (RIGHT) IRQ to Slot 4 (LEFT) IRQ. With these you can establish what numbers will be used for each of the four 4 PCI slots. If you're not certain, Slot 1 is the first slot next to the power supply.

In the Auto setting, which you should avoid, the BIOS will assign to each slot the first free IRQ it finds. That is won't help because it assigns an IRQ even to cards which do not need one (for example, video cards). So try to disable the mandatory assignment, particularly for all PCI video cards, by selecting NA. You'll then find out the next time you boot up whether the card will actually run without the IRQ. First disable each empty PCI slot with NA. When you install a new card, you can then manually assign it a suitable IRQ. The Windows 95 Device Manager can tell you which IRQs are still free (see the information in this chapter). You'll then avoid conflicts and use your precious resources more efficiently. Besides, only the upper 16-bit IRQs (9, 10, 11, 12, 14 and 15) are used for PCI cards, which means that IRQs 12, 14 and 15 are already occupied on EIDE systems with a PS/2 mouse. Only three IRQs thus still remain free for PCI cards, and certain ISA cards frequently also lay claim to IRQ 9. That can get very tight.

```
PNP OS Installed      : Yes
Slot 1 (RIGHT) IRQ  : NA
Slot 2 IRQ              : NA
Slot 3 IRQ              : 11
Slot 4 (LEFT) IRQ     : NA
```

The Plug & Play settings of the PCI slots are configured using the commands in the upper-left corner of the PnP and PCI Setup. Disable the IRQ assignment for video cards and assign an IRQ to each of the other cards manually.

ID	Device Class	IRQ
0	IDE Controller	15
8	Mass storage controller	10
D	Display controller	NA

PCI device listing.....						
Bus No.	Device No.	Func No.	Vendor ID	Device ID	Device Class	IRQ
0	1	1	8886	7111	IDE Controller	14/15
0	1	2	8885	7112	Serial bus controller	NA
0	10	0	10B7	9001	Network controller	11
0	12	0	5333	8BC0	Unknown PCI device	NA

Most of the new motherboards will display a configuration list of the PCI bus when you boot up. The image with Device Class and IRQ shows the devices and their IRQ assignments. As you see, the video card ("display controller") needs no interrupt. The mass storage controller is a SCSI controller.

Chapter 6

The IRQ and DMA configuration of the ISA bus is used mainly for the remaining options in PnP and PCI Setup. However, keep in mind that both the IRQ and the DMA assignments are valid only for ISA cards without Plug & Play capability. You can reserve an IRQ or DMA channel for conventional ISA cards from the list of commands (IRQ x Used By ISA or DMA x Used By ISA). Then it will not be grabbed by the PCI bus (which only occurs with the Auto setting).

The possible settings for the commands are Yes (reserving an IRQ or DMA for non-PnP cards) or No/ICU. The last option assumes you have a PnP card whose IRQ or DMA is assigned automatically by Windows 95 or by the ISA Configuration Utility from Intel. You can probably download this utility from the website of the motherboard manufacturer (for example, http://www.asus. com/downloads/bios-dl.asp#utility). This utility is installed as a driver in CONFIG.SYS. It configures the ISA card if the operating system can't do it. Our point here is that if you don't have problems with old ISA cards that cannot be assigned an IRQ or DMA under Windows, then reserve the desired value here. In most cases, however, the settings can be left at No/ICU.

We've already talked about the settings behind the ISA MEM Block BASE entry relevant for the ISA bus. This command can reserve an area in memory in the range between 640 K and 1,024 K (Adapter Segment) for ISA cards, if necessary. However, isn't necessary very often — normally you can leave the setting at No/ICU.

```
PNP OS Installed      : Yes
Slot 1 (RIGHT) IRQ : NA
Slot 2 IRQ            : NA
Slot 3 IRQ            : 11
Slot 4 (LEFT) IRQ    : NA
PCI Latency Timer   :  32 PCI Clock


IRQ  3 Used By ISA : No/ICU
IRQ  4 Used By ISA : No/ICU
IRQ  5 Used By ISA : No/ICU
IRQ  7 Used By ISA : No/ICU
IRQ  9 Used By ISA : No/ICU
IRQ 10 Used By ISA : Yes
IRQ 11 Used By ISA : No/ICU
IRQ 12 Used By ISA : No/ICU
IRQ 14 Used By ISA : No/ICU
IRQ 15 Used By ISA : No/ICU
```

Reserving IRQs, DMAs and a memory address in the PnP and PCI Setup is valid only for non-PnP ISA cards. Windows 95 is capable of correctly assigning resources in the BIOS for most cards of this type. So in normal cases, leave the settings disabled.

Overclocking—Risky Or A Stroke Of Tuning Genius?

Overclocking is intentionally speeding up the clock used by the processor and/or system bus to levels above the values which the manufacturer has found acceptable. But before we continue with this section, please read and understand the following note/warning. It is <u>very</u> important that you understand it.

> **NOTE**
>
> **Overclocking is dangerous: Proceed with caution**
>
> Overclocking is the term for intentionally speeding up the clock used by the processor and/or system bus to levels above the values which the manufacturer has found acceptable. Overclocking must be considered and carried out with extreme care. You'll void warranties and guarantees by overclocking and damaging a processor. **We're assume no responsibility for the information in this section or wherever overclocking is mentioned in this book.** Again, overclocking must be considered and carried out with extreme care.

The politics of overclocking

Overclocking is not new. Users since the 486es were "new" have managed to pump up their processors with all sorts of clock frequencies. However quite a stir was caused recently when a few motherboard producers brought out motherboards with the option of 75 or even 83 MHz. Asus was the first with its P55T2P4-board and others have since followed suit.

However, there have been rumors behind the scenes at Intel. Therefore, many motherboard have held back or even issued recall notices. Intel may not worry too much whether users overclock CPUs (when they break, you then have to buy a new one), its reaction to the topic *faster clocking of the system bus* is highly sensitive. According to Intel, from which all important specifications for processors, system bus and PCI bus originate, the clock frequency is 66 MHz for the system bus and 33 MHz for the PCI bus, period. Any more than that is unacceptable because the computer can't keep pace.

Then Cyrix, for example, released its 6x86M1 and simply introduced 75 MHz for the system bus. The new 6x86MX, too, demands these higher clock frequencies. And apparently it works, if a few small changes are made in the motherboard (for example, an asynchronous coupling of the PCI bus).

Chapter 6

However, now apparently higher processor clock frequencies are no longer taboo subjects at Intel. A Pentium MMX with 233 MHz was suddenly "developed" following the introduction of the AMD K6. Also, the new Pentium II processors can suddenly also be driven with 300 MHz and even faster in the future. Best of all, however, is the fact that new boards will probably be developed for the Pentium II or its successors in 1998, which will very likely work with a system clock of up to 100 MHz. As already discussed in Chapter 4, Intel is apparently attempting to divide the market into a small, economy Pentium segment with lower performance and a clearly distinct high-end market for the Pentium II. The intent in that case is to reserve higher system-clock frequencies for the high-end market.

The basics and prerequisites for overclocking

We talked about the general principles for setting the processor and system bus timing in Chapter 4 so we won't repeat that information here. You can overclock your PC in two ways. They have the following goals and effects:

◆ By resetting the internal processor clock with a higher conversion factor (for example, by increasing the factor from 2.5 for a Pentium 166 to 3.0 for 200 MHz). That would be the old, let us say, trivial method.

◆ By increasing the external processor frequency (system-bus clock) from the current 50 MHz to 60, 66, 75 or 83 MHz. This works only on one of the new boards which support the higher frequency.

On nearly all motherboards, the multiplier and system clock are set by means of jumpers near the processor socket. A few of the new jumperless boards, such those from Abit, do this through the BIOS.

Anyone wanting to skillfully overclock should note very carefully how the two methods mutually influence one another and how they affect the other PC components. We're already mentioned many times how the internal processor frequency is determined from the multiplier and the system-bus frequency. As a reminder, the PCI bus is tied to the system bus with a factor of 0.5 (at least on most motherboards). An increase in the system frequency thus leads also to an overclocking of the PCI bus, which is frequently the critical element for overclocking.

> **NOTE**
>
> **Illegal motherboards?—Which boards play along**
>
> As already explained, new clock generators (PLL chips) are apparently necessary for faster clocking. Whereas most chips with the label ICS are found on old boards, the label on the 75- to 83-Mhz boards is PLL. In addition, the new boards usually have four instead of three jumpers for setting the clock frequencies. Buying according to the manufacturer makes little sense. The BAT boards are already frequently built with the new PLLs, but the ATX versions aren't yet (so it is with Asus). Most Pentium boards with the 430TX or VIA-VP2 chipset usually support at least 75 MHz, because this is also necessary for the Cyrix 6x86MX. Careful questioning of the dealer is necessary. Probably the two best-known boards at present with 83 Mhz are the Asus P55T2P4 and the Abit IT5H (both initially only in the BAT version).

The most important lesson to be learned from the new overclocking possibilities is that increasing the frequency of the system clock produces an increase in speed for the entire PC greater than that from an increase in the processor frequency. For that reason, a P166 (settings 83 MHz x 2 and 41.5-MHz PCI bus frequency) is at least equally as fast as a classic Pentium 200 (66 MHz x 3 and 33-MHz PCI bus frequency). In fact, the processor frequency starting from 166 MHz has only a slight effect upon total system performance, because the remaining components of the motherboard have a restrictive effect upon the speed. Thus also the strong influence of an increased system-bus frequency, from which, among other things, the L2 cache, main memory and PCI bus benefit.

The new motherboards provide many options allowing you to overclock your computer. Let's take the Pentium 166 as an example, for which the following settings are appropriate. Whether the very last of these settings, which have particularly high clock frequencies, will also really run in a stable manner remains an open question (and will be discussed very shortly).

System bus in MHz	Multiplier	Result in MHz
66	2.5	CPU= 166, PCI = 33
66	3 (Processor overclocked)	CPU = 200, PCI = 33
75	2.5	CPU = 187.5, PCI = 37.5
75	3	CPU = 225, PCI = 37.5
83	2.5	CPU = 207, PCI = 41.5
83	3	CPU = 249, PCI = 41.5

Chapter 6

What the manufacturers have to say about overclocking

It's little wonder motherboard producers have officially distanced themselves from overclocking. Intel's position is well known: Overclocking brings only misery but no blessing. We'll mention the dangers soon.

It is amazing, however, that ever increasing numbers of boards are nevertheless being supplied with this option. It seems a bit contradictory that, for example, the popular motherboard producer Asus warns on its home page against using 75- and 83-MHz clock frequencies and expressly points to the risks. At the same time, however, these boards are being built and even listed in the Internet pages where overclocking is discussed in a positive manner. The following is an original sentence from the Asus Internet site: "What you do is your business, but Asus won't be held responsible for any damage done due to 'overclocking.'"

At least the 75-MHz clock rate is supported by a few producers, especially for certain Cyrix 6x86 processors (see Chapter 4). A few well known PC chains are offering such computers, the motherboard of which usually has one peculiarity: The PCI bus is asynchronously timed, so that it is possible to set it to the official 33 MHz.

Overclocking lies, rumors and truths

There is, for good reason, a lot of talk about overclocking and its risks. We've summarized the risks below that you should consider.

◆ All elements of a motherboard are sensitive to overclocking. The main risk is overheating. This affects not only the processor but also voltage regulators and chipsets and expressly points to the risks when the frequency of the system clock is increased. Too many users overlook this point. To ensure proper cooling, these components should have access to moving air. Intel does not test either its processors or its chipsets at frequencies above 66 MHz. So there are no guarantees on how these processors work or behave, for example, at 83 MHz. Intel competitors SiS or VIA, on the other hand, tests and approves 75 MHz for their components.

◆ The temperature increase from overclocking rises exponentially at high clock frequencies. Processors are specified and tested up to a temperature of 176 degrees. When cooled with a standard heatsink-fan combination, a Pentium at 66 MHz achieves room-temperature values of 86 - 140 degrees (see picture below). Without cooling, the temperature of a P100 rapidly rises to about 1400 degrees and a P166, on the other hand, increases in a very short time to more than 176 degrees. The processor will then be destroyed within a few minutes.

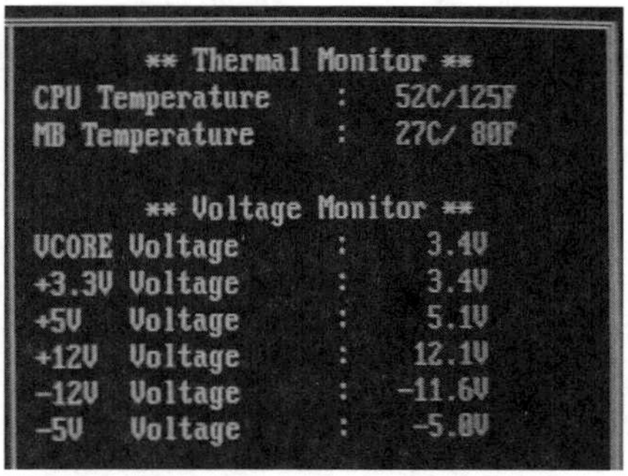

```
          ** Thermal Monitor **
   CPU Temperature    :   52C/125F
   MB Temperature     :   27C/ 80F

          ** Voltage Monitor **
   VCORE Voltage      :      3.4V
   +3.3V Voltage      :      3.4V
   +5V   Voltage      :      5.1V
   +12V  Voltage      :     12.1V
   -12V  Voltage      :    -11.6V
   -5V   Voltage      :     -5.0V
```

The new TX motherboards from Asus (Type TX97) seem to be made for overclocking. Several sensors on the motherboard check not only the voltage, but also the temperature of the board and of the CPU. The values are displayed in the Power Management BIOS or can be displayed in a Windows program. This picture shows the normal temperature of a Pentium 133.

◆ The basis for processor overclocking is the fact that all manufacturers produce their processors from a common basic series. Only after production is a processor's maximum stable clock frequency determined. But it must cast doubt upon the high quality of production at Intel, if there is really a difference between Pentium 150 and 166 or 120 and 133. It seems highly likely in this case that the same processor is applied to a broad market segment. The fact is, in any case, that not all processors from the Pentium series are really the same. In particular, the current 233 models of the Pentium and K6 are definitively different. That is seen already from the different conversion of the timing factors (a P233 interprets 1.5 as 3.5, being thus jumpered as P100 on the mother board).

◆ Normal BIOSes don't show the external, but only the internal processor frequency during booting. Only the MR-BIOS (see the information in this chapter) is an exception. A Pentium 166 is thus displayed as P166 by normal motherboards at 2 x 83 MHz and at 2.5 x 66 MHz.

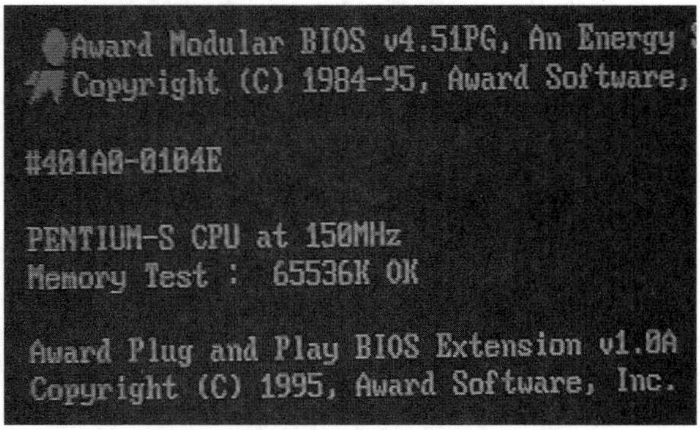

```
   Award Modular BIOS v4.51PG, An Energy
   Copyright (C) 1984-95, Award Software,

   #401A0-0104E

   PENTIUM-S CPU at 150MHz
   Memory Test :   65536K OK

   Award Plug and Play BIOS Extension v1.0A
   Copyright (C) 1995, Award Software, Inc.
```

When a Pentium 133 is overclocked with 2 x 75 MHz to 150 MHz, the Award BIOS will recognize it as a normal Pentium 150 during boot-up.

Chapter 6

◆ Why does overclocking of the system bus produce so much more than overclocking of the processor? Because a P200 doesn't access memory more rapidly than a P166; each uses the 66-MHz system clock. With a 75- or 83-MHz system clock, the main memory and L2 cache are likewise overclocked, which clearly yields more performance.

◆ You may have heard that normal DRAMs (FP or EDO) can only be driven to 66 MHz, and that SDRAMs are necessary beyond this. That is not correct, as practical experience with overclocking shows. High-quality 60-ns EDO RAMs can also produce 83 MHz without relatively major problems. Under some circumstances it is necessary to reduce the timing values in the BIOS somewhat (which should not be a problem thanks to the last chapter), but when all is said and done, its operation will be quite stable. For all practical purposes, 75 MHz seldom causes problems with RAM.

◆ The components most sensitive to overclocking are the PCI bus and certain PCI cards. Many SCSI controllers and some video cards experience heat stress at 41.5 MHz (83-MHz system frequency). The only remedy is a reduction in the frequency of the PCI clock. If the motherboard cannot do this asynchronously relative to the system bus, that's the end of your overclocking.

◆ An increased PCI frequency does not result in more speed on the SCSI bus. The PCI controller has its own clock generator, with which it clocks the SCSI bus. An increase on the PCI bus, on the other hand, will scramble the data transfer between the two buses all the more easily (see next point).

◆ Not all video cards will benefit from an increased PCI frequency. The gain in speed will depend greatly upon the kind of video card. In the cases of many, usually cheaper cards, it is not the maximum bandwidth to the PCI bus which is limiting, but the internal processing speed of the card itself. In this case, raising the PCI frequency produces nothing. Only very high-performance cards, which are not limited by the PCI bus (for example, the Matrox Millenium), will benefit from the higher clock frequency.

◆ Is it possible to overclock other PC components? In principle, each processor is driven by a clock generator and can therefore be overclocked. This is possible, for example, on many supplementary 3-D video cards, which make use of the well known Voodoo processor. The latter can be overclocked from 50 to 63 MHz by using certain programs (with all the notorious problems and risks). If the manufacturer has provided a corresponding function or the clock frequency can be increased using software, as in the case of the Voodoo chip, it is probably possible to overclock. However, in practice there is usually no access to such options.

◆ When will the higher system-clock frequencies officially arrive? This should happen very soon. Intel is expected to introduce 100-MHz boards before the end of 1998. It may be for the Pentium II but is more likely its successor. However, before then AMD and Cyrix will increase the frequency of the system clock on Socket-7 boards. The PCI bus on such boards, however, will continue to be driven asynchronously with 33 MHz. First of all, overclocking there brings little benefit and, second, the PCI bus really has problems with it.

Processor burns—Problems, risks and what can be done about them

Before we give you tips and suggestions for overclocking, you must know the risks, problems and possible fixes:

◆ The relatively simple problem of heating can be countered with cooling. It is easy to acquire a good cooling option for the processor. The chipsets, voltage regulators and possibly also the memory chips, however, also need cooling. If possible, use an ATX board with a good power-supply fan. That will provide better cooling for the chipsets and the voltage regulators, among other things. Older motherboards with linearly regulated voltage regulators become hotter during overclocking than the new switched-voltage types (see Chapter 4). Therefore, be careful with experiments if your motherboard is not up to it.

◆ The first line of defense against processor overheating is familiar. It consists of heat-conductive paste (frequently forgotten today but necessary since the P166) and a very good fan. Unfortunately, the usual fans sold everywhere as "Pentium coolers" for a few dollars aren't worth much. If you love your processor, go to an electronics store and buy it a proper, thick, high-quality heat sink, and couple this to a good fan equipped with an alarm function. Mail order houses are also a good source. Many of them offer special fans for Cyrix 6x86M1 processors because these were known for getting extra hot. It's sometimes difficult to mount a supplementary fan on a separately purchased heat sink.

If you combine a fan with a good heat sink (left picture) and install it on an ATX board having a large power-supply fan (right picture), your PC is set for good cooling.

◆ As stated, a good electronics store or mail order house is a source for a high-quality heat sink. This may be too large, but you can quickly take care of that with a metal saw. Otherwise check the Internet, under this address, for heat sinks and parts of all types: http://www.thermalloy.com/sga.htm. The heat sinks for Cyrix processors, mentioned above, are available from almost any computer dealer. Last but not least, active cooling systems based upon a Peltier element are also of interest. These air-conditioners for your processor are not bad, to be sure, but you also absolutely need a good fan, for heat conducted from the processor to the heat sink must be removed by air circulation.

◆ Be aware that air may still be unable to reach the processor in your computer despite all the neat heat sinks and other cooling means, if it is heavily shielded by a lot of flat ribbon cables. This easily happens in SCSI systems, where the 50-pin flat ribbon cable is easily passed over the processor on ATX boards.

Flat ribbon cables can block air circulation so make certain to avoid this situation.

◆ After heating, the second big problem is large data errors on the overclocked PCI bus. Unfortunately, there is no remedy for this problem aside from reducing the clock frequency. Don't underestimate this. The problems also occur, for example, with controllers for the SCSI or EIDE bus. Both of these connection types have precisely defined protocols which govern data transfer over the PCI bus. These protocols specify precise time intervals for data acceptance, which must not drop below a certain value. However, these limits are easily overstepped at 41.5 MHz (83-MHz system bus). The danger of (sometimes invisible) data losses when writing to EIDE or SCSI hard drives results. Remember, too, that overclocking offers you no speed advantage in the case of either system. Just like SCSI hard drives, EIDE drives will provide no additional performance internally, just because the nonlimiting PCI bus runs faster. And the SCSI bus is self-clocking, as already mentioned above. With that it becomes clear that a PCI bus coupled directly to the system bus is the main risk with regard to overclocking (if you have cooling under control). We advise against the 83-MHz clock frequency for the system bus. We use only 75 MHz ourselves.

◆ It is also frequently recommended that the PIO mode for EIDE hard drives be reduced from Mode 4 to Mode 3 in the case of an overclocked PCI bus. In most cases this leads to fewer crashes due to a PIO Mode 4 which has become still more susceptible to disturbances as a result of overclocking. But it changes nothing relative to the fact that data errors can occur as a result of timing problems with the transfer protocol. If at the same time the data-transfer rate should also decrease due to the PIO mode reduction, very little benefit will remain. So, the PCI bus is currently the main problem with overclocking.

Some final overclocking suggestions

We'll summarize a few suggestions for sensible overclocking on the next several pages. Overclocking is solely your responsibility. Always remember the opinion of all PC board and CPU manufacturers: You may void your warranty if you attempt to overclock your PC.

◆ Example 1: Processors that don't run with the maximum allowed 66-MHz system bus.

Most Pentium 75, 90, 120 or 150 processors can be increased — with good cooling — to at least the next processor level by increasing the frequency of the system clock. The suggestions from the table below assume that your (old?) motherboard is not capable of a 75- or 83-MHz system-clock frequency.

Present settings S = System clock P = PCI clock F = Multiplier	Recommended setting (first overclocking)	Try out (second overclocking, may not be stable)
P75 (S= 50, P = 25, F = 1.5)	P90 (S= 60, P = 30, F = 1.5)	P100 (S= 66, P = 33, F = 1.5)
P90 (S= 60, P = 30, F = 1.5)	P100 (S= 66, P = 33, F = 1.5)	P133 (S= 66, P = 33, F = 2)
P120 (S= 60, P = 30, F = 2)	P133 (S= 66, P = 33, F = 2)	P166 (S= 66, P = 33, F = 2.5)
P150 (S= 60, P = 30, F = 2.5)	P166 (S= 66, P = 33, F = 2.5)	P200 (S= 66, P = 33, F = 3)

◆ Example 2: Setting the multiplier of your processor one step higher (two would perhaps be a bit too much).
Most interesting here are the chips running at 60 MHz (P90, P120 and P150) because they can jump up about two processor steps by simultaneously increasing the system-clock frequency to 66 MHz. Most popular at present is increasing a Pentium 166 to 200 MHz. We must confess that ours failed under these conditions—up to that point it had been running absolutely great.

Chapter 6

Present setting	Recommended setting
P90 (S= 60, P = 30, F = 1.5)	P133 (S= 66, P = 33, F = 2)
P100 (S= 66, P = 33, F = 1.5)	P133 (S= 66, P = 33, F = 2)
P120* (S= 60, P = 30, F = 2)	P166 (S= 66, P = 33, F = 2.5)
P150 (S= 60, P = 30, F = 2.5)	P200 (S= 66, P = 33, F = 3)
P166 (S= 66, P = 33, F = 2.5)	P200 (S= 66, P = 33, F = 3)

◆ We still advise against overclocking the AMD K6 and especially the Cyrix 6x86MX. Both processors are already being driven so high by the manufacturers that they are putting out about all they can. Only AMD K6-166 is perhaps worth the attempt to jumper it to 200 MHz. The settings correspond to those of a Pentium. But likewise for the K6: cooling, cooling, cooling!

◆ The Pentium Pro or Pentium II is also an interesting tuning target. Thus far there are no motherboards with a higher system-clock frequency for these processors, but increasing the processor multiplier is worth a try (don't forget cooling). Optimal targets here are the Pentium Pro 150 and P180, which should in no case be raised to 200 MHz. The Pentium Pro can also be set with confidence to 233 MHz on most newer boards and usually handles that quite well. Because the L2 cache in this case is integrated with the full clock rate into the processor core, overclocking has a much greater effect than with a normal Pentium.

◆ Remember: You can't get the lower models clocked up to a regular 233-MHz Intel (with a 66-MHz system clock). That speed is only achieved with true 233 units (Pentium or K6). These interpret the BF assignment for the P100 with the factor 3.5 (66 x 3.5 = 233).

◆ The last and currently most important dimension of overclocking is increasing the system-bus clock frequency to 75 or 83 MHz. This can only be done with motherboards that support it. You can get the jumper settings from the manual or from information printed on the board. As mentioned, we strongly recommend against the 83-MHz system-clock frequency. Even if it seems to run well, you still risk possibly unnoticed data errors on your hard drive However, we have had good experiences with 75 MHz, especially with a Pentium 133 that cannot otherwise be further overclocked. With 150 MHz and 75 MHz external, our computer ran just as smoothly as a normal P166.

> **NOTE**
>
> **And yet it works—83 MHz with Asus boards**
>
> Since Revision 3.0, the well known Asus motherboard P55T2P4 supports the higher bus frequencies (only the BAT version, not the ATX board or the version with the integrated SCSI-UW controller, which will perhaps still be changed). You recognize the new, faster-clocked boards from the additional third jumper, J8. Formerly there were only two jumpers for setting the bus frequency (J9 and J10). The newer boards with Intel's TX chipset from Asus (TX97-serie) can still set 75 MHz as the system frequency. The 83-MHz setting of the P55T2P4 is, of course, documented neither in the manual nor on the motherboard. For those who want to test it come what may, the settings are: Set both J8 and J9 to 1-2, J10 to 2-3 (for 75 MHz: J8 and J10 to 1-2, J9 to 2-3). Naturally, as always, with no guarantee ;-)

◆ A hot tip for problem-prone processors is to increase the processor voltage. Higher voltages produce clearer signals for the CPUs and work like tranquilizer pills on fast-clocked processors. Our P166 ran, for example, stably at 200 MHz, only after we raised the voltage setting from Standard (3.3-3.46 V) to VRE (3.4-3.6 V). A slight increase of about 0.1-0.2 V will pump up most processors without problems. AMD expressly indicated only for the old AMD K5 that the processor would give up the ghost at 3.6 V. The Standard or VRE settings are valid in any case only for the older non-MMX CPUs. For the new MMX processors, you can increase the core voltage precisely in 0.1 V steps (see Chapter 4 on the topic of processor voltage). You can give the processor core of your souped-up MMX unit 0.1 V more juice with confidence.

◆ If you have considered everything, the next step is the big moment of booting and testing. Here's two tips on how to do the best test. Run a demanding application benchmark, such as WinStone or SysMark32 (see Chapter 1). You should be encouraged if the computer survives this. We have yet another tip for SCSI users from our experiences: Install a large program from a CD-ROM. In particular, if the well known InstallShield is used as a setup program, an unstable processor will nearly always crash during the execution of such a program. Our P166, which we have juiced up to 200 MHz, exhibits this charming caprice, for example. Everything seemed to be in order. However, always, when installing from our SCSI CD-ROM, that was the end of it. Funny, sad, but true. The remedy then, as mentioned, was to increase the processor voltage.

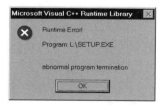

Overclocked processors react sensitively to running the InstallShield setup program from SCSI CD-ROMs. Anyone receiving such an error message will know exactly why.

NOTE

Turbo Switch—convenient overclocking by pressing a button

Because most jumpers for setting the system bus are three-pole, and the change between 66 and 83 MHz is achieved with only one jumper (JP8) on the well known Asus boards, for example, a three-pole cable and an outside switch can be installed and switched over as needed (naturally with the PC turned off). For this you can employ an unused three-pole cable of the housing (for example, the turbo-switch) or lead a new one with switch to the outside. Such cables are available in all electronics stores or via mail order. The advantage: you use the higher clock frequency only for important applications, for daily typing you continue with the "Intel-crawl." With that you will still have something left of your Pentium in ten years.

Chapter 7

SCSI And EIDE In Plain English

Deciding whether to use SCSI or EIDE is the question that users considering a new system ask themselves. Like the question about whether to use Windows 95 or Windows NT, the answer is clear to many: the professional system is the winner (i.e., SCSI or NT). One obvious thing is that most systems include EIDE when they are sold for good reason. Under certain circumstances, EIDE is, by far, the better choice. But some users, including us, argue that SCSI is better.

In other chapters you'll find instructions and tips on using hard drives, floppy drives and CD-ROM drives. We kept this information separate from the basic information on SCSI and EIDE because, in practice, it won't matter whether a hard drive or CD-ROM is running on a SCSI or EIDE bus. Partitioning, formatting or burning CDs works relatively the same on both. We'll talk about the information particular to the bus system in this chapter.

SCSI AND EIDE ADVANTAGES AND DISADVANTAGES

We'll start by saying the more devices and the higher the demands you place on your system, the more SCSI pays for itself. Besides, you may be able to purchase SCSI without paying extra—we'll show you how in the following examples.

We would only get EIDE if the PC is equipped relatively simply with a standard hard drive and CD-ROM and will be used for simple applications. Soon, USB will be one of the biggest advantages of SCSI, i.e., ending the troublesome expansion with peripherals such as scanners and removable drives (see Chapter 5). Here are some facts and background information for and against SCSI or EIDE:

◆ SCSI is more expensive than EIDE and not just because you will need an additional controller (EIDE connections are integrated on the motherboard). SCSI devices themselves always cost more than their EIDE counterparts. That's really inconsiderate since, with the exception perhaps of greater numbers in series production, manufacturing a SCSI CD-ROM is hardly more expensive than the same ATAPI version. However the manufacturers are aware of the fact that users who want SCSI are also prepared to pay more for it. In 1996, SCSI hard drives were just as expensive as the corresponding EIDE models. In the meantime, this has changed dramatically. SCSI hard drives in particular are a good 10-30% more expensive than the same EIDE components.

◆ SCSI is not necessarily faster than EIDE. In both instances, the bus protocols or controllers are capable of much more performance than the attached hard drive. Presently, there are hardly any hard drives that can achieve a data transfer rate of 10 Megs/sec. Most can only achieve a mere 4-7 Megs/sec. But the Ultra Wide SCSI can handle 40 Megs/sec, and even EIDE can handle at least 16 Megs/sec (PIO Mode 4) or 33 Megs (Ultra DMA). Nevertheless, you can only get the really high-performance hard drives that perform at 7,200 or 10,000 rpm for the SCSI bus. The same holds true for the high-quality scanners, portable hard drives or CD burners. While some of the devices have EIDE or ATAPI versions, these were designed for a different market segment and may have lower performance. The bottom line: access to the high-quality devices is possible only with SCSI.

◆ By the way, you may ask, "What good does supporting the high transfer rates of Ultra Wide SCSI or Ultra DMA do if there isn't a hard drive available to deliver this quantity of data?" We couldn't agree with you more.

This question is less concerned with making sense than exploring better purchasing options. It only makes sense for the controller to support more than 10 Megs/sec if several devices simultaneously exchange data. Imagine, if you will, that you have two hard drives operating at six Megs/sec and you want to copy files from the one to the other. Then a Fast SCSI arrives and is able to handle 10 Megs/sec and EIDE with the PIO Mode 3 is already in trouble. However, for the time being, a controller or bus system with more than 20 Megs is pretty useless. The same holds true for the fact that Windows 95b supports hard drive sizes all the way to the terabyte zone with FAT32.

◆ When more devices can be attached, SCSI shows just how good it is. EIDE can only handle a maximum of two devices on each of two ports. And each port requires an interrupt. Okay, with special controllers you can use up to eight devices, but this has zero effect on the market. The average profitable Fast SCSI controller, on the other hand, can handle up to seven devices. Other than for the controller itself, you don't need any additional interrupts or I/O addresses. Besides, slow and fast devices operate together without any problems on a common SCSI bus, whereas with EIDE this would only cause problems.

◆ SCSI is more stable than EIDE especially if you don't consider the new Ultra DMA since this finally has a reasonable protocol and bus termination.

◆ SCSI does have some disadvantages. For many beginners, SCSI seems to be more complicated than EIDE but only because of the business with the termination and the ID numbers. However, SCSI can be <u>less</u> complicated because you have to work with the BIOS installation with EIDE. When you understand a few basic rules of SCSI, we think it's much easier. New devices are simple to attach. However SCSI devices do have one problem that cannot be ignored. The devices (especially the hard drive boards) become hotter with SCSI than with EIDE. These devices will require some more cooling to prevent overheating.

Chapter 7

COMPARING SCSI STANDARDS AND CONTROLLERS

Users who have made up their minds to purchase EIDE have it comparatively easier because the interfaces are standardized on the motherboard. All you need to do si choose the size of the hard drive. This isn't the case with SCSI since there are so many standards and controllers available. For example, which is the right one, the Ultra or the Ultra Wide controller? Or is my old standard SCSI controller still good? With a little bit of background information, the decision is not so hard to make. By the way, the term "SCSI controller" is not correct. They are really called "host adapters" but the general term is SCSI controller and that is what we'll use here.

Finding the right SCSI standard for you

There are many SCSI standards and even more labels. You'll see terms such as Fast, Ultra, Wide, SCSI-1, SCSI-2 or SCSI-3.

◆ There are many **SCSI standards** and more become available daily. The old ones (such as SCSI-1) are still impressive but new ones such as optic fiber channel are appearing on the horizon. For now, however, there are only three standards on the playing field. Fast SCSI, Ultra SCSI and Wide SCSI. Since Wide SCSI is just the 16-bit enhanced variation of Fast or Ultra SCSI, it can be combined with either.

◆ **Fast SCSI** (also called "SCSI-2") is the classical standard for us and has been on the market for a few years. The normal model works with 8-bit data width, can accommodate seven devices on the

A typical Fast SCSI controller like the AHA 2940 has a 50-pin internal and external port.

controller and performs at rates up to 10 Megs/sec. With the well known SCSI controller manufacturer Adaptec, the designation for the classic Fast SCSI controller for the PCI bus is AHA 2940. This model is perfectly adequate for all normal desktop PCs that have up to two hard drives and five additional devices.

◆ **Ultra SCSI** (also called "SCSI-3") is a new variation of the Fast SCSI, with 20 Megs/sec throughput. This enhancement was achieved by doubling the bus frequency. The corresponding Adaptec controller is the AHA 2940U. As a rule, using an Ultra SCSI device at the increased bandwidth hardly makes a difference. For this reason, the bus is more sensitive to disturbances. The total cable length should not exceed 1.5 m, and it is imperative to use active terminators. Otherwise, there isn't any difference between the Ultra model and Fast SCSI. There are 8-bit and 16-bit models.

◆ Wide SCSI is not actually a standard in itself, but the 16-bit variation of the other two models. Correspondingly, there are Fast Wide and Ultra Wide controllers (AHA 2940W or 2940UW). Since the controller on the bus works in 16 bit, not only is the data bandwidth doubled (from 10 to 20 or 20 to 40 Megs/sec), but the controller is able to accommodate 15 instead of 7 devices.

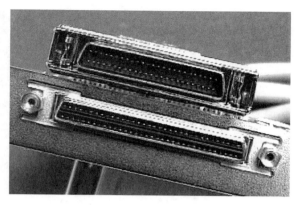

Only the Fast SCSI controller (type 2940) and the Ultra Wide controller (type 2940UW) are important. Since the price difference between an Ultra and an Ultra Wide controller is low, most buy the Ultra Wide if they think the usual 10 Megs bandwidth of a normal controller

Wide SCSI works with 68 pin connections (below) instead of with the usual 50 pin connections of Fast SCSI (above).

isn't enough. That's why stores mostly carry these models and you should choose between them.

Tips on buying a SCSI controller

Choose between a standard Fast controller or the UW variation. The standard type is adequate as long as you don't want to operate more than seven devices and if an interruption in the controller's output when simultaneously using several devices doesn't bother you too much (see illustration). Ultra Wide only makes sense for users who are running at least two very fast hard drives with 7,2000 rpm or for servers and other high-end computers.

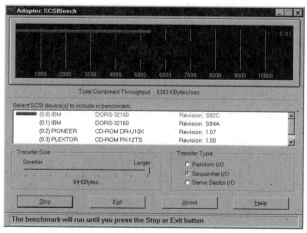

Use the benchmark program SCSIBench from Adaptec to measure how the bandwidth for a Fast SCSI controller, type 2940, drops when using several devices. In this picture, the first hard drive is running alone in the PC and relays approximately 5.3 Megs/sec.

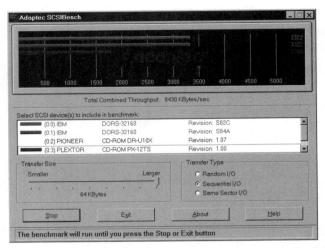

In this picture, a second hard drive and a 12x CD-ROM were connected to it. The hard drives' relay rates fell to approximately 3.3 Megs/sec. If you conduct this test using Ultra Wide disks on an UltraWide controller, the drop is far less dramatic.

Don't let all this talk about the Ultra and Ultra Wide make you crazy. A good Adaptec 2940 or similar Fast SCSI controller is sufficient for a single drive PC in 90% of the cases. On the contrary, you'll not only save money but also a lot of future aggravation. This is because the Ultra SCSI is not exactly insensitive to disturbances due to the increased speed. There are minor problems associated with cables that are too long. And external cables must, by all means, be tested for Ultra SCSI and are quite expensive. Wide SCSI has, in addition, it own difficulties, as you'll learn in the next section.

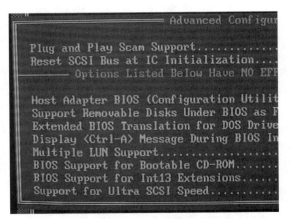

Support for the Ultra SCSI must be enabled in the controller BIOS.

But before this, here are a few buying recommendations for the Fast SCSI controller. You definitely buy brand names because support for the SCSI driver is absolutely essential. The market leader

is Adaptec. The most affordable solution would be a
SCSI controller supported by the manufacturer of the
motherboard, which already has the SCSI functions
integrated into the BIOS. The PCI-SC200 from Asis is
just such a controller with a SymbiosLogic Chip for
approximately $80.00 (see Chapter 6).

Avoiding the Wide SCSI trap

The connections on a Wide SCSI controller, such as the
Adaptec 2940UW, can't be used in the conventional
fashion, and this often leads to misunderstandings and
problems. The controller has a 50-pin internal plug for
normal SCSI devices and a 68-pin one for Wide SCSI. So
far, so good and just as expected. But what causes
problems is the fact that the external plug is also available
in 68-pin Wide variations (refer to the illustration above).
That's why you may not be able to connect your external
SCSI devices, such as scanners or ZIP drives, with the
usual cable. There are no external Wide SCSI devices
(other than hard drives in external cases). Through the
use of a special adapter, normal SCSI-2 devices, such as
scanners, can be connected to the 68-pin external Wide
port, but experience has shown that this makes the bus

*Quality and good driver support are
characteristics of Adaptec PCI controllers
(such as the AHA-2940UW, top, and AHA
2940, bottom). Furthermore, every operating
system and hardware manufacturer of SCSI
devices supports them.*

unstable. It's not coincidence that the controller has an internal Fast SCSI connector with 50 pins
to connect such devices. If that's not enough, there's still another roadblock. Only two of the three
ports may be used simultaneously to prevent the SCSI bus from splitting into a "T" shape. But
since both ports can be used in practically every PC (most people have normal SCSI CD-ROMs and
hard drives), there is no way to connect devices to an external plug.

If both of the internal ports of the UW controller are covered, as shown here, with flat ribbon cable
(on the right is the 68-pin UW cable), no other device can be connected to the 68-pin external plug,
because otherwise the SCSI bus would split into a "T" shape. Don't worry, because there is a
relatively simple and uncomplicated solution to this problem. With the aid of an adapter (see

following illustration) you can bring the 50-pin flat ribbon cable outside with the corresponding cable, to which you can then attach your devices. Your dealer can probably get you such an adapter.

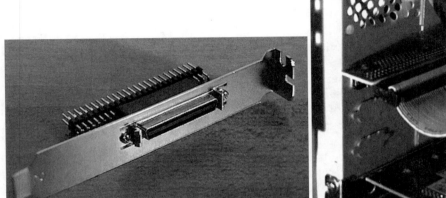

By using an adapter you can run your 50-pin flat ribbon cable externally to connect with external devices. Either use the slot panel or screw the adapter, left, directly into the corresponding recesses in the housing.

By the way, the P55T2P4 Motherboard by Asus, which comes in an "S" version with integrated Adapted UW controller on the board, hides another Wide SCSI trap. This board costs approximately $270.00 less than the combination package of a normal P55T2P4 and a 2940UW controller from Adaptec. But even if it's easy to get along without the external 68-pin Wide connection, it's still a nuisance that each of the two SCSI connections (50 pin and 68 pin) require an interrupt. One is normal. Besides, you cannot simultaneously use the SCSI connections and all four PCI slots. As always, we advise against such combinations if you have a well defined operation and do not wish to upgrade or change over later.

Practical solutions to achieve greater compatibility

You can upgrade an existing EIDE system with a SCSI controller and, in so doing, enjoy the best of both worlds. In any event, there are enough ways to get started in the big, wide SCSI world. If you'd like, you can make the switch to SCSI with your next PC purchase. Here are a few examples and suggestions:

◆ If you have a system with EIDE hard drives and you want to continue using these to boot the system, you do not need a SCSI controller that has its own BIOS. This is only necessary for the automatic support of hard drives and for booting. Eliminating the BIOS makes the controller's purchase price more affordable (between $70.00 and $100.00). The best known example of this is the AVA-1505 from Adaptec for the ISA bus. There's also a similar controller available for the PCI bus from Adaptec, the AHA-2920.

The Adaptec AVA-1505 is a simple SCSI controller for the ISA bus that operates without the BIOS and is very affordable. It'connects scanners, ZIP drives and other devices. You can also connect SCSI hard drives using a driver (ASPIDISK.SYS) but you can't boot from them.

◆ Many SCSI devices, such as scanners or internal ZIP drives, come with an 8-bit ISA SCSI controller. The manufacturers readily admit that these controllers have not been tested for other SCSI devices, but a SCSI ZIP drive ran without incident on the plug-in card for our HP scanner, which contains a SymbiosLogic chip. One big advantage of the 8-bit cards is that, in contrast to most 16-bit ISA and 32-bit PCI cards, these can also be assigned very low IRQs (*e.g.*, 3 or 4). If you experience significant IRQ problems in a EIDE computer and don't know how to link an additional device, this option offers some new possibilities.

Place the 8-bit controller on IRQ 3 (you will have to do without the serial interface) and attach a SCSI CD-ROM, portable hard drive or scanner. Then you can get rid of your ATAPI CD-ROM and gain the secondary EIDE port of IRQ 15.

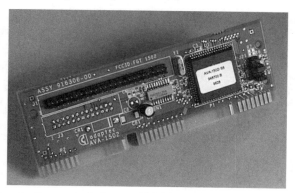

Even the internal ZIP drives by Iomega include a small SCSI controller for the ISA bus, which has an internal connection and requires a 16-bit slot.

◆ A frequent argument for buying a ZIP drive for the parallel port is that you can't connect a SCSI drive to any EIDE computer. You may do this with the parallel ZIP port, however, because every computer has a printer port. However, this argument is only partly true. Even external SCSI devices can attach using the printer port on every computer. You only need an adapter for this or, even better, a special parallel-to-SCSI controller. Once again, you can get such an item from Adaptec, among others. At approximately $217.00, the cost is rather high, but keep in mind that you will be able to work on any PC with the significantly faster SCSI devices. What's more, there are quite a few devices, such as the Iomega JAZ, that don't even have a parallel port. This adapter lets you go around that, which is also perfect for connecting such devices on a Notebook. However, the speed limitations of the printer interface are still a factor.

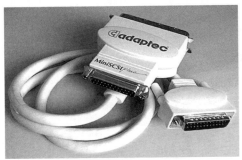

The MiniSCSI Plus adapter from Adaptec is a parallel-to-SCSI controller, which you can use to connect external SCSI devices to any PC via the parallel interface.

PARALLEL-TO-SCSI CONTROLLERS FROM ADAPTEC

If you attempt to install the Adaptec parallel-to-SCSI controller in Windows 95 and want to use the Windows proprietary driver, you won't find a driver listed under "Adaptec controller" in the hardware list. But if you check under the controllers listed for the company Trantor, you will find them. This is because Trantor manufactures the controllers as well as the drivers; Adaptec only distributes them.

Aside from taking advantage of these inexpensive or special solutions, you can also install a "proper," up-to-standard PCI SCSI controller that has its own BIOS for connecting hard drives in an EIDE system. If your BIOS does not support the accommodation of the boot sequence (see Chapter 6), the EIDE will still be the first place your system boots from. Blending both systems and their hard drives isn't a problem, but compared to a solution using one system, it's not as fast because of the greater load from drivers and two bus master devices on the PCI bus.

TRICKS FOR MASTERING SCSI HARDWARE

This section talks about what you need to know about combining a SCSI controller with its corresponding SCSI devices for group installation. The SCSI Manufacturer's Association has drastically reduced the number of possible arrangements and combinations. Only clear, straight connections are permitted with SCSI. Wandering off into "T" shaped cable branches is not possible. Nevertheless, the SCSI controller is allowed to keep up to seven devices. Anyone who uses it very wide is permitted up to 15. But we've already been over that. So now we hope that you're in a good mood, because here we go.

Assemble your SCSI system step-by-step

We recommend that you do not try to connect all the devices at once. Instead, start with the controller, the hard drives and perhaps even the CD-ROM. After you have these running and they've been integrated into the operating system, then connect additional devices, such as portable media (ZIP drives) or scanners. This dramatically reduces the risk of problems. Besides, you'll be able to find any problems much faster this way.

What to look for when building a stable SCSI system

We've already talked about the essential basics that you will need to build a stable SCSI system. The following summarizes the most important facts:

◆ Be careful when buying a SCSI cable. Because of the high frequencies carried over the SCSI bus, the physical characteristics of the cable are a major factor. With internal flat ribbon cables, you can't make too many mistakes. But with external cables, cheap product or increasing the length of the cable can cause a conflict with adapters. Occasional relay errors, SCSI devices not found and disruptions result from this.

The problem lies in the fact that you can't always judge the quality of an external cable. All good SCSI cables are of the "twisted pair" variety, i.e., every data line has its own ground wire. You can recognize these cables because they are at least one cm thick (including the covering) and by the fact that they are also difficult to bend.

Poorer quality cables are usually only half that size and are soft and flexible, like printer or modem cables. When all else fails, remember the following tip: buy your cable from a company that understands something about SCSI, not from just anyone. A good external SCSI cable, depending of the type of connection, costs $25.00 to $50.00 and is the worth the money.

Chapter 7

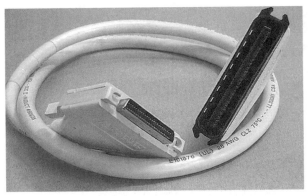

A high-grade cable like this one, with good screening and stable connectors, is extremely important for a stable SCSI bus, especially with the Ultra SCSI.

◆ Because of its double frequencies, the Ultra SCSI bus is very sensitive to interferences and, consequently, to bad cables and to terminating. Don't experiment with bad cables and passive terminators! Keep in mind that the entire cable length for the Ultra SCSI is limited to 1.5 m total, counting the internal and external cables! That can get a little tight in the tower cases, for instance. If you want to test the stability of your system, the same testing standards mentioned in Chapter 6.

◆ The controller must identify all devices attached to the bus relatively easily. Otherwise, they would communicate indiscriminately amongst themselves. With 8-bit systems (Fast and Ultra SCSI, not Wide), the numbers 0 to 7 are available; for Wide SCSI, the numbers 0-15. These are listed as SCSI IDs (identification). Each ID can only be assigned once. If two devices on the bus have the same ID, the bus will become very unstable and will crash.

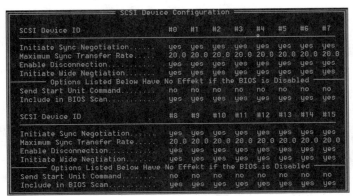

The assignment of IDs occurs in the devices. However, the configuration takes place in the controller's BIOS, which in a Wide SCSI controller such as the 2940UW, adds up to a lot of settings.

♦ The ID also controls the access priority to the SCSI bus. The controller queries the bus in ascending order (from 0 to 7). The IDs are usually issued in the following manner: the controller is assigned 7, boot drives are assigned the IDs 0 and 1, and the remaining numbers are assigned to all other devices. Old, slow or seldom used devices should be assigned the higher ID numbers. Incidentally, a few companies (such as Future Domain) do it exactly the opposite way.

♦ Older controllers could only boot from the ID numbers 0 and 1 but this has changed with the new controllers. Nevertheless, in most instances the ID number 0 is (or should be) the boot drive and the first partition on the boot drive is listed as the C: drive.

```
#401A0-0105

Award Plug and Play BIOS Extension v1.0A
Copyright (C) 1995, Award Software, Inc.

Initialize Plug and Play Cards...
Card-01: TerraTec Maestro 32/96
PNP Init Completed

Adaptec AHA-2940 BIOS v1.23
(c) 1996 Adaptec, Inc. All Rights Reserved.

◄◄◄ Press <Ctrl><A> for SCSISelect(TM) Utility! ►►►

    SCSI ID:LUN NUMBER #:# 0:0 - IBM       DORS-32160    - Drive D  (81h)
    SCSI ID:LUN NUMBER #:# 1:0 - IBM       DORS-32160    - Drive 82h
    SCSI ID:LUN.NUMBER #:# 2:0 - PIONEER   CD-ROM DR-U10X
    SCSI ID:LUN NUMBER #:# 3:0 - PLEXTOR   CD-ROM PX-12TS
    SCSI ID:LUN NUMBER #:# 4:0 - HP        C2500A
    SCSI ID:LUN NUMBER #:# 5:0 - IOMEGA    ZIP 100

BIOS Installed Successfully!
```

The controller initializes and shows all the devices
during booting that are connected and switched on according to the order of their ID.

♦ The assignment of ID numbers for external devices is done primarily using a small dip switch. Conversely, this is done over three jumpers called "ID pins" with internal devices (hard drives, CD-ROMs, etc.). If you remember the simple rule above, you'll soon see three jumpers—each one either plugged in or not—account for eight combinations and, as a result, eight numbers. The combinations are not entirely fixed but usually appear as indicated in the table. We omitted ID number 7 because this is always reserved for the controller.

Chapter 7

Present setting	Recommended setting
P90 (S= 60, P = 30, F = 1.5)	P133 (S= 66, P = 33, F = 2)
P100 (S= 66, P = 33, F = 1.5)	P133 (S= 66, P = 33, F = 2)
P120* (S= 60, P = 30, F = 2)	P166 (S= 66, P = 33, F = 2.5)
P150 (S= 60, P = 30, F = 2.5)	P200 (S= 66, P = 33, F = 3)
P166 (S= 66, P = 33, F = 2.5)	P200 (S= 66, P = 33, F = 3)

◆ Remember a SCSI bus is a chain. It always has two ends and branching out isn't possible. The controller, like every other device, is considered a member of the chain and can be placed anywhere. Both ends of a SCSI chain must always end electronically with a terminator. This prevents signals at the end of the bus from reflecting and returning as interference.

◆ One of the 50 or 68 wiring pins on the SCSI bus is the term power supply voltage for the terminators. It's the duty of the terminators to stabilize this term power voltage relatively uniformly. Passive terminators only do this within certain tolerance ranges, while active terminators use their own circuit to stabilize the voltage (see below). Under certain conditions, you may have to deal with the term power setting, since only one device on the bus should supply this voltage. The SCSI controller normally performs this function itself, but there are also lots of SCSI devices that have a term power setting. Ordinarily, you need to disable this setting. Only when problems occur should you enable this setting on a bus device.

◆ You can incorporate several SCSI controllers into one system. Yes, you may even use one external SCSI device through two SCSI controllers (refer to the information box). It makes sense to use two controllers, for example, if you are running Fast and Wide SCSI devices on separate buses, or if you wish to run more than seven Fast SCSI devices in one PC. Many CD burner manufacturers also recommend that you run this device on its own SCSI controller parallel to a SCSI system. As you can see, there are numerous possibilities. During installation, you only need to keep an eye out for the allocation of different resources (IRQs), and then install the appropriate drivers into the operating system.

NOTE

Pretty clever—one device, two controllers

Hardly anyone realizes that you can run one SCSI device simultaneously on two SCSI controllers in different computers. This doesn't work with most mass storage systems (they lack a locking mechanism, and so data loss is a foregone conclusion). But if you want to run a SCSI scanner on two computers, for example, this trick works wonderfully. To do this, connect both of the SCSI scanner ports to the corresponding SCSI ports on the controller. Also, disable termination on the scanner. If you don't run any additional internal SCSI devices on these controllers, termination will be enabled on both controllers, because they are now at the end of the SCSI bus. It's important that one of the two controllers is assigned the SCSI ID number 6, instead of 7, which you can set either via a jumper or in the BIOS. Of course, the scanner is assigned an entirely different ID and can be addressed by each PC via driver software.

Terminate your SCSI bus correctly

Termination is the source of most problems with SCSI devices. Termination is the technique of maintaining a specified voltage level at open cable ends. The required voltage is fed from a SCSI device (usually the controller) over the term power wire (see note above). Often small, passive resistance networks in internal SCSI devices function as terminators having nine, eleven or more pins, and in external SCSI devices as special terminators, primarily in the form of an empty plug housing. Many devices have a built-in circuit for active termination.

With many external devices, such as with this scanner, the IDs are easily set using the switch. On the right, there's a small switch for this marked with a plus '+'. An illustration of the ID jumpers appears further below.

A terminator must always be installed at the beginning and at the end of the SCSI bus. This means the following:

◆ If only internal SCSI devices have been installed, the last internal device and the controller must be terminated.

◆ If only external SCSI devices have been installed, the last external device and the controller must be terminated.

◆ If internal and external SCSI devices have been installed, the last external device and the last internal device must be terminated; the terminators on the controller must be removed or turned off.

◆ Terminating a Wide SCSI controller is more complicated. These have two terminating wires (Low and High) that can be used in three different settings, since both the 8-bit and the 16-bit bus need to be terminated. The Low setting on the controller only controls termination on the 8-bit Fast SCSI bus. The Low and High settings together control termination on the 16-bit Wide bus. The following table shows how the settings must be made on the controller. There are only three combinations. Newer controllers come equipped with automatic termination so you only have to worry about problems with the settings.

Connection type on a Wide controller	Low termination	High termination
Wide internal alone	Enabled	Enabled
Wide external alone	Enabled	Enabled
Wide internal and external	Disabled	Disabled
Fast internal alone	Enabled	Enabled
Fast and Wide internal	Disabled	Enabled
Fast and Wide external	Disabled	Enabled

Chapter 7

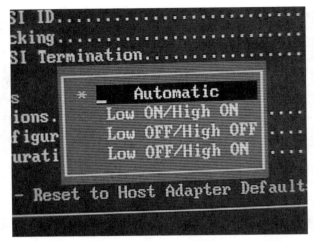

*Modern SCSI controllers terminate in the BIOS, which you can reach
(with Adaptec) during booting by pressing* Ctrl + A.

Modern controllers terminate either through manual readjustment in the SCSI BIOS or automatically by means of the controller. A jumper or dip switch can only be found in the cheap, simple controllers. SCSI devices are different. Most internal CD-ROMs include simple, passive plug resistance, just like the ones found in the older hard drives. In the meantime, most newer hard drives are actively terminated using a jumper.

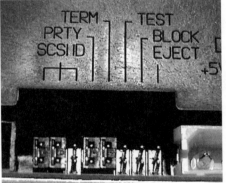

*Terminating internal SCSI devices is often done with small, passive resistance bridges (left) or by setting jumpers
(right). The polarization of the resistance bridges is characterized by a point (top left).*

Passive jumper terminators need to be placed in their socket according to the correct pin location. The outside pins are used to connect ground and power supply, and if they are mixed up, the SCSI bus won't perform properly. Make sure that the resistance marking (usually a point on the terminator, see figure) is on the same side as the corresponding marking at the socket of the controller.

> **NOTE**
>
> **Fully automatic termination with the new Adaptec 2940 controller**
> Granted, terminating is a chore, particularly if you don't always have devices connected externally. Previously, you always had to reset the termination on the controller. But not any more, since the BIOS version 1.20 supports automatic termination, at least with Adaptec. The controller recognizes whether devices are connected to its plugs. If you believe that automatic versions are unreliable because they make your SCSI computer unstable, you can still switch the terminating by hand to enabled or disabled.

Some of the common errors made when terminating are forgetting terminators, having too many terminators, or incorrectly polling the terminators (three instead of two) at the physical end of the SCSI chain. Open plugs within the chain, which can easily occur when using a seven-ribbed flat ribbon cable, are not critical, however.

Active and passive terminators

The quality of the terminators in most SCSI devices is very poor. Only newer hard drives are an exception. If you're using a controller that has Ultra SCSI support you may have move up to the higher priced active terminators. External ZIP drives are a typical example of bad termination. The following is an example. In all computers with a ZIP drive that we have tested so far, the drive always had to be turned on to terminate halfway decently. If the ZIP is turned off, the controller is usually left hanging during the boot process. But even a lot of CD-ROMs and a few of the older hard drives are able to make it with poor-quality, old, passive resistance outlet plugs.

However, everything is different with active terminators. They contain a circuit which holds the bus voltage at a constant 3.6 volts. By comparison, passive terminators permit a fluctuation between 1.2 and 3.5 volts. The terminator supply voltage is delivered over the SCSI cable on the term power wire, which is why the terminators don't require an additional power supply. You can purchase high-quality, external terminators in all types of models from most dealers for a few dollars each.

Chapter 7

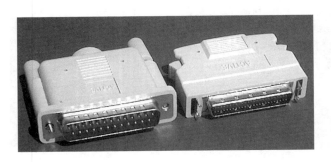

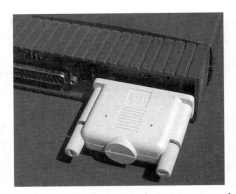

Active terminators are available in a variety of models (SCSI-1, SCSI-2, Centronics, etc.). Attachment to external devices is easy, as shown here with a ZIP drive.

Equip your last external device with an active terminator, especially if it's a ZIP drive. This is absolutely essential, especially with the Ultra SCSI. After attaching an active terminator, the aforementioned booting problem is eliminated. From that point on, the ZIP doesn't need to be turned on when booting the PC. Besides, the entire bus now runs more stably as a result.

However, the ideal situation is if you also actively terminated the internal section of the SCSI bus. Of course, you cannot attach the designated terminators directly to a hard drive, a CD-ROM or the flat ribbon cable, but there are terminators for this. Simply attach your flat ribbon cable to the device so the last port is left free. Then buy a direct adapter for the internal terminator port. A better option is using the adapter for Wide SCSI controllers that was mentioned earlier that you can use to bring a 50-pin flat ribbon cable outside the case. You can easily plug an active terminator using a SCSI-2 mini port to this newly created external port. Of course, you must disable termination on all the internal devices. We did this and the SCSI bus is noticeably more stable and has experienced no problems. The additional $40.00 in adapters and terminators was worth it.

To equip the internal section of the SCSI bus with an active terminator, place the end of the flat ribbon cable over an adapter facing outward (left picture), and attach the terminator.

You can now boot from the ZIP, CD-ROM and elsewhere

A useful feature in most of the new SCSI controllers is the ability to freely determine the boot ID in SCSI BIOS. Instead of having to choose between 0 or 1 for the ID number, as was previously the case, you can now boot from ID 3 or ID 5, where the ZIP drive or the CD-ROM is attached. Naturally, you must have a bootable medium and operating system in the drive. The well known Adaptec controllers in the 2940 series have supported this function since BIOS version 1.20. Another limitation concerns sectoring of the media. You're only able to boot from media that work with sectors that are 512 bytes in size, conforming with DOS. A few of the larger MO drives (for example, the 640-Megs 3.5-inches media) are hard sectored with 2048-bytes sectors. Therefore, you cannot boot from these drives.

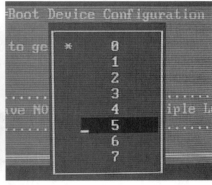

To switch from the default boot drive (hard drive, ID 0) to a ZIP drive (as an example), you simply need to select the new ID (picture on the right) in the controller BIOS under the Boot Device Options menu (picture on the left).

A practical option is booting from a SCSI ZIP drive. Here you won't have any problems with the sector sizes, since ZIP diskettes are formatted with the usual 512-bytes sectors. But you will first need to make a bootable ZIP diskette with an operating system. Using the DOS Sys X: (x = drive designation for ZIP), this isn't a problem. Then you can set up your own start configuration files on the ZIP diskette and /or even install Windows 95 on it.

We tried copying our Windows index on a ZIP disk and then booting from there but it didn't work. Windows 95 crashed. However, after we booted from the ZIP in DOS and re-installed Windows 95 on the ZIP disk, everything worked superbly. Now we have a super boot diskette for emergency situations (hard drive crash, virus attacks, etc.) that we can use to directly access the long file names in our hard drive and all of the essential utilities (such as virus scanner, Disc Doctor, etc.).

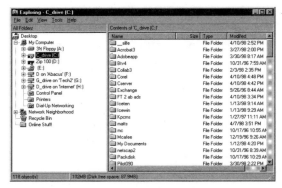

Windows 95 can be installed without a problem as boot drive C: on a ZIP diskette.

Incidentally, booting from a CD-ROM is a special case. This works only if the corresponding function for the SCSI controller has been enabled specifically for this purpose in the PC's BIOS (with ATAPI CD-ROM). You will, of course, still need a specially designed bootable CD-ROM, manufactured according to the El Torito specifications by IBM and Phoenix. The Microsoft Windows NT 4.0 CD-ROM is a an example (please see Chapter 6).

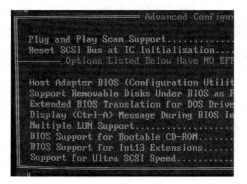

The SCSI controller BIOS must give added support to the boot functions in the same manner as the PC BIOS does for ATAPI CD-ROMs. You can find the setting for Adaptec listed under Advanced Configurations Options. To boot from the CD-ROM or the floppy drive, you need to switch on the function Support Removable Disks under BIOS as Fixed Disks, and open All Disks or Boot only. This is the default setting from the factory, so no other changes need to be made.

SCSI Hardware tuning & troubleshooting

SCSI is normally pretty uncomplicated, providing you don't make any errors in termination or assigning IDs. In the following section, we've compiled the most important tips and problem-solving solutions for SCSI hardware:

◆ The Adaptec controller comes in two versions, Bulk and Kit. The major difference between the two is that complete software support and a cable are supplied only with the Kit version. However, most people don't know that the Bulk version has another, older BIOS version. The Bulk version was designed for exclusive use with Windows NT. Its own SCSI drivers, however, don't work with the new BIOS versions from Adaptec, so an old, compatible version is used instead. Until now, this version unfortunately lacked expanded options such as selection of boot ID numbers and auto termination. You'll find more on the installation of Adapted 2940 (UW) in NT later in the section on software and driver information.

◆ When possible, avoid interchanging Wide and Standard SCSI devices or controllers. Don't use an adapter to attach normal SCSI devices to a Wide bus and, conversely, don't use an adapter to attach wide hard drivers to a standard controller. Many dealers entice their clueless customers into purchasing their surplus Wide drives with adapters (68 to 50 pins) at a reduced price by telling them that everything will run "just the same." Unfortunately, this works sometimes, but not always. And more and more often, it's a case of not always. This is because the bus timing for most Wide SCSI drives is specially designed for 16-bit. If you run this type of drive on an 8-bit controller, you can, under certain conditions, reduce your performance level by as much as 30%.

◆ A few devices, such as portable drives and older hard drives, take some time after being switched on to conclude the self test. Before this test, they're unable to respond to commands from the SCSI controller. This can result in the computer not detecting these devices until the entire system has been re-booted. To solve this problem, extend the period of time between turning on the computer and calling up the SCSI BIOS. If this doesn't work, you could slow down the boot sequence some other way, for example, by repeatedly running the memory test in the BIOS. Sometimes you discover a command specially designed for just such applications, such as Delay for SCSI/HDD (Secs), which extends the period of time in seconds. See Chapter 6 for more information.

◆ If, despite what appears to be correct termination, SCSI devices don't function and can't be located by the controller, then either the terminators are not in the correct sockets (refer to the second to last tip) or the fuse on the controller or SCSI device is defective. Every SCSI device contains a wire fuse which is used to carry the supply voltage to the terminators. These fuses often fail. That's why in the more expensive controllers (such as Adaptec) they are socketed and easily exchanged. The fuse on every controller is usually labeled "F" or "F1." When in doubt, check the fuse with a multimeter to see if it's intact. If not, you'll have to replace it. You can get the appropriate fuses (the Adaptec socket type is called "TR5," the fuses can generally be loaded with 2 A) from computer or electronic dealers. Never bridge defective fuses with a wire—an incorrectly placed SCSI cable could destroy SCSI controllers, devices, portions of the network and the motherboard. Don't underestimate this warning — a 20-A short circuit flow turns a flat ribbon cable into a hot wire!

Chapter 7

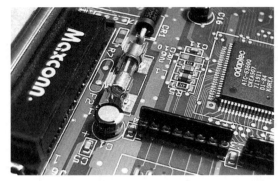

The more simple controllers come equipped with soft fuses—you can instantly tell if they are defective.

◆ SCSI controllers haven't experienced any problems with the **larger hard drives** for a number of years. By default, you can run drives up to one gigabyte in size, anyway. And within the past few years, hard drives up to eight gigabytes can be supported on the SCSI BIOS via a special conversion process. You just need to activate the function in the BIOS (just like the option for running more than two hard drives). The most recent controllers (Adaptec after BIOS 1.24) have enhanced functions for managing hard drives even bigger than eight gigabytes.

```
Peer Concurrency          : Enabled
PCI Streaming             : Enabled
Passive Release           : Enabled
Chipset Global Features   : Enabled
```

All the relevant settings for booting, BIOS and support for hard drives are located in the Advanced Configuration Options menu on the Adaptec BIOS.

◆ You risk losing massive amounts of data if you exchange hard drives bigger than one gigabyte between two different controllers that use different translation methods. Let's assume you previously ran a two gigabyte hard drive on an NCR controller and have recently purchased a brand new computer with an Adaptec 2940UW. When attempting to run the old hard drive (containing the saved data) on the new controller, the FAT and all data will be destroyed because of the different conversion method. Afterwards, the only things that will help are to completely reformat using the new controller or enlist the aid of a specialist to retrieve the data. Our suggestion is don't attach hard drives to a controller without first testing them with unimportant data, especially not if they come from different manufacturers. But even then you're not safe, since the AHA-2920 and AHA-2940(UW) controllers from Adaptec also use different methods, so that you're still not able to upgrade without worry. It's best to ask the manufacturer before you do something irrecoverable.

◆ If the SCSI bus is unstable, first eliminate the most common errors. For example, check to see that you have correct termination, ID allocation and a quality cable. Use the analysis software provided by the manufacturer (EZ-SCSI from Adaptec) to check the ID settings. Then go into the BIOS for the SCSI controller and test the complete settings for every device.

Did you mix Wide and Standard SCSI devices or ports? If nothing helps or gets corrected, try running the bus from just one hard drive and the controller. If this works, then install each device individually, step by step, and attempt to isolate which one caused the error. If you've narrowed it down to just one individual device and all other parameters are otherwise OK, a defective fuse is usually the cause. As far as the software is concerned, always install only the latest drivers. Adaptec offers an updated version for Windows 95 and NT 4 on its home page on the Web. But don't use the driver from the operating system! At the present time, there is hardly any device that won't work in both operating systems with 32-bit SCSI drivers. Even most scanners (for example, HP scanners) can be attached. You won't need the old DOS drivers in Windows 95 for this. You'll read more on this in the next chapter.

◆ The manufacturers deliver their devices and controllers almost always configured to optimal standards. Even overclocking the PC system bus or PCI bus doesn't benefit SCSI, but only causes problems because the bus is clocked by its own quartz crystal (see the section on overclocking in Chapter 6). As long as there aren't any old devices giving you aggravation, just check to see that the settings for Parity check and Initiate Sync Negotiation have been activated in the controller BIOS. The BIOS function Enable Disconnection still has some potential. This allows individual devices to log off from the controller when they are not in use, which then releases them. Enable this function when two devices are in use; if there is only one device attached to the controller, it must be disabled.

The settings for sync negotiations, maximum transfer rates and disconnections are located in the SCSI Device Configuration Menu for the Adaptec BIOS.

◆ Another tuning feature is disabling the BIOS. If you do not have boot hard drives attached to your controller, you can turn off the BIOS support under Advanced Configuration Options (see the next to last picture). That not only saves memory in DOS, but simultaneously increases the boot speed. This also allows you to address the hard drives using a driver (for example, ASPIDISK.SYS). If you haven't attached any hard drives, most SCSI controllers detect this automatically and do not load the BIOS under these circumstances.

◆ In the controller BIOS you can install a **Maximum Sync Transfer Rate** for every SCSI device. This is usually set to the maximum value supported by the controller (10, 20 or 40 Megs). Decrease this value only if you have devices that cannot operate with the higher transfer rates. Sometimes it's recommended to reduce SCSI burners to five Megs/sec to avoid buffer overlap.

SCSI SOFTWARE AND DRIVER GUIDE

Hardware configuration for the SCSI bus is, as you saw in the previous pages, a matter unto itself. But even if you gladly have that all behind you now, you still have the task of getting the controller, as well as the individual devices, up and running in the operating system via the driver software. The following section contains a collection of selected information and tuning tips to help you with this. You'll see a few things remain that you can optimize.

SCSI adjustments and optimizations for DOS and Windows 3.x

Configuring SCSI devices in DOS and Windows 3.x was, we admit, often more demanding than working with EIDE. But this is only at first glance. The trouble that people have with the BIOS in EIDE can be transferred to the drivers in SCSI. It's easier in Windows 95 because its 32-bit driver automatically supports CD-ROMs and portable drives. Besides, most SCSI controllers are detected as Plug & Play and include several drivers.

◆ If you want to use SCSI in DOS or Windows 3.x, you need to assign each device type (*i.e.*, not each individual device, other than the hard drives) a driver in the CONFIG.SYS (examples listed below). The controller also belongs in this category. Hard drives and all basic functions already run without a driver since they are controlled by the BIOS. It's become common to use Aspi drivers, even with Adaptec components. They guarantee optimal performance and data security. The following table matches the designations for the typical drivers with their functions.

Driver name	Device type
Aspixdos.sys (e.g., Aspi2dos, Aspi4dos and Aspi8dos)	SCSI controller. The different numbers designate the different controller types. Only one is used at any time. The Adaptec 2940 uses the Aspi8dos.sys driver
Aspicd.sys	Universal driver for SCSI CD-ROM devices (regardless of which brand)
Aspidisk.sys	Universal driver for portable drives (such as ZIP drives) and hard drives
Sjiix.sys	Scanner driver for HP scanners, but it works with practically all other types as well

◆ Optimal performance is available only if you use the corresponding driver instead of the BIOS functions. Since you're using 8-bit to get to the slower ROM BIOS and 16-bit for the DOS driver, they end up performing at a faster rate. This is most noticeable with hard drives. You can run these without using a driver for the controller (Aspixdos.sys) or for the disk (Aspidisk.sys). But if you add both of them to the Config.sys, the performance level in DOS and Windows visibly increases. Since Windows 95 uses its own 32-bit driver, the BIOS functions aren't accessed, eliminating the need for the ASPI drivers.

◆ The performance losses caused by not using a driver for the controller are particularly drastic when using the simple SymbiosLogic controller for motherboards with SCSI BIOS support (see Chapter 6). If you do not add the enclosed CAM controller driver to the CONFIG.SYS, it will only run in asynchronous mode, which limits the sync negotiation rate to five Megs/s.

◆ As we mentioned, many portable drives (such as Iomega and SyQuest) can run without a driver solely through the BIOS functions. However, there's another reason beyond performance to use a driver. Not using a driver in DOS and Windows 3.x can cause complications if you change a medium in the drive. This is because DOS and Windows 3.x do not recognize portable hard drives. As a result, it's possible that the operating system will transfer the FAT from the old disk to the new medium when the file structure is changed. In so doing, not only will the FAT for the new medium be destroyed and, consequently, all of the data on it, but the changes made to the old disk will be incorrect. In any case, enter Aspidisk.sys (with Adaptec) into the Config.sys and simultaneously avoid configuring the devices as the boot hard drives with an ID of 0 or 1. Other than that, nothing else can go wrong.

◆ You can load all the SCSI drivers into high memory, at least with Adaptec controllers. This also applies to the Aspi manager of the controller. The corresponding lines for added memory can be optimized in the CONFIG.SYS in DOS or Windows 3.x as follows. A SCSI CD-ROM and a SCSI scanner driver are added in this example.

```
device=c:\windows\himem.sys /testmem:off
device=c:\windows\ifshlp.sys
device=c:\windows\emm386.exe noems ram
devicehigh=c:\scsi\aspi8dos.sys /d
devicehigh= c:\scsi\aspicd.sys /d:aspicd0
devicehigh=c:\scsi\sjiix.sys
installhigh= c:\dos\mscdex.exe /d:aspicd0 /l:e /m:16
```

◆ Many SCSI controllers maintain **four drive names** for each attached portable drive. This can be quite annoying when the names of the other drives are displaced as a result. The reason for this behavior is that at the time of booting, the controller doesn't know how many partitions there will be in any portable medium that is inserted at a later time. Since the drive names are allocated during booting, the driver software must keep the required drive names available; otherwise, you wouldn't be able to access the additional partitions from a medium inserted at a later date. If you only use media with a partition, Adaptec controllers allow you to insert the parameter "/r<x>" behind the Aspidisk.sys driver. The variable "x" represents the number of driver names to be reserved per portable drive. The complete entry reads: *Device=Aspidisk.sys /r1.*

Chapter 7

◆ **With optimized driver configuration**, you can also tune many other devices. An example of this is the control of bus mastering for the ISA bus with Adaptec SCSI controllers. The well known Adaptec 1542C controller stops simultaneously running devices in the bus master operations. This affects simultaneously running floppy streamers, which for example, could occur when you are performing a hard drive backup. To remedy the situation, use the parameters */n04 /f11* behind the Aspi Manager in the Config.sys file. The entry for the 1524C would then read: *Device=Aspi4dos.sys /n04 /f11*. In so doing, the priority, or time process, of the remaining devices in the PC becomes more accommodating towards bus mastering.

◆ **Double buffering**: If a software cache driver is used with SCSI hard drives, double buffering must be employed. This feature, which was previously used to prevent data loss when writing to the hard drive, is no longer needed with the newer controllers that have Aspi drivers (for example, all Adaptec versions). For this reason, you won't need to enable double buffering, since it slows down the cache performance and consumes additional memory.

◆ **Two SCSI CD-ROMs in DOS and Windows 3.x**: Using multiple CD-ROMs is child's play with Aspi drivers. Compared to the ATAPI devices, where you have to install a separate driver for each device and register them using parameters to Mscdex.exe, you'll only need to call up Aspicd.sys and Mscdex.exe once when using multiple SCSI CD-ROMs. The second CD-ROM is automatically detected and gets a drive letter designation that is one letter before the letter used for the first device.

SCSI tips in Windows 95 and Windows NT

SCSI has eliminated the need in Windows 95 to use old DOS drivers. Instead you have stable and fast 32-bit drivers that support all of the controller functions and, by bypassing the BIOS, do so at the utmost speed. Normally you don't need to install a DOS ASPI driver in the CONFIG.SYS in Windows 95. One exception is for the scanners that don't include a 32-bit Windows 95 driver. CD-ROMs and floppy drives are automatically supported without additional drivers. The following summarizes the best tips, tricks and information.

◆ Definitely pay attention to the manufacture date of the driver in use. All manufacturers have provided newer versions for both operating systems than the ones in use in the Microsoft CD-ROMs. Adaptec, in particular, has been diligent about driver updates. The most current version for AHA 2940(UW) runs very consistently and without glitches. (As an aside, Adaptec uses a combination driver which supports most controllers of the same make.) Use the Add New Hardware Wizard of the Control Panel to install new drivers. However, first remove the old one by deleting the controller entry in the Device Manager. Then, after calling up the Add New Hardware Wizard in the Control Panel, disable the automatic detection and select SCSI Controllers from the device list. By clicking on Have Disk, you can select and install the new driver. Or you could go directly to the Device Manager to update the driver. Don't be intimidated by the new dialog boxes in Windows 95b (OSR2) because you can install a new driver using the Drivers tab. Simply click on the Update Driver command and use the Yes (recommended) option to search for the new driver or specify the target directory manually.

◆ Windows NT 4.0 and the Adaptec controller 2940(UW) usually make a great team, but there are a few points to keep in mind to insure trouble free installation. As previously stated, you will need to use an Adaptec driver suitable for the complete 2940 version. Only the Bulk version controller works directly with Microsoft drivers. To attach an Adaptec driver, you have to start the installation program for Windows NT without the usual /b switch (in other words, not Winnt /b) to have the installation performed from the boot diskettes. Only then will Windows NT prompt you for other, optional drivers.

◆ All manufacturers of normal SCSI controllers include special 32-bit drivers for Windows NT that, as just stated, need to be added when setting up the operating system. And just like their Windows 95 colleagues, they also support these CD-ROMs and floppy drives. You only need to install special 32-bit Aspi drivers (called Aspi Layer) when using scanners. But even these are included in the program and driver package from your manufacturer. Adaptec calls their version ASPI32.EXE. The file can be downloaded from the Internet home page and automatically adds itself when called up. Then the only thing left to do is install the specific 32-bit driver for the scanner, similar to the manner described below for Windows 95. If, despite all this, it still doesn't work, try calling up the Aspi Layer driver again after installing the scanner driver, but prior to re-booting Windows NT. This is because sometimes a scanner driver that hasn't been properly programmed will overwrite the Aspi Layer's important files, or configurations settings. With Hewlett Packard models, use the older Deskscan 2.2 version, since this version has fewer problems in Windows NT than the more current Deskscan 2.30, which was especially optimized on Windows 95.

◆ While CD-ROMs and portable drives (*e.g.*, ZIP drives) are automatically supported by the driver, the manufacturer needs to supply an additional 32-bit driver for scanners. If this isn't present, you'll have to continue using the old DOS drivers in the CONFIG.SYS. This normally won't have negative side effects, but don't run your computer in MS-DOS compatibility mode. If you have problems, look for the newest driver version and check your entire SCSI system for termination errors and bad cables.

◆ The popular scanner from Hewlett Packard (HP Scanjet) includes 32-bit drivers for Windows. However, the installation isn't properly documented and usually runs with problems. You may want to do the installation yourself. The necessary driver files are located on storage media (usually diskettes) or in the Deskscan (Version 2.31 and higher) scanner main program, as well as in the copier program Scancopy (Version 2.0 and higher). You'll find updates on the Internet at the following address: hpcc887.external.hp.com:9000/cgi-bin/awss/awss.cgi. Copy the following files from the storage medium on which you have the program into the specified directories:

ver files for HP Scanjet	Target directory
All .DLL files beginning with Hpsc* or Hpsj*	Windows\System directory
Hpscnmgr.hlp	Windows\Help directory
Scanjet.inf	Windows\Inf directory
Vhpscand.vxd	Windows\System\Iosubsys

Chapter 7

Then install one or both of the programs in the usual manner using the setup program. The next time that you start Windows, it will automatically detect the scanner using Plug & Play. Windows will prompt you for the source directory of the files previously copied by hand. After specifying the directory where the Scanjet.inf file is located (source index for Deskscan or Scancopy), Windows 95 then attempts to install the files listed above. All too often this process is error laden, but since you already copied the files by hand into the correct directories, the installation proceeds more or less successfully. The next time you start Windows, you'll find a new entry for the scanner in the Device Manager and the HP Scanjet icon in the Control Panel, which primarily is used to test the settings (see figure).

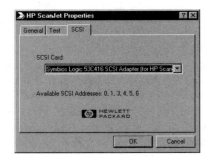

To function properly in Windows 95, an HP Scanjet and the SCSI controller must be entered into the Device Manager with their own 32-bit drivers. It doesn't matter if it's the original controller or another (for example, Adaptec 2940). You can check the scanner settings in the Control Panel by using the new HP Scanjet icon to run a function test.

◆ You may be familiar with the annoying problem that SCSI devices can only be used in Windows 95 when they have been switched on during booting. Since scanners or external CD burners are often turned on after booting, many users have to re-boot Windows. But that's not necessary, since the Windows 95 Device Manager has a function that registers the newly switched on devices even when running Windows. Consequently, you don't have to re-boot in order to use the scanner. Just go to the Device Manager and click once on the Refresh button (see picture above). Your SCSI device should now be activated and appear on the Device Manager list.

◆ Hard drives have their own cache memory that functions in read and write mode in the same manner as the cache programs (for example, Smartdrive). Many SCSI hard drives arrive on the market with disabled write caches. The manufacturer does this primarily for safety reasons. An enabled write cache is always at risk for data loss. Users who want to use the write cache can enable it themselves at their own risk. Other manufacturers don't see this in such narrow terms and usually this is not a big safety risk.

By all means, check to see if your write cache has been enabled and, if not, enable it using the corresponding utility. One such tool for DOS is Aspi-wd.exe by Seagate. It's freeware and is usually run with the analysis program Aspi-id.exe. You can get it on the Internet at a variety of locations. The EZ-SCSI package from Adaptec is much easier. The recent EZ-SCSI 4.01 version has the setup options built into the SCSI Explorer program (see following illustration). The older EZ-SCSI 3.1 version has a separate tool, Fastscsi.

We already covered the double buffering function of the Microsoft cache programs (Smartdrive, *e.g.*) for Windows 3.x and DOS. Similarly, it's possible in Windows 95 to run the cache program when using SCSI drives that have the added feature of double buffering. Windows 95 automatically loads the DBLBUFF.SYS driver using an entry in the MSDOS.SYS. However, as a matter of fact, the functions for this driver are rather unclear and undocumented in Windows 95. Disabling the function in the Msdos.sys or deleting the driver has, as far as we could determine in testing, no effect on the performance of the hard drives, so you can leave it enabled. Maybe in the future Microsoft will provide more information on this dubious driver. Incidentally, the appropriate entry in MSDOS.SYS reads DoubleBuffer=x, with x being either 0 or 1 (disabled or enabled).

IMPORTANT SETTINGS AND AVOIDING EIDE PROBLEMS

The BIOS chapter already covered EIDE information in detail so we won't repeat that information. However, we will mention two problems common to EIDE: the different operation modes (PIO or DMA) and overcoming the 504 Megs BIOS limit to run larger hard drives. All settings that affect, for example, selecting the PIO mode or configuring an EIDE hard drive, were discussed in Chapter 6.

If you already know what a bus master driver is and what it really does, or you were able to get your large hard drive up and running thanks to your new motherboard, then you can skip this section. The same holds true for all SCSI users. All others, however, who want to set up a new EIDE computer or upgrade an old one will get the definitive information to avoid the stress usually associated with EIDE.

Going beyond the 504-Megs limit

Most people are aware of the problem associated with the BIOS limit for hard drives larger than 504 Megs. Nevertheless, many users are always uncertain how to get a hard drive that has larger capacity to run in older or even new computers. But the principal is simple and once you know it, the solution is within reach.

◆ The original PC BIOS could only manage hard drive disks having a maximum of 1,024 cylinders, 16 heads and 63 sectors. As a result, the limit in DOS was established at 504 Megs (DOS can handle 512 bytes per sector, which works out to be $1024 \times 16 \times 63 \times 512 = 528,482,304$ bytes = 504 Megs). In the meantime, EIDE hard drives have reached sizes of eight gigabytes, so a quick solution had to be found.

Chapter 7

◆ With the help of clever conversion methods (translation modes), the operation system is able to address all data by using the old cylinder-head-sector system. The data blocks on the hard drive are managed by other procedures, either by the BIOS or by a special driver (*e.g.*, through sectors that have been continuously numbered from zero up). Think of it as a window with a limited view. The operating system can only look through this window, but the driver simply pushes the window around to view whatever area the OS needs to see. There is also a kind of translation or interpretation going on between the hard drive and the operating system.

◆ More important is the result and possible solutions: Up to 504 Megs, every BIOS can operate with a hard drive. But if you put a larger disk into an old motherboard, it will cut the hard drive capacity to 504 Megs. The remainder no longer exists. Partitioning won't help. Users who want more will have to switch to some type of translation method.

◆ Users who have a new motherboard or BIOS with a built-in translation mode are very lucky. There are two versions in BIOS: **Extended CHS** (also called Large) and **LBA** (Logical Block Addressing). As previously stated in the chapter on BIOS (see Chapter 6), Extended CHS is an older method; the new and uncomplicated LBA is preferred. Set Extended CHS, or Large, in the BIOS only if your hard drive previously ran with it in another computer. But be careful, there is a **risk!** Changing the translation method immediately leads to a drastic loss of data. If you want to change the translation method, you need to save all of the data and partition and format the disk with the new method.

◆ Users who decide to keep their old computer and outfit it with a new hard drive are at a loss because there aren't any more hard drives that are 504 Megs or smaller in size. In this case, there are three solutions:

1. First, set the previously mentioned maximum values into the BIOS and only use the first 504 Megs of the hard drive.

2. Use a **special hard disk driver**, the kind offered free by companies like Seagate or Western Digital (Seagate DiscWizard, previously called EzDrive and Ontrack Disk-Manager). These drivers attach themselves to the Masterboot Record (MBR) in the hard drive and are called up before the operating system. They operate just like the BIOS as a translator between hard drive and operating system. You'll have to use the most recent 32-bit driver versions for Windows 95, which doesn't exactly speed up the hard drive. Naturally, you can forget these types of solutions with Windows NT. We would advise against using such drivers. Not only because they are slow, but they've shown themselves to be troublesome in use. Especially if the hard drive crashes, you will no longer have an easy time retrieving your data with a diskette. This is because the translation driver in the hard drive's MBR was not loaded.

3   For about $83.00 you can buy an EIDE controller that has its own BIOS and translation mode to replace the computer BIOS.

So, you see, the problem is really easy to solve. Even for old computers. Another elegant solution that we didn't mention is, of course, exchanging the motherboard, new BIOS included. However, then you still have to fool around with a video card that is no longer suitable. What most people don't know is you can use your ISA video card in a PCI motherboard. Be that as it may, if you wish and if you've understood the problems as stated thanks to the information supplied, then using a larger hard drive will no longer be a problem.

Plain talk about PIO mode, bus mastering and Ultra DMA/33

You're probably familiar with the PIO modes 0 to 4. DMS modes 1 and 2 are less well known and they're important for bus mastering. At the same time, there is the brand new standard, Ultra DMA/33, and there remains a word or two to say about it. In the final analysis, everyone is plagued with the burning question: does the new standard have so much going for it that it's worth changing?

◆   Selecting the right PIO mode in the BIOS is determined by the maximum data transfer rate that the EIDE interface can transfer from the hard drive. PIO modes 0, 1 and 2 are completely outdated. Except for the brand new versions that have Ultra DMA/33 support, all of the latest hard drives use PIO modes 3 or 4, just like some of the CD-ROMs. Don't be misled by the maximum transfer data rates (e.g., 16 Megs/sec with PIO mode 4). Currently, there isn't an EIDE hard drive that is capable of a transfer rate over six Megs/sec. PIO mode 3, with about 11 Megs/sec, is perfectly adequate for this. The transfer of data in the disk's cache is correspondingly fast. Nevertheless, it makes sense to at least set up PIO mode 3 (if possible) in the BIOS. PIO mode 4 is not entirely out of the question, but the bus is very much prone to error in this mode. For this reason, very short cables (approximately 45 cm long) are recommended, even though a maximum length of 50 – 70 cm also works. Meanwhile, things are critical with PIO mode 4. Bottom line: find out from your hard drive specs which PIO mode is supported and attempt to set the highest value in the BIOS. If problems occur, reduce the setting to the next lowest value.

EIDE Modes and Data transfer rates	
Mode	Transfer rate, Megs/sec
PIO 0	3.33
PIO 1	5.22
PIO 2	8.33
PIO 3	11.11
PIO 4	16.66
DMA 0	4.16
DMA 1	13.33
DMA 2	16.66
Ultra DMA 0	16.66
Ultra DMA 1	25.00
Ultra DMA 2	33.33

Besides the PIO Mode, EIDE drives govern DMA modes (DMA 1 or DMA 2). In DMA mode, an EIDE hard drive works at a slower pace than in the comparable PIO mode, but the data transfer takes place by bus mastering functions over the expanded functions of the PCI bus (see Chapter 5 on the corresponding PCI functions). This results in a DMA mode that is more stable and a processor that is less stressed. The data can also be directly exchanged between the hard drive and the main memory without burdening the CPU. Unlike PIO mode, DMA is not directly supported by the BIOS. To enable this mode, you'll need, beside a chip set capable of bus mastering (all Triton and Natoma boards, and others), a driver specific to the chip set, the notorious bus master driver. You can usually get these drivers from the manufacturer of your motherboard, but you can also download the newest version from the Internet. Even Intel has a bus master driver available from their website (developer.intel.com/ design/pcisets/busmastr/index.htm). Another possible source on the Internet is web2.airmail.net/ksm/software.htm. Just be careful to use the right driver for your motherboard or chipset.

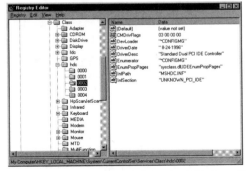

The bus master driver Ideatapi.mpd replaces the standard driver for Windows 95 for hard drives, Esdi_506.pdr. You can check, or even correct, the settings in the appropriate branch of the registry.

◆ The bus master doesn't do as much as people are saying. That's why there are so many problems. When installing the IDEATAPI.MPD driver, you enable the support for the EIDE bus through the bus master chip PIIX3 (or PIIX4 on the new HX-Boards). However, the function is only used if the EIDE hard drive is able to work in DMA mode. Even then, there's no advantage in enabling the function, because eventually the program and operating system need to make use of it. You only notice an advantage when multi-tasking, or when in multi-threading operations, if Windows wants to do something in addition to accessing the hard drive. The bus master driver only relieves the CPU during hard drive operations, but the actual transfer rate is not definitively influenced. On the contrary, the PIO mode is faster. The bus master driver could be interesting for multimedia freaks. Anyone who watches CD videos simultaneously burdens the EIDE and the CPU. On slower computers, this can result in strongly distorted pictures. Bus mastering is clearly an advantage in this situation. Users interested in all of the details can find a wealth of information on these Internet sites: http://www.quantum.com/products/whitepapers/ perform2.html#fast and http://developer.intel.com/design/motherbd/ideinfup.htm.

Typical problems with bus mastering

The bus master driver (BMD) only offers a few advantages in selected instances, but it also creates quite a few problems. One such problem was indicated in Chapter 6, the possible disappearance of CD-ROMs. Another problem is the fact that, after installing the BMD for both of the EIDE ports, an IRQ is forcefully engaged in Windows 95, even if the secondary port is not in use. So definitely avoid installing the driver if you're using the secondary port IRQ 15 for another card. You can remove the driver in two ways. First, use an uninstaller program that the motherboard manufacturer included with your driver (that's usually the case). Second, switch the driver back to the original Windows driver (ESDI_506.PDR) in the registry (see the picture above).

◆ An excellent feature was introduced for hard drives in the Device Manager of the new Windows 95 version: the ability to enable DMA mode. Even though a driver having the same name (Esdi_506.pdr, but with re-worked functions) has been used previously, Windows 95b can switch directly from PIO to the DMA mode. To do this you won't need to install the usual bus master driver provided by the manufacturer of your motherboard. But only use this function if you are certain that both your motherboard and the hard drives support DMA mode. Otherwise, this can lead to problems and even data loss after the function has been enabled. Don't underestimate this.

```
Onboard PCI IDE Enable    : Both
IDE Ultra DMA Mode        : Auto
IDE0 Master PIO/DMA Mode  : Auto
IDE0 Slave  PIO/DMA Mode  : Auto
IDE1 Master PIO/DMA Mode  : Auto
IDE1 Slave  PIO/DMA Mode  : Auto
```

◆ The newest Ultra DMA/33 mode, which was introduced this past spring by Intel with the newest 430TX chipset (Triton III), can be regarded as a positive development compared with the old PIO and DMA modes. In addition to Intel, VIA

The optimal setting for the PIO mode depends on the BIOS and is covered in Chapter 6.

Chapter 7

271

and SiS support Ultra DMA mode on their chipsets. The fact that the maximum transfer rate of 16 Megs (PIO 4) has been raised to 33 Megs is relatively unimportant. As has been stated previously, these dimensions exceed that which a hard drive can currently handle. No, Ultra DMA is interesting because it has a new protocol with error correcting functions, and the EIDE bus is at last protected from resistance as is customary with SCSI. This increases the safety of the data and the stability of the bus. Complete downward compatibility was achieved: Ultra DMA disks can be attached to the normal EIDE motherboards in exactly the same manner as the EIDE hard drives attach to an Ultra DMA board. That the ports and cables weren't changed is evident. If you have a new motherboard that has Ultra DMA/33 mode, try to purchase one of these hard drives. These are available at capacities of up to eight gigabytes from all of the leading manufacturers. You won't need to worry about space.

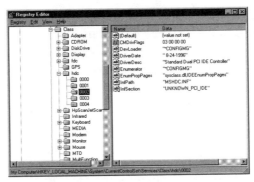

In the BIOS of the new motherboards there is a new,
additional item in the Chipset Features Setup for enabling UltraDMA mode.

Chapter 8

Hard Drive And Removable Drive Secrets

Hard drives always follow two truths: they are always too small and too slow. It's usually the component that limits overall performance the most for today's PCs. This is especially true when combined with insufficient RAM. If you want your PC to work at peak performance—assuming you don't have a Pentium 100 or 133 chugging away in your system—seriously consider a fast hard drive. You'll be amazed at how much of a boost Windows 95, for example, will get from an extra-fast SCSI disk spinning at 7200 rpm.

We talked about two common hard drive bus systems (SCSI and EIDE) in Chapter 7 so now we'll turn to the hard drive and other storage devices. We'll give you some buying tips and configuration recommendations and how to optimize the devices in DOS and Windows. We'll also talk about software caching, defragmenting hard drives and organizing your data better.

Avoiding Problems When Buying A Hard Drive

Buying the right hard drive isn't always easy. The outside of the hard drive does not list or show anything about workmanship or performance features. This is unfortunate because the hard drive plays an important role in how your entire system performs. It's arguably the most important component —if for no other reason than it contains a valuable possession: your data. If a graphics card dies, you replace it and the problem is solved. But when a hard drive gives up the ghost and you have no backup for your data, you could be in deep trouble.

So the choice of a hard drive should not be based only on speed and cost but also on reliability. But again, you cannot tell the reliability of a hard drive simply by looking at it. You'll eventually need to rely on test reports, the experience/recommendations of friends or the dealer and magazine/Internet web reviews.

What really makes a disk fast

A fast interface (Fast-ATA2, Ultra-DMA/33 or Wide-SCSI), a large cache or low mean access times are not what make a hard drive truly fast. The speed of a hard drive depends mostly on the areal density (AD) and the rotational speed of the disk itself. AD is defined as the packing density in bits per square inch. The internal data transfer rate (or throughput), the maximum potential rate at which you can retrieve data, is derived from the AD and the rotational speed. This is the figure you need to look for in the product specifications. It's given in megabits per second and should not be less than 88 Mbps.

Unfortunately, however, this theoretical value doesn't tell us much. The only good way to compare hard drives is by using the test results from benchmark programs (see Chapter 1). These programs use various test procedures to obtain an average of the data transfer to the operating system, in Mbps.

For a rough estimate of the performance class, we can use the rotational speed (in rpm). When combined with the areal density, this will tell us the maximum possible transfer rate. The faster a hard drive turns its magnetic heads, the faster they can access a particular data point and the more data per second can be positioned under the read/write heads for transfer.

A good hard drive should not spin at less than 5400 rpm. Plus the packing density should not be less than 90,000 bits/inch (bpi). State of the art disks spin at 10,000 rpm, but 7200 is also considered high-end and is only found in top-of-the-line models.

With areal density and speed, you should also understand the technology the hard drive uses. All newer, high-performance models use Magneto-Resistive heads (MR heads, or MRX heads on the newest versions) and a PRML read channel. These two processes make it possible to store and read data on the hard drive at a higher density, which in turn increases the data transfer rate.

So, before buying a hard drive, keep the three most important questions in mind. They are what is the rotational speed, how high is the areal density and are modern technologies such as MR or MRX heads used? Do not buy a hard drive which spins at less than 5400 rpm or does not have at least 2 Gigabytes of storage capacity on a single 3.5-inch magnetic disk (3.5 inches has become the standard for hard drives). The 5.25-inch hard drives are still available but are intended more for the mass market with a favorable price-to-storage capacity ratio. (Avoid 5.25-inch hard drives if you're expecting high performance.)

Special cases call for special hard drives

You may need to consider other criteria when shopping for a hard drive. This criteria depends on how you'll be using a hard drive. As mentioned above, the mean transfer rate is the most important value in most cases, but access time is more important in some applications (such as databases or compiling programs). Both factors do not necessarily have to coincide in a high-quality hard drive but here again it's true that hard drives with high rotational speeds will provide faster access.

However, if you'll be working with larger, self-contained data quantities such as graphic images, sounds or videos, you'll need to consider another criterion. This is the problem of thermal calibration. Normal hard drives compensate for minimal expansion of their components due to operating temperatures by using intermediate calibration. During the short calibration phase the read/write heads cannot read or write data. This is almost unnoticeable under normal conditions. However, when you have to continuously write long video sequences (hundreds of megabytes)

Chapter 8

from a video capture card, then the calibration can interrupt the data flow. Many manufacturers have special models with different calibration routines for this situation (for example, the AV models from Micropolis). However, consider a disk of this type only if you really are working continuously with large data chunks of at least several hundred Mbytes.

High speed problems of hard drives with 7200 rpm

Although most hard drives (and nearly all EIDE drives) turn at 5400 rpm and access four to five Megs/sec, there are real high-end speed demons that spin at 7200 or even 10,000 rpm. At present these are only applicable to SCSI bus applications and it's unlikely that EIDE disks spinning this fast will be available in the near future.

We've mentioned that the rotational speed has an important effect on the performance of a hard drive. (Popular models from the market leaders in this area — IBM, Seagate and Quantum — achieve transfer rates of six to eight Megs/sec with an access time often under 10 ms.) The difference is one you'll notice everyday.

Higher rotational speeds comes with a price of course compared to a normal model (four-gigabyte models spinning at 7200 rpm still cost considerably over $575). However, there is another, even more significant factor to consider here. It applies even more to the new Seagate models running at 10,000 rpm (Cheetah drives) than to the "normal" 7200 rpm versions:

◆ The high spin rate results in a somewhat loud operating noise. Many hard drives squeal when they are accessed. Some can give off a high-pitched sound even at rest. This noise can be so bad that it has prevented many from buying these hard drives. One exception is the Atlas models from Quantum. But even these, like all the others, are really suited more for servers than desk machines.

◆ The increased rotational speed leads to higher temperatures of the hard drives. This in turn requires more frequent thermal calibration. Depending on the application (for example, video processing), this can be a significant disadvantage and makes these hard drives a less than ideal choice even for general applications.

◆ The thermal problem is in fact so critical that you cannot install these hard drives without excellent ventilation. Never use an enclosed removable frames for these drives. Install the drive far from other devices and hard drives. Also, put it as deep in the rack and close to a PC fan. The best solution is to spend a few dollars on an auxiliary hard drive fan. For this to be effective, you'll also have to provide sufficient airflow. One or two small holes in the computer case in front of the hard drive compartment should do the job.

Buying the right hard drive

Buying a hard drive is often a matter of luck, especially if you aren't familiar with the various manufacturers and current models. The following tips will help you find the right model and not fall for the usual traps and shell games the manufacturers and dealers play.

◆ Make sure you're buying an original model designed to be sold to an end-user. in other words, you'll often see OEM versions for sale. These are units intended to be installed computers by manufacturers and not by end users. Avoid these for several reasons. The installation manual and other information material—even software—may be missing. It's not uncommon for the specifications of an OEM version to differ from those of a true series model. For example, you may find that an OEM hard drive comes with less cache or spins at a slower speed than the series model.

◆ Even the best hard drive manufacturers produce defective drives.. The problem is they aren't always destroyed but are sometimes sold at special prices to certain dealers or manufacturers. Although most manufacturers are candid about the inferior quality of these drives, they nevertheless can still somehow appear for sale to end users. So be suspicious of hard drives for sales at a special price or deal. Reconsider your purchase if the original manufacturer's name isn't clearly marked or if there are even additional company names indicated. Hard drives, like most computer components, are priced down to the penny. Margins are so small that you won't find great price differences from one dealer to another. Be skeptical when you suddenly see a model offered at a 10% or 20% or an even greater discount compared to other dealers.

◆ When you buy a new hard drive, pay close attention to the exact model number. Many manufacturers offer several variations of one model that often differ by no more than one letter in the model number. However, these may differ in cache size (usually reduced by half) or, less often, in rotational speed. For example, a magazine review will test model "XYa." You may soon afterwards see dealer ads for model "XY" at a great price. Unfortunately what they're really selling is a slimmed down cheaper model, perhaps the "XYb" model. However, you think that you're looking at the faster model.

◆ It's difficult to recommend a model or explain the criteria you should use when buying a hard drive. Specifications, models and versions change regularly. Manufacturers can disappear through a merger (Conner into Seagate, for example) or by going out of business. We recommend staying with the known, accepted brands and then considering rotational speed. Don't even consider a drive under 5400 rpm. On the other hand, 7200 may be a little tricky (see above). You should probably stay away from the Cheetah series with their 10,000 rpm, as they are really only suitable for use in a server. The leading manufacturers today are IBM, Seagate, Western Digital, Quantum and Maxtor.

The following table shows recommendations based on models which were available as we went to press. Look for a successor version if one of these models are already discontinued. Incidentally, "Ultra" now applies to virtually all hard drives, which means that EIDE Ultra-DMA/33, SCSO devices can in fact support Ultra-SCSI. "Normal" (non-Ultra) drives are no longer available. All types can however be connected to the old controllers.

Hard drive xx = Model numbers, by size	Remarks
Maxtor xx DiamondMax series	Various EIDE disks with 5,400 rpm and 5 to 8 GB. Fast and very economical
Quantum Fireball-STxxAT series	EIDE disks, similar to Maxtor. From 2 to 6 GB with significantly higher than 4 Megs/sec
Seagate Medalist STxx series	EIDE and SCSI at 5,400 rpm; very good and economical. Also available in various storage capacities.
Western Digital ACxxx Caviar series	The classic among the EIDE units, made in various capacities. Very fast (5,400 rpm) and good. The AC35100 version with 5 GB is especially fast
IBM DCAA or DCAS and the new Deskstar Ultra-DMA/33 series	EIDE and SCSI hard drives with 5,400 rpm, high speed, quality, but somewhat expensive. The favorite among professionals. The SCSI version almost reaches the level of 7,200 rpm disks. The new Diskstar 8 EIDE disk has 8.4 GB and a record data density of 1.74 billion bits per square inch. With 5.8 Megs/sec and 9.5 ms access time, currently the fastest EIDE disk
Quantum Atlas II (soon to be Series III) and Viking series (SCSI only, preferably used in the ultra-wide configuration).	High-end disks with 7,200 rpm and very high access speed. Sound level still bearable. Sizes 2.4 and 8 GB
Seagate STxxx Barracuda	Similar to Quantum's 7,200 disks, but somewhat noisier and with similarly high performance

TIPS AND TRICKS FOR INSTALLING AND OPTIMIZING

Now that you bought the right hard drive, it's time for installation and hardware configuration. The necessary steps are basic and simple. You just need to keep a few rules and tuning traps in mind.

Avoiding conflicts between the old and new hard drives

If you want to equip your old PC with a new, larger and faster drive, the question remains: "What do I do with the old one?" Here are some things to help you decide:

◆ Use ScanDisk or Norton's Disk Doctor on the old drive. If errors are reported, especially serious errors, you may want to consider removing the old disk. If your old drive is otherwise perfectly functional, but simply too small, consider compressing the drive using Drivespace.

◆ Determining whether the old drive will be compatible with the new one depends on your system. You'll only have problems when old (E)IDE controllers are running on the same port as devices with different operating modes (PIO vs. DMA). So for old (three to four years) motherboards, you have to hang old, new/fast and slow devices on their own EIDE ports.

This is not necessary for newer motherboards. You can even see this in the BIOS settings. If individual settings for each master and slave device are possible on each port, you can mix the devices without any problem. This is also true for connecting slower CD-ROMs with PIO mode 2 and faster hard drives with PIO mode 4. In fact, even Ultra-DMA and normal PIO devices can be mixed on a single port.

```
Onboard FDC Controller      : Enabled
Onboard FDC Swap A & B      : No Swap
Onboard Serial Port 1       : 3F8H/IRQ4
Onboard Serial Port 2       : 2F8H/IRQ3
Onboard Parallel Port       : 3BCH/IRQ7
Parallel Port Mode          : ECP+EPP
ECP DMA Select              : 3
UART2 Use Infrared          : Disabled
Onboard PCI IDE Enable      : Both
IDE Ultra DMA Mode          : Auto
IDE0 Master PIO/DMA Mode    : Auto
IDE0 Slave  PIO/DMA Mode    : Auto
IDE1 Master PIO/DMA Mode    : Auto
IDE1 Slave  PIO/DMA Mode    : Auto
```

Today's motherboards allow mixed operation of EIDE devices at different speeds, which can be individually configured in BIOS.

◆ SCSI, like the new EIDE controllers, is fairly friendly when mixing hard drives with different speeds. If possible you should try to avoid running 50-pin standard devices on a wide connection. Only the very newest Ultra-Wide II controllers, with up to 80-Megs/sec transfer rates, do not allow mixed configurations, since the transfer protocols on the new busses work differently. But it won't be long before these devices becomes the standard in every normal PC.

◆ Mixing small capacity and large capacity hard drives (up to 504 Megs and larger) is also no problem. You need a BIOS or a special driver to communicate with the new large disks, which also allows the old disk to be handled with no problems.

Tips for connecting the new hard drive for optimum installation

Installing a hard drive is more than tightening four screws. For example, the usual 3.5-inch drives often don't fit into the 5.25-inch slot of many housings. In addition, SCSI hard drives especially are very sensitive to insufficient ventilation. Here are the main points you need to keep in mind:

◆ All PC cases have accessible 3.5-inch slots for installing hard drives. The problem is they provide little room for adequate ventilation. Your best bet is to spend a few dollars on a set of simple spacers from 3.5-inch to 5.25-inches that you can find in any better computer store. This will enable you to install your disks with plenty of room in the large and easily accessible 5.25-inch bay, just as you find them in tower configurations.

Chapter 8

To prevent your hard drives from sitting too close to each other in a narrow 3.5-inch bay as shown left, use the spacers shown right to install them in the 5.25-inch bay.

◆ As we said earlier, it's imperative that you provide good ventilation for your hard drives. SCSI hard drives in general, and especially the fast-spinning varieties (7200 rpm and higher) get quite hot. The disk temperature is critical, and should under no circumstances be allowed to reach 122°F. This can be approximated using a simple hand test during operation. A hard drive above 122°F will be painful to the touch. When installing a 7200 rpm drive, you must provide an auxiliary fan to direct the air flow at the disk.

◆ If you intend to continue using your old hard drive, the question is in which combination you should use the two. A simple answer is to use the new, faster hard drive as the boot disk and for the operating system and/or programs. Use the old hard drive to store data (documents, tables, etc.). You'll get the most out of your new disk with its higher speed if you use it as a boot and program disk. In the case of SCSI disks, this means you need to set the new one to ID0 and the old one to ID1. For EIDE disks, the new one is configured as the master and the old one as slave.

◆ Old and new EIDE disks can, as mentioned above, always be connected in combination to newer controllers on the same port. This even has an additional advantage because the cable length and/or number of cables is reduced if you connect

EIDE devices can be configured as single, master or slave, which is usually done using jumpers. The jumper settings are usually shown on a sticker on the unit. "Single" is for exclusive operation, and "master" or "slave" is used as the setting for one of the maximum two devices in combination operation.

both to a single port as opposed to separate ports. Since many motherboards have the primary expansion port internally connected to the secondary EIDE port already, the maximum cable length of 17.75 inches for PIO mode then applies to both connections together. Unfortunately, there is no easy way to tell whether your motherboard connects the two ports. In any case, if you have problems when connecting the devices to their own port, first try reducing the PIO mode. If this eliminates the problem, then it's probably a cable problem. Then connect both devices together on a single cable and to a single port. Then PIO mode 4 should also work properly again.

◆ Interchangeable drives that can be inserted in the computer housing as desired are a great feature for those who want to work with various operating systems or configurations. When you decide you want to work with Windows NT or Linux instead of Windows 95, simply insert the corresponding hard drive. However, you may have problems using hard drives with different storage capacities. This is not a problem for SCSI, since the controllers are flexible about reporting the new devices. For EIDE, however, the BIOS should have an Auto Detect function. Otherwise, you need to update the new values in the BIOS every time you change drives. If the hard drives vary only slightly in their capacity, you can leave the parameters of the smallest disk in the BIOS and use the somewhat larger one with this setting. All you sacrifice is a little disk space in favor of fast and easy interchangeability.

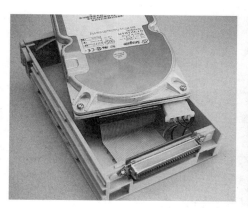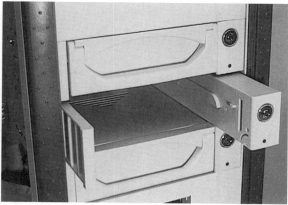

Removable versions of both EIDE and SCSI drives are available, which are screwed into a case (as shown at left) with adapters for the power and data cable. This does inhibit ventilation, though. The case is then inserted into the latchable 5.25-inch slot shown at right.

◆ It's no secret that caching data when reading from and writing to data storage devices creates a significant advantage in speed. Even MS-DOS and, of course, Windows have caching programs built-in (SMRTDRV, V-Cache, etc.). But in addition to this software cache, which works with the main memory and uses the processor for processing, hardware caching is also an option. There are special hard drive controller cards (to our knowledge, only for SCSI at present) which cache using their own static RAM. Such cards offer no great advantages in mainstream PCs. The speed gain compared to a software cache is virtually negligible. However, on professional systems, where every bit of speed matters more than price, these cards do make sense, especially because of the load they take off the main memory. If a PC is already maxed out with SIMMs and no further enhancement is possible, a cache controller with eight Megs of memory will be the equivalent of the same amount added to main memory.

Tips On Partitions, Boot Managers And File Systems

If you never considered your PC's partitioning, perhaps it's time you did. Subdividing the hard drive into data ranges (partitions) accessible as separate drives lets you get much more out of your PC. Smaller partitions allow better use of the hard drive's storage capacity because the cluster size shrinks. More importantly, data, programs and operating systems are handled much better in parallel on a partitioned PC.

Admittedly, partitioning using the programs supplied with most of the operating systems (for example, FDISK for DOS) isn't very user-friendly. However, we know of an alternative that you should consider. It's called Partition Magic and is from PowerQuest. For around $80.00 this program is well-named.

Partitioning alone isn't the whole answer, of course. The next logical step is a program for managing the various partitions or for selective booting of the operating systems installed there. For this we use a boot manager.

FDISK for DOS does work, but it's an absolute horror to use and offers too few options.

When partitioning makes sense

You probably already know that partitioning means to divide the hard drive into several areas that can then be accessed under normal drive letter designations. When partitioning, you separate the space on your data storage device into small, manageable morsels. Most users disliked and seldom used partitioning. The fairly complicated subject could only be implemented using cryptically operated and barely documented programs (such as FDISK for DOS or OS/2). Since the introduction of Partition Magic (PQ-Magic), it's now much easier. But first some information about partitions:

◆ Partitioning offers two main advantages. The first advantage is that it allows data to be arranged throughout the various partitions, or drive letters. Applications, for example, can be placed in partition 1 and data in partition 2. The second advantage is the smaller partition size reduces the cluster size for most file systems (especially FAT). While partitions up to 512 Megs in size with a normal FAT/VFAT file system for DOS or Windows 95 use clusters of up to 8 K, they will expand to 32 K with two-gigabyte partitions. This is not good because each file which is smaller than the cluster size itself still occupies a complete cluster as its disk space. On a 2 gigabyte hard drive, such disk space losses can add up to as much as 100 Megs and more if you use a lot of small files (for example, URL links in Internet Explorer). So partitioning increases your available disk space.

◆ Another justification for partitioning is that many operating systems can't handle large partitions. For example, DOS and most versions of Windows 95, or more precisely the VFAT file system, are unable to manage partitions larger than 2 Gigabytes. Only the new FAT32 for Windows 95b (OSR2) and NTFS for Windows NT eliminate this problem. So if you want to use a 4 gigabyte hard drive with normal Windows 95, you need to subdivide it into at least two 2 gigabyte partitions.

◆ Sometimes there are so many unknown problems that nothing runs anymore. You've reinstalled Windows 100 times, fooled around until you want to scream and everything is just getting worse. Maybe there were even a couple of viruses and the hard drive is still having trouble reading certain sectors. Plus, you'd just love to get rid of that despised hard drive manager in the Master Boot Record. Well, simply do some house cleaning. Delete everything in one shot by reformatting the entire hard drive and partitioning. You won't delete the hard drive manager in the MBR simply by formatting. For this you'll have to use partitioning to reset the boot sectors or rewrite them using the FDISK/MBR command. This action also happens to destroy any boot sector virus, though only if you have not booted from the disk. If the system boots from the infected disk, the virus still resides in memory and will reinfect the boot sector.

◆ One thing that sometimes caused total crashes with old IDE hard drives is also possible with the newest hard drives is low-level formatting. This might make sense, for example, if defective sectors suddenly appear on the disk and you want to check them. Or if for any other reasons (for example, changed translation procedure) you simply can't get the disk to run any more. Check the Maxtor website on the Internet (www.maxtor.com/idx2.html) and download a program called LLFUTIL.EXE that you can use to do low-level formatting of Maxtor EIDE hard drives. Since all EIDE hard drives should use the same command set, it should also work with disks from most other manufacturers. It's worth a try if all else has failed.

> **NOTE** **Partitioning jargon**
>
> Three terms come up again and again when partitioning: primary partitions, extended partitions and logical drives. The differences lie only in the way in which the corresponding partitions are recognized in an operating system. Primary partitions are always assigned the first drive letter and are bootable for DOS and Windows 95. You can have a maximum of four primary or three primary and one extended partition per disk. An extended partition is not primarily bootable, but rather can be used for booting only from special programs like Windows NT. To be precise, you don't even really boot from an extended partition, but rather from a logical drive within it. Because an extended partition should be considered like an area or a container on the disk, which must first be subdivided into logical drives. In the simplest case, the entire extended partition becomes a logical drive, but this in turn can be subdivided again into almost any number of drives. If you have more than one hard drive, the drive letters are assigned first to the primary partitions of disk 1, 2, 3, etc., then to the logical drives in the extended partitions. This system lets you play some interesting games with the drive letters.

FAT32 is more curse than blessing

Now we should say a few words about the new Windows 95b (OSR2) file system called FAT32 since it was created by Microsoft in direct response to the problems just mentioned.

FAT32 has two good features, one of which is that: it eliminates the old size limitation of two Gigabytes. This allows partitions up to two terabytes in size to be accessed. PC video enthusiasts happy are happy about this feature since they work with video files that are often over 2 Gigabytes. The second feature is the old FAT/VFAT problem of clusters being too large is solved. Instead of 32 K clusters with 2 Gigabyte partitions, FAT32 uses a maximum of only 8 K.

You can even configure the cluster size with an undocumented switch of the format command, Format/z:n. Here "n" represents a factor of 512 bytes, so that using the instruction Format/z:2 a hard drive can be divided into clusters of 1,024 bytes each. But this also means that a four-gigabyte drive has over four million clusters, which of course first have to be organized. Even with cluster sizes of 2,048 bytes, there will still be two million clusters. 4 K clusters is the standard, by the way.

> **NOTE** **Caution: Risks with old hard drive tools**
>
> FAT32 is not compatible with older programs which independently access the hard drive, such as DEFRAG or SCANDISK. You can only use the new programs from Windows 95b or specially released programs for FAT32 (such as Norton Utilities 2.0). Otherwise you are looking at major data chaos.

However, if FAT32 were all good, there would be no need for an update or Windows NT. So FAT32 also has its weaknesses and problems:

◆ FAT32 is incompatible with all other operating systems, including Windows NT4. The only way to create a boot diskette is with the help of DOS 7.1(included), allowing you to access data when a problem comes up.

◆ Many plug-in cards which work closely with the hard drive (for example, video capture cards) have problems with FAT32. Here your only recourse is an update from the manufacturer.

◆ Any programs which directly access the hard drive (disk editors, defragmenters) have to be FAT32 versions if you want to avoid data loss.

◆ Another thing which can be a problem is that FAT32 no longer supports disk compression with DriveSpace. Microsoft apparently has no plans for an update in the future.

◆ When it comes to notebooks, FAT32 often has problems with power management. Disks in sleep mode take too long to get back to full speed when enabled, which can lead to faulty data access with Windows 95. Worst-case scenarios even result in lost data.

◆ Perhaps the biggest weakness is that FAT32 is significantly slower than the previous file system. This is primarily due to the increased administrative complexity for the larger number of clusters. During normal use, the performance loss of around 5% may not be very noticeable. But as soon as you run hard drive utilities like ScanDisk, Speed Disk or Defrag, your performance goes right out the window, even more so the smaller the clusters. This is a good reason not to work with clusters smaller than four or even eight K in size.

NOTE
Tips on converting to FAT32
The simplest method is to use PQ-Magic 3.0 (see below). It lets you convert normal FAT and VFAT partitions into FAT32 and back again without formatting and with no data loss. You just select the properties of a drive and change the sector size. When you select one of the lower values (two, four or eight K), PQ-Magic tells you that it is automatically converting to FAT32. If you don't want to use PQ-Magic, the only alternative is the new FDISK in OSR2. First install Windows 95b as usual with VFAT. Then create a boot disk including the new FDISK. Finally, you have to repartition and format the hard drive from the boot diskette. FDISK automatically offers you the choice between the old file system and the new FAT32. The ability to convert existing data like PQ-Magic does will not be available from Microsoft until Windows 98 comes out, and even then you'll only be able to convert in one direction. !

The bottom line here is to stay away from FAT32 unless you absolutely need drives over two Gigabytes for video films. Instead, use the advantages of smart partitioning, as described below with PQ-Magic.

Chapter 8

Masters of the system—Boot managers handle multiple operating systems

Boot managers are a great thing. They enable themselves during the booting process and let you select from different operating systems for the start process that follows. These operating systems do however have to be installed in their own respective partitions. Certainly one of the best-known boot managers is for OS/2. Using the OS/2 FDISK program, you can set up one-Meg boot partitions, for example, at the beginning of your hard drive, where the boot manager is installed. Using OS/2 FDISK, you then enter the various partitions and operating systems installed there in a boot menu. The next time the computer is started, you can select the desired system (for example, OS/2 or Windows 95) and start using that one.

The OS/2 boot manager is getting a little long in the tooth, however. This is evident in the cryptic way in which it is operated. Unfortunately it's also not very cooperative when it comes to the newer Microsoft operating systems (or vice-versa, as you might expect). Fortunately there are alternatives:

◆ The first one is the PTS boot manager, from the developers of the popular PTS/DOS system, also known as "Russian-DOS." This tool (less than $30) allows you to manage up to ten different operating systems (DOS, Windows, NT, Linux OS/2, etc.) and selectively boot from one of them. Plus if you want to try one other than Windows, this is exactly what you need. The only disadvantage is that you can not run the same operating system in various configurations. This is because the weak link of the PTS boot manager is that it isn't really a typical boot manager (like the one with OS/2). It just stores various versions of the boot sectors for various operating systems and then when needed writes them back to the same partition. This also prevents working with two versions of the same operating system since the program won't save the same boot sectors twice.

◆ If you need to work with various Windows 95 versions, or in general want to use a real boot manager which can work with different partitions, the BeckerTOOLS boot manager from Data Becker might be for you. Available for around $15.00, you get a genuine boot manager which makes it easy to manage two versions of Windows 95, one Windows NT and one MS-DOS, for example, in separate partitions.

Boot managers vs. Partition Magic—Which tool is better for multiple operating systems?

Not many people know this by using Partition Magic as described below, you can also manage various operating systems using multiple partitions, just like with a boot manager. Every program or method has its advantages and disadvantages:

◆ A maximum of four primary partitions or three primary and one extended partion can be created on a hard drive. Both DOS and Windows 95 can only be started from primary partitions. Windows NT, OS/2 and Linux, on the other hand, can be run from extended partitions. Only one of the primary partitions can be the active one. The others must be set to hidden mode by the partitioning program.

♦ A boot manager will reserve one of the primary partitions for itself. So remember this if you want to use a boot manager. This leaves only two or three (depending on the example above) for the operating systems. But with PQ-Magic you get a tool, PQ-Boot, which you can use to switch between different primary partitions (the active one is hidden, a hidden one is enabled), without the program needing its own partition. Specifically, this means you gain a primary partition for an additional operating system, as compared to using a boot manager. This could be important depending on your requirements.

The bottom line is that if you want to work with more than two constellations of Windows 95 or DOS, you won't get by without Partition Magic. Only if you can get by with two primary partitions, and therefore two Windows 95/DOS combinations, is a boot manager perhaps the better alternative due to its simplicity.

However, keep the following in mind: while a boot manager comes up every time you boot and offers you a selection of various operating systems, you only need to open PQ-Boot when you want to switch to a different partition. Otherwise the PC runs normally: the hidden partitions are exactly that (it's like they are in quarantine), and the PC also boots faster. Our preference is for PQ-Magic and PQ-Boot as being significantly more flexible and in the long run a simpler solution.

PQ-Magic in practical application

In the following section you'll see a clever example of how you can work with three Windows 95 and/or DOS configurations or versions, as well as with a Windows NT workstation. The example also organizes your data optimally. Using the configuration shown, you'll be able to use your PC more flexibly and reliably than you thought possible. You must, however, use either Partition Magic or one of the imitation programs (like Quarterdeck's Partition It). Some of the features could be implemented using FDISK but more work is required with. Another important advantage of PQ-Magic compared with FDISK is that: you can change the partition size after the fact with no formatting or data loss. Should you run out of data space, for example, simply reduce the program memory.

Our configuration offers the following benefits:

♦ When we're done, you'll be working with drives C: (Windows), D: (data), E: (programs) and F: (Windows NT—this is of course optional). In addition, you create three primary partitions on the first hard drive where you can use three various combinations of DOS, Windows and/or Windows 95 (all primary partitions are on drive C:). You cannot exchange data between them nor can viruses from one directly infect another primary partition. You can even use FAT32 and VFAT since each Windows has its own partition. The only disadvantage is that you have to install all the applications on the extended partition E: and repeat this for each of the DOS or Windows versions in the primary partition. But this is a small price to pay for the benefits you'll get.

♦ Your data on drive D: are clearly separated from the programs. This gives you a better overview, increased data security and makes backup much easier.

Chapter 8

◆ You use one extended partition with one or more logical drives (F:, G:, etc.) for a Windows NT workstation, NT server, Linux or similar programs. This means you can try every possible operating system on your computer without having to worry about conflicts or any other kind of problem. You can even work with different file systems (FAT32, NTFS), since each operating system gets its own partition.

◆ Unlike using removable drives, here you take virtually full advantage of all your disk resources (except for the loss resulting from the two primary partitions which are always disabled). In addition, you don't have to play around with your hardware when you want to run a new operating system. Simply start PQ-Boot, select the desired boot partition, and reboot. That's it.

Returning now to the details and how to proceed, the normal Windows PC has three types of data which need to be distinguished for dividing into partitions: the operating system (Windows), applications and data (documents). Therefore you need to create at least one dedicated partition for each of these data types.

Let's take the following example. Say you're using Windows 95 but would like to run DOS or Windows 3.x in special configurations in some specific cases. Since a lot is happening now with Windows 95, you would also like to experiment with different Windows 95 configurations, service packs, updates or beta versions. Plus you wouldn't be a true power user if you weren't curious about Windows NT or Linux. Even these programs can be easily incorporated into the given configuration. Also, since you are always able to work with only one of the programs at a time, you can forget about any licensing difficulties.

The following partitioning example assumes a PC configured with two two-gigabyte hard drives, which today is completely economically justifiable and optimal for parallel working with the mentioned operating systems. If you have just a single, large-capacity hard drive, set up drives D: and F: on this disk as additional logical drives in the extended partition. The main thing is to end up with the same combination of drive letters. But as we said, two hard drives are more practical.

To create the partitions as shown in the lower table and illustrations, you'll need Partition Magic 2.0 or preferably 3.0. Then you can reduce or expand your existing partitions without having to reformat. The whole thing is amazingly safe, but of course you should make a backup anyhow. We have not witnessed a single crash or error function, even after frequent use of the program. You can also run PQ-Magic from the hard drive. If you really have to change all the partitions as in the following example, copy the program to a boot diskette or a ZIP drive and do the changes from there, which gives you truly unlimited access. Since operation is very intuitive, the help section is excellent and the manual is even better, the whole process should be a breeze.

But first back to our example. Using the illustration or the data in the table, divide the first hard drive into three primary partitions (each drive C:) as well as an extended one with a logical drive (drive E:). Each primary partition gets its own DOS or Windows version, whereby these can be set up in any way you want. All the applications will be installed later on the E: drive. To enable the desired primary partition, you can switch over to them either with PQ-Magic or PQ-Boot; the other two are then automatically hidden. PQ-Boot does function somewhat unreliably only if you disable a FAT32 partition and want to enable one of the other, normal FAT partitions. If this happens, the FAT32 partition is not hidden, but rather is displayed as an additional drive the next time you boot (which naturally leads to shifting). In addition, many operating systems cannot access multiple primary partitions. To get around this, carry out the switch manually in PQ-Magic and then explicitly hide the FAT32 partition. You'll find the corresponding command in the Special menu. However, it's best not to use FAT32 at all, since it offers only disadvantages with a partition size of 300 Megs.

Sectioning the first hard drive			
Name	Partition type	Size	Remarks
Win95A	Primary, drive C:	300	Working partition
Win95B*	Primary, drive C:	300	Test partition
Win97/98*	Primary, drive C:	300	Test partition
Programs	Extended partition with a logical drive E:	1,100	For applications
* Only one primary partition can be active at a time; the others must be hidden			

Now separate the second hard drive into one primary (D: drive) and one extended partition. The primary partition will contain all your data (documents). The extended partition is used for creating one or more logical drives (F: drive and so on), where Windows NT, other operating systems or other data can reside.

Sectioning the second hard drive			
Name	Partition type	Size	Remarks
Data	Primary, hence D: drive	1,400	Documents
Win_NT	Extended partition with one or more logical drives	600	Windows NT, Linux, OS/2, etc.

Since you can use the last drive letter for a primary partition (D: drive), you can also format this drive with NTFS. It disappears under Windows 95 (because Windows 95 can't recognize NTFS) but at least the drive letters are not shifted. You'll then have to carry out the installation of Windows NT using the roundabout method of a primary partition on the first hard drive. For example, if you set up Windows NT from the second primary partition (Win 95b), the NT dual boot manager will be installed there. NT itself however is put on the F: drive. If you later want to use NT, the second primary partition must be active so that you can use the boot manager installed there to start NT on the F: drive. If you enable one of the other primary partitions (where the NT boot manager is not installed), you won't be able to start NT. But you're still rid of the generally annoying NT boot manager in your daily work with Windows 95.

Chapter 8

Finally a way to make a backup copy of Windows 95

If you're following the advice above for hard drive and data organization, you'll get an additional benefit: now you can create a backup copy of the complete Windows 95 installation. In other words—no more reinstalling Windows because something or another is preventing the whole system from running.

It's well known that Windows is not exactly the most stable operating system available. In cases like this it would be much better if you could create a complete backup copy of the Windows and program files. You would ideally do this at a time when everything is still running as it should. Afterward, you can play with your active Windows 95 partition, install any program and carry out any test you like. Then if at some point the predictable, non-recoverable errors occur, just copy the saved installation to the active boot partition, delete the defective directories in DOS, and you're back up and running.

You might have had the same idea once but you hit the three usual stumbling blocks:

◆ The Windows 95 and Programs directory in the usual hard drive structure (Windows and all programs on a single hard drive, often with everything even located under the Windows main directory) is much too large to even consider making backup copies. The hard drive structure we showed you above clears this up, since here the operating system is consistently separated from all the programs. Furthermore you probably won't have more than 100, maximum 200 Megs of data, which you can easily back up on ZIP diskettes or somewhere on the hard drive.

◆ When you tried to use Explorer to copy the Windows 95 directory to another location, Explorer gave you a Share-error message because the active swap file prevented copying. The solution: a permanent swap file. Then the whole Windows 95 and Programs directory can be copied with no problem.

◆ You didn't know how to replace the existing, defective version with the backup copy because you recognized that some actions had to run in DOS, which then causes problems due to the long file names. But even for this there is an easy solution, so continue reading.

Here is how to handle your Windows 95 backup

Here are step-by-step instructions for creating the backup copy and then copying back or recreating the functional version:

1. Create a permanent swap file so that Windows 95 can be copied . You could alternatively disable the swap file entirely but this is neither necessary nor desirable.

2. Configure Windows and your hard drive as described above: all other applications (for example, MS-Office) should whenever possible be placed in a separate partition (E:) and not, as Microsoft suggests, in the Programs directory. Both directories should be no larger than 150-200 Megs. If the copy process is interrupted by an error message, it's usually a share

error which prevents an opened file from being copied. Check to make sure you have closed all your programs possible. Copy the Programs and Windows directories (with all subdirectories) to another storage device or another directory on the hard drive.

3. Rename the backup copy of the Windows main directory to any desired name, such as "Winsave." Just be sure the name doesn't contain more than eight characters, since you'll be working with it in DOS. The renaming is essential, because later you'll have to copy the complete backup copy directory parallel to the existing Windows version to one and the same partition. For this reason they may not have the same name.

> **NOTE** **Creating a backup copy with Xcopy32**
> If you don't enjoy fooling around with Explorer and still actually prefer the unwieldy DOS programs, you can also use xcopy32 from the \windows\command directory to copy your files. This only works however in the DOS window of Windows 95, since only then will long file names be supported. Using the command parameter c:*.* d: /h /e /c /k all the files and (sub)directories (including empty and hidden ones) are copied with no further prompting to the D: disk. The /c switch also copies if error messages such as share conflicts occur. If you click a small batch or PIF file using this command, next time you'll be able to backup the complete C: hard drive by double-clicking.

That was the whole process of creating a backup copy. Now we look at the reverse, the recovery action. Consider this example. Your active Windows 95 partition is having problems, something or another is wrong, and you want to recreate the old, functional backup copy.

1. The most important prerequisite is that your archived Windows 95 partition must be able to run in the backed up mode. This is because the long file names will require you to use Windows 95 to restore the backed up directories.

2. Start the defective Windows version to be removed (in Safe Mode if nothing else is working) and close all programs except for Explorer.

3. Save all the important data which have been created in the meantime in the two affected directories and their subdirectories (Programs and Windows), assuming they are not part of the backup copy. This applies especially to the desktop and Start menu settings to which the subdirectories under the Windows main directory correspond.

4. Delete the entire Programs directory in the active partition. Don't panic by the number of "Do you REALLY want to...?" messages. You do have a backup copy.

5. As soon as this is complete, copy the saved Programs directory to your active partition. Now this directory has been recreated, or rather replaced.

6. Now we come to the Windows directory itself. Check the free space available in the active partition: Will the Windows backup copy fit along with the existing one in the partition? If

not, delete all unnecessary files and sub-directories in the existing, active Windows version (help files, BMPs, text files, backup copies, favorites, etc.). You won't need these anymore. Actually, you can delete almost everything because the active Windows 95 only has to make it through this copy action.

7. Next copy the renamed, saved Windows version (Winsave) to the active partition. You should now have two directories named Windows and Winsave.

8. Go to the DOS level and give the old, still-active Windows directory some other name like Winold. Use the DOS command Ren (e.g., Ren Windows Winold).

9. Now rename the Winsave directory to Windows (Ren Winsave Windows).

10. You can either now or later delete the "old" Windows directory (now called Winold). The DOS command Deltree is ideal for this (Deltree Winold). But be careful, because Deltree deletes complete directories in one fell swoop without much prompting. Don't make any typing mistakes. Incidentally, deleting the Winold directory in DOS can take one or two minutes even on fast machines. This mainly because of the long file names and all the little files which keep the program busy.

11. Start your "new/old" Windows again either by rebooting or simply enter "Win," and everything will be the same as the day you created your backup copy. Sometimes Windows 95 forgets the position of the icons on the desktop so you'll have to rearrange them. Finally, there is the option of transferring any still saved files and settings from the Winold directory into the restored backup copy. The whole recovery action normally takes five to ten minutes. Compare this with the normal time required to completely reinstall Windows, including all the programs.

HARD DRIVE TUNING IN DOS AND WINDOWS

Once you have properly installed, connected, configured, partitioned and formatted your hard drive, all that remains is installing the operating system. However, we still have some optimization possibilities remaining.

Tips and tricks for accelerated booting

The boot process is what most irritates us about the PC. If you're like us, you are always experimenting with different hardware and software configurations that requires restarting the computer or Windows several times. The following are interesting tuning tips on we have collected for this.

◆   The BIOS is a real treasure for optimizing the boot process. All these tips were discussed in the BIOS chapter. You won't want to miss that section.

◆ If fast booting is especially important to you (using a fax server, for example), you should use EIDE and not SCSI as the interface. PCs take a lot longer to boot when the SCSI controller is used for initializing.

```
#401A0-0105

Award Plug and Play BIOS Extension v1.0A
Copyright (C) 1995, Award Software, Inc.

Initialize Plug and Play Cards...
Card-01: TerraTec Maestro 32/96
PNP Init Completed

Adaptec AHA-2940 BIOS v1.23
(c) 1996 Adaptec, Inc. All Rights Reserved.

◀◀◀ Press <Ctrl><A> for SCSISelect(TM) Utility! ▶▶▶

    SCSI ID:LUN NUMBER #:# 0:0 - IBM      DORS-32160    - Drive D: (81h)
    SCSI ID:LUN NUMBER #:# 1:0 - IBM      DORS-32160    - Drive 82h
    SCSI ID:LUN NUMBER #:# 2:0 - PIONEER  CD-ROM DR-U10X
    SCSI ID:LUN NUMBER #:# 3:0 - PLEXTOR  CD-ROM PX-12TS
    SCSI ID:LUN NUMBER #:# 4:0 - HP       CZ500A
    SCSI ID:LUN NUMBER #:# 5:0 - IOMEGA   ZIP 100

BIOS Installed Successfully!
_
```

This painfully slow initializing of all the devices connected to the SCSI controller is something manufacturers could really improve.

◆ If you mix SCSI and EIDE and only boot from the latter, you can switch off the SCSI controller BIOS and access the hard drives through the DOS driver (ASPIDISK.SYS) or the Windows 95 driver of the controller. This speeds up the boot process considerably. See Chapter 7 for more information.

◆ Under Windows 95, skip all the superfluous drivers and programs in the CONFIG.SYS and AUTOEXEC.BAT files. Reading these files only slows down the boot process even more. To separate the necessary from the superfluous files, see the descriptions in Chapter 4.

◆ Even in Windows 95, try to keep the SYSTEM.INI and WIN.INI start files as small as possible and free from old or incorrect entries. The registry files can grow to several Megs after a long period of time, which takes additional time when starting. Microsoft has a special registry cleaning program called RegClean which checks the registry for unneeded or erroneous entries and removes them. You can download the program from Microsoft's website.

◆ To check the boot process or to troubleshoot when problems arise, you should press F8 during startup to open the Windows 95 boot menu, where you can enable the Logged option. Then you can look for error messages (Loadfailed) in the log file (Bootlog.txt) and check all installed files. Here you may find all kinds of superfluous drivers which really should have been removed long ago.

Chapter 8

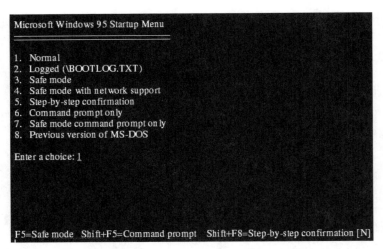

```
Microsoft Windows 95 Startup Menu

1.  Normal
2.  Logged (\BOOTLOG.TXT)
3.  Safe mode
4.  Safe mode with network support
5.  Step-by-step confirmation
6.  Command prompt only
7.  Safe mode command prompt only
8.  Previous version of MS-DOS

Enter a choice: 1

F5=Safe mode   Shift+F5=Command prompt   Shift+F8=Step-by-step confirmation [N]
```

Pressing the F8 key while the message Starting Windows 95 appears will display the Windows 95 boot menu. The second selection allows you to generate a report file of the boot process.

◆ Optimize the MSDOS.SYS Start file in the root directory of the hard drive. In this write-protected and hidden text file you'll find all kinds of configuration parameters that can affect how Windows 95 boots. The following table describes the most important settings in MSDOS.SYS, which you can process with any text editor. Just don't forget to deselect the attributes Hidden and Write Protected (in Explorer using File | Properties or the DOS command Attrib Msdos.sys -h -r). When you're finished, reset the attributes to the way they were. The settings shown in the table are in the [Options] section of the file. The values given generally correspond to the recommended settings.

BootMenuDelay=x	Determines how long the boot menu will be displayed until the menu item given under BootMenuDefault or the standard preset for start is enabled.
BootMulti=1	If you have installed Windows 95 parallel to the old version, you can press [F4] while Starting Windows 95 is displayed to start the old DOS/Windows version. Entering a value of 0 here disables this option. If you install Windows 95 in another directory than the old Windows, this option is automatically set to 1.
BootWarn=1	If a start in failsafe mode is required, this is automatically carried out if the value is set to 1.
BootWin=0	If you wish to work for a time only with the old Windows version, set the value to 0, which prevents Windows 95 from starting
DBLSPACE=0	A value of 0 means: the driver Dblspace.bin is not automatically loaded. Note that as a consequence, access to compressed drives is no longer possible
DRVSPACE=0	ditto., but for Drvspace.bin
DoubleBuffer=0	Disables dual buffering for SCSI disks, which is normally loaded (value = 1) to enhance data security when caching the data storage device. Dual buffering can also be set in Config.sys by entering Device=Dblbuff.sys
LoadTop=0	A value of 0 controls loading of the Command.com and the drivers for a compressed disk; they are not loaded on the upper end of the conventional memory.
Logo=0	Suppresses the start logo of Windows 95, which speeds up the boot process somewhat.
Network=0	The network components are not loaded.

Regardless, it makes sense to suppress automatic loading of all non-essential drivers (for example, DRVSPACE.BIN) using the appropriate setting. In addition you should disable any option which slows down the boot process, such as loading the start logo or automatic overlaying of the boot menu.

Disk caching: software cache programs offer solutions

The principle of caching is used in a computer whenever possible. The process is always the same: faster memory forms are used to make certain data available to a slower memory. The hard drive for example is cached by the main memory, and the latter in turn by the first and second level cache of the processor. Cache memories are also built into many hardware devices. All today's hard drives and CD-ROM players have a small, built-in cache RAM (usually 128 to 512 K). Caching also refers to buffer storage on the hard drive of programs like Web browser data which are used often (such as graphics or HTML code).

The cache does not have to be nearly as large as the memory to be cached. Clever algorithms are used to store often-needed data according to statistical rules. An example would be any data which was last read.

The program called Smartdrive, a software cache for data storage devices, first appeared in DOS. This is invoked in the AUTOEXEC.BAT file and caches the hard drive, floppy drives and CD-

ROMs with the help of the main memory. Four to eight Megs of reserved RAM is generally quite sufficient. Windows for Workgroups introduced the first 32-bit cache program (VCache) for Windows. Naturally Windows 95 no longer works with the 16-bit Smartdrive from DOS, but uses its own 32-bit drivers. Using Smartdrive only makes sense for the MS-DOS mode of Windows 95.

Besides these software programs, there are also hardware cache solutions for hard drives. In this approach, special controllers integrate RAM chips which are used for caching hard drive data. Solutions like this for EIDE disks have pretty much died out, and such expensive controllers are really only available now for the SCSI bus. However, for normal, single-station PCs, hardware cache controllers don't make much sense. Amazingly enough, the speed advantage is almost non-existent—amazing considering that both RAM and processor are unburdened. A cache controller makes sense only in servers — and then only with at least eight Megs of RAM.

The right way to use Smartdrive under DOS and Windows

The DOS program Smartdrive (SMARTDRV.EXE) should usually be switched off for straight Windows operation. But anyone who frequently works in DOS may well find it useful. Smartdrive can also cache CD-ROM drives, which makes it interesting for computer games. Remember, however, that video sequences are usually jerkier when a CD-ROM cache is enabled.

SMARTDRV.EXE is enabled either directly upon start using AUTOEXEC.BAT or it can be invoked at any time under the DOS prompt like any normal DOS program. It can also be integrated into CONFIG.SYS using the auxiliary command Installhigh. The parameters are simple: the following command line gives you an example for embedding in CONFIG.SYS when you have at least 16 Megs of RAM, whereby Directory refers to the memory location of Smartdrive (usually the Windows directory). With this simple command the program is loaded into the high memory and caches all available drives. The write cache is disabled for diskettes. The first number calls out the memory which is used in DOS and the second is used in Windows. If you set this to 0, caching is only done on the DOS level.

```
installhigh=c:\directory\smartdrv.exe 4096 4096
```

Depending on the type of drive, Smartdrive disables the write cache automatically. Diskettes and CD-ROMs are (naturally) excluded.

Use SMARTDRV /? to view the full set of command parameters for Smartdrive in DOS. Here are the most important ones:

/S	Displays expanded status information
/x	Disables the write cache for all drives
+x or -x	Enables or disables the write cache for the drive indicated by X (i.e., +d for the D: drive)
/r	Writes all data from the cache to the hard drive. Useful when shutting down if you want to be absolutely safe.

The following line enables caching only in DOS (which accelerates the boot process somewhat), but also disables the write cache for the D: hard drive. This increases data security and can be useful for partitions which contain mainly documents. This command line also causes all status information to be displayed upon start, which then slows the boot process down (which is why we would turn it off).

```
installhigh=c:\directory\smartdrv.exe -D 2048 0 /s
```

Note that to cache CD-ROMs, Smartdrive must be loaded **after** the CD-ROM driver (i.e., the CD-ROM must already be enabled). For verification, you should simply invoke Smartdrive again after the start without parameters (enter "SMARTDRV"), whereupon you'll see an information output similar to the following.

NOTE **Smartdrive and Windows 95, is it useful?**
Windows 95 has its own 32-bit cache driver (as does Windows for Workgroups). Smartdrive is no longer needed for Windows, and would in fact have a negative impact on speed. Now you might think that reserving 512 or 1,024 K cache memory for Smartdrive purely under DOS accelerates the boot and start routine for Windows. But this is not the case, as a comparison test easily shows. When Windows starts, most files are read only once, so a cache can't have much impact. In addition, by enabling Smartdrive you lose valuable memory. Therefore, use the program only for pure DOS sessions, when running games for example. In cases like this, of course, you can invoke it individually, not using the Autoexec.bat file. This is most easily done using the Dosstart.bat file in the Windows 95 directory, since all the DOS programs located there are automatically invoked when you exit Windows 95.

Chapter 8

The right amount of memory for Smartdrive in DOS

Anyone still working with Smartdrive in DOS or Windows 3.1 usually has precious little available memory. In these cases it is appropriate to determine the optimum amount of memory to reserve for Smartdrive.

Available memory	Typical Smartdrive settings for the DOS or Windows cache
8 Megs	1024
16 Megs	2048
32 Megs	4096
> 32 Megs	4096 (above this: diminishing returns)

But back to determining the hit rate. When you invoke Smartdrive in DOS using the /s switch, you'll see a message containing more or less the following lines:

```
C:\> SMARTDRV /S
Microsoft Smartdrive, disk cache program, Version 5.0
Copyright 1991,1992,1993 Microsoft Corp.
Space for 384 elements of 8,192 bytes each.
The    data    could    be    taken    25,431    times    from    the    cache
The data had to be read 1,313 times from the disk.
Cache size: 3,145,728 bytes
Cace size while Windows is running: 3,145,728 bytes

Hard drive Cache Status
Drive          Read cache        Write cache    Buffering
─────────────────────────────────────────────────────────
  A:                yes               no             no
  B:                yes               no             no
  C:                yes               no             no
  D:                yes               no             no
```

The above message tells you that of 26,744 (25,431 + 1,313) read tries, 25,431 were successful in the fast cache, while the hard drive only had to be accessed 1,313 times. The hit rate is therefore 95.1 %, an outstanding value. Here also you gradually expand the cache and check the hit rate, until expanding no longer has a significant affect on the rate. Now you have all the information you need for the size of the optimum cache. Windows 3.1 includes SMARTMON.EXE for similar purposes. Take a look at the program since it makes the optimum setting for Smartdrive even easier. The whole point is meaningless for Windows for Workgroups since only the size of the 32-bit VCache program can be set there and WfW takes care of the rest itself.

Possibilities and limitations with the Windows 95 cache

While in DOS and Windows 3.x you were able to easily set all the important parameters yourself using Smartdrive or VCache, things have changed with Windows 95. Everything runs automatically. But only at first glance. Besides, with Windows for Workgroups the 32-bit cache for CD-ROM drives was introduced, the size of which is also configurable. More on this in Chapter 9.

But back to the hard drive. The actual size of the data cache does not appear to be configurable in Windows 95. Automated features are supposed to have relieved us of the painful burden of optimizing settings. Unfortunately, it doesn't necessarily work out that way.

Tuning the PC into a server—The only cache setting in Windows 95 is defective

The convert from DOS or Windows 3.x will look everywhere for ways to set the hard drive cache. But except for an undocumented selection of three settings in the system control, the search will be in vain. There is a way, as we are about to show you. But first back to the settings options in the Performance tab of the System control panel. Click on the [File System] button as shown in the illustration to select from among three settings for the Windows 95 cache. The default setting here is Desktop computer.

These settings affect the cache size which Windows uses to buffer file and directory names, in other words, not the actual disk cache, but rather a kind of sub-entity of it.

If you have more than 16 Megs of RAM, you should change the default Desktop computer to Network server. The third setting Mobile or docking system is used for notebooks. As a Network server, Windows 95 now reserves 16 instead of eight K of Ram for caching 64 directories and 2,729 file names (the Desktop computer setting caches 32 directories and 677 file names).

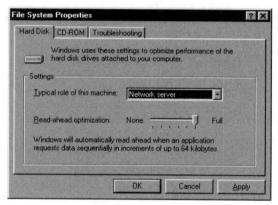

Configured as a network server, Windows 95 reserves more memory for caching directory and file names. But Windows 95 users must first alter the registry manually.

This is because the original version of Windows 95 (95a) contains a bug which prevents the cache settings from being automatically changed in the registry. As a Windows 95a user, to take advantage of the improved cache feature, make the following manual settings in the registry:

In the entry Hkey_Local_Machine\Software\Microsoft\Windows\Current Version\FSTemplates\Server the following entries must be set with the specified values:

```
NameCache    a9 0a 00 00
Path Cache   40 00 00 00
```

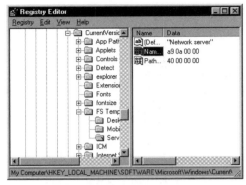

Anyone using Windows 95a has to enter these settings manually to configure a network server cache.

The best cache settings are hiding in the SYSTEM.INI

"Keep your hands off the cache," says Microsoft in an attempt to keep one of the most important tuning settings away from the Windows 95 user. No matter where you look, you can't seem to find any more settings which affect the memory for the complete disk cache. Instead, Windows again—as with the swap file (see below)—uses an automatic procedure in which the cache size is dynamically adapted.

What sounds good at first turns out to be an annoying speed bump in practice. The administrative complexity of dynamic settings uses processor resources, and usually the disk cache reserves far too much of the main memory, so working with large programs doesn't run as smoothly as it should. You can check this easily with the help of the Windows 95 system monitor.

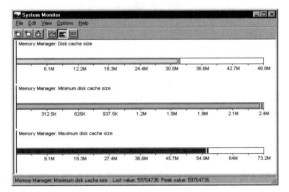

The system monitor offers you three displays for cache size (actual, maximum and minimal memory size). With the automatic setting, Windows 95 reserves large amounts of memory and doesn't release them fast enough.

However, it can be done. Amazingly enough, a minimum and maximum cache value can be set in the SYSTEM.INI. It's almost funny that these settings, which are so important and system-critical, are made in the old SYSTEM.INI and not in the Windows registry. However, what is important is that works.

After the corresponding change in the SYSTEM.INI file, all the cache memory values are set to a fixed size.

Our experiences regarding the optimal settings are straightforward. Reserve an identical, fixed value for the minimum and maximum value using the entries minfilecache and maxfilecache in the [VCache] section of the SYSTEM.INI file. This will finally put a stop to the automatic setting which Windows 95 would do otherwise. The best values are shown below.

PC main memory	Optimum cache setting
16 Megs	2048
32 Megs	4096
64 Megs and higher	8192

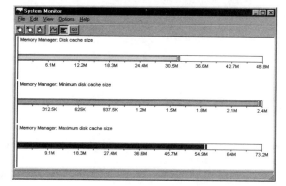

With these settings you can set the disk cache size in SYSTEM.INI to a fixed minimum and maximum value. For optimum performance, it's better to keep both the same size.

Chapter 8

By the way, if your data is more important to you than every bit of speed, disable the software write cache in Windows 95. This eliminates the risk that after a crash, the data you thought had already been written to the hard drive is actually still in RAM. Do this by double-clicking the System icon in Control Panels, select the Performance tab and click [File System], then select Troubleshooting. There, enable the option Disable write-behind caching for all drives as shown in the illustration. However, bear in mind that all modern hard drives have a built-in hardware cache with write-cache function, which can likewise be disabled with SCSI hard drives. (see Chapter 7).

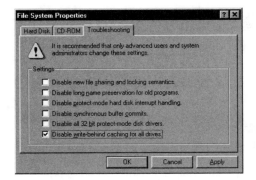

The Windows swap file

With the introduction of the 386 processor, the hard drive could now be redefined as a main memory device. However, it wasn't until Windows 3.0 when the idea of a file swapping (also called "paging") was implemented and that real use could be made of this function. The swap file is used to virtually expand a too-small main memory and allowing a PC to execute programs and manipulate data files larger than main memory. Although terribly slow (after all, a hard drive is much slower than RAM), this is one solution if there's a memory shortage.

Using the swap file is quite simple in practice. Even Windows 3.x generated it automatically, as does Windows 95. But there many ways to optimize the swap file.

◆ You should use a swap file even if you have sufficient main memory available. Windows 95 simply expects that this file exists and routinely copies certain elements there. If you disable the swap file completely in Windows 95, the most peculiar error conditions will result. In addition, Windows 95 will hang much more frequently than usual. So regardless of how much memory you have, generate a swap file of around 60 Megs, which is sufficient in most cases.

◆ Wherever possible, create a permanent swap file with a fixed size instead of a temporary one. Whereas the second option is thriftier when it comes to the hard drive, the first is significantly faster. This is because the file doesn't have to be created and later shrunk every time you need to use it. Using a few tricks (see further below) will allow it to be written to the disk in one contiguous segment, which also increases speed.

◆ In Windows 3.x you can accelerate the 32-bit read and write accesses to the swap file by going to the [386enh] section of the SYSTEM.INI file and increasing the value of the PageBuffers= entry from 4 to 8 or 16. You should also try the maximum value of 32. This will reduce the amount of available main memory (each buffer requires four K), but could be just the thing for a machine with little memory. Don't be afraid to experiment. If the entry isn't present in your version, simply create it using a text editor.

◆ If you have Windows 3.x or WfW and insist on continuing to use a temporary swap file, you should still consider setting a maximum size limit. Especially when working with a server in the network, WfW sometimes creates a very large swap file. Using the command MaxPagingFileSize=xxxx in the [386eng] section of SYSTEM.INI allows you to limit the maximum size to a fixed value. Simply enter this amount for xxxx (for example, 30,720 for 30 Megs).

◆ In Windows 3.x you still had the corresponding menus in the control panel for setting size and type of swap file; this is all supposed to be automatically controlled in Windows 95. Automatic means that Windows creates a temporary swap file every time the machine is started and constantly varies the size while the machine is running. This is more flexible, but also takes a real toll on performance and the hard drive. You eliminate all that by again defining a maximum and minimum size. The result is a permanent file which is not deleted even when you exit Windows. To enable this function, proceed as follows: Open System properties by double-clicking the System control panel icon. Click the Performance tab and the [Virtual memory] button at lower right. Now, as shown in the illustration, you can select fixed Minimum and Maximum values for virtual memory. It's best to select the fastest hard drive in your system as the target.

Chapter 8

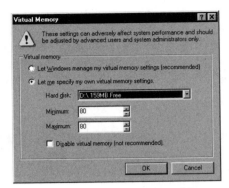

A permanent swap file with a fixed size, if possible on a second drive,
prevents the constant exchanging of data segments to the hard drive.

It's fairly important that you enter a large enough minimum value. We use a 64 Megs minimum and 300 Megs maximum. This generates a permanent swap file of 64 Megs, which is generally sufficient. In certain cases this can be expanded to 300 Megs but watch for the trap. As the Maximum selection, Windows offers you the maximum available memory space of the selected drive. If you don't enter at least one Meg less than that, Windows 95 doesn't accept the settings and switches defaults back to the default, temporary scheme when you close the dialog box. Many people have fallen into this trap and later wondered why nothing seems to have changed.

◆ You can improve access to the swap file by doing the following: if you have one, use a second, fast disk or a partition where Windows (95) doesn't reside as the swap drive. In this way Windows can access both its data and the swap file at the same time. If possible, the file should reside in its own partition at the beginning of the disk (outer range), since this is the fastest area. In addition, the swap file won't be fragmented in its own partition. Speaking of fragmenting and defragmenting, the swap file should, as we mentioned, be a continuous segment on the disk. How you accomplish this and how you defragment a disk in general are worth a discussion of their own.

Defragmenting the right way

Nearly everyone is familiar with defragmenting but hardly anyone takes full advantage of it. You may not know that MS-DOS based systems with the FAT file system (for example, Windows 95 including FAT32) have the habit of not necessarily writing data in a spatially continuous way to the disk. Instead, they simply distribute it wherever there happens to be space available. Plus, frequent deleting and saving means that available space quickly gets strewn all over the magnetic surface. This is a consequence of the FAT file system.

Fragmented data cost not only additional time when reading and writing (after all, the magnetic heads first have to assemble all the data), it also puts a considerable strain in the disk mechanics. Help is available here from the defragmenting tools which for some time now have been part of the operating system.

> **NOTE**
>
> **What about NT? Defragmenting with NTFS**
>
> Fragmenting is especially a problem for all systems using the FAT file system (i.e., DOS and Windows 3.x/95). Fragmenting also occurs with NTFS, but is far less of a problem, which is why Microsoft and other companies have so far opted not to develop corresponding tools. Recently this has changed, and now the program Diskeeper 2.0, from Executive Software (available from Megasoft (www.megasoft.com)), is the first NTFS degragger. Prices run around $80.00 for the workstation version and $400.00 for the server version.

However, defragmenting doesn't have to be limited to the simple reassembling of scattered data remnants. If the defragmenting program supports enhanced functions, you can sort certain data segments or position yourself at certain disk positions (for example, the beginning). Whereas Microsoft's ScanDisk does not have such additional functions, you'll find them in Norton Utilities's Speed Disk. Here the swap file is automatically optimized (in other words, defragmented).

◆ In the past defragmenting required specific tools (especially Norton Utilities with Speed Disk). However, Windows includes a basic defragmenting tool called DEFRAG.EXE. It is indeed a basic tool because it won't do much more than reassemble the existing files. There are no positioning functions.

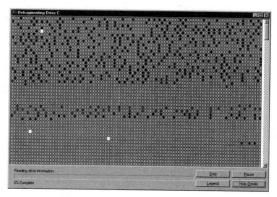

The Windows defrag program offers only rudimentary defragmenting functions, so you'll be better served with special tools.

◆ Use ScanDisk or Norton Disk Doctor to check the hard drive first for errors before you start defragmenting. Otherwise, the defragmenting programs will be interrupted with error messages.

Chapter 8

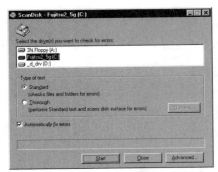 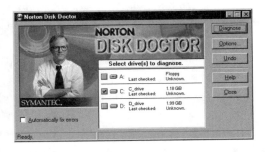

Defragmenting only works properly with error-free hard drives. First check the disk using ScanDisk in Windows (left) or better the Norton Utilities Disk Doctor (right). If file fragments are found, they will be saved on the disk as chk- or _dd files, which you should normally delete since you can hardly use them again. As described in Chapter 1, this can also be executed by means of a short command line in AUTOEXEC.BAT.

NOTE

ScanDisk-Trouble with copy protection

Some application software uses artifical defects on the hard drive as copy protection, which are entered into the FAT upon installation. Every time the program is started, they are used to check for any unauthorized copying attempts. If the program is copied to another computer, the specific defects are no longer present, which the program notices as soon as it is started the next time. So far, so good (or bad). The dumb thing is, ScanDisk and similar utilities can look for just such errors and correct them. To get around this, you have to tell ScanDisk to prompt before correcting such errors. To do this, deselect the entry Automatically fix errors in the main window of ScanDisk.

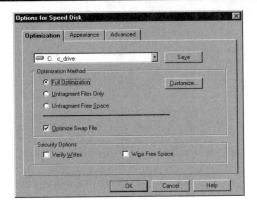

◆ As mentioned, Speed Disk in Norton Utilities offers far better degragmenting functions that can be used for tuning hard drive performance. Compared with Defrag from Windows, it offers the following enhanced, practical functions:

1. After defragmenting, all available memory areas are deleted. In this way they are marked for the operating system as free for continuous writing.

Using the Configure command in the Properties | Options menu of Speed Disk, you can specify that all free memory areas are deleted (lower left).

2. Speed Disk offers—unlike DEFRAG—the possibility of incorporating the swap file into the defragmentation process, which means significantly improved performance in the data exchange between main memory and disk. This option is located in the same dialog as the setting for unfragmenting free space (see illustration).

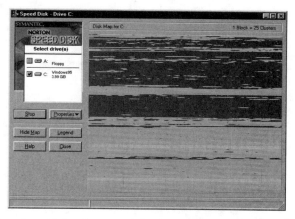

Speed Disk at work—at left a fragmented hard drive is optimized; the result is at right.
The swap file, set off in color in the center, was integrated as a complete block.

3. But perhaps the best option is the ability to position folders and files on the hard drive according to certain criteria during defragmenting. Ideally this is used to place frequently used files at the fast beginning (outer edge) of a partition. The corresponding settings are again reached in the Properties | Options menu. One recommendation is to place all the folder entries and the swap file at the beginning of the disk. Although there is a separate option (see illustration) for shifting the files, to shift the swap file you must enter it (win386.swp) in the list contained in the Files first register.

Chapter 8

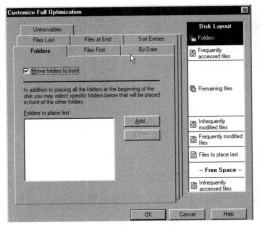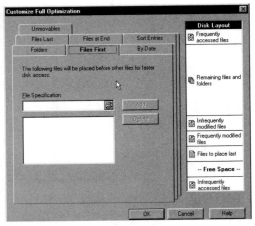

The Full optimization option gives you the ability to place the folders (left) and the swap file (right) at the beginning of the hard drive.

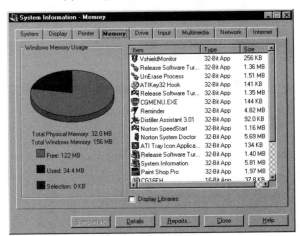

After Speed Disk has shifted the folders and the swap file, the graphic overview gives you a clear view of NOTE0085.

> **NOTE**
>
> **Unexplained disk chatter even after defragging ?**
>
> Maybe you've experienced this: the PC isn't supposed to be accessing the hard drive (like while you're typing), but suddenly you're getting disk chatter like crazy. Even after you've defragmented? The two aren't necessarily related. For one thing,, Windows 95 includes a write cache buffer, which can write data to the disk only after the fact. To turn this write cache off, you only need to double-click the System icon in the control panel, select the Performance tab, click the [File System] button, and select the box check next to Disable write-behind caching for all drives. If Office 95 or 97 is installed, the chattering may be a result of the indexing function, which loads the files of the Office pacakge into an index, which is then used for the Find Fast feature in the Open dialog. This index is automatically loaded through the Autostart group, and is configured from the Create Index icon in the control panel. This function has nothing to do with the Windows 95 Find File function, by the way (even though people will tell you it does).

Memory defraggers for RAM

While we're on the subject of defragging, it's also possible to defrag your RAM. Windows 95 is famous and infamous for its mixed memory management with 16 and 32-bit code. If you have opened and closed several programs during a session, the still-active addresses are distributed in the memory. Windows reserves heaps of RAM in its resource management that are released again after some programs are closed. Using a memory defragger helps the PC to run somewhat faster but the main gain is in stability.

At least three programs are available to help bring order to your RAM. One is a clever freeware program by Alexander Peter Kowalski called APK NT95 Memory Compactor Defragger32. It automatically defrags the memory in the background for both Windows 95 and NT4. However, the latter isn't so much in need of a tool like this as is Windows 95. You can download this program from the Internet (http://nic.zcu.cz/ftp/pub/win/ winsite/win95/miscutil/) or searching for "apk" from Shareware Central (www.shareware.com).

A commercial program called WinCheckIt Pro 4.0 is available from Touchstone (www.touchstonesoftware.com). It works similar to APK NT95 Memory Compactor Defragger32 but costs around $50. It does, however, also offer a collection of additional analysis tools useful for Windows 95.

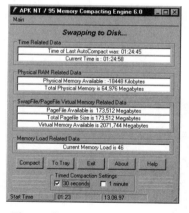

The small APK icon is usually in the system tray. From there you can open the overview shown above. A few settings can be made in the Main menu but are unnecessary since APK runs automatically.

Chapter 8

More hard drive tuning tips from application cache memory to ramdisk

In this section you'll find additional tips for optimizing your hard drive performance. Here again we're talking about indirect functions, in other words, those which take some of the load off by optimizing use of the main memory.

◆ Windows isn't the only program that uses a cache memory for often-needed data. Many applications do this as well. Plus sometimes you can even configure it. Without giving you a complete list of all the programs with all the cache settings, we do want to use Word for Windows as an example of how this works in detail. Look for the corresponding functions in your manual, the program Help files or the menus, and feel free to experiment with this. Graphics programs also frequently use these techniques. Unfortunately, most graphics programs require almost all RAM for themselves. A reduction here to 10-20 Megs often results in a significant speed increase for the entire system.

◆ But back to Word 6, 95 or even 97. This program manages two cache memories. One is for graphics (Bit map cache size) and the other for general representation of data in the window (Cache size). These are set quite small by default so if you have 32 or 64 Megs of RAM, you can feel free to select larger sizes. When you're working with large documents and many graphics, for example, this speeds up scrolling considerably. In Word 6 you still had to make the settings in the Winword6.ini file's [Microsoft Word] section. Enter "CACHESIZE=2048" there and "BitMapCacheSize=2048," so that two Megs each are used as cache. Practice has shown this setting to be best. In Word 95/97, these entries have to be made in the registry. To do this, use the identical or similar parameters CacheSize=2048 and BitmapMemory=2048 in the branch HKEY_CURRENT_USER\Software\Microsoft\Word\7.0\Options (for Word 97, Version 8.0). That's it. The standard values for Word are 1,024 K for the graphics and only 64 K for the general data cache.

*For Word 95 you need to make the settings for
the general and bitmap cache in this branch of the registry.*

◆ Bear in mind that removing and keeping your hard drives free of unnecessary data is also something that improves performance. Steps include disabling the Windows Recycle Bin function or deleting temporary files, perhaps by using a batch entry in AUTOEXEC.BAT (see Chapter 1). Any superfluous files and programs should not be exempted from such housecleaning (there are plenty of programs which sniff out duplicate files). Other typical space hogs are old chk-files left over from a ScanDisk rescue operation. And for users with a network connection, think about using hard drive resources in the network more efficiently. Programs and documents can easily be stored centrally on the server.

◆ Finally, we need to include the Ramdisk function in this list. This refers to the creation of a virtual drive using the main memory. Obviously, this only makes sense if you have sufficient RAM available (at least 64 Megs). However, then you'll be able to reach speed dimensions you didn't think possible. After all, a RAM disk is approximately a thousand times faster than hard drive drives. This function makes sense for storing temporary files or frequently accessed programs on the RAM disk. Many power users copy the entire Windows directory to a RAM disk before startup and start from there.

One problem has always been that the usual RAMDISK.SYS driver for Windows or DOS, which is loaded simply with the command device=ramdisk.sys xxxx in CONFIG.SYS demands an exact specification for the memory amount to be reserved (xxxx = memory amount in kilobytes, e.g., 2,048). This is very inflexible and wastes memory. But not all is lost, because there is a clever shareware tool called Vramdir available on the Internet (www.accessone.com/~virtual/vramdir.htm). This program uses Windows 95 to manage a virtual, dynamic RAM disk whose memory size adjusts to the corresponding data quantity. If more data need to be copied to the RAM disk, Vramdir automatically expands the size. The program doesn't create an additional drive, but rather takes a certain directory which is normally used for temporary files and reroutes it to its RAM disk. This means it works completely transparently, with no external evidence to the user that it's running. The only thing you notice is the gain in speed, for example when working with large documents in Word. The only catch is that if you experience a crash, all the data in the RAM disk are lost that otherwise could have been used for data recovery.

COMPARING ZIP DRIVES AND OTHER REMOVABLE MEDIA

Hard drives, as everyone knows, are always too small. The best solution may be to store data externally. Removable drives were considered faily exotic only a few years ago and few were available except for SyQuest and MO drives. However, things have certainly changed since. The ZIP drive even seems to be positioning itself as an eventual successor to the normal floppy diskette drive.

The removable drive market has, to be sure, grown significantly with ever more economical solutions, but at the same time you find a huge number of completely different technologies battling for market share: magnetic, magneto-optical, or pure optical are the basic technologies, with any number of variations. It's at the point where an overview is hard to get. Once you've made your decision on which technology, there's still the big question of optimum installation and use. The following tips are designed to help you decide what to buy, how to configure it and how to make the best use of your purchase.

Chapter 8

Decision-making aids for the right removable drive

Believe us, one of these removable drives in addition to the hard drive is really a great thing. You can get an internal ZIP drive for about $100. However, as good as the ZIP drive is, it's not the best solution for all cases. Finding the best one is not that easy. It depends a lot on what you do with the medium. Following are a few facts and points to consider when making your selection, followed by more detailed descriptions of units which we find really interesting.

There are two criteria you should take into consideration when selecting your medium:

1 **Data security**
   Are you going to use the medium for permanently storing important data? Or will you use it just for data exchange, fast intermediate backup and/or running programs? For the former, you should consider the reliable magneto-optical (MO) or pure optical technology. Only in the second case are purely magnetic technologies like ZIP or JAZ the best solution.

2 **Necessary storage space**
   If you want to store very large quantities of data, e.g., sound files, graphics or videos, you have to consider the cost of memory. Here again, the MO and pure opticals offer an advantage. For very large amounts of data consider the MO drive instead.

The drive speed is of course also important. But this often depends less on the actual technology and more on the interface. If you run devices on the parallel port, everything will run at a comparative snail's pace, likewise for tapes, which are connected to the diskette drive controller. Otherwise, the magnetic devices (ZIP, JAZ, SyQuest) are always somewhat faster than their counterparts in the MO and purely optical camp.

If you frequently exchange data with other people, the medium or drive type is also of great importance. The following devices and technologies have gained wide use:

1. The ZIP drive. According to Iomega, it has around 80% of the market share for removable drives.

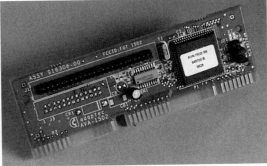

An internal SCSI version of the ZIP drive (shown at left) including its own controller (right) can be had now for around $120.00. This makes it interesting for just about anyone.

2. Iomega's JAZ drive is also popular but more expensive compared to the ZIP drive.

3. The old 5.25-inches SyQuest drives with their storage capacities of 44 and 88 Megs are still used for service bureaus, printing shop, photo studio and others. This is the device you'll frequently need in order to exchange data with these people.

4. Probably the broadest range of read drives is represented by the CD-R drive (Compact Disk-Recordable drive). A CD-R is a disk drive that can create CD-ROMs. It gives you not only one of the most economical forms of media, but also the greatest odds of the other party being able to read your data. Virtually every computer has a CD-ROM drive today. You could only burn a CD-ROM once but even this is changing with the introduction of re-writable CD-RWs, which will be discussed separately in the next section.

NOTE **The right interface for your removable drive**
At present removable drives have three possible interfaces: SCSI, ATAPI (EIDE) and the parallel port. You should opt for SCSI whenever possible, which is the standard interface for the better devices anyway. There is only one reason to buy a parallel port device: if you are always connecting it to other machines, like a notebook. But even here there is a (admittedly somewhat expensive) solution which enables you to work with SCSI. ATAPI is also an alternative, though not as good, and it is only available for a few devices.

Tips, tricks and all the latest on the ZIP drive

Iomega has filled a big market need with their ZIP and JAZ drives. Several million ZIP drives have been sold in the last few years. The following summarizes a important points and tuning tips for you concerning these two versions:

◆ The ZIP drive is a strictly magnetic drive. The disk media each contain 3,000 rpm magnetic disks, which are scanned by normal read/write heads. The whole thing functions quite reliably. Confidence is also bolstered by Iomega's five-year warranty for its JAZ media. Reports of data errors or defective media are practically unknown so far. Sure, these media aren't designed for eternity or extremely important data, but for daily use, as an intermediate backup and for data exchange, they're ideal.

◆ If you look for a ZIP drive, you'll have to choose between internal or external versions and select an interface option (parallel, ATAPI or SCSI). The internal versions, at around $115.00, are a little more than $55.00 less expensive than the external versions. But for that, it's easier to work with the external version on your desk, especially since they can be stood up on their side next to the monitor. We personally would always go for the external SCSI version, which does require its own SCSI controller, but this should not be a hindrance. However, the internal version be better for users with cluttered desks or who want all their computer components in the box.

Chapter 8

◆ And speaking of SCSI interfaces: the external version is supplied only with the old SCSI-1 standard, with 25-pin connectors. You can't connect these directly to the normal PCI-SCSI controller using the 50-pin SCSI-2 mini-connectors, so you'll have to get a new cable or adapter in any case.

 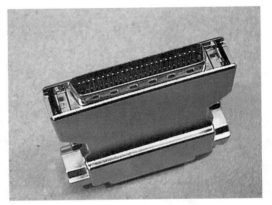

Connectors and cable for the external SCSI ZIP drive also aren't compatible with the usual SCSI controllers, so an adapter to the 50-pin SCSI-2 interface (right illustration) will also be required.

◆ There is no significant difference in speed between the ATAPI and SCSI versions, just a little under one Meg/sec. The parallel version is unbearably s-l-o-o-o-w (around 300 K/sec). We really recommend against getting this version for that reason alone. Besides, it happens frequently that a parallel ZIP won't connect to the parallel port of a SCSI machine. Especially some versions of the Adaptec 2940 controller seem to conflict with the internal SCSI-to-parallel chip in the ZIP drive. We've seen this peculiar problem on several machines, unfortunately without being able to find the exact explanation for it.

◆ Another tricky problem is the difference between the IDE version supplied to OEMs and the ATAPI version sold through retail. Although very similar, the instruction sets differ. The IDE version comes up like a hard drive but the ATAPI version acts more like a CD-ROM and can't be used without drivers or a specially adapted BIOS version. The IDE version should however be used with a special driver which tells the operating system that a medium has been changed. Because in the case of a "hard drive" (which it considers the IDE ZIP to be), the OS doesn't assume that media were changed. Without the right drivers, significant data losses could result. Incidentally, both versions are only supported by Windows 95 and NT 4; if you're using OS/2 or Linux, you're out of luck. Although the IDE version is only supposed to be installed by OEMs, you can still find it for sale. Make absolutely certain you aren't buying one of these instead of the expected ATAPI model. You'll have the problem we just mentioned (especially without the appropriate driver) plus Iomega doesn't offer any support for these IDE models.

At least there are some places where you can optimize the parallel ZIP to get a noticeable increase in speed:

1. Go to the BIOS and enable the markedly faster EPP+ECP transmission protocol for the parallel interface (see Chapter 6).

2. In Windows, don't use the Guest.exe program for linking to the drive, but rather the fixed PPD driver which is either supplied or available over the Internet at the Iomega homepage. Here use the supplied .INF file (click on Explorer with the right mouse key and select install) or install the driver using the hardware assistant (manual setting) as Iomega SCSI-to-Parallel-Driver. Be careful that you don't use the out-of-date driver integral to Windows 95, but rather select the directory for the new driver by clicking on the [Diskette] button. Speaking of out-of-date: even the PPD driver which Iomega normally supplies with the ZIP drive is usually an old version. Get the most current version over the Internet.

3. You should also go to the Windows 95 registry, and see if you can enable a higher speed for the EPP+ECP mode. Here you need to check the settings of the sub-point AdapterSettings in the branch Hkey_Local_Machine\Enum\Root\Scsi\Adapter\0000. The number value behind the entry /speed:x should be 5 or 6 (0 to 6 are possible to define the speed). The default value is 4. If you have problems with your ZIP driver after storing the settings and restarting, just replace the original value.

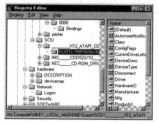

This branch of the registry is where the speed settings for the EPP+ECP mode of Windows 95 are set.

4. If you're in a real hurry and want the copy process to speed up a lot, try continuing the action in DOS instead of Windows 95. Thanks to the guest program, your ZIP will also run in DOS. It is rather peculiar that copying actions run noticeably faster in DOS than in Windows 95. Sometimes you can take advantage of this. By the way, the DOS program Xcopy32.exe in the \Windows\Command directory also copies long file names, although only in a DOS window in Windows 95 (and not in pure DOS mode).

5. The final tuning tip applies not just to the parallel ZIP, but also to all the other versions: use the Windows 95 disk compression program Drivespace to compress the ZIP diskettes.

But let's get back to the SCSI version. Here again you'll find some interesting information and tips. We already mentioned that you can boot both from a SCSI ZIP and a JAZ drive under some circumstances. You should really take advantage of this possibility and create a boot diskette containing Windows 95 and all the important rescue and anti-virus programs on it. Also interesting are the possibilities of using the SCSI devices portably, for example with notebooks. We also showed you how to connect these through a special adapter to the parallel port of other

Chapter 8

PCs in Chapter 7. Besides this SCSI-to-parallel adapter, which you can use to connect the devices to virtually any PC (including notebooks), there are also special notebook adapters. The ZipCard-PCCard-to-SCSI adapter available from Iomega as well as Adaptec is something worth considering for any notebook with a PCMCIA slot (see illustration). It's not exactly cheap, but does offer high performance. Iomega's adapter also allows other SCSI devices to be connected to a notebook.

And there's even this: The rechargeable ZIP unleashed! from Iomega allows you to take the ZIP drive on the road.

A closer look at Iomega's JAZ

Whether you should consider the JAZ drive depends on many factors. The fact is, it's currently one of the fastest removable drives on the market, together with the SyJet from SyQuest (see below). It performs at just over two Megs/sec, putting it in a class with hard drives, and is around twice as fast as a ZIP drive. It's also quite economical. Current prices are around $450.00. The disks, with one gigabyte of storage capacity, aren't bad at just under $115.00, but they ought to be a little more reasonable. In any case, the disks come with a five-year warranty, and all the user experiences so far have been amazingly positive. As this book goes to print, there will probably already be a new JAZ version with two Gigabytes of storage, which will then dethrone the SyJet from SyQuest as the biggest magnetic portable drive.

The JAZ drive does however come with some drawbacks: it makes more than its share of noise when accessing, too much for many ears. We can only hope that the new two-gigabyte version will be somewhat quieter. After 60 minutes without accessing, it also goes into sleep mode, from which it awakens rather slowly. The data security of the disks does seem to be quite high (though we advise against throwing them out a window), but the JAZ is still not comparable with an MO or PD drive in this respect. You shouldn't use the disks for archiving, and anyway they're too expensive for that. For archiving, you would be better off with backing up to a CD-R, which is significantly more cost-effective and much safer. Its size and speed make the JAZ more suitable as a hard drive substitute. As a SCSI device, the bus also offers enough performance, for example, to start Windows NT from a JAZ. Many parents also use a JAZ drive to provide their children with a computer environment which will prevent damage to the main configuration. With the new two-gigabyte version, this drive will look even more attractive.

NOTE **Videos and JAZ, soon even better**
The JAZ drive is actually ideal for video processing, at least for storing the finished products. For direct recording, the speed has been still too slow for high-quality, low-compressed capture processes. Iomega has thought this over, and will soon bring out a new auxiliary card for the JAZ called "Buz" (can someone tell me how they come up with these names ;-)). Buz is a PCI-Ultra SCSI controller with a built-in MPEG encoder. All this should only cost around $250.00! There's been nothing like it before. Now you can record MPEG videos directly on a JAZ disk, especially with one of the new two-gigabyte drives. That could be just the ticket.

Here's a last word on the JAZ/SyJet comparison (see following section). Both devices are no slouches when it comes to speed; the one reads faster, the other writes faster. The nice things about the SyJet are (currently) the higher data capacity of 1.5 Gigabytes and the significantly lower noise level. Still, the SyJet will probably offer little competition against Iomega, as we have already seen with the ZIP drives. The reason lies in the mostly negative experiences which users and dealers had with the latest generation from SyQuest, who were the former market leaders in this area. The SyJet could be the greatest thing since sliced bread, but the market doesn't forget so easily.

The SyJet from SyQuest beats the competition with speed and storage space

Marketed as the competition to the JAZ drive from Iomega, the SyJet also uses two rigid, magnetic platters enclosed in a removable 3.5-inch cartridge. The platters are spun (again like the JAZ) at 5400 rpm, which provides high performance often at way over two Megs/sec. A total of four magnetic heads handle the necessary read and write operations. The write speed depends greatly on a verify function (which can be disabled).

With a very high storage capacity (for magnetic disks) of 1.5 Gigabytes, the SyJet is certainly impressive. Only the 5.25-inch MO drives can surpass this at the moment. Internal and external versions of the SyJet are available, for SCSI and the EIDE bus, plus a model for connecting to the printer port.

This technical background begs a direct comparison with Iomega's now well-established JAZ. Although it can store nearly 1 ½ times as much data per disk (than the old one-gigabyte version of JAZ) and reaches about the same levels of performance, SyQuest is likely to have a difficult time reasserting itself against the established JAZ after all the negative experiences of recent times. The JAZ's advantages are that it is known to be reliable, like its little ZIP brother, return rates are quite

Chapter 8

low, and it has a five-years warranty on the disks. Data on the reliability of the SyJet still needs to be gathered. On the other hand, the SyJet is significantly quieter than the sometimes grating JAZ; for sensitive ears, this could be a deciding factor. Cost-wise, there isn't much difference. Both devices hover around $450.00. The SyJet disks, at $115-$140 dollars, are somewhat more expensive than the JAZ disks, which cost under $115. But since they also hold 500 Megs more, the SyJet is more cost-effective in the long run.

The new SyJet offers high speed and 1.5 Gigabytes of storage at an attractive price.

The SyJet has a neat write protection feature, with corresponding programs supplied for DOS, Windows 3.x and Windows 95. Software is used in the solution, although it can be configured for media and for the drive. By using a write-protected drive, you cannot write to any cartridge.

NOTE

What's the problem with SyQuest and the old drives?

For years SyQuest was the leader in the portable drive market. But then Iomega came along and took over the market with their ZIP and JAZ, with barely a whimper from SyQuest. It's hard to believe. Return fire didn't come until too late, with the EZFlyer 135 and 230. Although the prices are comparable, the media is higher capacity and the drive speed is higher, SyQuest had no success against Iomega. Along with inferior design and handling, the source of their misery was the alleged poor reliability of the media and drives. Too bad, actually. All the older SyQuest devices like the SQ3270S with 270 Megs have disappeared totally from the market. It will be interesting to see what develops with the SyJet.

Why MO is currently the hottest portable drive tip

MO drives (Magneto-Optical) may be less popular with the average user but they are quite popular with professionals. As the name implies, magnetic and optical and even thermal techniques are used in combination to write to 3.5-inch and 5.25-inch media. This results in extremely high data security which, when you also consider the mechanical stability, even beats the CD-Rs.

NOTE

Nitpicking—disc and disk aren't the same thing
Just a side remark: by convention, "disc" is used for all media with magneto-optical or pure optical technology. "Disk," on the other hand, refers to purely magnetic media. But how many of us stick to convention ... ;-)

There used to be two main drawbacks to MO drives:

1. The first is cost. Although the media have a favorable cost per Megs ratio compared with CD-Rs, the drives were too expensive. It's just like what happens when comparing the consumer and professional markets: in the former the devices are inexpensive and the consumable parts expensive (e.g., the ink jet printer and ZIP drive); in the latter you have expensive devices with low usage costs. These devices continue to carry a high price tag (over $1000), but only for the 5.25-inch versions with 2.6 and 4.6-Gigabytes storage capacity per disc. The newest generation of the 3.5-inch drives with 640 Megs however, cost about as much as a JAZ drive (around $450-$525), which makes them really attractive.

2. The slow speed especially when writing. Before now, MOs always had to write in two steps (first delete the old data before writing the new data), which reduced the performance significantly. The newest versions use the LIMDOW process (Light Intensity Modulation—Direct Overwrite), which does the write in one pass and makes it nearly as fast as reading.

Fujitsu and Pinnacle Micro are two of the first manufacturers to use MO devices with the LIMDOW process. These do require special MO media, but are still able to work with the old, traditional ones. MO media are available in various sizes, and for the new LIMDOW versions you currently find 640 Megs for the 3.5-inch format and up to 4.6 Gigabytes in the 5.25-inch format. At a cost of $22-$28 (3.5-inch) or $45-$55 (5.25-inch), MO technology has the most cost-effective media you can get.

Chapter 8

*Already inherently safe, the MO media also come protected in a cartridge
for inserting them into the unassuming-looking MO drive.*

The hottest unit currently for the normal user is the new 3.5-inch MO drive DynaMO 640 from Fujitsu. It's available in both internal and external configurations. The current SCSI version will soon be followed by a parallel version. The drive is between a SCSI-ZIP and a JAZ drive for speed. This is possible due to a respectable 30ms access time and a two-Meg cache memory and the LIMDOW process.

The new DynaMO from Fujitsu is the ideal portable drive for personal use.

Also considering long-term archiving, the size of the media also makes it easy to simply burn a copy on to a CD-R with its 650 Megs of storage capacity. The energy-save mode is also practical, whereby the device puts itself to sleep with very little current consumption.

> **NOTE**
>
> **Booting from MO? Not always...**
> As already described in Chapter 7 for the ZIP drive, generally you can boot from any portable drive using the new SCSI controllers. But, they have to be formatted with the 512 bytes per sector which is typical of the PC, which doesn't apply to some MO media. This is because MO media are hard-sectored by the manufacturer, namely according to media type with different sizes. The 3.5" media with 640 Megs storage, for example, work with 2,048 bytes/sector, which means they aren't bootable.

For more information check out the page on the Internet devoted strictly to MO technology (www.mo-forum.com). It's set up jointly by ten MO manufacturers and should tell you everything you need to know.

Finally, for all of you who are eyeing a 5.25-inch drive maybe because you need to store really large quantities of data (videos, audio files, etc.). Pinnacle Micro has the most ingenious MO drive currently available: 4.6 Gigabytes on one disc that also offers high performance. Again, however, the full capacity is possible when data is written to both sides.

PD drives are frequently overlooked but they shouldn't be

Finally, let's introduce a particularly interesting portable storage device called PD drives (Phase Change Disc). Unlike MO, the PD drive uses a purely optical process in which data is written to CD-like media using a laser beam. (See below for more information on the very similar CD-RW.) The two most important differences compared with the CD-RW are a different data format and the ability to rewrite the media freely over 100,000 times.

This logo is used to identify PD media and drives.

PD technology has some unique features and advantages. PD drives are not only a unique portable storage device, but also a normal 4x CD-ROM. This is because the PD is basically a type of rewriteable CD which uses a hard drive-like file format which is incompatible with the traditional CD. This means you can write to a PD medium without any extra drivers or special software. The drives, which are almost exclusively SCSI, are simply connected and then work like a ZIP or JAZ drive. Depending on manufacturer and model, the data transfer rate is around 300-600 KB/sec for writing and 600-1,000 KB/sec for reading.

Chapter 8

Perhaps the biggest advantage of the PD is its extremely high data security, which even exceeds that of the MO. Since a purely optical process is used, whereby the data points are created using a laser and high temperature (several hundred degrees), only severe mechanical damage will result in data loss. But since the discs are supplied in a caddy sleeve, even this risk is slight. Prices are also attractive for the 650-Megs media: around $28. Availability of supplies is guaranteed for at least the next ten years. All the big manufacturers, such as 3 M, offer these media, although you won't find them in every store. Drives are currently available from Compaq, Panasonic and Plasmon (PD2000e at around $575), as well as TEAC (PD 518E). The latter is a real price-buster at around $285, and offers 8x performance for reading and 2x for writing.

PD media are supplied in a protective caddy sleeve, but otherwise look like a normal CD-ROM, except for the visible formatting structure.

If data security is your highest priority, then your best bet is an MO or PD. Based on its higher speed and the somewhat less expensive media with equal data security, the MO wins the race for normal conditions. However, the fact that the PD actually gives you two drives in one might tip the scales in its favor. Especially if you've run out of room on your PC. The PD is also ideal for notebooks, where there is usually room for only one drive anyway. With the PD, you then have not only a CD-ROM, but also a great backup medium. Also, anyone who has a PD drive in his or her notebook will surely want one in his or her desktop PC. In this case we recommend the new TEAC.

Chapter 9

About CD-ROMs
And CD-RW

CD-ROMs have experienced incredible growth in recent years, and have become indispensable in PCs. Many new software programs are available only on CD-ROM. Now that you can buy a CD-Recordable drive for far less than $1000, the dream of making your own audio or photo CD has become a reality. The technology and development for one CD standard are rapidly superseded by the next breakthrough. The rewritable CD-RW is the latest.

It's hard to keep track of all the developments and to know what you might be able to use and what not. If you only use your CD-ROM to install software, you probably won't care about new standards and speeds. But if you want to run multimedia CDs, databases or application software directly from the CD, you can't get enough speed.

Fortunately, CD technology has a lot of potential for improvement. The following tips are useful for all those who just can't get enough speed. Of course, we're not just talking about the rotation speed (which in our view can be idiotic at times). We'll be dealing with all aspects of optimizing your CD-ROM player. The first part of this chapter contains general information about buying and optimizing traditional CD-ROM drives. The end of the chapter discusses all of the topics dealing with CD burners and the new CD-RW devices.

LOOKING CLOSELY AT THE CD-ROM

You don't have a CD-ROM at all, or you need a newer, faster one? Today's CD-ROMs are loaded with features, so you have to be careful to know which ones are useful and where there are differences among the models. This chapter will give you the necessary insight. We'll also talk about tuning and troubleshooting after you have your new purchase at home on your desktop..

CD-ROM lies and truths about the speed mania

What was the latest CD-ROM speed: 24X or was it 30X...why not 40X? The manufacturers seem to be releasing new CD-ROMs regularly. At the same time, many of us remember the problems of vibration when switching to 8X, 10X and 12X drives.

Vibration has been a main problem with the speed demons of the CD-ROM world. It's the result of CD-ROMs that are not perfectly round. Anything above 8x or 10x makes the smallest imperfections on the CD immediately noticeable in the form of strong vibrations, which are not only aggravating, but they also affect the reading accuracy and the drive stability.

This can be critical with the new 12x to 24x models. These devices are almost useless without decisive measures to protect against vibration, such as a breaking sensor, stabilizing mechanics, etc. The best thing would be to grab an out-of-round CD and simply test the new device with it.

You need to be very clear about the fact that the increased speed of rotation is only advantageous for a few types of applications. In actual practice, you won't notice any difference above 16x speed. So a 24-speed drive is humbug. At the same time, note that the interface you're using (ATAPI or SCSI) will definitely make a difference with transfer rates above three Megs/sec. If you have an ATAPI CD-ROM operating at the same time as a hard drive, things will get pretty tight with EIDE. And if the BIOS doesn't play along, under certain conditions some ATAPI CD-ROM drives won't run at full capacity. And if that's not enough, the increased speed of rotation will create problems, especially with error correction. First of all, the timing gets off far faster when the devices run at high speeds (try reading a house number while driving by at 120 mph). And if an error shows up then, the machine has to put on the brakes.

NOTE

CLV or CAV—Sales hype or useful?

Even when the audio CD premiered, there was a stipulation that a CD must rotate with a constant data transfer rate. However, since there are more data along the outer edge of a disc than the inner edge, the speed of rotation of a CD-ROM must vary along the longitudinal axis, so that the data flow always remains constant. This old CLV process (Constant Linear Velocity) has also been used with CD-ROMs up to now, until some manufacturers came up with the idea of operating CD-ROMs at a constant rotation speed, like hard drives. Of course, this produces different data rates, depending on the position. The constant speed of rotation also speeds up the access. The new process is called CAV (Constant Angular Velocity) and is used by almost all manufacturers. However, usually they use a mixture of CLV and CAV in an attempt to achieve optimal performance, depending on the application and the track used. So, CAV improves the access time and the rapid jumps between different positions. Therefore, it is optimal for rapid searches for data. However, if you are loading multimedia files (e.g., videos), you want a constant transfer rate, and pure CAV is aggravating. Also, almost all 16-24x drives only rotate with approximately 8x speed along the inner tracks, making them slower there than the previous 10-12x generation. Since most CDs primarily have data on the inner tracks, these "faster" drives are in actual practice often even slower than their predecessors. Therefore, CAV or CAV/CLV mixed operations aren't the final answer, and they don't necessarily make a good CD-ROM drive. But they are great for advertising

The bottom line is that if you still have a good 4x-8x drive, don't buy a new one just for the sake of the "faster" speed. You'll be disappointed because you'll only notice a difference with long copying and installation operations. Plus, the new drives have problems with error correction and vibration, they are noticeably slower when reading a CD and they still cost too much. If you do buy a new drive, look especially for good anti-vibration protection and error correction. If it's got that, go ahead and get a 12-20x or a 16x drive. A 24x drive won't give you anything more, except probably aggravation. You'll find a tip for reducing the vibrations at least a little in the next section on CD-ROM practical tips.

Differences among CD-ROM drives are noticeable

Features are the big thing with CD-ROM drives. One standard and enhancement follows right after the last one. It's enough to make you see red instead of the rainbow when you are bombarded with all the specifications of the CD-ROM books, which contain the established CD-ROM standards. And meanwhile, it has actually become obligatory to support the different standards with new drives. What is more important to look for are the newer features, some of which are quite useful, such as digital output or support for the new CD-RW media. The most important points you need to look for when buying a new drive are summarized below:

◆ Actually it is quite rare for a CD-ROM drive to not support the entire spectrum of CD-ROM formats. Still, it can't hurt to double-check this, perhaps by looking through the user's guide. The cornerstone of all CD-ROM formats is the Red Book, which was defined by the inventors of audio CD, Sony and Phillips, in 1982. It specifies how the data are to be laid down on the CD. This nomenclature was continued with the Yellow Book, then the Green Book was added for the CDi format selected by Phillips. The most current supplement is the Orange Book, with standards for CD-Rs, CD-RW and photo-CD (so it actually only applies to CD burners). In addition to these standards, your CD-ROM should also carry the XA label, which indicates compatibility with an expanded recording format. A lot of things happen at the same time with modern multimedia applications. Text appears on the monitor, a video is running somewhere and a musical piece is playing in the background. CD-ROM XA was developed so that all these data streams arrive at the processor at the appropriate time and can be read from the different files concurrently. By using the technique of interleaving, similar to the memory access technology, these data are nested within one another directly on the CD, just like the presentation requires.

◆ The quality of the error correction is particularly important. After all, most CDs have at least a slight fault, and this is even more true for CD-Rs. A device with poor error correction may completely refuse to read data, and it frequently becomes unbearably slow when it comes across faulty locations. The models differ enormously with respect to error correction. Frequently, you can't even rely on proven manufacturers. For example, Toshiba was well known for very good error correction with its 4x drives, but it had considerable problems keeping these quality standards with its faster models. Unfortunately, when evaluating individual models for this property, you will have to rely on test reports in the current trade journals because it would be very rare that you could test them personally.

◆ If you want to use the CD-ROM drive as an audio device in your PC, look for audio buttons. If you want to use it strictly as an audio device, that should even be the most important feature for you. After all, you don't need to connect that kind of a device to the bus, only to the sound card. That way it doesn't load down the PC when playing CDs.

◆ Since we are talking about audio data and replay, it is unfortunately still not the norm for manufacturers to supply their CD-ROMs with a suitable audio cable for connecting the drive to the sound card. If you don't have one yourself, you can often find a suitable one at your dealer's. By the way, the audio cable only provides an analog transmission of the audio sound to the sound card. It only has one purpose: to regulate the volume via the sound card. Depending on the sound card, you can also use this connection to record, which means converting analog to digital. If you can't establish a connection using this internal cable, you can also connect the headphone jack of your CD-ROM drive with the line input of your sound card using a mini-jack cable. This will work the same way.

◆ We've been frustrated in the past because the data on an audio CD, which are of course stored in digital format, can't be copied digitally to a hard drive or transferred to a digital recording device (DAT, MD). But things can be done differently, because for the first time, some new CD-ROMs have a digital output. This is one feature we'd really make sure our new drive had. An alternative is the digital readout of the audio data from the CD using special software via the normal PC bus. Unfortunately, this does not work with all devices, usually only with the high-end SCSI drives. In addition, you also need a special program for this (see side bar), which has to work with your CD-ROM. Especially if you have a CD burner and you want to create your own audio CDs, it is extremely important to have the support of one or both functions.

> **NOTE**
>
> **Extracting audio data from the CD to the hard drive**
>
> Toshiba, with its 4x CD-ROM drives a few years ago, was one of the first manufacturers to make it possible to digitally read out audio data as .WAV files to a hard drive. Even today, though, that is the exception, because not all drives support this. However the software is just as critical. There are some shareware programs (CD-Worx95, CD-Grab Audio, DAC (Digital Audio Copy) and CDT (CD Tools) that make this possible, although some of them do so only under DOS. In addition, some CD burner programs offer the function, but only if the CD-ROM drive supports it. Currently, the best of class in this area are the CD-ROMs from Plextor (Plex12-20x), because they are the only devices on the market that can extract audio files with the help of an included tool (see figure) to the hard drive at 8x speed. That is part of the reason why the Plextor CD-ROMs are currently so popular among professionals

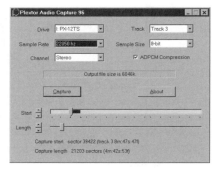

The Plextor Manager, bundled with high-grade Plextor CD-ROM drives, has many features for controlling audio CDs (left) and a clever audio capture program (right). This program can even process audio files relative to the sampling rate and it can process ADPCM compression during extraction.

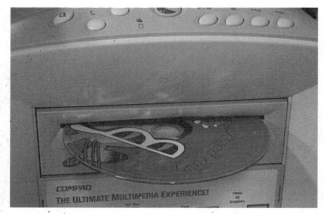

While the caddy is being replaced as a protective cover (left), some manufacturers are moving a step further: CD-ROMs with automatic feed, like car audio CD players (right, CD-ROM drive from a Compaq Presario).

CD-ROM TROUBLESHOOTING AND OPTIMIZATION

Right after you install the new CD-ROM drive, nothing works like it's supposed to. First, you can't figure out how to hook up the ATAPI drive. Then Windows 95 won't recognize the CD-ROM drive. Plus, you would like to operate both your new and old drives under DOS (e.g., for computer games).

Or maybe everything did finally work, but it vibrates excessively. Can't you do anything about that? Even if you've overcome all the challenges, the drive still refuses to eject a CD-ROM. Do you know where the emergency eject button of your drive is?

Optimal installation

Probably everyone understands the basic procedures involved in installing a new CD-ROM drive: remove the front panel from a 5.25" bay, and screw the drive into the bay with the (hopefully) supplied flat screws. Then connect the data and power cables and the sound card cable, if applicable.

◆ Even during installation you can counteract troublesome vibrations by wrapping the outside of the device with several layers of adhesive tape. Use just enough so that you can still insert the device into the bay using a little pressure. The increased resistance and the buffering effect of the tape cause a significant dampening of the vibrations that develop. Your CD-ROM drive and your hard drives will thank you.

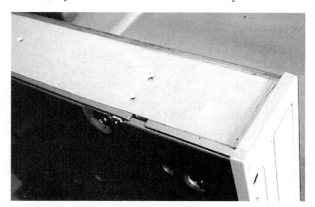

Before you install it, wrap up your high-speed CD-ROM drive with several layers of adhesive tape, but don't forget to leave openings for the mounting screws.

◆ Sometime in your life your CD-ROM drive will swallow a CD and won't spit it back out. If the problem is electronic in nature, you're lucky. Usually there is a small hole somewhere on the front or back side of the housing for manually unlocking the drive, also called the emergency eject button. To use it, you have to straighten a paper clip and poke a small button with it. But note carefully any recommendations from the manufacturer. Not all holes in the housing are suitable for paper clips. <u>If you poke around in them, it is possible that you can damage your drive.</u>

Sometimes poking around does help. You can use a paper clip to activate the emergency eject button of a CD-ROM drive, but sometimes you have to hit exactly on the pressure point inside the device.

◆ Connecting the connection to the data bus (SCSI or ATAPI) follows the hardware installation, SCSI is straightforward since you only need to note the ID setting (see Chapter 7) and termination. It won't hurt with an ATAPI CD-ROM to attach the IRQ 15 exclusively to the secondary EIDE port on the motherboard (except for using IRQ 15). We already discussed the pros and cons of possible connection combinations in Chapter 6. The same is true of the (normally not necessary) BIOS notification also in Chapter 6. Note again that the EIDE controllers of all current motherboards can very easily merge a slow CD-ROM drive with a fast hard drive on the same port. The frequently given recommendation to operate a CD-ROM drive alone if at all possible, because otherwise it would slow down hard drive access, is only true for old motherboards which cannot individually adjust the PIO modes of master and slave. If you attach the ATAPI CD-ROM exclusively to the motherboard, you should also check to see if the drive is operating in slow 16-bit mode (see Chapter 6). To do so, determine the maximal data transfer by copying a large file under Windows.

NOTE **Toothpaste as correction fluid—Salvaging defective CDs**
Scratches in the protective layer can render a CD-ROM useless. However, if the scratches are not so deep that they reach the data layer, often you can still save the CD. First, clean the CD with water and a cleanser that doesn't affect plastic. Do not use alcohol under any circumstances! If this doesn't help, lightly polishing the protective layer at the scratch can often work miracles. Often the inability to read is simply due to the laser beam scattering. If you smooth out the scratch without creating new ones or damaging the data layer, the laser beam will be reflected without scattering. You can find appropriate polishing kits in specialized stores. One alternative that is also cheaper is to try it with toothpaste! It is important that you stroke from the inside to the outside, and not concentrically so that you don't do even more damage to associated data.

CD driver under DOS

After the hardware installation, next on the agenda is linking the driver. Although this happens almost automatically under Windows 95, in DOS there are a number of tricky spots. But even those people who use Windows 95 exclusively or primarily won't be able to avoid working with DOS drivers. After all, Windows will be installed from DOS, and some games or programs still won't run under Windows 95. Therefore, here are the tips you'll need to get a handle on DOS driver problems:

◆ Linking the driver under DOS and/or Windows is easy. You just need a hardware driver from the manufacturer or, with a SCSI CD-ROM, you need the universal CD-driver of the SCSI controller (for example, ASPICD.SYS). The hardware driver of the ATAPI CD-ROM should be bundled with the drive on a diskette. It's best to link the driver with the DOS software driver Mscdex.exe in CONFIG.SYS see Chapter 4).

When linking the drivers in CONFIG.SYS, there are several things to optimize or to note:

1. There is an updated version 2.50 of Mscdex.exe that you can download from the Internet from the Microsoft homepage. You should always use the newest version that your DOS accepts.

2. If you use the DOS cache program Smartdrv.exe, keep in mind that this program can also cache your CD-ROM drive (which Vcache in Windows for Workgroups can't do). To do so, you just need to make sure that Smartdrv.exe is invoked after both CD-ROM drivers. With Windows for Workgroups, you might find it better to only activate the CD-ROM caching via Smartdrive.

3. If you use Windows 95, but also have to have the CD-ROM drive automatically activated at the DOS level, then we have a really great tip for you: Load the hardware drivers in CONFIG.SYS, but not Mscdex.exe. Loading the 16-bit driver without the DOS program doesn't bother Windows 95 operations, and this way there is no chance for the CD-ROM to be loaded twice under Windows 95. Subsequently, you should load the Mscdex.exe driver with all the necessary parameters in the batch file Dosstart.bat in the Windows 95 directory. This file is always executed automatically when you leave Windows 95 and call up DOS. This way your CD-ROM drive is automatically linked in DOS, but it doesn't disturb Windows 95 operations due to the activation of the 16-bit driver. This solution could be a little ticklish for SCSI users, because in addition to the SCSI CD-ROM driver, the 16-bit DOS driver of the controller (e.g., Aspi8dos.sys) must also be loaded in CONFIG.SYS. However, even this driver doesn't normally bother Windows 95 operations. I say normally this is true, because depending on the SCSI controller and driver, Windows 95 can start working in MS-DOS compatibility mode after loading the DOS driver.

4. You should be aware of the command switches of Mscdex.exe: /L:x and /M:yy. Whereas /L:x specifies the drive letter of the CD-ROM (e.g., /L:G), with /M:yy you can reserve a buffer memory somewhat like a small cache, which improves performance. However, if you use

Smartdrv.exe, this function is relatively unimportant, and you don't need to use it at all. Otherwise /M:16 is a value that produces very good results.

◆ Things get a little trickier if you want to link two (or even more) CD-ROM drives per driver via CONFIG.SYS. But don't worry, it can be done, and very easily to boot. This allows you to easily use your old drive as an audio player or for permanently having a CD-ROM encyclopedia on hand. With Windows 95 the registration is as easy as pie. Stick in the CD, call up the Add New Hardware Wizard, and the rest is done almost automatically. Afterward you just need to check the drive letter assignment in the device manager. In DOS or Windows 3.x you must give each CD-ROM drive its own name when the drivers are invoked. A CONFIG.SYS for ATAPI devices would look like this (with sample driver names, which you need to replace with the particular names of your drives):

```
device= c:\driver\atapi1.sys /d:cdlw0
device= c:\driver\atapi2.sys /d:cdlw1
install=c:\dos\mscdex.exe /d:cdlw0 /d:cdlw1 /L:g /L:h /M:16
```

If you use two SCSI CD-ROMs, you only need to call up the hardware CD driver (Aspicd.sys) once, instead of two times with ATAPI devices. The drives are automatically recognized by the controller, and they are allocated a drive letter via the SCSI ID number. In other words: For a second SCSI CD-ROM you don't need any additional driver calls or modifications; the settings for the first device are sufficient. You only have to invoke the driver two times as shown above when you do not want to explicitly allocate the second CD-ROM drive the drive letter which comes directly after the first one.

CD-ROMs under Windows 95

You don't have to have a Ph.D. to get a CD-ROM drive to run optimally under Windows, because as a rule, the device will be recognized by Plug & Play and will be linked without any errors. However, that's only a general rule, because there are still plenty of traps and problems, especially with ATAPI drives. The most common problem is that Windows 95 simply won't recognize the device, regardless of what you do. But there are solutions for this problem.

◆ Windows 95 usually recognizes ATAPI drives during setup via Plug & Play. SCSI CD-ROMs are supported directly by the driver for the SCSI controller, so they require the least amount of tinkering. It's a little more problematic with the ancient CD-ROM drives with a proprietary interface (e.g., old 2x Sony and Panasonic drives). Plug & Play recognition doesn't work with these drives, so during setup you have to tell Windows that this device is present. Many users misunderstand when the system asks about a CD-ROM drive during setup, thinking it is a general question about a CD-ROM drive, and they click on the option even if they have a SCSI or ATAPI drive. But the question only concerns those ancient CD-ROM drives. As a result, Windows gets confused, it looks for one of those drives, and it hangs up too long during setup. Sometimes it can even lead to crashes.

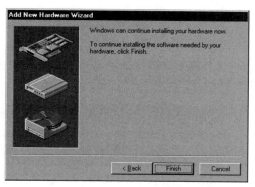

Installing a CD-ROM using Windows 95 Hardware Wizard.

◆ DOS CD-ROM drivers, which must used before you can even install Windows 95 from a CD, are another frequent source of problems during installation. But the very presence of these drivers sometimes causes Windows to fail to load any Windows drivers for ATAPI drives or ones with a proprietary interface. If you remove the DOS drivers after successfully installing Windows, then the device itself disappears under Windows 95. By the way, this isn't a problem with SCSI drives, because the CD-ROMs are controlled by the controller driver. Here is the best solution: Copy the folder Win95 from the Windows CD to your hard drive (using the loaded DOS driver). Then disable the DOS drivers with a REM command in the CONFIG.SYS file and install Windows 95 from the hard drive. That's the only way you can be certain that all 32-bit drivers have been correctly loaded.

◆ If you use Windows 95, but you still need access to your CD-ROM drive in DOS, then you still need to have the DOS drivers loaded in CONFIG.SYS, although in certain circumstances this can cause Windows 95 to work in compatibility mode. The best solution for this problem is the one we just gave above on using DOS drivers. If you skipped over that, you might want to flip back to it.

◆ Loading the bus master driver is useful especially for using the drive with multimedia CD-ROMs. Of course, there are the known problems which were discussed earlier. If you are using Windows 95b (OSR2), you can activate the same function (called DMA mode in this case) in the device manager (see Chapter 7).

◆ If everything has gone smoothly and the drive is finally registered by Windows 95, you should check the cache settings in the Control Panel. Unlike Windows for Workgroups 3.11, the software caching in Windows 95 finally also supports CD-ROMs. You will find the appropriate setting in the System Properties window, which you can access by clicking on the System icon in the Control Panel or by clicking on Properties in the workspace. Select the option File System in the Performance tab. Under the second tab there, CD-ROM, you can adjust the supplemental cache size with the slider in 214 K increments up to 1,238 Megs. In the combo box "Optimize access pattern for" you can also optimize the access by selecting the rotation speed of your CD drive. However, Windows 95 will only optimize up to a quad-speed drive.

NOTE

CD-ROM caching in Windows 95—How much is best?

A lot helps a lot? Not necessarily, and definitely not with CD-ROM caching in Windows 95. If you select the highest setting, more than one Meg of space will be reserved for CD-ROM optimizing. If you only rarely work with CDs and you only use them to install software, it will be better for you to reduce the cache size in favor of the entire system. And anyway, CD caching only helps if data are read multiple times, like with databases. You won't gain much with installations or especially with multimedia CDs. In fact, if you are playing video segments, you might see jumpy pictures. In this case, reduce the cache size.

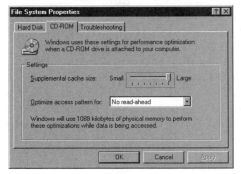

Click on the System icon in the Control Panel to access the Properties of the File System,
where you can adjust the cache size for the CD-ROM drive.

◆ Speaking of speed, keep in mind that using a CD-ROM drive with Windows 95 really burdens the processor. ATAPI CD drives are the king of the hill in this regard, because depending on the model, they can tie up as much as 90% of the processor resources during operation. Listening to audio CDs is also important in this regard, again more so with ATAPI drives than SCSI drives, because depending on the model, this can use up 10-50% of the resources. Surprisingly, the new, fast drives use up more resources than the old 2x or 4x CD-ROM drives. In addition to this, many CD drives have the annoying habit of not shifting back up from single speed after playing an audio CD. A restart is the only thing that helps in this case. The best solution for this problem was already described above: Use a drive with audio buttons, and attach it only to the sound card and not to the controller.

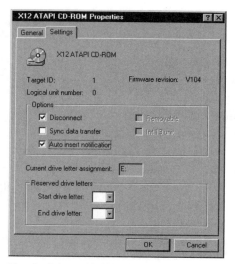

The check box "Auto insert notification" is enabled/disabled in the Windows 95 Device Manager under the Properties of the particular CD-ROM drive (as is the assignment of the drive letter). It causes Windows to automatically recognize and refresh inserted CDs, and if they are auto-start CDs, it performs this function as well.

◆ Here is a tip for those people who have an eye on a CD changer. They are actually great tools, since you always have a large repertoire of CDs at your fingertips. If you open the Desktop in Windows 95, or bring up the Explorer, then the system has nothing better to do than to inform the user about all of the CDs that are present. Even if you already know which CDs you have inserted, a computer is very thorough. Windows 95 simply insists on taking every opportunity possible to check whether there is a CD in each compartment of the changer, and what kind of a CD it is. You can put a stop to this super-diligence by turning off the "Auto insert notification" in the CD-ROM properties of the Device Manager. The entire magazine will still be read when you start up, but after that you can work in peace. In the meantime, many manufacturers have recognized this problem, and they offer special devices or drivers so that the problem doesn't occur even if you have "Auto insert notification" turned on. If possible, test this at your dealer's before buying a particular model, because this function can become a real nuisance in a hurry.

CD BURNERS AND CD-RW

Burning CDs is the new amateur sport. Wherever you go, anybody who has a burner is excited about it. And most users would like to have one too. The newsgroups are full of questions like "Which CD-Rs are better for audio CDs, the green ones or the gold ones?" And by the end of the year, everything will be even more interesting, when the new sound cards with digital input and output (like the Terratec EWS 64) take hold in the market place. Then nothing will stand between the seamless and perfect transfer of data between stereo system and PC. The ultimate goal of many hi-fi fans: immortalize the old black vinyl records on high-quality CDs. It will be a dream come true for many. Five years ago, who would have thought that possible?

All the same, CD burners aren't just used for making audio CDs, but above all for making data CDs of all kinds. Since the prices for CD blanks are dropping rapidly right now, the CD-R is working its way up to a cost-effective and in some cases ideal backup medium. Even MO can't keep up.

But the latest thing is the rewritable CD, or CD-RW for short. The new technology is fascinating, since it actually makes it possible to erase and write on special blanks up to 1000 times. A slight modification (a light amplifier) is all that's needed to make normal CD-ROM players capable of reading the media. Unfortunately there won't be any way to upgrade old players. But more about that in a minute.

As usual, in this chapter you'll find a buyer's guide with exactly the important facts that you need to look for when selecting your equipment. In particular, we discuss the latest options, like packet writing and CD-RW. Finally, we have compiled a collection of valuable tips about CD burning. There's a lot to talk about, so let's get going right now.

Buying your first CD burner

Soon there will be as many CD burners on the market as there are CD-ROM drives. All of the notable companies like Sony, Philips or Mitsumi have one or more models on the market. The prices for almost all 2x models (2x write and 4x or 6x read) have slid to $400-600. Only the 4x models (4x write and 4x, 6x or 8x read) are still above the $600 mark.

On the outside, there is very little difference among the models to the user, and if you don't happen to be interested in all the technical mumbo-jumbo, you won't know which criteria to use in making your selection. All of the models can do all the basics, of course, like producing multisession CDs on all of the usual blanks on the market, but the models do sometimes differ considerably in special features. If you just watch out for a few typical sticking points, you should do just fine.

◆ Particularly with CD burners, many manufacturers don't make the devices themselves, but rather they market OEM devices from a few primary manufacturers under their own label. If you want to save a lot of money, it's better to get an original model. Not only is it (almost always) technically identical, often you'll get better support for it. Take for example the Philips CDD series, which are also sold by HP, Plasmon, Grundig, and who knows who else. The original model from Philips (currently CDD2600) can often be found for several hundred dollars less, and Philips even provides very good support, which can't necessarily be said of the other manufacturers. Of course, sometimes the cheaper price might be due to the lack of a (or a cheap) SCSI controller and worse software.

◆ Sufficient cache is essential for CD burners. The bigger, the better. During the normal burning process, the devices have to rely on a continuous flow of data. But if the data aren't fed fast enough from the hard drive, without a cache as intermediate storage there would be a loss of data (the dreaded "buffer underrun"). So the size of the cache is very important for reliable writing, and at the same time, it is dependent on the speed of the device. For example, one Meg cache at 2x speed is enough for just about three seconds of buffering. One Meg offers a shorter buffer for 4x models. Don't buy any model that doesn't have at least one Meg with a 2x and two Megs with a 4x writing speed. Of course, twice that amount would be preferable.

◆ What do 4x burners really give you? A significant time advantage! Figure out how long it would take to duplicate a 74-minute audio CD. Most CD players can only read audio CDs at single speed. Then if you use a double-speed model for writing, the whole thing, including working time, takes about two hours. Now, if you use a Plextor CD-ROM drive to read the audio data at eight-speed, and then burn the data on a four-speed device, the whole process only takes about 30 minutes! So if you burn a lot of CDs and don't have a lot of time, you should definitely get yourself a faster burner.

> **NOTE**
>
> **Details on four-speed burning**
>
> If you're eyeing a four-speed burner, right now you have a choice between models from Yamaha and Teac. Since the prices and the technical data are almost the same, it comes down to the processing and user experience. Yamaha clearly wins out in both areas. Also, there was a recent report that CD pressing companies supposedly often have problems with master CDs (CD-R masters for pressing CDs in a CD company) that were produced with the Teac model. We can't confirm that, and it's supposed to depend on the blanks that are used as well. But the fact is that the Yamaha model is currently bundled with the better software package from CeQuadrat (see further below for CD software). And keep in mind that your computer has to provide a high, constant data rate of more than three Megs/sec for successful four-speed burning, so a fast Pentium with a SCSI system is required.

◆ Which interface— SCSI or ATAPI—should you use? Our recommendation is not to use ATAPI. The risks of problems due to interference on the bus and low speed are much greater with ATAPI or EIDE (see Chapter 7). Even if you only have an EIDE computer, you can still upgrade to SCSI for not much money (see Chapter 7).

On the outside, CD burners don't differ one iota from normal CD players. They even have audio buttons, but because of all the heavy-duty mechanics inside, don't misuse these devices for that purpose.

Be careful of heat build-up. Don't burn your fingers on equipment that is too hot. A relatively large amount of heat develops when burning a CD due to the writing laser. Depending on the design, the machines can react to heat build-up during operation or in the long term with thermally induced deformations and maladjustments. In other words, if the burner gets too hot, sooner or later it will develop a problem. The models of the Philips series (CDD2600, burners from HP, Plasmon, Grundig, etc.) are especially well known for this, which also explains their relatively high failure rate. These models in particular, and all others if possible, should be housed in an external case, or you should buy them directly as external models. After all, note that the manufacturer's listed maximum ambient temperature is usually only 86-104°F (30-40°C). You'll easily surpass that in a PC after just a few minutes.

You should use a standard commercial SCSI case with its own cooling fan for your CD burner. This costs around $60-100.

One way of differentiating the CD burner "wheat" from the chaff is their support of special burn formats or standards. Most notable in this regard are the support of CDs with variable sector sizes and the ability to use packet writing (also called incremental writing). There is a separate section on packet writing further below. Let us just say here that your burner should definitely support packet writing, or it should be upgradeable via firmware. Now back to variable sector size. There are certain CDs (especially game CDs) that are written with different sector sizes. If you want to make a copy of these CDs, a lot of burners won't work. The key point is whether your CD burner is capable of writing all possible sector formats (CD-ROM sector mode 1 and 2, and CD-XA sector mode 1 and 2). Sectors in mode 1 always contain additional bytes for error correction which are not present in mode 2 sectors. So more data can be stored in the latter. With CD-XA CDs it is possible that mode 1 and 2 sectors are mixed together on a CD, which places significant demands on a burner. There is a firmware update for the popular burners of the Philips CDD series that supports burning with variable sector sizes. The four-speed burner from Yamaha is another model that can handle all of these functions.

Speaking of firmware: It has become commonplace with almost all models, but you still definitely need to make sure that your future CD burner can be updated via flash-ROM. After all, there's not a single device that's placed into the market that works completely error-free, but the errors can be fixed with new firmware.

Another very important function that needs to be supported by the CD burner and the burner software is Disc-at-Once. This process is important for producing audio CDs, since more data fits on a CD than when using Track-at-Once. The bottom line is, CD burners write data sequentially on the blank. Therefore, it's difficult to make an uninterrupted recording; in fact, it's only possible if the CD can be burned in a single operation with a particular technique, namely Disc-at-Once. In contrast, the usual Track-at-Once method adds a two-seconds pause after every track. With data CDs, that is immaterial, but with audio CDs, each song corresponds to a track, so that a forced two-seconds pause is added between each songs. In addition, the pauses delimit the amount of data for the actual music. And when you copy CDs which already have pauses built in, these pauses are enlarged. Not all CD burners or burning software support Disc-at-Once. But you can avoid these forced pauses by using Easy-CD Pro, GEAR 4.x and Win On CD 3.0 or 4.0, assuming of course that you were smart enough to check for Disc-at-Once support when you went shopping.

For all of you who want to create audio CDs with your burner, you might be interested to know that the CD burner, like some CD-ROM players, makes it possible to digitally extract audio data from a CD to your hard drive. If you don't have another CD-ROM drive or it doesn't support this function, it would be important for your new CD burner to support it.

◆ Here is another royal pain: In Windows 95, some models (including the Philips CDD series) don't show up as a normal CD-ROM drive, but instead as a WORM (Write Once Read Many). The result is that the device can't read a normal CD-ROM unless a special driver is loaded. Fortunately for the Philips models, the driver (Cdd2000.vxd) is bundled with almost all burner software. Still, we don't think this is a very elegant way of solving the problem. Other manufacturers, such as Ricoh, don't have this problem: Windows recognizes the device immediately as a CD-ROM player and assigns it a drive letter.

◆ Our next point for discussion is the support of CD-RW media. Since these media reflect too little light for normal drives, they can only be read by new drives with a built-in amplifier (called AGC). These drives are also called multiread-capable. Look for this feature, because it's not all that common and it wasn't used until mid-1997 in the new 16-24x models. The new 20x drives from Plextor and Hitachi (including the Hitachi 16x) definitely are multiread-capable.

> **NOTE**
>
> **Specific CD burner recommendation**
> Well, which one should I get? If money isn't a priority (again), we would get the original Philips CDD2600, but be sure to put it in an external case. However, if possible, we would go straight to a CD-RW drive. Currently, the Ricoh MP6200S is the only SCSI recorder, so it gets our prestigious Tuning Seal of Approval ;-). If you don't have any time, but you do have too much money, get the four-speed burner from Yamaha instead.

CD-RW is finally here

There's been a lot of talk and speculation about the rewritable CD, or CD-RW, for a long time. It's finally here, and you could easily ask why it took so long, because the technology, a variant of the PD process (see Chapter 8), has been known for a long time. Anyway, the CD-RW comes along just at the right time to provide support for CDs during the current transition to DVD. At the same time, you could view it as a transition medium to DVD, because in contrast to traditional CD-R discs, which DVD players can only read if they have an additional laser, CD-RW discs are immediately recognized by DVD players.

Much of the speculation about CD-RW is nonsense or will only be possible in future models, such as writing to and erasing the media at will. By the way, we know exactly what we're talking about, because we just bought one of these drives ourselves ☺. Here are the most important facts about CD-RW:

◆ All CD-RW drives can process not only the new media, but they can also burn normal CD-Rs, and of course they can read CD-ROMs. That makes them universal drives. Since the prices are around $600-800 (and they're falling), you shouldn't buy a traditional 2x CD burner any more.

◆ Amazingly, Ricoh beat the competition (Philips CDD3610, Sony and Yamaha) by months, and in the spring of 1997 they produced the first available CD-RW drive, the MP6200S. Its big advantage over the competition's drives that came out in the fall of 1997 is that it's a SCSI drive and not an ATAPI, like the others. In my mind, that makes it a winner in comparison.

The Ricoh MP6200S is a 2x-write, 6x-read CD-RW drive with a SCSI connection. Its one-Meg data cache and its good write protection don't leave anything to be desired. And it supports all other important functions. Only the CD-RW functions aren't quite perfect yet, but that will be significantly improved with the firmware update to version 1.2 which will be available on the Internet. You'll find the update at www.ricoh.co.jp/cd-r/cgi/e-/00_dos-e.html. We strongly recommend that you update your burner. Note also that an update from Direct CD is also available on the Internet, as will be described below in the section on UDF packet writing.

*Except for the color, the silver **media** don't look much different than traditional CD-Rs. However, they are considerably more scratch-resistant, because the data layers on both sides are coated with protective layers. The prices for the media are still high at $25, but they're acceptable.*

*The new CD-RW media aren't just better optically;
they are especially more scratch-resistant than normal CD-Rs.*

The main difference compared to the PD technology is the CD-compatible file format. This means that it isn't possible (yet) to freely write to the CD like a normal hard drive or removable medium. As usual, you need a CD-R-compatible drive and corresponding burner software. The data are written in CD format, and therefore they can also be read later by multiread-capable CD players (see the last point in the section above with our general recommendations for buying a CD). The situation is similar with audio CD players; only the newer higher priced models, such as those from Sony and Rotel, are CD-RW-compatible.

> **NOTE**
>
> **The technology behind CD-RW**
>
> CD-RW is based on phase-change dual technology (PD). Although PD drives can read CD-ROMs, the PD media have a format which is not compatible with a CD. That will change with the definition of the CD-RW standard in the Orange Book III, which was established by a consortium consisting of Ricoh, HP, Philips, Sony, Yamaha and Verbatim-Mitsubishi. In the PD process, the data are coded optically on an alloy made of silver, indium, antimony and tellurium. The crystallization state of this alloy can be switched exactly between two phases (crystalline and amorphous = high and low reflection, respectively) by differential heating with a laser. In CD-RW media, the PD material is embedded sandwich-like between several auxiliary layers. The process results in a high level of data security, and the silver-colored media make a robust, scratch-resistant impression. The manufacturers guarantee 1000 erasing operations, but in actual practice, probably 10,000 or more are possible.

◆ As will be described in more detail in the next section, the new technology of packet writing is well suited for CD-RW drives, but it doesn't have anything specifically to do with CD-RW. With the aid of a special UDF driver, during packet writing the data can be transferred in smaller blocks, and they can be written to the medium at any time. Otherwise there is no need for any burner software; for the writing process, the device is addressed via the drive letter like a removable medium.

◆ Erasing a CD-RW is currently possible only in larger blocks. Right now it's only possible to erase one session, one track or the entire CD. The new 2.0 version of UDF (see next section) or Adaptec's Direct CD will make it possible to actually physically overwrite data during packet writing.

Although there aren't too many multiread-capable CD players out there, that will change soon, and then they will be an optimal medium for exchanging data. The big advantage to using CD-RW right now is the ability to finally test all of the features of your burner and your CD burner software to your heart's content. If something goes wrong, you just erase the test CD-RW. How about a test with CD-R blanks? No, probably nobody has tried that. Anybody who buys a traditional 2x CD-ROM burner now can only blame himself, when you can get a CD-RW recorder for just a little more money. Only 4x CD burners still have a chance.

Packet writing and UDF—The new way to safely and comfortably burn CDs

Are you tired of complicated and tiresome CD burner programs? Then perhaps you should switch over to the new packet writing. Using a special driver, the CD burner (CD-R and CD-RW) is addressable just like a normal removable data carrier. You can simply use Drag & Drop in Explorer to copy or move files. Another plus is the data transfer method, which, as the name indicates, uses small packets of uniform or varying size. The decisive advantage of this method is it greatly reduces the risk of a buffer underrun error. With packet writing you can even transfer files from a network or a compressed drive to the CD-R(W).

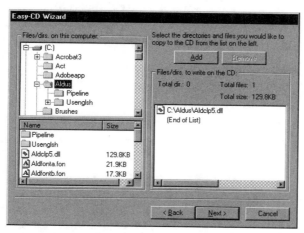

Thanks to packet writing, you can address a CD burner
like a normal drive and use Drag & Drop to move files for writing.

Sony started out with its CD-R-FS, but it was only made for Sony's own drives. Besides, CD-ROMs written with CD-R-FS could only be read using a driver which also had to be integrated into the CD-R. Sony's proprietary file format was at fault.

Packet writing only really took off after the manufacturers agreed on a new universal file format, UDF (Universal Disc Format). In the spring of 1997, Adaptec was the first to bring a corresponding program to the marketplace, i.e., Direct CD. Then CeQuadrat, known for their professional CD burner software WinOnCD (see below), came out with Packet CD. In contrast to Packet CD, Direct CD 1.0 seems to have a lot of bugs and generates more errors. Adaptec does have an update to version 1.01 available on the internet (www.adaptec.com/support/ BBS_EZSCSI.html), which fixes some of the bugs. Version 1.2 should appear in the fall of 1997. By the way, if you're having problems with Direct CD, you should make sure that the "Auto insert notification" is turned on, in contrast to normal burner programs. Otherwise, long file names are often not enabled for writing. In addition, never write to a CD with Direct CD and other CD burner programs, even if this is possible by converting to ISO format. And one final tip: Disable the Direct CD task if you are writing to a CD-R with a normal CD burner program. If you follow all these tips and use the newest versions of the programs, things will work out just fine.

NOTE

Problems with Direct CD

Adaptec's Direct CD does create some genuine problems. For example, all of a sudden long file names won't be supported on the target drive. That's usually just the start of the problems because the CD doesn't get completely written. The next time you boot, suddenly the whole CD-R(W) doesn't get recognized and the data are lost. However, the bug only appears sporadically and only with certain drives. To avoid it, be sure you enable the "Auto insert notification."

However, both programs are similar from the standpoint that they load themselves invisibly int the system and they make the recorder writable like a normal drive. Assistants help wit formatting in the UDF format. To read a UDF CD in a normal CD player later on, the software ju has to convert it into the usual ISO or Joliet format. It's even possible to rewrite to the free are of the CD later with packet writing. The table of contents from the previous session is simpl transferred into the new common table of contents (TOC).

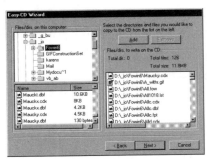 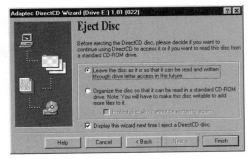

Wizards lead you through all the important steps such as formatting (left) and converting UDF into ISO format (right).

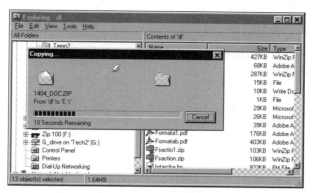

*After you've properly installed Direct CD,
you can use Windows Explorer to copy files to your CD-R.*

One final word on packet writing, CD-RW and the erase function of UDF. The current version of UDF (1.5) does not support the ability to use a CD-RW any differently than a CD-R. Although erasing is possible on a UDF CD, it isn't physically performed. Only the file entries in the TOC are removed. So the erasure is actually virtual, and it doesn't free up any room on the disc. The same is true with renaming files. But at the end of the year, new programs will appear (first of all Adaptec's Direct CD 2.0) that support UDF 2.0. Then the new file system will allow the physical erasing of data for the first time on CD-RW media. So then working with CD-RWs will almost be like working with a normal removable data carrier medium.

The optimal burner software

If you want to use the more extended features of your CD burner, like making audio or photo CDs, packet writing won't help at all. You'll need burner software for that. The question is, "Which software?," since more and more programs are coming out. As is often the case, the programs only differ after you look closely; after all, almost all of them support the basic functions.

While some of them emphasize extremely simple operation, others concentrate on supporting all CD formats and all possible extras. Of course, even the makers of professional software, like CeQuadrat, do everything they can to make the user interface as simple as possible. We've picked out some of the most interesting and important programs for you below. Our recommendation is clearly the same as that of many other users: WinOnCD from CeQuadrat. You'll read why below. First of all, an overview of the different programs:

◆ Whereas a year ago there were only just a few burner software titles, and most of them were very expensive (Corel CD Creator, Easy CD, GEAR and a few others), now every couple of weeks there are new titles offered, in some cases at dumping prices. Overall the prices have really gone down; even professional programs like WinOnCD only cost around $100-200. So when you buy a recorder, don't even take the bundled software into account. Focus instead on the recorder itself. Then buy the best software for your personal needs after the fact.

◆ When selecting the program, look for the following features in particular, which absolutely should be supported and which will be described in the course of the subsection: Disc-at-Once, multisession support with acceptance of the data from the previous session, Joliet format for long file names and the ability to digitally extract audio data from an audio CD. If one of these features is missing, we wouldn't buy the program.

◆ The Adaptec company, which is well known for SCSI controllers, has obviously decided to enter this market in a big way. After buying up different CD burner programs (like Corel CD Creator), in late summer 1997 Adaptec brought out its new product, Easy CD Creator Deluxe. This program is the successor to the well-liked Corel CD Creator and can be updated. Insiders weren't too surprised to see that this program was strongly oriented on WinOnCD from CeQuadrat in terms of handling and features. And just like CeQuadrat, the package is rounded out with a packet writing component (Direct CD; see above). Like WinOnCD, CD Creator lets you combine CDs of all formats using a double window with the help of Drag & Drop: in one window you select the data, in the other you produce the future CD. A nice feature is the addition of some tools for producing audio CDs, like CD Spin Doctor, which is supposed to remove noise from old vinyl records when recording them onto CD. But if you know anything about the complexity and difficulty of a feature, you can already suspect that something like this can't be completely resolved with just a little tool. After all, professional programs like DART or SoundForge, which also have this feature, rightfully cost several hundred dollars, and they still aren't perfect. Of course there is also the obligatory CD case wizard, which you don't need if you have a good drawing program like Corel DRAW! But there's no question that in the future, Adaptec's CD Creator will share the upper end of the market with the new WinOnCD version 3.5, and for a price of $100-200 it offers good, attractive features.

◆ However, there are also lots of users who don't really care about supporting all possible this-and-that CD functions and a few add-on tools with mediocre performance. Instead, they would rather have an easy and fast interface. A program for these users is called CD Wizard (from VOB). It's a good inexpensive alternative to larger programs (CD Creator and WinOnCD). CD Wizard uses the wizard idea and takes you through CD production with step-by-step queries. This approach takes a little getting used to for those switching over from other CD burner programs (and the online help is very limited and Disc-at-Once isn't supported).

If you are looking for the right combination of professional software and easy operation, you definitely need to look at the new WinOnCD 3.5, from the CeQuadrat company. It is the best burner program there is. Naturally, WinOnCD provides complete support for all possible CD formats. And the practical interface with four directory and file windows is easy to learn; after all, it has been adopted by Adaptec for the new CD Creator and by other companies for a good reason. WinOnCD is also praised for its first-class integrated audio functions. It really is impressive to see everything that is possible with audio CDs and to learn what you didn't know anything about beforehand. WinOnCD also enables you to work with extra features such as pre-emphasis or CD copy protection. The integrated audio editor is ingenious. You can use it to adjust the volume of musical pieces, or you can automatically blend them in and out. Music fans who want to use their burner especially to produce audio CDs don't really have any alternative to WinOnCD.

In addition to an improved interface, the new version 3.5 offers several new, attractive features, such as a Booklet Editor (makes CD cases), a tool for reducing pops and clicks when recording analog records (like Adaptec's CD Creator), optimized speed via special support of the available SCSI hardware, and the automatic recognition of attached CD recorders. One useful feature is the ability to convert a project that has already been created into another format (e.g., an ISO CD to a bootable CD). The Plug-In function, which makes it possible to add more functions at a later date, is very clever. For example, soon multirecorder support and different DVD functions will be provided as Plug-Ins. When it comes to features, you can't beat WinOnCD 3.5. You can even convert AVI videos to MPEG, or produce ISO/Mac HFS hybrid CDs in the full version. Full Windows NT support is also provided.

By the way, if the $150 price tag (recently drastically reduced) is too high, you can get WinOnCD's smaller and very economical brother, ToGo. It offers the same interface and supports all basic functions. Missing features are the expanded audio functions, although they can also be replaced to a degree by different shareware programs, like Cool Edit 96.

PRACTICAL TIPS FOR BURNING CDS

Thanks to the previous sections, hopefully you are now equipped with the right recorder and suitable software. The only thing missing are the corresponding practical tips. The most common problem when burning CDs is the buffer underrun error, which always occurs when the data flow stops while you're burning. Unfortunately, the CD blank and the stored data are lost once this happens.

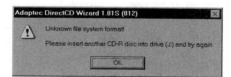

The great fear—buffer underrun error when burning CDs!

So that you're not plagued by too many errors (and there's no such thing as problem-free CD burning yet), and to make the result even a little better, we have compiled a few practical tips for you again.

Checklist for burning CDs

Before you start burning CDs in earnest, or whenever problems occur, go through the following checklist. It lists the most important basic prerequisites for successfully producing a CD.

1. Give your burner software the PC's full attention. Turn off any programs running in the background, including screen savers. A defragmentation process that automatically starts during the burning process, for example, guarantees a buffer underrun.

2. Don't ignore the system requirements. Burning CDs with a slow 486 won't cut it. Quadruple burners desperately need a fast Pentium system with a SCSI bus. If available (e.g., with WinOnCD and ToGo), let the burner software test the performance and the recommended burning speed.

3. Disable or be aware of possible performance reducers, such as the use of compressed drives or a network connection. Both of these can hinder the burning process. Never read data from a compressed drive on the fly, since this will certainly lead to a buffer underrun, especially with slower machines.

4. If you are burning at quadruple speed, you will bump up against the performance limits of current computers. It might be necessary in that case to use especially high-grade components. Using a wide SCSI controller to connect to the originating hard drive, for example, provides a maximal data transfer, especially since it lets you read and write at the same time. To really avoid data errors, also buy an AV hard drive without normal thermal calibration (such as Micropolis makes). They are the only models that really guarantee a continuous data flow with large amounts of data.

5. On the other hand, the read speed of the originating CD-ROM when copying directly from CD to CD isn't a problem with current CD-ROM models. It just needs to be a little higher than the writing speed. Quadruple and 8x CD players are quite sufficient, and they're the most common by now. Naturally, place an especially high emphasis on error correction. Because if you get delays due to errors, then the result will be a coaster.

6. The auto-insert notification must be turned off for CD burners. Many burner programs (including WinOnCD once again) check for this when they start up, and they ask if you want to turn it off. Otherwise do this by hand (select Device Manager, then Properties for the CD burner and inactivate the "Auto insert notification" option). Notice, though, that if you record your CDs with packet writing, using Adaptec's Direct CD or a similar program, you have to leave the auto-insert notification switched on so that you don't generate errors during operation.

7. The SCSI bus should be optimally configured for the burning operation. Naturally, all of the settings of the IDs and the termination should agree. In addition, only the SCSI controller should provide the Term-Power signal (see Chapter 7). Some manufacturers recommend that you attach the burner to its own SCSI controller (in addition to the present one). We're not convinced of the positive effect, but if you have a lot of problems, it's worth a try.

Otherwise, it's best to attach the burner to a bus master-capable PCI controller. Many people also recommend that you limit the maximum transfer rate to five Megs/sec in the BIOS of the SCSI controller. That's still much higher than the actual capabilities of the recorder. We're not convinced that this recommendation makes much sense or has much effect, but again, if there are problems, try it out.

Green, gold or blue: The role of the blank CD

Now that most of the initial problems with CD recorders seem to be overcome, the optimization-hungry computer community is busy philosophizing about the utility of the different CD blanks. Even well known audio magazines are running tests with high-end equipment: "Do green blanks sound better?" "Yes" is the clear answer from the magazine. Green is a whole five sound points better.

However, for normal ears or stereo equipment, little or no difference can be heard. In principle there doesn't seem to be any significant difference between the different blanks. Besides, it's pretty hard to clearly distinguish between the three basic types anyway (cyanine = blue-green, phthalocyanine = gold, and metal complex azo dye = blue). More and more manufacturers use their own combinations, so there's really no way to keep them straight. The manufacturer's quality control seems to be much more important anyway. So it would be better to buy name-brand blanks rather than cheaper no-name products.

There is one point that you need to pay attention to, though: There are special blanks that have been tested and certified for quadruple speed. They have fundamentally higher quality than the double-speed blanks, but they don't necessarily cost more. So pick them up whenever you can.

By the way, the manufacturers are claiming that their blanks will keep for 50 years guaranteed, and probably for even 200 years. Of course, nobody can really test that. Naturally, the stability depends very much on the storage conditions, because temperature variations in particular are hard on the material. Chemical reactions with things like the coating resins can at least partially destroy the data.

CDs with long file names—The Joliet format makes it possible

The normal CD format, ISO 9660, ensures compatibility of a CD with almost all computer systems. Of course this comes at a price, because file and directory names can only consist of the first 128 ASCII characters with a maximum of eight letters in length and three letters for the file name extension (8+3 rule). Also, the maximum directory depth is limited to eight levels. This is particularly stupid when you're trying to use a CD-R as a backup medium of a data carrier with long file names. When using the ISO format, the file names are unmercifully abbreviated (as in DOS by using the tilde ~).

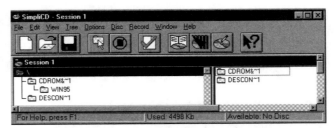

In the lower window you can easily see how the long names of a hard drive are cut off on a CD in ISO format.

As a solution for this, there are different variations or extensions of the ISO format, but they aren't standardized. Currently the best solution, but unfortunately only in Windows 95, is to use the Joliet format. This format works with the expanded Unicode character set and allows file and directory names up to 64 characters in length. In addition, directory names can have extensions.

CDs burned with the Joliet format can only be read in Windows 95 with the long file names. However, since a table of contents following the ISO format is also generated at the same time, theoretically other systems, such as DOS, should be able to read at least the short versions of the names.

Unfortunately, not all programs follow the exact specifications of the Joliet format, and they don't create an ISO 9660 copy of the files, for example. When Joliet CDs made with the popular Corel CD Creator program are read in DOS, they only show a readme file with a remark about an "outdated operating system." Test your CD burner program to see how compatible the Joliet format is with other operating systems.

Avoid packet writing

If a CD has been produced using packet writing, as described in detail above, this can lead to significant performance problems on older CD-ROM drives. You'll have the fewest problems if the software will allow you to use a fixed packet size, since many packet writing programs allow you to specify either fixed or variable packet sizes.

Sometimes "multisession" is only "multivolume"

Multisession is a process in CD burning whereby a CD can be produced in several parts. This makes is possible for you to put your data on the CD blank in separate burning operations. The finished CD will have several sessions on it, each of which basically represents a separate CD on the CD. The advantages to this are obvious, although you lose about 15 Megs on the CD per session.

The important thing is that there are two different ways to generate multisession CDs. In the Incremental Multisession process, the transition from one session to the next is generated by references from the old file system to the new one. When a new session is created, the contents of the previous TOC (Table of Contents) are imported into the new one.

In the Multivolume process, on the other hand, the individual sessions are kept separate and are each treated like separate CDs. This kind of CD can result if you forget to import the data from the last session when you are creating a new session, or if you use a program that can only work with the Multivolume process but not the Incremental Multisession process. So when you buy a program, definitely make sure that it completely supports the Multisession process.

If you put a Multivolume CD in a drive, at first you will only see the last of the available sessions. You need a special driver, sometimes called a Multivolume mounter, to access the others. With the driver you can switch between the different sessions, but you can only see one at a time.

Bootable CD-ROMs

You can boot from a CD-ROM but only if certain prerequisites have been met:

◆ The BIOS of the PC (see Chapter 6) or of the SCSI controller (see Chapter 7) must support the function and it must be switched on.

◆ You have to have a bootable CD-ROM based on the El Torito process.

◆ Right now, you can only boot from a CD in DOS and Windows 3.x, since other operating systems bypass the BIOS routines necessary for booting.

So the prerequisite for booting from a CD is the El Torito standard. To create a bootable CD based on this El Torito process, you have to use a burner program that supports this standard to completely transfer a bootable partition of the hard drive (DOS and possibly also Windows 3.x) over to the CD-R. In another session, you can also record files on the CD using the ISO format, but they will only be visible if you don't boot from the CD. Conversely, if you boot from the CD, only the boot session will be visible. That's how it works.

```
SCSI ID:LUN NUMBER #:# 0:0 - IBM      DORS-32160
SCSI ID:LUN NUMBER #:# 1:0 - IBM      DORS-32160
SCSI ID:LUN NUMBER #:# 2:0 - PIONEER CD-ROM
SCSI ID:LUN NUMBER #:# 3:0 - PLEXTOR CD-ROM

A BOOTABLE CD-ROM IS DETECTED IN YOUR CD-ROM DRIVE...

The boot sections on your bootable CD-ROM are:
  0. DEFAULT ENTRY
SCSI ID:LUN NUMBER #:# 5:0 - IOMEGA  ZIP 100
```

Probably the first bootable commercial CD-ROM was the Windows NT 4.0 CD, as you can see from the message when you boot from it. Of course, you can't actually boot Windows NT itself; just a DOS partition on the CD.

One final detail: You can determine whether the CD should be addressed like a diskette as drive A: or like a hard drive (drive C:). Normally you should use the latter option, because if the CD is "masked" as a diskette, the mirroring of the boot partition on the CD can't be larger than 1.44 or 2.88 Megs (depending on the diskette setting in the BIOS).

Giving your CD-ROM a custom label

There are a lot of methods nowadays for professionally imprinting CDs or for putting a self-adhesive label on them. If you want to label your CDs by hand, only write a few comments on the back side with a soft felt marker. If the resin layer is dissolved, you will destroy the data. Never use stickers, because not only can their adhesive damage the CD after a while, but they cause a tremendous imbalance in fast CD players.

Now, back to the real labels. There are special printers for professional users which can imprint the CDs very professionally using thermotransfer. However, those printers cost several thousand dollars. You just put the CD in, use a program to design the label, and you print. That's it (except for the high costs). Of course, that's really out of the question for a single individual. But now there is a whole series of pre-made stick-on labels for individuals to use; they are placed on the CD exactly centered using a supplied special tool. You can print on the labels with any normal printer (ink jet or laser) using a program like CorelDRAW!

Super tips for home-made audio CDs

Making your own audio CDs has become a real hobby for a lot of people. Naturally, people rapidly move beyond simply wanting to copy CDs or compile songs from CDs they already have. Ideally they would like to record the digital data of a DAT or MD recorder, and of course to record their old, dearly beloved vinyl records on CD. But in the meantime, the manufacturers have intentionally set up many hurdles in this regard. Here are some interesting tips for hard drive recording.

To copy all of an audio CD, all you need is the CD copy function found in most burner programs. The data are simply copied sector for sector. It gets more complicated if you only want to transfer individual songs digitally to your hard drive and from there to the CD-R. You can do this with the following methods:

1. Your CD-ROM drive has digital output and transfers the data to a special card with digital input in your computer. We'll talk about this more below.

2. With some CD-ROM drives (practically only SCSI drives), you can digitally extract the songs as .WAV files via software. This method was already discussed earlier in this chapter.

3. You direct the analog data from the Line Out connection of the CD-ROM drive to the Line In connection of the sound card and digitize the data all over again using the card's A/D converter.

Method #2 is the best and easiest of all, but unfortunately it only works with a few drives. If this method isn't possible, most users go with method #3, which almost always leads to notable degradation in the quality, since sound cards simply don't have as high-grade and low-noise A/D converters as good hi-fi systems. Besides, the multiple D/A-A/D conversions introduce additional losses as well.

So we're left with method #1, which will also be of interest to all those wanting to digitally transfer the audio data from a DAT or MD recorder. But since normal sound cards haven't been equipped with digital input/output so far, you have to use special cards (see figures) that have the appropriate connections. On the other hand, the first sound cards with digital input/output are coming into the market now. The hottest one of all is the Terratec EWS 64, which has video and coaxial connections on a front panel and only costs about $600. Read more about this super sound card in Chapter 11. The new Sound Blaster AWE 64 Gold also has a digital connector for the first time, but unfortunately, it's only a digital output, which makes it useless for hard drive recording. The only other product is the Pinnacle sound card from Turtle Beach, for which you can get an upgrade kit with digital input/output. However, the price is over $600, so it's not very attractive and it doesn't compare with the EWS 64.

Digidesign, with its Audiomedia III card, is probably the best known maker of a purely digital I/O card with input/output for audio files. You'll find more information about it on the Internet: http://www.digidesign.com/ Newdigiweb/Diginews/Digireleases/Prodrelease/audiomedia_IIIpr.html.

The second well known maker of a digital I/O card is Digital Audio Labs, with its Digital Only CardD. They offer a special digitizing card, the CardDplus, which works with the other card. You'll find more information on the Web at http://www.rfspec.com/ digaudla/cardd.htm.

If you want to save money but not scrimp on performance, your best bet will be the EWS-64 from Terratec (right). This is more than just an all-around sound card; it also has digital input/output in coaxial and video form via a 5.25" module. Unfortunately, it doesn't have a scanning rate converter, although you can make up for that by subsequently processing the recordings by software.

The Multi!Wav Digital PRO card from the AdB company is an absolutely high-quality, but correspondingly expensive, digital I/O card. This card is used by sound studios and, in contrast to the other cards, it has video input and output. You'll find more information about it on the

Digital obstacles—Copy protection and sampling rates

NOTE Two problems keep cropping up when making digital copies: first, the copy protection bit, which is added to the recording by all digital hi-fi devices (DAT, MD) with the first copy of a CD. This bit prevents any attempt to make a second copy. Second, there are the different scanning rates, which prevent direct dubbing from DAT (48 kHz) and digital radio (32 kHz). You can buy copy protection crackers for the copy protection bit, of which the Hucht ICP 1 CE from the Hucht company is the best, because unlike all other models, it doesn't destroy the title markers of a digital recording. A scanning rate converter helps with the varying scanning rates, although it's not really necessary with digital I/O cards for the PC. That's because almost every decent sound processing program (e.g., Cool Edit) can convert to other sampling frequencies. The Hucht device also has the advantage of being a converter between optical and electric digital connections. The device costs around $180. By the way, most PC cards, including the EWS 64 from Terratec, ignore the copy protection bit. You have to ask yourself how much longer the music industry will accept that.

The bottom line is thanks to relatively inexpensive cards with digital input and output that are finally available, and to the drastically reduced prices for CD recorders and media, the PC has become an excellent recording machine. However, if you want to record your analog records on CD, definitely use a hi-fi device (DAT, MD) for digitizing, because the quality and noise reduction of the A/D chips on PC sound cards don't come close to such devices. Then transfer the data digitally into the PC via a special card. Special programs like DART Pro of SoundForge 4.0 let you do special editing, like removing noise and pops. And you can use standard sound editors (such as the shareware program Cool Edit 96) to do the other editing, like converting the sampling rate. Some CD burner programs, like WinOnCD, sometimes offer other useful functions, like the ability to softly fade songs in and out, or to adjust the differing loudness of different songs. In some cases, the end product, the self-recorded audio CD, is actually of a higher quality than the original record.

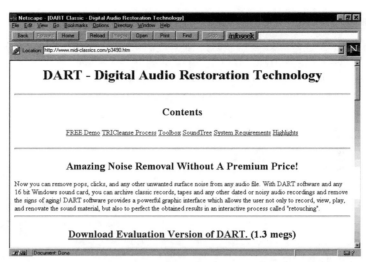

You will find more information about DART on the Internet at http://www.midi-classics.com/p3490.htm.

Make it a hit—There are special requirements for producing master CDs

If, for whatever reason, you want to have your home-made CD mass-produced by an actual CD manufacturer in the form of normal CD-ROMs, there are a few other things you need to know:

To press the CD, the CD manufacturer needs a different, high-grade CD-R as a master, called a "glass master." You can only make the glass master using the Disc-at-Once method, since CD-Rs made with Track-at-Once generate errors in the press. In addition, you should definitely talk to the company about different types of media and potential type-specific problems. There was a recent report that Teac's popular quadruple recorder apparently generated glass masters that presses couldn't use when certain types of blanks were used. So you see that sometimes there are unpredictable problems in these kinds of special cases.

Chapter 10

Video Cards And Monitors

Even the best computer isn't worth much if it doesn't have a good video card and monitor. The monitor is your system's most important output interface. Your monitor should be the best and highest quality element in your system that you can afford.

◆ Perhaps the most important indicator is the horizontal scanning frequency. Monitors are often advertised with many numbers, but don't get discouraged; one parameter will quickly tell you where you stand: the horizontal scan rate (in kHz). This defines the maximum refresh rate (in Hz) at which a monitor can run at a particular resolution. At the same time, you can assume that a monitor with a high scan rate is a high-grade device in other technical aspects as well.

Typical Monitor Sizes	Scan Rate (max., in kHz)	Effective Resolution	Refresh Rate (max; in Hz)
14 inches	35 or 38 (fixed)	640x480	70 or 75
14 inches	48 (multisync)	640x480	96
15 inches	48 (multisync)	800x600	72
15 + 17 inches	64 (multisync)	800x600 1024x768	96 80
17 inches	82 - 85 (multisync)	1024x768	100
20-21 inches	82 - 85 (multisync)	1024x768 1280x1024	100 77 - 80
20-21 inches	112 (multisync)	1280x1024	100

Fortunately, there aren't that many variations here. Only a few different types of monitors are on the market. A quick glance at the monitor's spec sheet will quickly tell you which class it belongs. The table summarizes the most important classes and their associated resolution and refresh rates at this resolution. Often inexpensive monitors are advertised at prices below the normal prices in their class. These include 15-inch monitors for about $300, 17-inch ones for $600 or 20-inch ones for $1200. These are usually models with a low scan rate (48, 64 or 82 kHz, resp.). If you're sensitive to flickering images, stay away from these models. Also note that the larger a monitor is, the more distracting the flickering is. Whereas 80 Hz on a 15-inch model is just fine, it's not nearly enough for a 17-inch monitor. As a general rule, a 15-inch model should run at least at 64 kHz, a 17-inch model should have 82 kHz (86 is better), and a 19-inch to 21-inch monitor should run at least at 96 kHz (110 is better). If you're only going to run a 19-inch to 21-inch monitor at 1024x768 (which makes a lot of sense), then 85 kHz is acceptable.

◆ Note the fineness of the shadow mask since it determines the definition and maximum resolution. The mask pitch has a very decisive effect on the picture quality. It determines the color purity and the sharpness, especially at higher resolutions. Although there's not much difference in the quality of well-made shadow masks and the alternative aperture grille (Trinitron tubes)—each has its advantages and disadvantages—the matrix, that is the distance between the pixels for red, green and blue, is decisive for the maximum resolution. This is especially important for monitors 17-inches and larger.

In this case, the frequently used 0.28 mm isn't quite good enough to display a resolution of 1024x768 pixels very well and definitely not for even larger monitors at even higher resolution. A general rule is a 17-inch monitor should have at least 0.26 mm; a 19-21" model should have 0.22-0.25 mm. Unfortunately, it is exactly the larger monitors that are often made with large mask pitches (0.28 or 0.31 mm).

◆ A monitor works in analog and true color. So, it doesn't have problems when the color depth is increased, like a digital video card does. Yet, more colors and high resolution and refresh rates really put a monitor to the test. In addition to the horizontal scan rate, the pixel frequency (in MHz) is a second important indicator of the ability of a monitor to draw new pixels on the screen as rapidly as possible. It should be at least 135 MHz or higher, if possible. Cheap monitors often have a high scan rate indicated in the catalog, but a glance at the low pixel frequency (e.g., 105 MHz) shows that the monitor won't cut it at higher resolutions and color depth.

◆ Choosing the type of screen mask is less important than the quality of the particular type of mask. Each of the mask types currently used has notable advantages, but they are starting to merge.

◆ The popular shadow mask. The pixels for the different colors are arranged in triangles. This has the advantage that the pixels are located at defined points, which prevents waviness. Due to the small holes, on the one hand the light efficiency is limited, but on the other hand it provides the best sharpness. Misconvergence doesn't occur very often, but the picture often seems a little dull. The advantage of the shadow mask is the low manufacturing price and the high clarity out to the edges due to less misconvergence. But, there is reduced color brilliance and contrast.

◆ The Trinitron tube from Sony is typical of the aperture grille technology. Since the patent has expired, now there are imitators like the DiamondTron mask from Mitsubishi. Instead of dots, both use small stripes running parallel to the longitudinal axis. This provides improved luminous efficiency and contrast. Misconvergence, however, can be a disadvantage, especially along the edges. The increased luminous efficiency can also be tiring to light-

Chapter 10

sensitive eyes after a long time. These tubes are also popular because they are slightly curved only in the horizontal direction, since the design is strictly cylindrical. By the way, the DiamondTron tube from Mitsubishi doesn't have nearly as good picture quality as the Sony original, but the former is considerably less expensive, so a lot of manufacturers are switching over. Another plus is that Mitsubishi uses a separate focusing lens for each of the three cathode rays, while Sony only uses one large lens. This allows the picture tube to be shorter, and thus the monitor is more compact.

◆ Right now, only NEC makes the newer slot mask, called ChromaClear. This represents a new type of combination of the shadow mask and the aperture grille. Theoretically, it achieves almost the luminous efficiency of an aperture grille and the same clarity, without misconvergence.

There's just not much difference between the displays of good monitors with the different types of masks. Plus, the new slot mask isn't the promised cure-all, either. Brand name manufacturers often use both types in their product lines today. The Trinitron tube does have a slight advantage in the user's judgment, since the better color brilliance and the high contrast have a more animated and pleasant effect. Text in particular is easier to read on it. With an aperture grille, don't let yourself get disturbed by the almost always present misconvergence in the corners and the well-known suspension filaments in the display. The price is usually about $150 higher than with standard masks.

5. No monitor is adjusted absolutely correctly after connecting to your video card, aside from a few complete systems which only high-priced dealers provide with the correct configuration. This is not due to poor quality so much as the fact that all electronic devices are subject to some scattering due to the manufacturing process. Therefore, all monitors should be able to adjust the pincushion and trapezoidal distortion that are often indicated on the case simply as "Geometry." This is , of course, where cheap manufacturers like to cut corners. So, be careful because if your monitor doesn't have this adjustment feature, you might have to live forever with a skewed pincushion distorted picture. This will get even worse when the monitor gets older and you want to install some new cards in your PC.

6. Many manufacturers like to save a few pennies by using cheap image intensifiers. The video signal must be processed several times before the picture appears on the screen. The bandwidth of the amplifiers plays a key role here. If it's adjusted too low, they will wash out the signal, and the picture becomes blurry at higher resolution. So don't be impressed strictly by technical data. The eyeball test at the resolution and refresh rate that you plan to use is absolutely essential.

7. A good anti-glare coating is just as important with monitors as it is with eyeglasses. Studies have shown that glare specifically from a monitor greatly tires the eyes, because it continually distracts you and makes it difficult to focus on the actual image. Detecting low-glare monitors is fairly easy. If a light source falls on the dark glass of a monitor that's turned off, it isn't clearly reflected, but instead it refracts in a diffused fashion. You can only see a fuzzy region of light. Also, run your hand lightly over the surface of the glass. If it feels

slightly roughened, you've found the kind of screen you're looking for. So ask the salesperson specifically about anti-glare.

8. Unfortunately, the problem of misconvergence occurs with inexpensive monitors. If the convergence is out of line, the electron beams for the three basic colors—red, green and blue—don't focus exactly on a single point any more. An example of what happens next is that a white point doesn't look pure white but it shows color edging with the three basic colors (RGB) on the edges. This is especially noticeable on the borders between bright and dark areas, like a thin black line on a white background. As a result of the misconvergence, fine objects become fuzzy and hard to read, which can be painfully obvious with text. With fine lines you notice that they are usually bordered with a blue or red parallel line. With a good monitor from the factory, you should hardly see misconvergence, or only slightly in the corners. However, you practically can't make an aperture grille (Trinitron) monitor entirely without misconvergence. Also, all high-grade monitors should provide convergence correction in the horizontal and vertical directions if possible. Again, to make the adjustment, you should orient yourself on a thin line on a white background and turn the knobs so that the line doesn't have any color edging. By the way, if you adjust the picture too much, you can restore the factory settings by pressing the Reset button on the monitor.

9. It's well known that monitors generate radiation. The very strict MPR II standard guarantees a good level of protection. The crackling due to static charges so familiar from TV screens is totally absent. The TCO '95 doesn't provide much in the way of radiation protection, but it provides particular support for energy savings.

10. Your monitor should also have a power-saving feature that puts it into sleep mode with minimal power draw after a preset time. The monitor should support general standards such as DPMI or the old VESA energy-saving functions so that the sleep mode can be controlled with the computer. Then the BIOS, the video card or the operating system can put the monitor to sleep or wake it up again. If your monitor sports the TCO '95 sticker, it is guaranteed to support the latest energy-saving modes.

11. Your monitor should be a multisync model with memory for at least ten settings. This means that the monitor will automatically adapt to the settings fed to it by the card, and if there is an overload a defense mechanism will turn it off immediately. At the same time, you should be able to store the geometry settings like size and image orientation, and they should be automatically activated when you use the machine. Let's say you frequently switch the resolution from 1024x768 to 1280x1024 in Windows. The monitor will automatically recognize the change and will activate the appropriate settings that you previously set up.

12. If you buy a monitor now, you definitely need to consider how important USB technology will be for it in the future . If you opt for USB, you will also need a USB monitor, because it will serve as the central connection point for all of the other USB devices (keyboard, mouse, etc.) on your desktop.

Chapter 10

13. Newer monitors have all kinds of features and bells and whistles that aren't really important, but they're certainly fun or desirable. These include the ability to select color temperatures or other settings that are necessary for professionals in a pre-printing operation. The average user will use the normal default color settings. But it's nice to be able to adjust the monitor using an on-screen menu or via software from the computer. Whereas the on-screen menu is stored in the monitor itself and is accessed using the normal control knobs, software-based control requires a special connecting cable usually attached to the serial port. But as we said, these features alone shouldn't be a reason to buy a particular monitor.

Monitor specifics and our shopping recommendations

We recommend a 17-inch monitor for working with Windows 95. Don't even consider a 14-inch monitor and consider a 15-inch monitor only if your budget is tight. The new 19-inch monitors now available have an ideal ratio of price, performance and size. They are considerably cheaper to make than the previous 20-21-inch models and they take up almost the same amount of deskspace as a 17-inch model. Unfortunately, only a few companies, like Philips, Miro or Hitachi, have manufactured these models. The Philips model already has USB connections. Based on technical specs, the Hitachi CM751 ET with its impressive 0.21 mm mask pitch is very convincing.

Other than that, look at companies that have a reputation for making excellent monitors: Nokia, ELSA, Samsung and Iiyama.

◆ Iiyama, the market leader in Japan, always markedly undercuts the competition in price, with almost the same quality. Iiyama also has a large selection of models so you can always pick out your monitor based exactly on the desired criteria (scan rate, TCO standard, length of guarantee, service package, etc.).

◆ ELSA monitors have an excellent price-performance ratio, and they are also synchronized with the manufacturer's video cards. Combining the two high-grade components gives an excellent picture quality. One attractive model is the 17-inch Economo 17H97, which only costs about $900 thanks to the use of the DiamondTron tube. Except for some very slight geometry errors which sometimes appear at the upper edge of the screen, this model is simply perfect for the price. The same is true for the larger 20-inch and 21-inch Economo models, but they're not as economical.

◆ The 17-inch models from Samsung are also superb. The current model 700p stands out because of its excellent clarity, but it's considerably more expensive than comparable models from ELSA or Iiyama. However, if you work with text a lot, consider whether it wouldn't be worth spending a hundred dollars or so more.

*The Samsung 700p is convincing due to its slick design,
simple operation and high picture quality. But all of that has its price.*

NOTE

Monitor and TV in one package?

Many users ask for it, but there are still very few monitors that are also television sets. This is because the technical requirements are fundamentally different, so the conversion has always had to be a compromise, like with the 17-inch Nokia 447 V with TV tuner, video text decoder, loudspeakers and remote control. The technical specs for the PC aren't overwhelming (horizontal scan rate only 64 kHz, mask pitch of only 0.28 mm). Instead, it would be better to buy a TV card for about $100; then you can watch TV on your PC.

Information on the new flat display monitors

The first flat display monitors for desktop PCs are available. The manufacturers have the technology to the point where they can produce larger screens of 14-inch and 15-inch now and soon even larger. When evaluating the screen size, note that TFT CRTs use the entire screen up to 100% unlike traditional monitors (which have a least a thin black border). Therefore, a 15-inch TFT screen has almost the same amount of viewing area as a classic 17-inch monitor. A 17-inch TFT is almost the size of a 20-inch monitor.

Many are wondering what's the point in buying this kind of monitor. Although the picture is flatter compared to current monitors, many already believe the latter are flat enough already. Plus having a straight picture, undistorted out to the corners, isn't a problem any more for normal monitors today. A reason may also be the steadiness of the picture, which is admittedly better on TFTs. However, then they are more sluggish in their image painting, which is not ideal for animations and similar applications.

A side view shows how much thinner the new TFT monitors are compared to traditional monitors.

The main argument for flat displays is the absence of radiation. However, that isn't too critical any more either, because all new displays that follow the MPR II or TCO 92/95 standards are so radiation-free that it's no longer a concern.

Although, or perhaps because, we put the most emphasis on good picture quality, ergonomics and protecting our health, the TFT monitors don't seem to be attractive to us yet. They have a notably poorer picture quality than good regular monitors. The problems with the angle of view, oft-seen glare, and especially the poor contrast make these screens more tiring on the eyes than a traditional high-grade monitor. Unfortunately, these negative effects are overlooked by almost everyone in their excitement at the introduction of new technology. Keeping in mind that the cheapest 15-inch TFT CRTs cost more than $2000, we recommend that you buy a high-grade monitor with excellent anti-glare treatment.

Tips on working and using the monitor

The story's not over after you buy and connect the monitor. You'll spend a lot of time in front of it. The experience in the wrong conditions can be annoying or even painful. We have some recommendations for you.

◆ Take good care of the connecting cable. You can enhance the picture quality by using a high-grade, shielded cable. This is especially important with high resolutions and/or large monitors. Bad cables can lead to problems like shadows or blurring. Many monitors use 5-wire BNC cables with 17-inch and larger models. The signals in these cables for each color (RGB) and for the lines and screen end (Vertical and Horizontal sync) are fed into separate, shielded cables and connected to the monitor. This prevents mutual interference and notably improves the picture quality. If your monitor has this kind of connection (usually in addition to the normal 15-pin plug), you should definitely switch over to it.

◆ While you used to be able to distinguish high-grade monitors from cheap ones by their use of a BNC cable or connection, this is no longer the case with the current models. Now the manufacturers are so good at shielding the cable, for example by using ferrite beads on the end of the cable, that BNC isn't necessary any more and it's used less and less. You can recognize these cables by their thickness and rigidity. Check the cable quality when you're buying a monitor. If it's soft and flexible and it doesn't have these small ferrite beads at the end of the cable, that's not a good sign.

These BNC cables with the typical five bayonet connectors
are only needed for high quality transmission with older monitors.

A person needs resolution to make sense of the screen: The introduction of Windows has given greater significance to the resolution capacity of video cards and monitors. However, many users are uncertain which resolution is desirable under various circumstances. A 14-inch monitor with 640x480 pixels is certainly too small for Windows. A 15-inch model with 800x600 pixels is standard and inexpensive. Don't use higher resolutions on it, however, because the display will be too small, straining your eyes.

A 17-inch monitor represents the optimum price-performance ratio. At 1024x768 resolution, you have almost three times the display area compared to 640x480 pixels. This is where the fun and efficiency begins. A higher resolution has a positive effect on all applications. You can read the text much better in a word processor, for example. As a comparison, a resolution of 1024x768 corresponds to the 120 dpi commonly used in the printing industry, while 800x600 is equivalent to 96 dpi. That shows how low the detail clarity actually is.

Higher resolution is especially important when working with graphics. Since the presentation of the picture elements is directly associated with the monitor pixels, at lower resolutions you would hardly see anything of your picture. However, don't expect too much from resolutions higher than 1024x768. Hardly any monitor-video card combo can provide really sharp, clear pictures above that point. Sure, when working with graphics, you may want to switch to a higher resolution, but for normal work, 1024x768 is ideal on a 20-inch monitor. This large display greatly relieves the eyes, which you'll appreciate after several hours working at the screen.

◆ **Upgrade old or poor monitors.** Buy a high-grade filter that hangs in front of the monitor. You can get these from different manufacturers in computer stores or by direct mail. Make sure you look for quality products from reputable manufacturers, because there is a great market for unsuitable cheap products. A good filter isn't exactly cheap since they have to work with labor-intensive tricks like polarization filters. However, with a good filter, you can noticebly improve the picture quality in some cases.

◆ **Be careful with non-shielded speakers**: they can cause long-lasting misconvergence. Audio speakers are often positioned right next to the monitor. But if the speakers are not sufficiently magnetically shielded, the magnetic field will affect the monitor's electron beam, which deflects the beam and leads to misconvergence. If your monitor doesn't have an effective demagnetization feature (degaussing), you'll need to take it into a shop to have it demagnetized. So be careful that you only use specially magnetically shielded speakers next to your monitor.

◆ **Location can affect the picture quality**. Did you know that monitors are manufactured for regional viewpoints? A monitor destined for shipping to Canada probably won't have a really great display in a Tokyo living room. The earth's magnetic field is to blame. It affects the display relative to convergence. So don't bring a monitor home that you bought while on vacation overseas. By the way, large areas of misconvergence caused by the earth's magnetic field can be reduced on some monitors with a degaussing button. This dramatic example applies as well for small areas. The location in the room where you set up the monitor is important. Definitely avoid strong magnetic fields (e.g., from speakers). Also, consider the monitor's position relative to the nearest lamp or window. Avoid direct light reflection; your eyes will thank you.

◆ Think about ergonomics. This slogan that car clubs use makes sense for your monitor as well. If the distance between the monitor and your eyes is too small, working at the screen will be torturous. The distance should be at least 20 inches. Don't forget that a screen is a genuine "ray gun." To relieve the neck muscles, it is important to have the head looking down slightly, in a natural position. It is optimal if the monitor is an inch or two below eye level.

A SHOPPER'S GUIDE TO VIDEO CARDS

It's amazing how much the video card determines not only the speed of new PCs, but also the picture quality. Spending $100 or so gives you tremendous results. You could even say that video cards are one of the most important tuning sources right now. There's hardly another area where so much development is occuring. Plus, so many tremendous changes are expected in the near future. You could write an entire book about video cards and how to use them optimally.

Video card speed factors and speed traps

You can't go wrong with most of the video cards for 2-D acceleration or the functions for normal Windows programs. This technology seems to have reached its zenith some time ago. Naturally, the magazines still like to proclaim this or that card to be the "fastest 2-D card in the world." However, if you look carefully at the differences, they're really only a few percentage points apart. There's no reason then to be comparing video card speed, if you're not talking about true color and extra high resolution, because there are still drastic differences in that case.

If you aren't a power user working at 1280x1024 pixels with true color, you should pay more attention to other points, such as good driver software support, long guarantee, and especially good picture quality. Unfortunately, hardly anyone talks about the last point, and yet there can be some drastic differences in the picture quality from different video cards, as we will point out in detail below. With the aid of the following tips and background information, you should be able to buy the card for your needs.

◆ Decisive factors for a video card's speed include the performance of the video processor and the speed and manner in which the card's video memory is accessed. Not only does the processor have to access this memory at an extremely high speed, but so does the RAMDAC, the component that prepares the analog signal for the monitor. Manufacturer's efforts to speed up this bilateral data exchange vary widely, and in some cases they use a combination of methods. Some use special dual-ported RAM chips (VRAM or WRAM), which can be accessed simultaneously from both sides. Naturally this is faster than with the usual single-ported DRAM chips.

Another method is to increase the memory speed, which is made possible by new memory components like SGRAM and RDRAM. Usually they run at about 100 MHz right now. The third typical method is to expand the video bus from the old 32 bits to 64 bits, which is now standard, on up to the current peak of 128 bits, although only a few video processors support that. All of these methods can be combined, of course.

*Dual-ported VRAM memory on a video card doesn't differ
one bit from other RAM types except for the low speed of 50 ns, labeled on the chip above.*

◆ So, you can recognize a high-value video card by the type of memory used (especially VRAM or WRAM) and the width of the video bus (128 bits is currently the best).

◆ A wider data bus does have an important effect on the RAM chips used on the video card. Typical one Meg RAM chips have a 32-bit data bus. Therefore, a 64-bit video card requires at least two Megs of video memory, and a 128-bit card needs four Megs. Some video cards use special types of RAM which make it possible to access the full bandwidth with less RAM. For example, the 128-bit ET6000 video cards use MDRAM and allow access to the full bandwidth with only two Megs. However, this is the exception to the rule.

◆ Why does the card need memory anyway, and how much is necessary for which applications? The data for the display are processed and cached in the video memory. In addition to the minimum memory that a card needs, as was just discussed, the amount of memory also limits the maximum number of colors that can be displayed on the monitor. Too little memory also has a negative impact on the speed and the refresh rate. The table below shows how much memory you need to display a given number of colors at a given resolution. Since RAM prices for video memory have gone down considerably, don't buy a card with less than four Megs of RAM, unless you know for sure that you will never work with true color above 800x600 pixels. Also, think about the fact that some cards cache image data in the expanded memory, so that scrolling occurs noticeably faster in a word processor, for example. By the way, with 3-D cards you should roughly double if not triple the amount of memory needed, because the additional data for the 3-D information require incredible amounts of memory.

Video Memory Requirements Relative to Resolution and Color Depth					
Color Depth 16 colors	640x480	800x600	1024x768	1280x1024	1600x1200
4-bit 256 colors	150K	240K	390K	650K	960K
8-bit 65536 colors	300K	480K	780K	1.3 Megs	1.9 Megs
16-bit	600K	960K	1.5 Megs	2.6 Megs	3.8 Megs
16.7 million colors, 24-bit	900K	1.4 Megs	2.3 Megs	3.9 Megs	5.7 Megs
4.29 billion colors, 32 Bit	1.2 Megs	1.9 Megs	3.1 Megs	5.2 Megs	7.6 Megs

◆ By the way, the interleaving technology which was previously described for normal PC memory is also used for speed in video cards. And just like in the PC, both memory banks have to be filled symmetrically. This is another reason not to buy a video card with the minimum configuration (for example, two Megs).

◆ You obviously don't want to sell your house and home just to get a new video card, nor do you need to. But whatever you do, make sure the card can be upgraded with more memory modules. That's the only way you can enjoy more colors and a higher refresh rate. Also note whether and how you can add memory to your card. Recently a new standard has emerged here: SO-DIMMs, or Small Outline Dual Inline Memory Modules. Whereas before each manufacturer did his own thing, now more and more companies are offering memory modules usually with two or four Megs of SGRAM, which have been used in notebook computers for some time. Simply insert them in an adapter on the board. Of course, this only works for cards that use SGRAM.

◆ The RAMDAC is one of the most important components on a video card. It is especially well-suited to providing a rough estimate of a card's quality, because there are drastic differences in quality in this area. As we just mentioned, the RAMDAC reads the data from the video memory and converts it into the analog video signal. That's why it's one of the decisive components of the refresh rate and the picture quality. The most important technical specification is the maximum pixel frequency of the RAMDAC, which currently vacillates between 135 and 250 MHz. This provides direct information about the maximum refresh rate that a video card can pass to the monitor. Since faster RAMDACs are usually of higher quality, as a rule they have better picture quality, although that doesn't have to be the case. Currently, a card shouldn't be made with anything less than a 175-MHz RAMDAC; the really good cards start at 220 MHz. It's only with a 220-MHz RAMDAC that you can run true color at 1024x768 pixels with decent quality. By the way, a lot of video processor manufacturers have started integrating the RAMDAC directly with the processor chip. However, this usually actually degrades the picture quality, but here again the alternatives (external RAMDACs) aren't always any better. In the end, you need to test the desired card with your monitor.

◆ It's a little futile trying to pick out the best video processor. Scores of different processor types are on the market now. And right now, all of the typical 2-D processors are losing their ranking in the marketplace because they are being superseded by new ones with additional

Chapter 10

3-D functions (see the 3-D subsection further below).If you are only interested in 2-D, we heartily recommend the S3 Virge and the Matrox cards with the MGA64 chip.

◆ Look for DirectDraw or DCI support. DirectDraw support has come to be a standard for almost all video processors, but the quality of the conversion by the drivers varies greatly. DirectDraw (for Windows 95) or DCI (for Windows 3.x) enables the video card to use bus mastering of the PCI bus for data exchange with other PCI cards. This is done with video, MPEG and TV cards. We've even seen the first 3-D add-on cards that write their data to the video card's memory using only DirectDraw. Manufacturers well known for their abilities in this arena are Matrox, ELSA and Diamond. If this functionality is important to you, pay careful attention to this.

◆ It is also important for the card to support additional features which have become quasi-standards, such as full BIOS support for games via the Vesa 2.0 standard and the support of all new monitor functions. For example, the video card should be able to exchange data with new monitors via the DDC signals (DDC 1, DDC 2AB). It should be mandatory that it supports the new energy-saving functions according to the VESA-DPMS. With DPMS, the card can put the monitor into two levels of energy-saving mode in which it only consumes about five Watts. Although as we said, these features should be present in all current cards, there is the chance that you will come across a model where that's not the case.

NOTE

Work with two monitors with Windows?

If you want to work with two video cards and two monitors, like you can with a Macintosh, you don't have to wait until Windows 98 arrives. Windows 98 will support this function with almost every video card (you'll need two). But this is possible even now using special cards and drivers. ELSA offers this kind of solution with its Winner 2000 Pro/x, with which you can drive up to four cards in your PC in parallel.

A buyer's guide for 2-D applications

Providing specific buying recommendations for certain models is difficult because so much is changing so quickly. Instead, we'll give you the opportunity to determine for yourself whether a selected product is really suitable for you. Drivers that allow the card to be adjusted exactly to the attached monitor are absolutely necessary. In particular, you have to be able to adjust the refresh rate to the exact Hertz value.

Since the performance of all 2-D cards has become very comparable put more emphasis on the quality of the drivers and the manufacturer's support. In our opinion, look for ELSA, Matrox, Diamond and Hercules video cards.

The Matrox Millennium (now the Millennium II) is still one of the best 2-D cards on the market. It stands out due to its 220-MHz RAMDAC (soon to be 250), excellent drivers and high performance even with true color. But if integrated 3-D functions are important to you, buy a different card, because the Millennium can only handle just a few 3-D functions. Aside from that, it's still attractive for normal DOS games (without 3-D features) because its VGA kernel is laid out completely in 32-bit mode. After cards with the ET6000 chip, it's the fastest DOS card around. The Millennium also has another attractive feature: Matrox offers an upgrade module for the card for about $400. Called "Rainbow Runner," not only is it an MPEG decoder, but it also has video input and output, so you can use it to capture very high quality videos via the PCI bus and to conduct video conferences with high quality. Since there isn't any comparable stand-alone card right now with all these functions with the PCI bus, this card is very attractive for all video.

The Hercules Dynamite 128 with four Megs RAM only costs about $125 and is the ideal card for office machines. Only at higher resolution, refresh rates and color depths does the card rapidly lose ground.

If you're looking for a card with outstanding performance, very good driver support, and excellent picture quality, get one of the Winner series from ELSA. The current Winner 2000 AVI 3-D series with the S3 Virge chip has notably better picture quality than the Matrox Millennium. Although it's 10-20% slower, the better picture quality is worth a lot.

Another hot tip is the new card from Number Nine, the Revolution 3D. Number Nine uses the newly developed, proprietary chip Ticket-to-Ride, which works with 128-bits. In the 2-D range, this card is supposed to even beat or at least match the Matrox Millennium II. A 220-MHz RAMDAC and extensive driver support, along with high-grade 3-D features, make the Revolution attractive for all high-end users. If 3-D is important to you, you'd better get the Revolution rather than the Millennium, even if the drivers might not be quite as well developed yet.

PRACTICAL TIPS FOR THE BEST 2-D DISPLAY

Here are some general tips on this topic:

◆ The newest drivers are normally found on a video card makers web site. The big online services (especially AOL and CompuServe) are another source.

◆ You can get drivers for older card manufacturers on the Internet as well or from Microsoft. But with all generic drivers, you'll have the problem that you won't be able to adjust special parameters like the refresh rate any more. You'll find the Web addresses for processor manufacturers in the following table:

Manufacturer/Processor	WWW Address for Drivers
Tseng / ET3000-6000	www.tseng.com
S3 / 9xx-Chips, Trio, Virge	www.s3.com/bbs/0main/topindex.htm
Cirrus Logic / Cirrus Logic	www.cirrus.com/support

◆ If all else fails, you can usually resort to the VGA or SVGA drivers in Windows 95. This is also the setting you need to choose when you are installing a new driver or a new card. Enable one of the two drivers beforehand, shut down Windows 95, and install the new card. When you boot back up, the card will start immediately in its basic mode so you can then install the original drivers without any problem.

◆ Few cards designed for Windows allows you to change the refresh rate in DOS. Yet that is very desirable when playing DOS games, for example. At its basic setting, the monitor flickers with graphics at 60 Hz. However, sometimes manufacturers of the processors offer special tools for this purpose, such as S3 for all their cards. But some end manufacturers like ELSA provide these tools as well. You will find the ELSA program under the name "Vgarfsh" in the company mailbox. A Readme file explains how to link it to the AUTOEXEC.BAT file. Or download the program REFRES.EXEor S3REFRSH.EXE (the name varies) from S3's Internet site. The addresses are ftp://www.s3.com/pub/bbs/util (FTP server) or http://www.s3.com/bbs/util/index.htm (WWW server).

Correctly configuring the card and desktop

Even if the drivers are correctly loaded, it's not the end of the possible problems in Windows. Incorrect settings or desktop configuration can drop the speed of any card like a rock. Here are the appropriate tuning tips so that won't happen to you:

◆ **Run faster with a lower refresh rate**: The higher the refresh rate setting, the greater the load on the video processor and the video memory. The latter is often the limiting factor in these situations. If you don't absolutely need the highest rates of 100 Hz or more, try reducing the rate to around 80 Hz. In most cases the card will run faster as well. But this is true only if you are running the card at its upper limit, meaning with high color depth. Of course also consider whether one or two percent more performance is worth the increased eyestrain.

◆ **High color is often the fastest setting**: Most users run their video card at 256 colors, thinking that this gives them the fastest speed. And yet the video card's driver loses a lot of time at this setting due to dithering. Dithering is required whenever objects with more than 256 colors have to be displayed (for example, photos or videos). Whereas true color mode with 24 bits really does load the video processor too much, 16-bit color depth (high color) is the best setting that you should normally work with. The driver doesn't need to dither photos and videos at this setting, so in addition to the considerably improved display, performance is enhanced as well. Also, with 24-bit color depth, Windows often has problems displaying the desktop icons.

◆ **The optimum color depth for DOS**: On the other hand, if you often work with DOS machines, the 256 color setting is actually much faster and better, because Windows doesn't have to convert from the 16-bit to the 8-bit display in the DOS system.

◆ Though rarely necessary, if **true color**, then **32-bit**! True color mode is only necessary if you want to process images pixel by pixel while changing or correcting particular color values. There's not much of an increase in the quality of the display compared to high color, but the speed decreases significantly. You can make up for that somewhat by working in 32-bit mode when possible, if your driver supports it. In the meantime, almost all video processors work with 64-bit, so they can process 32-bit data better than 24-bit data. This doesn't have any effect on the color depth of your image during processing; that remains coded in 24-bit.

◆ **Disable typical performance reducers**: Each time you open or close a window, it's either placed in the Taskbar or pulled out of it with optical fanfare. If that bothers you, just turn it off. In the Registry under \\Hkey_Current_User\Control Panel\Desktop\Window Metrics, you can add a new string with the name "MinAnimate," to which you assign a value of 0. In addition to these animations, all of the other memory-hogging "sins" of a beautiful desktop are a real load on the video card. We mean all those beloved background images, animated cursors, high-color icons and smoothed fonts, some of which are found in the Plus! pack. If performance is more important than beauty, disable all of this stuff.

◆ Only a few video cards support being able to **change the resolution and/or color depth without having to restart the system**. But actually restarting the system is usually necessary if you have changed fonts at the same time. You might know that at 1024x768 pixels and above in Windows, it's best to work with the large display fonts. If you often change both of these parameters and it bugs you to be forced to restart, download the free **PowerToys** from Microsoft (www.microsoft.com/windows/software/powertoy.htm), which can also be found on a lot of magazine and shareware CDs. The PowerToys are a collection of small but useful utilities. One of them is the tool Quickres.exe, which stays in the Tray on the Taskbar after it has been executed.

If you click on it, it shows all of the combinations of resolution and color depth that are supported. Select the desired setting, and it is invoked immediately without a restart. By the way, if you have Windows 95b (OSR2), don't use that program any longer, because this functionality has already been integrated into the system. Quickres.exe doesn't quite work right in 95b. Instead, click on the box "Display icon in Taskbar" in the Settings tab of the Display icon in the Control Panel.

More deskspace with low resolution, better readability with higher resolution

It's funny that hardly any users notice the settings options on the Appearance tab in the Properties of the Display Control Panel. You can change the display of almost all Windows elements (icons, windows, etc.) and save the settings under different configuration names. This is especially practical and sometimes even necessary if you're working with different resolutions.

Whereas most of the pre-configured settings are pretty much just for show (mostly playing with colors), there are three usable settings for the basic configuration of Windows 95: Windows Standard, Windows Standard (large) and Windows Standard (extra large). The different pre-defined settings for the title bars and icons are of interest here.

<!image!> page 761

You can return to the Windows 95 default settings with the Appearance tab of the Display Properties. We recommend a higher resolution if you switch to Windows Standard (large).

Go ahead and test the settings "large" and "extra large" on large monitors with high resolution (1280x1024 and higher) so that the individual elements of the display, which are often too small, can be manipulated better. However, with small monitors or low resolution, create your own scheme; one which creates the maximum space for documents so that as much room as possible is taken from the window display. You'll have to do that by hand, and then save the scheme under its own name (for example, Maxspace). Of course you can do the same thing for individual settings with high resolution.

It's especially interesting to change the display items "Scrollbar," "Caption Buttons" (sets the size of the window title and the Taskbar) and the "Window Border." If you change resolution and display schemes, check or adjust the "Caption Buttons" in particular, because Windows often doesn't adjust them correctly. For example, a size of 22 is optimal for 1024x768 pixels; a value of 18 is good for 800x600 pixels. However, depending on the resolution, not all settings can be changed at will. If the "Apply" button is disabled, the settings you have entered aren't compatible. The preview in the upper part of the dialog window gives a preview of the changed settings, which is very helpful. Below is a list of the relevant display items and of some recommended settings for maximum room at low resolution or with small monitors. The sizes indicated depend greatly on the selected resolution, so "or less" is used in places; you'll have to find the correct size by trial and error.

Item	Size
Active Title Bar	18 or less
Active Window Border	0
Scrollbar	12 or less
Inactive Title Bar	18 or less
Inactive Border	0
Selected Item	18 or less
Menu	18 or less
Palette Title	18 or less
Icon	16 (instead of 32 as default)
Caption Buttons	18 or less

WATCHING VIDEOS AND TV ON YOUR PC

A PC and current video cards can do a lot more now than just scroll faster through Excel or show pretty, colorful pictures. A video accelerator (actually a misleading term) has been standard on all cards for a long time. Of course, that's not all there is to it, and all this doesn't make all that much difference, because who watches .AVI videos on their PC non-stop? Even with the greatest video accelerator, you can't work any magic with 320x240 pixels of information. And of course there are a number of interesting tips on this topic that we want to share with you.

The next step after AVI was MPEG. But even the MPEG wave died out some time ago, at least MPEG-1. Now the next wave is rushing toward us: MPEG-2, driven by DVD. There's little to buy or in the stores yet, but the 1997/98 Christmas season started things rolling in earnest. In this chapter, we have compiled everything that's important for you to know about displaying MPEG-1 and MPEG-2 on a PC.

Our favorite thing is neither AVI nor MPEG, but the ability to watch TV on the PC. In contrast to the usually boring and very passive viewing of AVIs and MPEG movies, watching TV on a PC is fun for other reasons: You can transfer video text, still pictures and in some cases even videos into your PC. So if you've always wanted to have your favorite celebrity as a background picture, you won't want to miss the recommendations and tips at the end of this chapter. Since you can buy TV cards for a little over $100 now, this is really an attractive option for everybody.

How to better play AVIs

Actually, watching AVI videos on your PC isn't really a hot topic anymore. It was just a few years ago that we were so enthralled with these first postage stamp-sized videos. Here are some facts and tips about AVIs that you might not have known:

◆ Most multimedia AVIs are produced using the standard compression technique from Intel, Indeo R3.2. That means at most 320x240 pixels, but always at 24-bit color depth (true color). However, to play the files as fast a possible, change your card to high color since this doesn't burden the video chip too much.

◆ Most video cards have a built-in video accelerator, but this term is misleading. The videos aren't accelerated; instead, when the small video window is enlarged, pixels are added by means of interpolation to improve the picture. Don't expect any miracles here, though, because if you enlarge 320x240 pixels to 1024x768 pixels, even the best "video acceleration" in the world isn't going to look very good.

◆ In Windows 95 you can set a fixed display size for all videos. The "1/4 of screen size" option is the best here. However, this doesn't work for videos in multimedia applications that come up in their own window (for example, with multimedia CD-ROM encyclopedias).

◆ If you have installed all the updates for Windows 95 and Internet Explorer, you have two options in your system for playing AVIs. The first method is the good old Media Player. The other is the new Active Movie Player Module, which can play not only AVIs, but also WAV files and QuickTime and MPEG movies (more about that below). You can also download ActiveMovie as a separate module from Microsoft's Web page. It's a good alternative to Media Player. After installation, it automatically associates itself with the appropriate data types, so it is automatically executed with every video. You can also start the program any time in the Accessories/Multimedia program group.

◆ Speaking of QuickTime movies: AVI is to Windows what QuickTime is to Macintosh, the difference being that you can also play QuickTime videos on a PC. Both processes have comparable quality, but videos created with the newest QuickTime format are clearly better than Indeo R3.2 AVIs. If you want to take advantage of the full quality and all the options of QuickTime, install the free QuickTime Player, which you can get from all the usual places (Internet, online services, shareware Cds, etc.) and of course on all CDs that contain QuickTime movies. But here too, the new ActiveMovie Player will work if all you want to do is replay QuickTime movies. Since CDs with QuickTime movies can be used on both Macintosh and Windows computer systems, more and more of them are being made. For example, most of the new enhanced CDs (audio CDs with videos) are made with this format.

Optimizing MPEG display for movies on your PC

MPEG is a compression standard for audio and video information. It provides clearly higher picture quality at high compression ratios than previous processes (for example, Intel Indeo R3.2).

Up until now, the simpler, lower quality MPEG-1 process was used to save data files on normal CDs and to replay them on a PC. The higher quality MPEG-2 will take off now with DVD and its significantly larger storage capacity. Whereas MPEG-1 was a little worse than VHS quality and showed noticeable compression artifacts, the quality of MPEG-2 is almost as good as that of a laser disc. By the way, both MPEG processes included audio compression standards as well, but they're rarely used just to compress audio files. Since there still aren't many MPEG-2 decoders that you can buy, and there's no sense to have them until the first DVD players and DVD movies show up (the prices for the drive and MPEG-2 are around $600), we'll just stick with a few tips that are still relevant for MPEG-1.

◆ MPEG decoder: Hardware or software solution, what is better? Since MPEG is a coded compression process, you have to decode it before replaying it. This can be done either by the PC's CPU or by a specialized MPEG card which contains a small special processor for this. These are the positives and negatives of each solution:

◆ The software solution means that you need a program that can decode MPEG (an MPEG player). Up until now these were special programs like the Xing MPEG decoder. However, ever since Microsoft introduced ActiveMovie (with Internet Explorer 3.x), you usually don't need the old MPEG player, for which you had to pay money. And ActiveMovie's MPEG capabilities are great. Still, keep in mind that you need at least a Pentium 100 to decode MPEG software. With faster processors than that, you don't need a special card.

◆ **Hardware MPEG decoders** make sense for slow machines. At the same time, some of the models have a decisive advantage, which we feel is the most important point of all: They have a TV output. We believe that MPEG only makes sense if you have a TV output.

◆ **The right MPEG decoder card**: It's hard to find MPEG cards any more. It was always hard to find a really good MPEG solution for the PC, and now it's even harder. The fact is that a hardware solution with special decoder cards usually gives a better picture quality. The connection to the video card is critical though. There are three procedures that will give you the best results:

1. Use a card with PCI bus mastering, which transfers the data directly into the video card memory via DCI or DirectDraw. Naturally the video card and the MPEG decoder have to be synchronized with each other to do this. The only card we know of for this is the MPEG Motion card from ELSA. Although it's the best solution, this card doesn't have a TV output.

NOTE

Fixing DirectDraw problems in the BIOS
The DirectDraw transfer from MPEG to the video card is problematic on some boards. You can avoid this by making the PCI settings in the BIOS a little more conservative. In the Chipset Feature BIOS, disable the entry "Chipset Global Features".

2. Cards that loop through the video card signal (**VGA loop through**) are another option. The video card output is connected to the MPEG decoder, which in turn drives the monitor. The few cards of this type usually have a TV connection.

3. The final alternative is plug-in modules for video cards. Some manufacturers offer special economical plug-in modules for their video cards, like the Scenic/MX2 module for S3 Trio64V+ cards. But these plug-in modules usually restrict the video card in other areas, so you couldn't really do much with them.

◆ Forget the Feature Connector idea. As an alternative to the three high-grade solutions, some processes work with something called the Feature Connector. This is a special plug-in on the video card to which you can connect an MPEG decoder. However, there is the limitation that the video card has to be run at 640x480 and 256 colors at 60 Hz in order to get a picture out of the MPEG card.

◆ Matrox offers an interesting solution: a plug-in module for the popular video cards from Matrox. Formerly called "Media XL," now it's called "Rainbow Runner," and it has an MPEG hardware decoder with a TV connector built in to it. By the way, the module for the Mystique card isn't identical to the one for the Millennium II. The initial problems with drivers and limited color displays in Windows 95 are supposed to be fixed now. If you have a Matrox card, the Rainbow Runner module is very attractive because of its video capture feature, in spite of the high price of $300-400.

◆ Solving problems with ATAPI CD-ROMs and MPEG: If you have an ATAPI CD-ROM and you aren't using the latest updates or service packs for Windows 95, you'll be disappointed if you want to play CDi-MPEG videos. The original CD-ROM driver for Windows 95 has a bug. With the combination mentioned above, the CD-ROM shifts down to single-speed operation, which is too slow for MPEG's large data volume. Of course, Microsoft has known about the problem for a long time, and there is a corresponding bug fix on the Internet homepage or in the newest Windows 95 versions (OSR2). So if you still have an old version and you have the problem, you should download the newest ATAPI CD-ROM drivers.

TV goes PC

Watching TV on your PC is really cool. You can capture the pictures that are shown either individually or in the form of small videos. And if your card has a video text decoder built-in, you can also access the video text and even capture it for use in your applications for further processing.

The cards are also interesting for those who have a camcorder or a small video camera for video conferencing. Most TV cards have VHS and/or SVHS inputs for connecting an external video source. If there is also an MCI driver for the Windows video interface, you can use the card for video conferences, for example, via the Internet with Netmeeting.

There are basically three kinds of TV cards:

◆ Older models for the ISA bus connect to the video card via the Feature Connector or a VGA loop-through cable. But both methods impair the video card's performance. With a Feature Connector the graphics card can't use more than 800x600 pixels with high color and 72 Hz. That's out of the question nowadays. Perhaps the most popular ISA TV card is the MovieMachine II from Fast. This card is also interesting because there is an MPEG upgrade module for it, which you can use for video grabbing with very high quality. You can find the card with the module for about $300. Since the connection is done through a loop-through cable, the impairment of the image quality isn't as drastic as it is with the Feature Connector, but it is still unpleasant. If you have a newer computer with a PCI video card, we recommend that you use the second solution, given below.

Forget about using a Feature Connector on your video card; you'll be disappointed with the results.

TV cards that use bus mastering to write the images to the memory of the PCI video card via the PCI bus are considerably better. Many manufacturers make these cards (Siemens, Philips, Miro, Hauppauge) and they usually cost between $125 and $250. At most they restrict the video card only when the card is activated, and then only to a slight, acceptable degree. They are currently the best solution, but you have to have a video card that supports DCI or DirectDraw.

◆ Special upgrade modules for individual video cards (like ATI's) are an exception. Their distribution is quite limited, exactly because they only work with a certain type of video card. And yet they do have the advantage of being better synchronized with the card. If this kind of module exists for your card, buy it. Otherwise, use a PCI bus mastering TV card instead.

TV Cards In Detail

If you have a newer PCI video card with a driver that supports DirectDraw, and you're interested in a TV card, look at the offerings from the Hauppauge company. In contrast to many other manufacturers (Siemens, Miro, Philips and many others), this California company specializes in this market. The product base is rich, and the driver support is also good.

Like almost all PCI TV cards on the market, Hauppauge also uses the popular Booktree chip as a video decoder.

Hauppauge has three versions of its WinTV card among the PCI bus-mastering cards: one strictly TV version for about $125, one with video text function ($150) and another one with video text and radio (about $200). The newest version of the WinTV-Radio is completely stereo-capable and has both VHS and SVHS video inputs. Since an MCI driver is also provided, you can run video conferences on the Internet without any problem using programs like Netmeeting or VDOPhone.

Whether using Netmeeting or VDOPhone, with the WinTV card you can even use a TV picture for video conferences.

The installation of the WinTV card is done as with any normal PCI card. Afterwards, you just plug in an antenna cable, install the drivers and the bundled programs, and you're done. Naturally the card is cable TV-ready. The sound is also carried via the PCI bus and can be broadcast from the sound card. The other connectors on the card are for inputting video and sound from external video sources.

The TV tuner can be readily seen above on the WinTV board (here the version without radio). Usually the TV picture is shown in a freely scaleable window. Depending on the video card, you can show a full screen picture up to 1024x768 pixels without tool bars and borders.

The card has its own entry in the Device Manager.

One of the best things about a TV card is the capture function for individual pictures and videos. The videos only have moderate quality, however. Individual pictures are stored in NTSC resolution with good quality.

Hauppauge Computer Works, Inc. web site demonstration.

VESA Standard And 3-D functions

Nothing in the computer market is experiencing the boom and rapid development of the 3-D video card market. Things aren't even happening as fast with the main processors for computers.

There are only a very few reliable tips to give about which card to buy and how to get the best 3-D display with which game. There are just too many versions and options. It's more important to get an overview of the general trends and technologies involved. If you want to dive in now, you'll have to be prepared to experiment and to accept a bad buy and an unstable system. So for all those who prefer a stable system and the least possible hassle with their video card, the first tip is definitely this: stay away from the first, and possibly even the second generation of these cards. If you don't play any 3-D computer games or use any "serious" 3-D applications (for example, CAD or rendering software), you don't need to worry about the entire development. In this case, you would be better to buy a good, fully developed 2-D card like the Matrox Millennium II or an S3 Virge video card. Then you'll be spared any ugly surprises for now.

The following tips are meant for all those who absolutely want to get the maximum playing fun out of their computer right now. Before we go to the newer 3-D functions, first a couple of tips for general games support by video cards.

Only full **VESA** support improves game graphics

If you try to play one of the newer computer games in DOS with an old video card, you will be disappointed with the lousy video quality. It's funny that it looked considerably better at an acquaintance's with a new 2-D card even without 3-D support.

The background for this is the expanded graphics modes that all newer computer games use so they can work with higher resolution and color depth. In DOS, the normal BIOS of a video card only supports 13 different display modes, the best of which can handle 16 colors with graphics at 640x480. With older video cards, many games only work with 320x240 pixels. Of course that is totally unacceptable, because at 640x480 it should be at least 256 colors or better yet, 65,000 colors (high color). Some games even support graphics modes with 800x600 pixels and high color, if only the video card would play along.

To make this possible, the VESA Committee defined corresponding expanded video standards that have to be supported by the BIOS on the video cards. The current version is VESA 2.0, which is supported by all new graphics cards directly via the BIOS. That way the higher resolution and color depth mentioned above can be displayed.

However, a lot of old cards either have no VESA support or they have a lower version (Version 1.0, 1.2 or 1.5) built in. Even the popular ELSA Winner 2000 card only has Vesa 1.2 built in. Cards with VESA 1.0 BIOS have been around since about 1990, but these are totally out-dated for all current games.

Unfortunately most cards don't have the ability to change the BIOS or get a version with higher VESA support. And yet for some cards there is a solution, because you can get special drivers for them, which make it possible to convert the VESA mode even without BIOS support. There used to be something like that with the old UniVESA driver, which made it possible for cards without any BIOS support to use the first VESA standards.

There are different drivers for S3 video cards that you can use to bump up cards with old VESA versions to the current VESA 2.0 support. The video processor company S3 offers a driver like this on its Internet site (www.s3.com/bbs/shrware/index.htm): a shareware program from Dietmar Meschede. The program specifically lets you upgrade S3 cards with VESA 1.2 support to version 2.0. It's also worth checking with the video card manufacturers themselves, who sometimes offer these drivers for specific cards, such as ELSA, for its Winner series (ftp.elsa.de/Anonymous/graphics/ELSAWARE/S3VBE313.ZIP or S3VBE20.ZIP). However, a lot of the drivers only work with S3's 64-bit processors, so old cards with the 32-bit S3 928 processor can't be upgraded that way.

The best-known driver may be the Sci Tech Display Doctor, sometimes also called the UniVBE/Display Doctor. The Display Doctor makes it possible for considerably more cards, especially those with S3 processors, to support VESA 2.0 games, so it is recommended by many video card manufacturers (like Hercules). You'll find the program in the Internet at SciTech's home page (www.scitechsoft.com).

What we can expect from the second generation of 3-D video cards

Right now a whole new, second generation of 3-D cards are entering the market; these cards work with totally new processors. It's hard to tell what effect this will have on the video card market. One thing that's obvious is that a lot of companies that worked exclusively with S3 in the past are suddenly using the new processors from other manufacturers. ELSA and Diamond are typical examples. In the fall of 1997, ELSA will introduce two new graphics cards (Erazor and Winner Office series), neither of which works with S3 chips any more.

The number of cards to choose from is increasing dramatically right now, and it's hard for the user to figure at a glance which one to buy. When you go shopping, look less at the manufacturers' creative names and advertising slogans than you do at the solid facts. It's especially important that you don't overlook the good old and much more important 2-D functions in the midst of all the hollering about 3-D.

The best way to find your way among the new cards is to group them based on the processor they use. If you do that, you'll suddenly see light in the video card jungle and you'll only have to decide among a few models. So first of all, look for the processor that seems to be best for your applications. Then you can consider from which company to buy the card with the desired processor. The usual criteria are important in this last decision: What's the driver quality like? Which RAMDAC is used?

Pay attention to the following points when you're trying to decide on the right processor:

◆ What is the ratio of the 2-D vs. 3-D performance?

◆ Are all important 3-D functions (about a dozen) supported?

◆ What's the graphics quality at which the 3-D functions are supported? This is especially true for the important filtering and fog effects that are responsible for making a 3-D image look so real.

◆ Which three APIs (standardized software interfaces) are supported? Direct 3D and OpenGL are the most important (see more below under separate items).

◆ Up to which resolution and color depth is the 3-D display possible? And is this only possible in DOS or also in Windows 95 in a window and/or full-screen mode?

◆ Do the processors have any unique functions? For example, the new Permedia 2 from 3DLabs supports video in and out.

◆ Which kind of memory is supported? Only dual-ported RAM (VRAM and WRAM) and SGRAM enable good 2-D quality at high resolution and color depth. This is important for all those who use their computer primarily for work.

The following table introduces the most important and interesting processors with 3-D functions that you should be aware of:

Processor/Manufacturer	Description
3D-Rage / ATI	2-D/3-D combo chip, only with ATI cards, up to 8 Megs SGRAM, good 3-D and 2-D performance
Permedia 2 / 3DLabs	New 2-D/3-D combo chip with good performance and up to 8 Megs SGRAM. Video input and output are supported
Voodoo / 3dFx	Pure 3-D chip, currently the best supported, very good performance and display quality. Used for 3-D stand-alone and combination cards
Ticket to Ride / Number 9	2-D/3-D combo chip with 128-bit and WRAM support up to 16 Megs. Very good 3-D and 2-D performance. Only for Number Nine Revolution card, which is designed for high-end applications in Windows NT
MAG 2164 or 1064 / Matrox	2-D/3-D combo chip, 64-bit, best 2-D, but poor 3-D performance, doesn't support a lot of 3-D features
Virge-GX / S3	2-D/3-D combo chip, 64-bit, poor 3-D but good 2-D performance, behind all other processors
PowerVR PCX2 / NEC	Pure 3-D chip with very high performance, used up to now only for 3-D stand-alone cards with 4 Megs SDRAM, Direct Draw for data transfer to the graphics board, performance depends on the computer's speed
Verite 2200 / Rendition	2-D/3-D combo chip, SGRAM up to 8 Megs, up to 120-MHz memory speed, video input and output
Riva 128 / nVidia	2-D/3-D combo chip with 128-bit data bus, SGRAM, but with a maximum 4 Megs and 205-MHz RAMDAC, 100-MHz memory speed, video input and output. Very high 3-D performance at a reasonable price. Not good 2-D performance with high resolution and colors. Soon probably faster than the Voodoo chip for game cards with optimized drivers

We can recommend these 3-D graphics cards

The decision as to whether you even need one of the new 3-D cards depends very much on what you want to use it for. If you mostly use your computer for work, meaning you want to have good 2-D performance, maybe you should buy a good, more stable 2-D stand-alone card (like the Matrox Millennium II). A 3-D add-on card with a Voodoo chip would be a good solution for game playing in that case. The 3-D display is very fast in certain circumstances, but there is no total 3-D effect that is displayed on the monitor like with a Voodoo card. Especially the absence of support for the so important bilinear filtering makes the surface textures look rough-edged and blocky.

Right now, an external Voodoo card is the best solution for game buffs. The new processors might be very powerful in theory (like the Riva 128), but if the drivers aren't refined yet and especially if the game manufacturers don't provide any corresponding software support. And the Voodoo chip from 3Dfx is the best supported 3-D chip right now. At the same time, it provides very good picture quality. So with these advantages, an appropriate card like the Monster 3D from Diamond will be the best.

3-D add-on card with the Voodoo chip—The Monster 3D from Diamond.

The only disadvantage to the Monster 3D is that the image of the 2-D video card is guided through the 3-D card using a loop-through cable, which distorts the picture quality somewhat in terms of sharpness.

> **Tuning the Voodoo chip**
>
> **NOTE** You can fine tune the Voodoo chip. Different programs are available that let you change the settings and especially the processor's clock frequency. And they keep making new tools. You just need to check out all the techie pages for the Voodoo chip in the Internet, and of course make regular visits to 3Dfx's own pages (see next figure). The best known tuning tool is Tweek for Voodoo, which you can use to overclock the processor from 50 up to 63 (with appropriate cooling!). In addition, you can change the refresh rates and turn the Direct 3D support in Windows 95 off and on without rebooting. There's also a gamma correction for the display. The program is freeware and can be found at www.wolf.demon.co.uk/.

The Stingray 128/3D is also interesting. The Hercules company has succeeded for the first time in integrating the Voodoo chip from 3Dfx, which is normally used on separate 3-D accelerators, directly onto the graphics board. At $250-300, the card is a very moderately priced all-around card with good 2-D and excellent 3-D properties. Another nice thing about the card is the luxurious amount of memory: six Megs of RAM, of which four are used for the normal 2-D displays and two for the additional 3-D data.

NOTE

Adding on 3-D functionality for games

So far, out of the huge number of computer games, there have only been a tiny number of programs that really support 3-D functions. Most of them work with 640x480 pixels and 256 colors. But fortunately, a lot of manufacturers offer game patches which up-grade existing games with 3-D support for certain cards or chips. Patches for the Voodoo chip are at the top of the pack. You should check the Internet addresses for the manufacturers of your games on a regular basis to see if a patch like this is available for your games.

The speed and ergonomics of the normal display in Windows are in the upper midfield, so they're not comparable with a Matrox Millennium or a good S3 Virge card, but they are clearly good enough for most users. For example, you can reach 100 Hz with 1024x768 and high color. And in 3-D, the card attains the usual performance for the Voodoo chip. The big advantage of this card compared to a 3-D add-on card with a Voodoo chip is that the 3-D display even works inside a window in Windows 95. So if game-playing enjoyment is more important to you than 2-D quality, this is the card for you.

If you are looking for a 3-D add-on card without a loop-through cable because that way the data are pushed through to the video memory by bus mastering (Direct Draw), look at the Apocalypse 3Dx from Videologic. This card works with the Power VR PCX2 chip from NEC, and theoretically it offers at least the same performance as a card with the Voodoo chip. The performance does depend greatly on the processor speed, however. It should be at least a Pentium 166. Also, support by games is still very sparse, with the result that almost all games will generate some kind of a faulty display on the screen. But when the drivers and game support are improved in the future, the Apocalypse 3Dx will actually be more attractive because of its better basic concept. It's funny that this card can already be used in parallel with a pre-existing Voodoo 3D card, so that way (if the drivers are compatible) the maximum 3-D power is possible. Otherwise, the market in the lower price segment will be ruled by the Riva 128 for now. For example, ELSA will offer this kind of card with four Megs of SGRAM in its Victory Erazor for about $250. It has video input and output, but you can't connect a TV in parallel with your monitor. There might even be a video text decoder for this card. However, due to the memory limits and the 205-MHz RAMDAC, the card won't have a chance with discriminating 2-D users.

Then there is the market segment of the cards with the Permedia 2 chip. Once again, ELSA has an interesting model, the Winner Office. Thanks to a 230-MHz RAMDAC and up to eight Megs of SGRAM, the card can be used with high color depths and refresh rates. Like the Erazor, this card has video input and output, so you can play games on a large monitor or run video conferences with this card.

The battle of the 3-D standards

The best 3-D card won't do you any good if the software (either a game or the rendering software) can't address it. With DOS, as usual, this was always a matter of every program for itself, but graphical interfaces like Windows provide general APIs for the addressing. With Windows, this is Direct 3D, a subset of the Direct X hardware acceleration API.

In addition to Direct 3D or Direct X, there are also other 3-D APIs, but they are less significant because they are so specialized. These include nice-sounding names like Heidi, or the more popular OpenGL. OpenGL was developed by Silicon Graphics for workstations, and it is supported by Microsoft with appropriate drivers for both Windows 95 and Windows NT. There are various animated 3-D screen savers that sit on this OpenGL interface. But OpenGL isn't designed for games and screen savers; instead, it's designed for professional rendering and CAD programs. That's why there's no support for any other multimedia acceleration.

Games that are written for Windows 95 or even Windows NT could theoretically base their 3-D acceleration on the OpenGL interface or Microsoft's own Direct 3D. It's interesting that we've been hearing recently about huge fights between Microsoft and some game programmers because the programmers have determined that it's a lot easier to program using OpenGL in games and that it usually yields better results. Of course, as usual, Microsoft is trying very hard to not support standards of other companies (Silicon Graphics in this case), but naturally they want to push their own standards instead.

After a few disagreements, a kind of settlement seems to have been reached. Microsoft has updated version 3 to 5 and built in considerable improvements in the process (see the next point). In addition, the support for game programmers is supposed to be improved. So we'll have to wait and see if Direct 3D games push through as the desired standard in the future.

And anyway, if you work with "serious" 3-D programs in Windows NT, in the near future either OpenGL or Heidi will be the decisive interface, which of course should also be supported by the video card and its drivers. Direct X for Windows NT 4 has been around since Service Pack 3, but it doesn't include any Direct 3D support. That's supposed to be introduced with Windows NT 5, so until then, games will continue to have to run in Windows 95.

DIRECT X 5 OFFERS MORE SPEED AND GAME PLAYING FUN

Microsoft introduced a new version of Direct X early in August, 1997, called Direct X 5. It provides new features, plus it has improved APIs for game programmers. The DrawPrimitive function in particular is supposed to provide better access to the graphics functions. This is supposed to allow Direct 3D to be the interface for 3-D games in the future, rather than OpenGL.

One highlight of Direct X 5 is the new feature called "Force Feedback," which is a component of Direct Input. It allows a game to provide feedback to the joystick in the form of vibrations. Of course you need a new joystick for this, one that can produce the appropriate vibrations. The new

Microsoft Sidewinder will be the first joystick of this type. It's also interesting that many functions are said to support or use MMX as well. But don't expect too much out of that.

Hands-on 3-D

And finally, a few tips to guarantee that your playing fun is undisturbed:

◆ **A coprocessor is important for 3-D display**: 3-D cards just don't make sense on a 486 PC without a math coprocessor (Floating Point Unit, FPU). The chips integrated on 3-D cards are dependent on a high floating point calculation rate for the 3-D coordinates (geometrical transformation), and these calculations are still performed by the CPU or the FPU. And satisfactory floating point calculation rates can only be attained with a Pentium or better. With or without an FPU, a 486 PC slows down the 3-D chip far too much because the chip isn't fed the needed data fast enough. However, games run faster on a 486 with a 3-D card than without one, because the 486 is relieved of all the 3-D calculations.

◆ Intel has the fastest game processors, with the Pentium II and Pentium Pro at the forefront. Due to the high speed of the L2 cache and a powerful FPU particularly in DOS, these chips are clearly superior to the Pentium and especially the AMD K6 and the Cyrix 6x86MX.

◆ **3-D display uses a lot of memory**. Two Megs is far too little for 3-D applications. 3-D graphics take up a lot more room in memory, since in addition to the coordinates (x and y), you also have to assign the depth (z) to a buffer. Also, the polygons and textures have to be stored in the card. The total of all these data which have to be stored in RAM exceeds the two Megs found on standard cards. And even four Megs are only enough for 800x600 pixels. So if you want to work with 3-D displays and 1024x768 pixels in Windows 95 and especially in Windows NT, you'll need to have eight Megs of video memory. Only a few video cards can handle that right now (Millennium, Number Nine Revolution, Winner Office, etc.).

◆ If you really want maximum 3-D performance, buy one of the new motherboards with **AGP**. Not only does the next graphics bus allow higher speeds, but the PC's normal working memory can be used for the additional 3-D data. At the same time, that makes the AGP 3-D graphics boards a considerably better value. At the end of 1997 you'll also be able to buy AGP for motherboards with ZIF-7 sockets. The new chip sets from VIA and SiS will make this possible.

Naturally, if you want to test the 3-D performance of different cards, you need a special **3-D benchmark**. The popular benchmarks PC Player 3D benchmark for DOS and PC Player Direct 3D benchmark for Windows from the PC Player magazine are somewhat outdated but still decent. You can download them from the Internet at www.pcplayer.de. ZIF-Davis has a new 3-D Winbench test, which not only tests the performance but also the support of different 3-D functions. Therefore, it's currently probably the best 3-D test. As usual, you can download the program from the Internet, at www1.zdnet.com/zdbop/3dwinbench/3dwinbench.html.

Chapter 10

Chapter 11

Sound Card Tuning

This chapter is about sound cards. Two great innovations are expanding the market: the support for 3-D audio and the integration of digital inputs and outputs on sound cards. A new sound card is light years ahead of what you could buy two years ago. This chapter explains what you need to know when you buy a sound card, what is possible with it and many practical tips for your daily routine.

How do sound cards make music?

To decide what type of equipment is important for you in a sound card, consider how music and sounds are made by a sound card. Then you will quickly recognize which method is sufficient for you. Basically, new cards use three methods for outputting sound to the speakers:

1 By Digital/Analog or Analog/Digital converter. Every sound card is like a DAT recorder. It can pick up sounds by A/D converter and save them as a WAV file on the hard drive. Naturally, you use the reverse route (D/A conversion) to output the sounds. No new or artificial sounds are generated by this method; you are always working with existing sounds.

2 By FM-Syntheziser. The frequency modulation method, introduced many years ago, makes it possible to generate sounds artificially with the help of a synthesizer. Well known chips such as OPL2, OPL3, 4OPL+, etc., are used for this purpose. These chips, found on all sound cards, make it possible to play back sounds defined under the MIDI standard.

3 By Wavetable method. Under the MIDI standard, specific instruments or sounds are defined by numbers in order to be artificially generated for playback, e.g., by a synthesizer. Since this synthesized sound is really quite synthetic, developers invented the Wavetable method. With this method, the defined MIDI sounds are recorded (sampled) from actual instruments (or other sources) and stored in a memory chip (the Wavetable ROM). When a MIDI file calls to have a violin played, the sound is generated from the sample in the Wavetable ROM with much better quality than a synthesized sound. The synthesizer is no longer necessary or is no longer being used in this method.

DSP, Sampling RAM and other sound card features

In addition to these three methods of sound production, you should know about a fourth sound-influencing chip on expensive sound cards, called the DSP (Digital Sound Processor). Cards equipped with this chip can mix in effects such as hall or chorus to the sound methods mentioned above. DSPs also make enhanced 3-D sound effects possible, which are nothing more than an artificial widening of the stereo roots. The results are usually modest and cannot be compared with proper 3-D. A DSP is especially interesting for computer games, because its effects really make sense in them.

The Sound Blaster cards with the Emu8000 chip
offer comprehensive effect settings, which you can also disable.

Additional RAM chips on the card are interesting for musicians. Into these one may load samples for enhancing or replacing the existing Wavetable samples. The first card on the market with this option was the Sound Blaster AWE 32. Since currently there aren't any computer games that use the memory on such a card to load their own samples, this RAM on the card really only benefits musicians. And even for musicians, using the function is labor intensive and requires much knowledge before something practical can be done with it.

Some Sound Blaster cards also feature a Compression Chip. These chips used to be referred to as "ASPs," though "CSPs" is more common today. This chip can compress wave files (via hardware) directly during recording. However good this sounds, it is hardly usable in practice. The sound interference is so great that it is only practical for voice recordings. Moreover, the compressed files can only be reproduced by a card with the same chip. Since software compression methods don't cause any problems and are more flexible, the need for hardware compression is very minimal. Windows 95 has built in some compression algorithms, so that exchanging files edited with them is much less complicated. Anyone who wants to have audio compression without strong sound interference is better off using special programs that permit an MPEG compression. All we can do is hope that future cards will incorporate the ATRAC compression method from Sony's MiniDisc. This offers very high sound quality and would make wide-scale compatibility possible.

Selection criteria for picking the right card

When selecting a sound card, consider which form of sound production is most important to you. While an FM synthesizer is standard equipment on all cards and doesn't have any special differences anyway, points one and three from above should be carefully considered. Wavetable MIDI sound makes a sound card $50 more expensive, on average. The larger and better the sound samples are in the Wavetable ROM (0.5-4 Megs are normal), the more expensive the card becomes. You will find other important quality differences with the A/D-D/A converters. The following questions will help you make a decision and give you more insight:

◆ Do you want to play back only other people's music or create your own? Only a small percentage of users are musicians. However, the most expensive cards have an added value that is interesting for musicians.

◆ If you only want to play back music, is a high sound quality in MIDI files important to you, for example, for computer games? And, do you also have the appropriate speakers, so that you can hear the difference? Many users have inexpensive $20 speakers that could never portray the sound difference between wavetable and synthesizer.

◆ If you want to record or create your own music, do you want these to be MIDI sounds, which are input by a keyboard? Or, do you want to record records and other recordings as wave files by A/D conversion? In the second case, it won't matter to you whether or not the card is equipped with a Wavetable.

As you can see, selecting a card depends to a great extent on what purpose you have for it. Anyone who only works with Windows 95 and occasionally plays a computer game without great sound requirements, definitely does not need an expensive $200 card with all the gimmicks. This type of user will be happy with a simple sound card for under $50 with an FM synthesizer. And even if the improved MIDI sound of a Wavetable card means something to you, 0.5 - 1 Meg sample ROMs are completely adequate for computer games. Only musicians require the expensive cards with up to four Megs of Wavetable ROM.

Users who want to digitize sounds as wave files with their PC, i.e., like a digital tape deck (hard disk recording), need to remember that the sound quality of very expensive cards approaches that of a good DAT or MiniDisc recorder. The poor screening and low operating voltage on the cards doesn't make high quality possible. As we already discussed you will get better results if you record the sounds with a good stereo and then digitize them into the computer for additional processing. However, good recording and playback quality is very important for many applications (voice recognition, voice output and video conferencing, for example).

> **The Full-Duplex function is needed for Internet telephony**
>
> **NOTE** All applications that both play back and record sounds using the AD-DA converter of the card (e.g., Internet telephones) require a full-duplex sound card. Most cards (and of course, some of the newer models) are only capable of half duplex, because the converter chips are only present in single. If you hold an Internet telephony conference with such a card, you won't be able to speak and listen at the same time. Some older Sound Blaster cards can be brought up to full-duplex capacity with a driver update. However, this still doesn't give the card complete full-duplex capability (also called extended full-duplex), because with extended full duplex, you can even work with different sampling frequencies for recording and playback through two separate converter chips.

Bottom line: Most users who only want to have background sounds for Windows and computer games, a simple sound card with a maximum of one Meg of Wavetable ROM is completely sufficient. Since currently all standard cards below $50 can also be upgraded later with a Wavetable add-on board, first buy a pure FM synthesizer card. If that sound isn't good enough for you, or if it sounds too artificial, later you can upgrade for about $50 to a MIDI module with one Meg of Sample ROM. Altogether, you will spend about $100.

Users who plan to make their own MIDI music will need cards with the highest possible quality Wavetable ROM, up to four Megs. In addition, the card should be upgradeable with RAM chips, into which you can record your own samples for enhancing the existing samples. For example, you could buy the more expensive AWE sound card from Sound Blaster.

The new sound dimension: 3-D audio

Recently, 3-D audio effects have become possible for sound cards — especially important for gamers. In contrast to artificial 3-D effects, which are created by a DSP and output through the conventional two speakers, the new 3-D audio is a genuine quadrophony standard. However, that means that your sound cards have to be able to run a second pair of speakers, and that you'll have to set up this second set on the back of your PC and connect them to the sound card.

On this card (a Terratec EWS 64), you can clearly recognize the two loudspeaker connections (L-1, L-2) for 3-D audio next to the three inputs (MIC, 0-1, 0-2).

However, up to now only Windows 95 supports the new 3-D audio functions, which require Direct X as an interface between software and sound cards. For example, when a computer game uses this new function, sounds can be placed exactly in space (called Positional Audio). A helicopter, for example, will fly from the rear right to the left front over your head, as you are familiar with from good surround theaters. The effect is simply fantastic. 3-D audio is an absolute must for game enthusiasts!

Unfortunately, there are few cards on the market that support this genuine 3-D audio function. Examples of cards that do support this function are the Monster Sounds from Diamond. You can easily identify a card that supports this function by the additional jack for the second pair of speakers.

The first sound cards with PCI and full 3-D audio support—The Diamond Monster sound cards.

Theater Surround Sound versus 3-D Audio on the PC

NOTE Many users are getting the 3-D audio functions of the new sound cards confused with the well known Surround Sound standards from theaters and videos, such as Dolby ProLogic, THX or AC3. 3-D audio uses genuine quadrophony, that is, 4 equivalent channels that are used for exact positioning of objects in sound space. The surround procedure, however, besides the normal stereo channels, uses only additional, sound reduced effect channels. With Prologic, two mono surround signals of low quality are mixed (coded) into the stereo signal. With AC-3 and THX, up to three additional surround channels and one center channel are used (5+1 method). In contrast to THX, AC-3 is purely digitally. However, the surround channels are not tonally adequate and contain only surround information. With new 3-D audio for the PC, however, a full signal can be distributed on all four channels.

Sound Blaster Compatibility

What do they mean by Sound Blaster compatible? You have to distinguish between hardware and software compatibility. There are sound cards that achieve the compatibility only by calling a driver in the AUTOEXEC.BAT, which is known as "software compatibility." Sometimes, that functions quite well. However, there will be problems with games that attempt to address the card from their own routines. Many computer games will refuse to start when some other memory resident programs are loaded along with them. Nearly all games that use the DOS extender (DOS4GW), and their number is increasing, use their own routines for addressing the card. The same also applies to all other operating systems besides DOS. If there is no separate driver present, the card will remain silent.

The Sound Blaster 16 offers CD quality for the first time in recording and playback of Wave files (not to be confused with Wavetable for MIDI). This card works with 16 bits and 44.1 KHz stereo sound for the first time. In practice, however, the sound in recording is far inferior to that of a DAT or MD recorder, because the converter chips used aren't exactly high quality. The Sound Blaster 16 uses the OPL3 synthesizer chip for the first time, which offers better sound than the old OPL2 (but still doesn't approach Wavetable).

What other manufacturers claim as 16-bit sound cards don't necessarily have to be Sound Blaster-16-compatible. In general, the 16-bit capability in recording and playback only applies if the supplied drivers and programs for Windows are used anyway. Since these are missing under DOS (and thus, also with the computer games), you must usually resort to the existing Sound Blaster compatibility.

Nearly all computer games work with 8-bit sounds at 22 KHz, for reasons of space, which is the old Sound Blaster standard. Yes, even stereo function (Sound Blaster Pro compatibility) is not always present. 16-bit quality is really only necessary for those who wish to digitize sounds themselves in CD quality.

MIDI sound

Sound generation via the MIDI standard is, next to using digital-analog conversion, the second great option for generating sounds with a sound card. As we explained at the beginning, MIDI files can be played back synthetically via synthesizer or realistically by using sound samples. The resulting sound is much better when created from actual samples. For example, the orchestra for Wing Commander no longer sounds like grandpa's phonograph in the cookie jar, but more like the London Symphony Orchestra. Wavetable sounds make a wonderful sound track out of the almost unbearable drone of many games.

So anyone who wants really good MIDI sound needs the Wavetable synthesis. Once again, though, there is much misinformation and confusion about the different standards and methods. The following information contains the most important points about MIDI and Wavetables:

◆ Wavetable synthesis needs sound samples, which correspond to the digitized sounds (e.g., from instruments) and are stored in memory (usually a ROM). The **Wavetable memory** can be integrated directly on the card (as in the AWE 64 or Terratec Maestro 32/96) or can be upgraded later through a Wavetable board. The sound card needs to have a slot for accepting add-on boards. Some boards even let you upgrade with a Wavetable board although there is already a sample ROM on the card (e.g., the Maestro 32/96)

◆ MIDI versus Wave files: Depending on the application, it can be practical to work with Wave or MIDI files. The advantages and disadvantages of these two fundamentally different sound file types are shown in the following table:

Advantages of WAV	Advantages of Midi
.WAV files sound equally good on almost any sound card / good for generating sounds / you can play back complete musical pieces regardless of what kind of card you have / mperative for sound creation	Natural sounds in real time / speed can be set freely / varied options of sound modulation / very small file sizes / does not burden the processor / standardized commands / possibility of sound studio in computer / editing is very simple and efficient
Disadvantages of WAV	Disadvantages of Midi
File sizes range from large to huge (up to ten Megs per minute) / requires high processor performance / hardly any options for later sound modulation / due to wealth of data almost no real-time editing is possible / editing is labor intensive	Sounds different depending on the output synthesizer / almost no noises can be generated / plays back only through a special synthesizer

◆ Wavetable add-on boards don't have to be from the same manufacturer, since MIDI is standardized. For example, you can get well known and high-quality Wavetable boards from Roland (SCB 15) or from Yamaha. These boards sound better than the directly integrated samples on some of the more expensive cards (e.g., the samples of Sound Blaster cards). That's why it is practical to buy a good card without sample ROM and then upgrade it with a Wavetable upgrade, e.g., from Yamaha.

◆ The MPU, or better the MPU-401 port, is a standardized MIDI interface from Roland company. You need the MPU-401 port for playing back MIDI sounds over Wavetable sounds. There are other interfaces for this purpose, but the MPU-401 is a standard. It is important for games, since they can only address the Wavetable sounds on the card via the MPU-401. Many older sound cards don't have a correct, hardware implemented MPU-401, but instead use a proprietary interface. That also prevents the use of a Wavetable board that you might have plugged in to the sound card. Your only solution: your game supports the proprietary standard of the card, which, at best, applies for one of the first Sound Blaster AWE 32 versions. With all newer cards of well known manufacturers, the MPU-401 should be present in hardware form. At any rate, this is the case for the new Sound Blaster cards as well as all the models from Terratec.

◆ Which MIDI standard do you need, GM or GS? These abbreviations refer to the number of available instruments and their classifications via MIDI. GM stands for "General **MIDI**" and defines 128 instruments and one drum kit. GS stands for "General **S**tandard" and defines 197 instruments and 10 drum kits. However, these differences are only important to musicians. Games and multimedia applications, the Wavetable samples are addressed almost only with the GM standard. That way you won't have the violin suddenly playing the notes of the trumpet, which thinks it's really a timpani. As long as you don't intend to make your own music, pay attention to full GM support, and don't worry about GS.

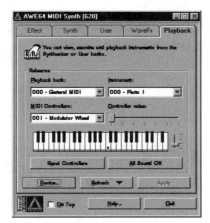

The 128 instruments of the GM standard are numbered consecutively from 000 to 127.
The first three correspond to the three different
piano variations that can all be addressed by a keyboard.

◆ Do Wavetable samples really sound different, and how do you recognize the good ones? Sometimes the sound differences are very strong. We were very surprised when we discovered in a comparison with a complex MIDI file how differently, e.g., a card with the well known dream sample (Terratec Maestro 32/96) sounds compared to a Sound Blaster AWE 64. We were somewhat disappointed, because the AWE 64 did not at all live up to our expectations. However, the AWE 64 uses one Meg sample ROM (instead of four Megs, which the Maestro uses). Proper sampling is a science in itself and requires much time and effort on the manufacturer's part.

The Dream company is famous for its high-quality MIDI samples, which are used on many sound cards.

◆ How do you recognize good samples? One mark of quality is well looped samples. For example, when you want to run a violin sample 16 bars without having it audibly stop, the quality of the sample will quickly be revealed. No sample this long is saved in the Wavetable card (it would require too much space), so a much shorter one is broken off at a good place and repeated from the beginning.

If you hear this process (a crackling or the sound suddenly becomes louder or softer), it means the sample is of inferior quality. Another mark of quality is the procedure of multisampling. An instrument from the Wavetable card is almost always put together from several samples (exceptions are drum sounds) that have to be recorded with similar stroke, hall, proximity to the microphone, volume, etc.

Otherwise, the piano, for example, will sound significantly louder and scratchier in the lower area than in the upper area, which can be very disturbing. There's no way of getting around the ear test. To determine the quality of a card, you need to test it extensively, and play *each* key from some of the instruments (e.g., piano, violin, trumpet, saxophone, bass and organ) paying attention to the quality features described above.

◆ Watch for incorrect memory specifications for Wavetable samples. The size of a sample ROM is a good, albeit rough measure for the sound quality. However, poor samples don't even sound good when there are eight Megs of sample. Many manufacturers use compressed samples, of which one Meg can correspond to two Megs uncompressed. Be careful: they often play tricks with inaccurate specifications on the size of the ROM. Specifications such as "8 MB" could also mean eight MBits, which only correspond to one Meg. Pay careful attention to the units of measure used on the sound card.

◆ What is the difference between Sample ROM and Sample RAM? More and more cards, starting with the Sound Blaster AWE 32, have RAM chips on the card, into which you can load your own samples. These could supplement the existing MIDI samples in ROM, or even replace them. Naturally, this is only interesting for musicians, since computer games or multimedia programs would only sound like nonsense with completely foreign samples. The latest cards (Terratec EWS 64) use only one big RAM chip, into which the samples are loaded from a file when you boot the computer. This makes a far-reaching modification of all samples, including GM and GS standard, much easier.

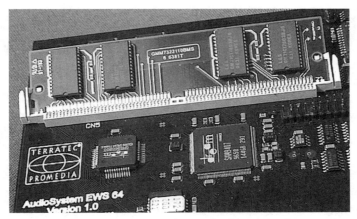

New cards like the EWS 64 use only RAM chips to load pre-defined or proprietary samples.

◆ Creative Labs was the first to promote its next generation of cards with a new, effective feature: 64-channel instead of 32-channel Wavetable synthesizer. The coherence of a synthesizer indicates how many sounds or notes it can play simultaneously. The best way for you to understand that is to picture a synthesizer keyboard. You can press exactly 32 keys simultaneously, but the 33rd key will no longer be played back. The fact is that currently no 64-channel sound card can actually play back a MIDI file with a full 64 notes simultaneously, because neither the hardware nor a normal MIDI player can play back more than 32 channels simultaneously. Only a sequencer program can select all the channels from two synthesizers with 32 channels each and play them in rotation.

In addition, the second 32 channels on the Sound Blaster AWE 64 can only be generated using a software Wavetable procedure (WaveGuide Synthesis). However, it is possible to select 64 channels for a MIDI file from the entire repertoire of the two synthesizers. While a sequencer program can do this without assistance, a special program called the Instrument Mapper was written for the normal Windows MIDI Player from Creative Labs. This program lets you combine your own sets of instruments from both synthesizers into a new allocation list, from which you can still only play back 32 channels simultaneously, but you can choose them from 64 different channels. Admittedly, the whole thing is rather confusing. In other words: you can play back only 32 channels simultaneously, but you can take the channels either from the repertoire of the instruments of the 32-channel hardware synthesizer (E-mu8000 chip) or from the repertoire of the 32-channel WaveGuide software synthesizer. You cannot do both at the same time, and even this solution is only possible if you organized the desired instruments in the Instrument Mapper by hand.

Sound Blaster AWE64 is installed (left) and the Sound Blaster AWE64 MIDI Synth (right).

Demystifying Sound Blaster cards

Everyone knows that the sound card market has been heavily dominated by Creative Labs Sound Blaster family. Only the Sound Blaster 16 and the AWE series are being produced currently.

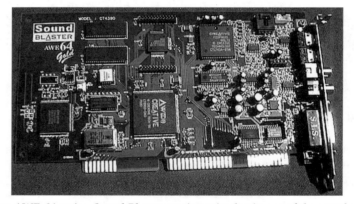

With the new AWE 64 series, Sound Blaster continues its dominance of the sound card market.

if you need background music for games and Windows, consider the SB 16 PnP and upgrade it with a Wavetable module from Yamaha. The AWE 64 Value card is also interesting, which has been trimmed down in software and the accompanying "goodies" (microphone, cable, etc.) compared to the full version. Since you can get these surplus items at reasonable prices yourself and sometimes with even better quality, we recommend purchasing this trimmed down version over the full version. All AWE versions now have an MPU-401 and complete Wavetable support, although the sound does not approach that of the Dream samples from Terratec.

The new AWE 64 Gold is also interesting, because it has a SPDIF digital output, which supports data up to 20 bits with a noise difference of 120 dB. It is on the card in the form of a small plug connection, to which a cable is attached with a mini-jack plug. The cable is screwed to the PC case via a slot plate. Using an adapter cable you can output digital sounds directly to a DAT or MD recorder.

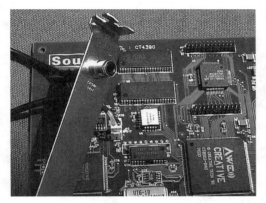 

Only the Gold version of the AWE 64 has a SPDIF digital output (left figure) as well as the analog Line-Out connection in Cinch model (right figure), which improves communication with a stereo set.

Description	SB 2.0	SB Pro	SB16	SB32	AWE32	AWE64*
Mono/Stereo	Mono	Stereo	Stereo	Stereo	Stereo	Stereo
Resolution	8 Bit	8 Bit	16 Bit	16 Bit	16 Bit	16 Bit
max. playback	44 KHz	44 KHz	44 KHz	44 KHz	44 KHz	44 KHz
max. record	15 KHz	22 KHz	44 KHz	44 KHz	44 KHz	44 KHz
FM synthesis	OPL2	OPL3	OPL3	OPL3	OPL3	OPL3
Wavetable	No	No	No	EMU8000	EMU8000	EMU8000
GM-compatible	No	No	No	Yes	Yes	Yes
GS-compatible	No	No	No	No	Yes	Yes
Sample-RAM	No	No	No	No	512K	1 Meg
RAM upgradeable	No	No	No	Yes	Yes	Yes
CD-ROM-port	No	Yes/No1	Yes/No	Yes	Yes	No
Mixer	No	Yes	Yes	Yes	Yes	Yes
MIDI-port	Yes	Yes	Yes	Yes	Yes	Yes
Waveblaster connection	No	No	Yes/No2	No	Yes	No
CSP or ASP	No	No	Yes/No2	No	Yes	Yes

1 Not available with older models
2 Not available with the Value edition
*Value without microphone, cable and only with simple software, Gold version with digital output and cinch connections for Line-Out.

> **Sound Blaster Audio Interrupts**
>
> **NOTE** Sound Blaster cards with a Wavetable function have a special feature, which can be either an advantage or a disadvantage, depending on how you use it: the MIDI port for controlling the Wavetable uses the same interrupt as for the normal audio function (A/D-D/A converter). All other manufacturers use two interrupts. Creative Labs achieves this through clever programming of the drivers, which are able to switch back and forth like lightning between the two functions. What proves to be an advantage in normal operation under Windows and with games, because a precious interrupt is being saved, can be a disadvantage in complex musical arrangements. In this situation Wave and MIDI files must often be played simultaneously, which can result in time shifting. Demanding musicians are better off getting a card with its own interrupt control for the MIDI port.

SOUND CARD TIPS FOR DOS AND WINDOWS 95

We hope that you now have enough insight to purchase the right sound card for your needs. Now let's talk about installation and configuration. Since sound cards are one of the few items still under DOS and Windows, you sometimes have more problems with these cards than with others. Problems between sound cards and computer games drive many users over the edge, because users want to have fun with their PCs, not aggravation. The following tips for installation and configuration under DOS, and then Windows 95, should save you all kinds of trouble and help you use your card better in the future.

Configuring sound cards for DOS games

This section deals with the hardware installation of sound cards and their configuration under DOS, which is necessary for playing DOS-based computer games. However, we'll start with some general information that will give you more insight.

◆ What is necessary for sound cards under DOS? If you purchased a card with high hardware compatibility, you actually don't need to install or configure anything more under DOS. Some cards expect only the one-time call of an initialization program, but this is not a memory resident driver. Almost all new games run in Protected Mode through the DOS4GW Extender and address the card through the known interfaces (Sound Blaster Pro for Audio, MPU 401 for MIDI).

◆ Above all, get rid of all drivers from the start files that have anything to do with CD-ROMs or the ASP or CSP chip (e.g., Csp.sys), because these don't work under Windows anyway, and they just disrupt things. You definitely won't need them under DOS.

◆ The Sound Blaster variable in the AUTOEXEC.BAT is only necessary for old games, which address the card via the addresses specified there (see below). New games no longer need this.

This Sound Blaster variable is only important for old games.

◆ Interestingly enough, under DOS it is not necessary to define or use an interrupt for MIDI playback. Playback of the MIDI data occurs in such small, regulated data blocks that it works without interrupt control. That is why you won't find an entry for the MIDI setting in the Sound Blaster variables.

All new sound cards are Plug & Play capable, i.e., the BIOS and Windows 95 automatically assign the necessary interrupts and addresses. If you are the unfortunate owner of an ancient, non-Plug & Play BIOS, you'll have to get help with the ICU (ISA Configuration Utility) from Intel, which simulates a Plug & Play BIOS. Only then can a Plug & Play card correctly initialize itself. You can also find out what you have to do to install a non Plug & Play card. Some manufacturers such as Creative Labs (Sound Blaster) have their own utilities with the same function, such as the CTCM (Creative Configuration Manager). For more information on how to use CTCM, check out the Internet under www.cle.creaf.com/wwwnew/tech/faqs/ctcm.html. Another alternative, that many users don't know about, but is really easy is calling the manufacturer to ask for a predecessor model without Plug & Play function. They may still have such models in stock.

◆ Nearly all new cards have a Flash ROM, in which the configuration settings are stored. Tools are supplied for configuration under Windows 95 and DOS; you can use them to change the interrupts and I/O addresses. So if you have problems on your computer with assigned interrupts or installation problems due to resource conflicts, then use such a tool to change the default settings under DOS. As an example, you can set the interrupt for the MIDI port permanently to IRQ 11.

◆ Which resource settings are the best? While the assignment of resources under Windows is completely free, for compatibility with games you have to use specific standards. Usually these are:

Chapter 11

Resource	Audio Function (Wave files)	Midi Function (MPU-401)
IRQ	IRQ 5, alternative IRQ 7 (Parallel Port)	No IRQ under DOS, doesn't matter under Windows, usually IRQ 9
I/O Address	220h	330h
DMA	1 and 5 (Low and High channel) (for full-duplex cards)	Does not apply

◆ The settings are then communicated to all the games through the Sound Blaster variable. However, as we said earlier, this only applies to the older programs. All the programs attempt to address the card themselves to find the settings. The variable is defined in the AUTOEXEC.BAT by the Set command, e.g., Set blaster=A220 I5 D1 T6. "A" and "I" are used to define the address and the interrupt for the normal audio part of the card. "D" defines the low DMA channel, which is used for playback. Since you don't record when you play a game, additional parameters are not necessary. "T" establishes the Sound Blaster model, but is relatively unimportant, because hardly any game can do anything with it anyway.

◆ There is a mixer program named "Sb16set.exe" for setting the volume of the Sound Blaster card under DOS, normally located in the Sound Blaster directory. You can set the mixer with the help of this program. If you don't find it in the Sound Blaster directory, check the Creative Labs web site at http://www.creaf.com.

◆ In the first versions of the AWE32, the MPU-401 port was not connected with the internal synthesizer, so that games that the card did not directly support could not play any MIDI music. You can solve this problem with a program named "Aweutil" that comes supplied with AWE. Aweutil connects the MPU port with the internal synthesizer by means of software. For this purpose, Aweutil must be called twice in the AUTOEXEC.BAT. The first time you call it with the parameter /EM:GM (Aweutil.exe /EM:GM) and right after that with the parameter /EM (Aweutil.exe /EM). After that, it should be possible for old games to address your Wavetable set. By the way, this doesn't work with the games Wing Commander and Comanche, since these games use a rare MIDI mode only implemented with Roland cards.

◆ More game sound for the AWE 32 and SB32: Enable more hall and chorus under DOS. For some games it would be entertaining if the music had a bit more three-dimensionality. This wish can be fulfilled. Simply call the Aweutil program with the following parameters: Aweutil /r:70 /c:30 /s. This sets the Hall to 70 and the Chorus to 30, and the music of the game suddenly resounds in a large hall with very beautiful acoustics.

Troubleshooting sound card installation

◆ Some cards, e.g., SCSI controllers (such as Adaptec's 1542B) or network cards also use the address *330h* of the MPU port. This can lead to crashes or failures. Sometimes it is difficult to detect the error, because some cards start with a deeper start address (e.g., *300h*) and in spite of this, also use regions above it. In any event, you've no other choice but to shift one of the addresses (if at all possible, the address of one of the other cards). For this purpose, you will have to change the configuration parameters according to the instructions of the card's manual. There are also new ROM versions for the Adaptec 1542B that make relocation of the memory addresses possible.

◆ It's possible that your sound card cannot play any 16-bit sound or can only play it back in very poor quality. In this case, you probably have a problem with the 16-bit wide, high DMA channel. With some motherboards this hasn't been implemented 100%, so that there can be hardware incompatibilities between sound cards and motherboards. The best way to solve this problem is to buy a new motherboard. Otherwise, you can use a trick which merely circumvents the problem: You have to transfer the high to the low DMA channel. With Sound Blaster cards this operation is performed with the help of the Diagnose program. However, on many cards this has the disadvantage that you can actually no longer edit any more 16-bit sounds (listen and play back), because ordinarily this only works with the high 16-bit DMA channels. The only way you can still work with 16-bit sound is if the manufacturer supplies special drivers that will reach the 16 bits with low DMAs also (e.g., the Terratec Maestro 32/96).

In the Diagnose program you can set a low DMA channel for your Sound Blaster card.

◆ Your sound card makes a humming noise? If you connect your sound card to the Stereo set, it can result in a deep humming (50 Hz). Frequently this is a ground connection, also known as a hum loop. Usually you can eliminate this problem easily. If your stereo has a tuner (radio), often the antenna connection is the culprit. Pull it out until the outer casing of the plug no longer gets any contact. You can also wrap the plug in paper so that only the middle pin has contact. If that doesn't take care of the humming, try the same thing with the plug of the sound card. If that doesn't help either, you can build a bypass filter into the antenna wire (costs about $5). Also try plugging in the plug of stereo or the computer the other way. If nothing helps, consider buying a computer speaker.

◆ The sound card makes disturbing noises, such as crackling. Crackles and similar disruptive noises usually are a result of poor electrical screening in the PC, caused by radiation from other cards. In general, it is advisable to install sound cards as far away as possible from other cards, and also from the power supply. However, crackling noises can also come from a defective ISA bus or DMA controller. If replugging doesn't help, try replacing individual components of your PC.

◆ The sound card makes noise? If there is noise during playback, it often has to do with unnecessarily opened inputs, which have nothing better to do than amplify the noise. Close all inputs on which there is no signal by switching off the microphone, the Line-In input and/or the CD input in the mixer of the sound card. By the way, the most frequent culprit in this situation is the microphone. Of course, another reason for excessive noise could be inexpensive speakers.

To reduce noise during playback, turn down the
input level for the microphone and/or Line inputs in the Mixer.!>

◆ You want to use two sound cards? Running two cards is no problem, as long as you use different resources (IRQs and I/O addresses). All you have to do is configure the cards accordingly. One of the two cards will no longer run with DOS computer games. However, under Windows, this is no problem. Set the first sound card to IO 220, IRQ 5, low DMA 1 and high DMA 5, then you can usually set the second sound card to IO 240, IRQ 10 or 7, low DMA 3 and high DMA 7.

Sound tuning for Windows 95

Sound cards under Windows 95 are not as complicated and prone to errors as they are under DOS. And Plug & Play frequently makes installation child's play. However, the key word in the last sentence is "frequently." Plug & Play can also cause trouble. The following tips will give you an overview of problem solutions and tuning options.

◆ Windows 95 Setup and Plug & Play cards actually don't get along very well. If you ever reinstall Windows 95, remove the sound card from your PC first. Then install Windows 95 completely. Only then can you install the sound card correctly. Otherwise, the Plug & Play card may snatch away important interrupts and I/O addresses, causing a resource chaos under Windows.

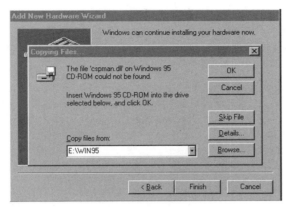

Adding new hardware in Windows.

◆ You are probably familiar with the second golden rule: Always buy the most up to date drivers. Naturally, source number one is the Internet.

A screen that appears while you're installing the software

◆ Almost all Plug & Play sound cards have a stupid habit during Windows installation: They want you to restart the computer after each partial installation of a driver component (for the audio part, the MIDI part, etc.). Since sometimes three to four such driver components are installed, this can really get annoying, especially if you are to comply with Windows' wishes. You'll save time and your nerves if you simply answer the Windows prompt with No, because the rest of the installation continues. Just restart the machine once after installation is complete.

◆ Many sound cards waste resources (especially interrupts). These are often reserved for components of the card that aren't even necessary. Example: a pure 16-bit sound card without Wavetable, but with MPU-401 support reserves an IRQ for the MPU-401, although this isn't even being used (see figure). The Terratec Maestro 32/96 is a special case, because it uses two MPU 401 or two MIDI ports. The second one is almost never necessary. It's

Chapter 11

possible that the Maestro will wind up reserving as many as three IRQs for itself. So, go to the Device Manager of Windows 95 and disable or remove the driver of the components. Windows 95b (OSR2) has a separate command for this in the Properties of the driver (right figure). In conventional Windows, try to remove the driver.

◆ Addressing two sound cards under Windows 95. Using more than one sound card under Windows is no problem. As we mentioned earlier for DOS, you simply have to assign each card its own resources. If you later wish to use one of the cards in a program, for example, the Windows 95 Sound Mixer, all you have to do is select the desired card from the Device List. To do this, choose the command Options | Properties | Device in the Windows 95 Mixer.

◆ Sound card-modems are an interesting solution or alternative. These two device types are closely related, because they use similar parts. Using such a modem always as an internal plug-in card is no big deal under Windows 95. The advantage compared to an external modem is the continued availability of the COM2 and less cable in the back of your computer. However, there are also disadvantages. Internal modems do have the reputation of causing significantly more problems than external modems. For example, an IRQ has to be free and the modem software has to work with a COM3 port on a freely selectable IRQ. Under Windows this usually works without any problems, only under DOS do you still have to tell the software the IRQ where the COM3 is located. If the DOS software doesn't play along, you will have to use a different one.

Sound card-modems are addressed via a third COM port and a separate interrupt.

◆ **Watch the MIDI setting in the Control Panel**! Many users are disappointed by the poor MIDI sound under Windows, without knowing that they probably haven't even enabled Wavetable support on the card. This does not occur automatically with most cards. You have to make the setting manually in the Control Panel. Double-click the Multimedia icon and then select the MIDI tab. Almost always you will find several entries there involved with the card's options for playing back MIDI files. If nothing else, you will find items here that have to do with the FM synthesizer and the Wavetable synthesizer. Unfortunately, the terminology is different for each card, and some of it is difficult for laypersons. Depending on which entry you select, you will hear drastic sound differences. If the terms aren't clear, you'll have to use the trial and error method to determine what sounds the best. If at all possible, do not choose FM synthesis (the Sound Blaster calls this item Stereo Music Synthesizer), because this doesn't use the Wavetables and doesn't sound as good.

Usually you have to choose the right MIDI synthesizer manually under Windows 95. The left figure shows the correct setting for the Maestro 32/96; the right figure shows the setting for the AWE 64 Gold with installed WaveGuide synthesis. Don't use the latter, because this causes as much as 10-15% processor load.

What you need to know about Wavetable upgrades

Sound cards that don't have any Wavetable ROM on board can often be upgraded by an external Wavetable board. You will find standardized edgeboard connectors on the cards for this purpose, which you plug into the upgrade board.

Simply plug the Wavetable board into the appropriate edgeboard connector of the sound card.

Chapter 11

An installation under Windows 95 occurs then by Plug & Play or supplied driver. The board must be addressed with the MPU 401 of the card. Otherwise it won't work. Here are some tips on this topic:

◆ Wavetable boards come with different memory amounts. One, two and four-Meg types are common, with the larger ones being usually better, but also more expensive. For computer games a one Meg module for about $50 is usually sufficient, if requirements aren't especially high. Pay more attention to quality when you buy one.

◆ If the Wavetable board won't run under Windows, the trouble often lies with a defective control of the MPU 401 on the card. In these cases, you will see an error message of the following type: A hardware problem has occurred. Reinstall the MPU401 driver. In this case, you can remedy the situation by using the proprietary MIDI driver of the card. For example, this would be the SB16 MIDI Out for the SB16. To do this, simply adjust the MIDI output to the sound card driver in the MIDI Mapper (Windows 3.1) or in the Multimedia Control (Windows 95). After that, this problem should no longer occur.

After installation of the card go to the Control Panel and change from the FM synthesis you have been using to the upgrade board. To do this, choose the entry External MIDI Port in the MIDI tab.

◆ One last, typical problem source is the simultaneous use of a joystick. The joystick and MIDI ports share common data lines on the sound card. Some joysticks with add-on functions (e.g., the CH Flightstick) short circuit the MIDI lines when they are connected directly to the joystick port of the sound card. The internally plugged in Wavetable card is also controlled through these MIDI lines, and due to the short-circuited lines, this card can also no longer receive any MIDI information. The result: No music can be heard from the Wavetable card. It refuses to cooperate. To solve this problem, purchase a MIDI adapter cable, which reliably prevents such a short circuit from occurring. You can buy one at almost any computer store; many sound cards also include a MIDI adapter cable in the package.

A typical MIDI connecting cable: On the right is the port for the computer, the flat plug on the left is the joystick port. The two round plugs are the actual MIDI connections. One each for input and output.

NOTE

More sample RAM for the Sound Blaster AWE 32

What an upgrade board is for the cards without any Wavetable, that's what an upgrade of the sample RAM is for the Sound Blaster AWE 32 card. However, which memory chips are required? Classic, 30-pin SIMMs (not PS/2), always two identical modules (e.g., 2 x 2 Meg modules).

Chapter 11

Index

PC catalog

Order Toll Free 1-800-451-4319
Books and Software

www.abacuspub.com

SHAREWARE, FREEWARE AND PUBLIC DOMAIN SOFTWARE

Because shareware is copyrighted, the authors ask for payment if you use their program(s). You may try out the program for a limited time, typically 10 to 30 days, and then decide whether you want to keep it. If you continue to use it, you're requested to send the author a nominal fee. Registration involves paying registration fees, which make you a licensed user of the program.

Check the documentation or the program itself for the amount of registration fee and the address where you send the registration form. Shareware benefits both the user and the author as it allows prices to remain low by avoiding distribution, packaging, and advertising costs.

You'll find program instructions as well as notes on registration for the shareware programs in special text files located in the program directory of each program.

Thanks again from the Abacus Editorial and Technical Staffs

Windows 95 is a trademark of Microsoft Corp.

The Companion CD-ROM

Thank you for purchasing PC Tuning. We hope this book will be an indispensable reference guide to upgrading your PC. The companion CD-ROM contains dozens of practical utilities for checking system information, performance checking, diagnostic utilities, benchmarks and much more.

The following table lists the directories you'll find on the Companion CD-ROM root directory:

Directory	Explanation
Symantec	Symantec's Norton Utilities Evaluation Edition
Adobe	Adobe's Acrobat Reader 3
Abacus	Abacus Latest Catalog
BookFile	Contains the complete book in Acrobat format.
And dozens of Diagnostic Utilities from the BEST shareware authors!	

Why use these programs? Perhaps you're uncertain what type of equipment your computer contains. Maybe a friend just bought a computer and they have no idea what the new PC has 'under the hood.' You can experiment with using the various utilities and diagnostic programs on the CD. You can install them from the CD-ROM or copy them to a new directory on your hard drive and then run them. The programs are commercial demonstrations, shareware or evaluation programs written and copyrighted by the respective authors and companies. Please register the programs you use with the respective authors.

The companion CD-ROM can be installed using Windows 95. The directories included on the companion CD-ROM are in the file called CDDIR.TXT. You can print or view this file.